This book tells the story of how a fertile European country, as a result of overpopulation and military armament, overexploited its fields and forests in a nonsustainable fashion. By the eighteenth century Denmark, along with other European countries, found itself in an ecological crisis caused by clear felling of forests, sand drift, floods, inadequate soil fertilization, and cattle disease. The crisis was overcome by a green biotechnological revolution that changed the whole pattern of agriculture, and by the abandonment of wood as a raw material and source of energy in favour of coal and iron. This development had wide, unexpected consequences for the landscape, patterns of disease, politics, social structure, art, and literature. The book outlines the background of the present-day ecological crisis, both in the industrial world and in developing countries, and is the first attempt to understand early modern Europe from a consistently ecological viewpoint.

The Danish Revolution, 1500–1800

STUDIES IN ENVIRONMENT AND HISTORY

Editors
Donald Worster   *University of Kansas*
Alfred Crosby   *University of Texas at Austin*

Advisory Board
Reid Bryson   *Institute for Environmental Studies, University of Wisconsin*
Raymond Dasmann   *College Eight, University of California, Santa Cruz*
E. Le Roy Ladurie   *Collège de France*
William McNeill   *Department of History, University of Chicago*
Carolyn Merchant   *College of Natural Resources, University of California, Berkeley*
Thad Tate   *Institute of Early American History and Culture, College of William and Mary*

Other Books in the Series
Donald Worster   *Nature's Economy: A History of Ecological Ideas*
Kenneth F. Kiple   *The Caribbean Slave: A Biological History*
Alfred W. Cosby   *Ecological Imperialism: The Biological Expansion of Europe, 900–1900*
Arthur F. McEvoy   *The Fisherman's Problem: Ecology and Law in California Fisheries, 1850–1980*
Robert Harms   *Games Against Nature: An Eco-Cultural History of the Nunu of Equatorial Africa*
Warren Dean   *Brazil and the Struggle for Rubber: A Study in Environmental History*
Samuel P. Hays   *Beauty, Health, and Permanence: Environmental Politics in the United States, 1955–1985*
Donald Worster   *The Ends of the Earth: Perspectives on Modern Environmental History*
Michael Williams   *Americans and Their Forests: A Historical Geography*
Timothy Silver   *A New Face on the Countryside: Indians, Colonists, and Slaves in South Atlantic Forests, 1500–1800*
Theodore Steinberg   *Nature Incorporated: Industrialism and the Waters of New England*
Richard H. Grove   *Green Imperialism: Science, Colonial Expansion, and the Emergence of Global Environmentalism, 1660–1860*
J. R. McNeill   *The Mountains of the Mediterranean World: An Environmental History*
Elinor G. K. Melville   *A Plague of Sheep: Environmental Consequences of the Conquest of Mexico*

THE DANISH REVOLUTION, 1500–1800

AN ECOHISTORICAL INTERPRETATION

Thorkild Kjærgaard

Translated by David Hohnen

CAMBRIDGE UNIVERSITY PRESS
Cambridge, New York, Melbourne, Madrid, Cape Town, Singapore, São Paulo

Cambridge University Press
The Edinburgh Building, Cambridge CB2 8RU, UK

Published in the United States of America by Cambridge University Press, New York

www.cambridge.org
Information on this title: www.cambridge.org/9780521442671

© Thorkild Kjærgaard 1994

This publication is in copyright. Subject to statutory exception
and to the provisions of relevant collective licensing agreements,
no reproduction of any part may take place without the written
permission of Cambridge University Press.

First published 1994
First paperback edition 2006

A catalogue record for this publication is available from the British Library

Library of Congress Cataloguing in Publication data
Kjærgaard, Thorkild.
[Den danske Revolution 1500–1800. En Økohistorisk tolkning.]
The Danish revolution, 1500–1800 : an ecohistorical interpretation
/ Thorkild Kjærgaard; translated by David Hohnen.
    p.   cm. – (Studies in environment and history)
Includes bibliographical references and index.

ISBN 0-521-44267-2

1. Natural resources – Denmark – History. 2. Conservation of
natural resources – Denmark – History. 3. Human ecology – Denmark –
History. 4. Environmental policy – Denmark – History. I. Title.
II. Series.
HC353.5.K5713   1994   93.46320
                                                                          CIP

ISBN 978-0-521-44267-1 hardback
ISBN 978-0-521-03043-4 paperback

Transferred to digital printing 2008

CONTENTS

List of Illustrations	*page*	vii
Preface		xi
Introduction		1

Part I Denmark, 1500–1750: A Country in an Ecological Crisis

1.	The Road to the Crisis	9
	1.1 Population Growth	12
	1.2 A Fiscal-Military State	13
2.	The Anatomy of the Crisis	18

Part II The Ecological Revolution

3.	The Green Revolution	33
	3.1 Sand Drift Is Arrested	33
	3.2 Land Reclamation	39
	3.3 Control of the Water Level	40
	3.4 Control of the pH Balance of the Soil: Marling	49
	3.5 Addition of Plant Nutrients through Better Utilization of Existing Resources	57
	3.6 Nitrogen from the Sea	64
	3.7 Nitrogen from the Air	65
4.	The Energy and Raw Materials Revolution	88
	4.1 The Energy and Raw Materials Crisis	88
	4.2 Relieving the Energy and Raw Materials Crisis by Economizing	92
	4.3 Increased Production of Energy and Raw Materials	106
	4.4 Use of Wood Substitutes	116
	4.5 Stabilization of the Forests, 1763–1805	129

Part III The New Denmark

5.	Landscape	135
	5.1 The Denmark Facing East	135
	5.2 The Denmark Facing West	142

v

vi   *Contents*

6. Labour Burden and Social Structure   145
    6.1   Labour Burden and Working Hours, 1500–1800   145
    6.2   Falling Marginal Production and Changes in the
          Social Structure, 1500–1800   157
    6.3   Factors behind the Rising Influence of the Farmer
          Class during the Last Half of the Eighteenth
          Century   173
7. The Disease Pattern   179
    7.1   Plague   179
    7.2   Malaria   182
    7.3   Tuberculosis   185
    7.4   Smallpox   191
    7.5   The Changing Pattern of Disease and Its Impact
          on Social Life   192
8. Power   198
    8.1   The Danish Power Structure from the Viking Age
          until 1766: The Rule of the Aristocracy   198
    8.2   The Breakthrough of Centralistic Government,
          1766–1814   216
    8.3   Conditions that Paved the Way for the Breakthrough
          of Centralistic Bureaucratic Government   228
    8.4   Winners and Losers   242

**Part IV   The Driving Forces behind the Danish
Revolution, 1500–1800**

9. Agrarian Reforms   247
10. Technology and Communication Systems   253
    10.1 The Danish Revolution, 1500–1800:
          A Chaotic Process   256

Part V   The Inheritance

11. The Social and Political Inheritance   261
12. The Ecological Inheritance   265

Appendix 1: Currency, Weights, and Measures   268
Appendix 2: Reigns of Danish Kings and Queens   270

Sources and Bibliography   271

Index   303

ILLUSTRATIONS

1. The Danish States: Denmark, Norway, Schleswig, and Holstein in the eighteenth century. *page* ix
2. Denmark in the eighteenth century. xii
3. Agricultural prices and population. 1650–1800. On the basis of *Statistiske Meddelelser*, 4th series, 15, 1st fascicle, 1904, and Bjørn Matsen 1978, p. 61. 17
4. Areas afflicted by sand drift in the eighteenth century. Mainly on the basis of Palle Friis 1967, p. 16. 20
5. Soil map of Denmark. Prepared by Knud Rosenlund. 55
6. Use of seaweed as fertilizer in Denmark. On the basis of Holger Rasmussen 1974, p. 397. 66
7. The expansion of cultivated clover in Europe ca. 1250–ca. 1750. Partly on the basis of Gertrud Schröder-Lembke 1978, p. 168. 73
8. Domesticated clover in Denmark, 1775. On the basis of the Danish edition of this book, pp. 270–4. 77
9. Domesticated clover in Denmark, 1785. On the basis of the Danish edition of this book, pp. 270–92. 78
10. Domesticated clover in Denmark, 1795. On the basis of the Danish edition of this book, pp. 270–309. 79
11. Domesticated clover in Denmark, 1805. On the basis of the Danish edition of this book. pp. 270–336. 80
12. Crop rotation in the village of Køng, Zealand, 1780–8. *Avis for Bønder* 1780–1, cols. 115–16. 81
13. Instructions for training tree growth according to the needs of the shipbuilding industry. Engraving by J. G. Fridrich. H. F. Becker 1804, facing p. 155. 107

viii   *Illustrations*

14. Coal and iron imported into Denmark during the
    period 1722–1986, converted into forest equivalents.   126
15. Areas covered by forest in Jutland, ca. 1800 and ca. 1950.
    On the basis of Jette Hellesen and Ole Tuxen 1988,
    p. 107.   132
16. Change in garden styles, 1740–1820.
    Ledreborg Park, Zealand, in the 1740s.
    Engraving by I. Haas.
    The Royal Library, Copenhagen.   140
17. Change in garden styles, 1740–1820.
    Ledreborg Park, Zealand, in the 1820s.
    Engraving by Søren Henrik Petersen.
    The Royal Library, Copenhagen.   141
18. Haymaking festival in June.
    Overdoor.
    Rydhave Manor, Jutland. Photo by H. H. Engqvist,
    Nationalmuseet, Copenhagen.   153
19. Amalienborg.
    Drawing by Steen Eiler Rasmussen.   215
20. Number of pages of law texts per year, 1683–1800.
    On the basis of *Forordninger og Aabne Breve
    1683–1800*.   230

Figure 1. The Danish States: Denmark, Norway, and Schleswig-Holstein in the eighteenth century.

PREFACE

The first draft of this book was made during the winter of 1984–5, when I held a scholarship at the European University Institute in Florence. In its original form it was inspired in important respects by the Danish economist Ester Boserup, particularly by her pioneering work *The Conditions of Agricultural Growth* (1965). In 1987 I was in the United States as a Danish Fulbright guest lecturer at the University of Kansas in Lawrence. Here I met Wes Jackson, director of the Land Institute in Salina, and Professor Donald Worster, Brandeis University (now at the University of Kansas). They – and their books – opened my eyes to fundamental ecohistorical correlations. Donald Worster also drew my attention to the great American pioneer in the field of environmental history, James C. Malin (1893–1979). This encounter with American historiography caused me to revise many of my ideas, and I rewrote the whole book.

The Danish edition, *Den danske Revolution 1500–1800. En økohistorisk tolkning,* was published in 1991 (reprinted twice in 1992). A sixty-seven-page appendix entitled "Domesticeret kløver i Danmark 1749–1805" [Domesticated clover in Denmark, 1749–1805] has been omitted from the present English translation. Elsewhere a number of factual errors have been corrected, and in some places the text has been slightly shortened or rephrased.

In connection with the publication of the English version I should once again like to thank Wes Jackson and Donald Worster, who paved the way for the book to be published by the Cambridge University Press. I also extend my thanks to Professor Arnold H. Barton, Southern Illinois University, Carbondale, Illinois. Finally, I thank Professor Ole Feldbæk of the University of Copenhagen for his never-failing interest and inspiring cooperation for more than fifteen years.

I am grateful to the Aage Krarup Lind Foundation, to George and Emma Jorck's Foundation, to Queen Margrethe and Prince

xii *Preface*

Figure 2. Denmark in the eighteenth century.

Henrik's Foundation, to L. Zeuthen's Memorial Foundation, and to Georg and Lole Malling for grants towards the cost of the English translation and new maps and diagrams for this edition.

Thorkild Kjærgaard

The Danish Revolution, 1500–1800

INTRODUCTION

When the Danish poet Poul Martin Møller was sailing across the South China Sea on his way to China in 1820, he let his thoughts wander back to his homeland in a poem that he called "The Joys of Denmark"; in his mind's eye he saw cattle standing "in grass up to their knees," and dreamed of "a clover-field for noonday peace."[1]

At about the same time, in the vicarage at Købelev on the island of Lolland, Møller's stepbrother, Christian Winther, wrote a poem about the blossoming, sweet-smelling hedges in the Danish countryside.[2] And in the capital, Copenhagen, the grand old poet of the period, Adam Oehlenschläger, praised Denmark as the land of the beech tree:

> There is a lovely land
> With spreading, shady beeches
> Beside the Baltic strand.
>
> Old Denmark will prevail
> As long as leafy beech trees
> Are mirrored in the waves.[3]

Luminous green beechwoods, sweet-smelling hedges, and fertile fields of clover were felt to sum up the character of the Danish landscape during the nineteenth century, not only for these poets and countless others but also for the Danish people as a whole.[4] In 1936, when Denmark was invited to let herself be represented by her national plants in an international 'garden of peace' in La Plata, Argentina, the choice fell on red clover and the beech tree. In the Nature Conservation Act passed the following year, stone fences and hedgerows were mentioned in §1 as being particularly worth preserving.[5]

[1] Quoted by F. J. Billeskov-Jansen 1985–7, II, p. 219. [2] Christian Winther 1828, p. 126.
[3] Quoted by F. J. Billeskov-Jansen 1985–7, II, pp. 75–6. [4] Christian Elling 1961, p. 11.
[5] Axel Lange 1937, p. 183; Act no. 140, 7 May 1937.

2   *Introduction*

This landscape, whose beauties were so highly praised by the poets and painters of Denmark's "Golden Age" (1810–48) and which all Danes have learned to love and regard as the very essence of everything Danish, was not an ancient landscape, but came into being around 1800. Oehlenschläger's description of cows walking in clover in the ancient Danish landscape (in his cycle of mythological poems of 1819 entitled *Nordens Guder* [The gods of the North])[6] is an anachronism. Clover came to Denmark as a pioneer plant immediately after the last Ice Age, some 10,000 years ago[7] and was undoubtedly to be found here and there in the fields of ancient Denmark. But at that time it was a wild species, completely different from the dense, luscious, cultivated red and white clover that sprouted up from the newly drained fields of Denmark in the early years of the Golden Age, when cattle waded "in grass up to their knees." The first documented reports of domesticated clover in Denmark date from the 1740s.

Like clover, the beech tree and the hedgerows were new features in the landscape at the beginning of the nineteenth century. It was not until after 1750 that hedges began to make a crisscross pattern all over the landscape, nor was it until this time that the beech tree began to dominate the forests. Until then, insofar as any forests had been left to grow at all, the oak had been the predominant species. It was regarded as a national tree, and people liked to think that its hard, durable timber and mighty trunk symbolized Denmark's strength and age.[8]

Major changes in building methods also took place towards the end of the eighteenth century. Whereas wood formerly had been not only the most important material for building houses but also by far the largest source of energy and raw materials, it was now gradually superseded by clay, iron, and charcoal. Around 1500, most houses were made of wood, but by the end of the eighteenth century they were nearly all being built of mud-and-wattle and half-timbering, or of bricks. The open fires at which people were still warming themselves throughout the seventeenth century had gone: Iron stoves had replaced them, and coal began to be used for heating. In agriculture, wooden ploughs were discarded; iron fittings and reinforcements became common on carts and other implements. The first steam engines, made of iron and steel and fired with coal, made their appearance at the end of the eigh-

---

[6] Adam Oehlenschläger 1896–9, XII, p. 102.
[7] N. L. Taylor 1985, p. 2.   [8] V. J. Brøndegaard 1978–80, I, p. 324.

Introduction 3

teenth century. Ships were soon given iron hulls, and railways were built. The age of wood gradually came to an end and gave way to the age of iron and coal.

It was not only the immediately visible world of the countryside, of houses, of farm implements, and of machines that was transformed. The invisible world was also changing. In 1800 the infinite microworld of bacteria and tiny parasites was different from what it had been. The significance of this development extended into human society, where it affected the pattern of disease. Old diseases such as plague and malaria, from which the population had suffered for centuries, had disappeared, or were on the point of disappearing, only to be replaced by tuberculosis, which became the dominating disease of the new period.

New social patterns and norms of behaviour and work appeared in the life of the community. New social groups arose, and other groups, previously dominant, found themselves on the defensive. At the bottom of the social ladder, a new lower class began to emerge. These changes had repercussions all the way through society and influenced the political power structure. As the oak began to disappear from Danish forests, the old decentralized power of the aristocratic landowners was gradually undermined. In the same way that the beech tree was ready to take over from the oak, a new class of bureaucrats was ready to assume control of Denmark.

There can hardly have been any contemporary – or, for that matter, any later – observer who did not feel that the world at the beginning of the nineteenth century had changed. But the changes involved have been regarded too narrowly, consideration being given as a rule only to the more striking changes in the life of the community. Furthermore, these changes have been seen as being bound up almost exclusively with political events: on the domestic front, most notably with agrarian reforms, and internationally, with America's independence, the French Revolution, and the Napoleonic Wars. The deeper structural causes bound up with the ecological, economic, sociological, psychological, and political long-term developments of the period have not been given the attention they deserve.[9] The purpose of this book is to rectify this state of affairs by describing the changes that took place between 1500 and 1800 in their full complexity and by giving a more satisfactory analysis of their causes. Unexpected correlations will appear. For example, connections will emerge between coal, iron,

[9] For recent discussions of Danish historiography, see in particular H. Arnold Barton 1988, and Claus Bjørn 1988a.

4   *Introduction*

domesticated clover, and beech forests; between the number of cattle and the disappearance of malaria; between earth-fast fences and the undermining of the power held by the old aristocratic elite; and between the development of communication systems and agrarian reforms. The agricultural, or 'green,' revolution that resulted in increased production of foodstuffs, and the industrial, or 'energy and raw materials,' revolution during which wood was replaced by coal and iron, will be shown to have been mutually supportive and interdependent.

Conversely, other correlations that hitherto have been regarded as being of major importance either dissolve or fade into the background. Among these is the commonly accepted relationship between agrarian reform legislation – the abolition of adscription, enclosure, freehold, and so forth – and the dynamic development of agriculture and industry during the nineteenth century. Whereas the agrarian reforms are normally credited with having been of decisive importance to the emergence of modern Denmark, in the present examination they are seen as having played a more limited role. They should be understood only as the conclusion of a long struggle for political and social power among competing factions of the Danish elite.

The development that took place in Denmark during these centuries was part of an overall pattern that occurred in most European countries. It was a process that resulted in Europe's rebirth and that gave Western civilization the upper hand both economically and politically throughout the world. The history of Denmark between 1500 and 1800 is a typical and clear example of this European development.

Unless otherwise specified, 'Denmark' is used in this book to cover the kingdom as it was until 1920, when the northern part of Schleswig, following a plebiscite held in accordance with the Treaty of Versailles, was united with Denmark. During the period from 1500 to 1800, Denmark formed part of a larger, multinational and multilingual united monarchy whose capital was Copenhagen. In addition to Denmark, it included the richly forested kingdom of Norway and the two predominantly German-speaking duchies of Schleswig and Holstein. Finally, there were the North Atlantic territories – Iceland, the Faeroe Islands, and Greenland – and a few overseas possessions, including the three West Indian islands of St. Croix, St. Thomas, and St. John (the Virgin Islands), which were sold to the United States in 1917. The provinces of Skåne, Halland,

Introduction 5

and Blekinge – which make up the whole of the southern part of present-day Sweden – were separated from Denmark in 1658. Nevertheless, because of Denmark's considerable extent and strategic position at the entrance to the Baltic, the Danish monarchy represented, throughout the period dealt with in this book, a not inconsiderable factor in European politics. It was not until the loss of Norway in 1814 and of Schleswig and Holstein in 1864 that Denmark was reduced to a minor state.

Part I

DENMARK, 1500–1750
A Country in an Ecological Crisis

1

THE ROAD TO THE CRISIS

The kingdom that Christian IV took over in 1588 was in excellent condition. Almost a quarter of the country was covered in forest and there was an abundance of big game – wolves, wild boars, and red deer.[1] Agriculture was flourishing. In 1539 Frederik I's chancellor, Wolfgang von Utenhof, described Denmark as

> a very fertile, useful, splendid and merry kingdom that has fertile fields, lovely forests and groves and endowed moreover with excellent cattle-breeding, a wealth of fish, all manner of game in the forests, and poultry and fowl aplenty.[2]

In 1622 the Danish scholar Ole Worm gave his country a testimonial that was in no way inferior:

> Had Aristotle known the fertile and splendid islands in the Danish sea he would have been highly justified in calling this kingdom the larder and inexhaustible barn of all Europe and the wet-nurse of all peoples; for, had not foreigners fetched from it, as from the richest of warehouses, all the necessities of life, so many thousand oxen, such myriads of fish of all kinds and such an abundance of crops, many must needs have died of hunger. Then there are the vast numbers of the most noble horses – so much in demand for purposes of war by Germans, Frenchmen, Spaniards and Italians – that are annually despatched hence. No kingdom, no empire, hath supplied a greater quantity of gold and silver pieces than this kingdom's customs office at Kronborg Castle alone. Were I to weigh all things justly, then the Danes have no need of others, but all have need of them.[3]

Although Worm may have been biased, this can hardly be said of the Italian Torquato Recchia, who came to Denmark at the end

[1] Troels–Lund 1879–1901, I, pp. 68–71; C. Weismann 1931, pp. 76–9, 90–8; V. J. Brøndegaard 1985–6, III, pp. 134, 211–12, 226; C. F. Bricka 1870–2.
[2] Wolfgang von Utenhof 1539, p. 12 (". . . ein sehr fruchtbar, Nutzlich, herlich und lustigk reich, welches Iar ein fruchtbaren acker, schone welde, und holtzer, darzu ein treffliche fihe zucht, darzu sehr fysch reich, mit allerley geschlechte des wilprechts, in welder, und sehr vil geflochelten tiren und fogeln, begabet").
[3] Ole Worm 1965–8, I, p. 62.

9

10 Denmark, 1500–1750

of the 1620s as majordomo to a general in the army of the Austrian warlord Wallenstein. Recchia described Denmark as being

> very rich in forests, replete with all manner of game in such large quantities that on occasion one sees them in the open fields, excepting wolves, and accordingly there is excellent hunting. . . . The country is very fertile and well suited to trade, both on account of her shipping, being protected by the ocean as well as by the Baltic Sea, and on account of her rich soil, which is cultivated in peacetime. Here, large quantities of grain are produced for human and animal consumption, cows, lambs, pigs and butter, in such wise that in addition to supplying her domestic needs the country can also export to Holland and other countries; 100,000 oxen are exported annually.[4]

Although the young Christian IV's Denmark was in many respects in good shape and sound condition, there were still some vulnerable points. Thanks to a much-needed pause enjoyed by the ecological system after the decline in population during the Black Death in the fourteenth century, the forests were larger and better than they had been for centuries. Large areas that had been open countryside during the Middle Ages were once more overgrown: In Zealand, for example, the stretch between Kalundborg and Ringsted, an area once characterized by the medieval chronicler Saxo Grammaticus as thinly forested, was described by the topographical writer Arent Berntsen four hundred years later as one of the most important forest districts in Zealand.[5] However, the forests were still not fully developed after their decline in the Middle Ages. For example, in Zealand it was not possible to find timber of sufficiently large dimensions for repairs to Antvorskov Palace near Slagelse (the wood had to be brought from Norway);[6] and although the moors had been decreasing since the fifteenth century, they were still far from having been reduced to their very modest extent during the period before agriculture began to take its toll on the ecosystem.[7]

Finally, there was the weakest link in the ecological chain, the sand dunes, which had never completely settled after the Middle Ages and might start drifting at the slightest pressure on the ecosys-

---

[4] Johannes. Lindbæk 1909–13, pp. 358–9.   [5] Svend Gissel 1968, p. 236.
[6] A. Opperman 1923–31, p. 14.
[7] Pollen analyses reveal a decline for xerophytes (i.e., plants that grow on open land) and heather during the period 1400–1600, whereas the beech curve rises. Bent Aaby and Bent Odgaard 1988, p. 10. The original extent of the moor: Johannes Iversen 1979–82, p. 444; Bent Aaby and Bent Odgaard 1988, p. 19, cf. Kim Aaris-Sørensen 1988, p. 188.

Road to Crisis

tem. It was precisely here that problems had arisen in the decades prior to Christian IV's accession to the throne. In 1539, Christian III, with the aim of preventing sand drift, had prohibited the pulling up of dune plants, which were used as winter fodder and thatching material by the inhabitants along the North Sea coast.[8]

The Danish coastal dunes are not, as might be supposed, a spontaneous product of nature. Originally the forests extended right out to the water's edge all over Denmark, especially alongside the North Sea, where they protected the coastline and its hinterland from erosion by wind and waves.[9] With the advent of agriculture these coastal forests were felled, whereupon the wind and the waves were able to commence the long-drawn transformation of the coastline and its hinterland in the manner that continues to this day.

Sand drift started about 3000 B.C. which is to say 1,000 to 1,200 years after agriculture had taken hold,[10] and recurred repeatedly throughout antiquity, the Viking period, and the Middle Ages.[11] There are signs that it followed the rhythm of agriculture, increasing in periods when agriculture expanded and decreasing when it declined. There is evidence of heavy drifting during the Iron Age and again, around 1200, during the period of Valdemar the Great and Valdemar the Victorious. In Thy there are migrating dunes whose position around 1880 – assuming that drifting had been continuous – indicates that they must have been formed around the year 1200 ± 50. Correspondingly, Dansted Dune and "The Church Dune," which covered Skagen Church with sand at the end of the eighteenth century, can be calculated as having started to drift in the years 1230 and 1300 respectively.[12]

---

[8] Hans Kuhlman 1979–82, p. 185–6.

[9] Johannes Iversen 1979–82, p. 445. Cf. *Trap Danmark* 1953–72, 14, p. 32, and David Liversage and David E. Robinson 1988, p. 264. Unlike the coastal dunes, the inland dunes (inland sands) in Central and West Jutland constitute an original characteristic of the postglacial landscape, cf. *Trap Danmark* 1953–72, 1, pp. 47–8. But as the changing appearance of the inland dunes in historic time was determined in a way similar to that of the coastal dunes they are grouped together.

[10] Agriculture since about 4200 B.C.: Jørgen Jensen 1979, p. 55. Sand drift from about 3000 B.C.: David Liversage and David E. Robinson 1988, pp. 266–87. Sand drift caused by human activity: P. V. Glob 1949, p. 6.

[11] David Liversage and David E. Robinson 1988.

[12] Sand drift during the Iron Age: Palle Friis 1970, p. 37; Gudmund Hatt 1937, p. 93. The migrating dune at Thy: Viggo Hansen 1957, pp. 79–80, 1976, p. 56. Dansted Dune, "The Church Dune," et al.: Viggo Hansen 1964, pp. 75–6. Among other examples of sand drift in the Middle Ages was Lindholm Høje at Nørre Sundby. Between 1040 and 1076 there was a sandstorm here that suddenly covered the fields with 35 cm of sand. Sand drift was possibly the reason why the settlement was finally abandoned around 1100. Thorkild Ramskou 1960, pp. 31–9.

12   *Denmark, 1500–1750*

There is reason to believe that sand drift decreased during the so-called late Medieval crisis of the fourteenth and fifteenth centuries, and that many dunes were gradually tied down beneath an unbroken cover of stiff lyme grass and other dune plants that were now left in peace because they were no longer needed. However, sand drift did not cease entirely; it is likely, as just mentioned, that some of the largest migrating dunes, displaying formidable dynamism, were in constant movement from the thirteenth century until far into the nineteenth century.

Increasing pressure on the ecosystem – as evidenced by the peasants' interest in the dune lyme grass in the time of Christian III – was a forewarning of the ecological crisis that would cause the young Christian IV's once so prosperous kingdom to totter during the ensuing one hundred fifty years. The two most important factors behind the crisis were population growth and the building up, during the seventeenth and eighteenth centuries, of a modern, fiscal-military state.

1.1 POPULATION GROWTH

It is uncertain by how much Denmark's population decreased during the demographic plunge in the fourteenth century. However, it is beyond all doubt that the figure dropped to well below one million, this figure being approached when nature, assisted by the Black Death, finally took pity on the Danes (living, at the time, "in a state of misery without parallel in the country's history"[13]) and delivered them from an impoverished, worn out, and overpopulated world. Deserted farms and a pronounced 'population shortage' in the middle of the fourteenth century point to a considerably smaller population and reduced pressure on resources;[14] the same applies to the ecological recovery that took place during the fifteenth and sixteenth centuries, including reforestation, reduction of the moorlands, and partial stabilization of the dunes.

During the fifteenth and sixteenth centuries, population figures began to increase in Europe again and perhaps also in Denmark.[15] Around 1650 the population of Denmark was about 550,000, still no more than just over half what the population is assumed to have been around the year 1300.[16] But from 1650 on the increase gathered mo-

---

[13] Helge Paludan 1977, pp. 412, 414–15. [14] Ibid., p. 176; Svend Gissel 1972.
[15] Colin McEvedy and Richard Jones 1978, p. 18 (fig. 1.2); Helge Gamrath and E. Ladewig Petersen 1980, p. 379.
[16] This and subsequent figures for Denmark's population from Aksel Lassen 1965, pp. 11, 530.

Road to Crisis

mentum. The white race's "tremendous willingness to procreate" (as the Danish historian Erik Arup so enthusiastically expressed it)[17] ran true to form. By 1735 the figure of 550,000 had become 715,000, and in 1774 just over 815,000, that is, a growth of about 50 percent in the course of roughly a hundred years. In 1800 Denmark's population was just over 925,000, about the same as it had been five hundred years earlier. Since Christian IV's days, pressure on resources had almost doubled because of population growth.

1.2 A FISCAL-MILITARY STATE

Along with population growth, the most important factor behind the pressure on resources that led Denmark into her ecological crisis was the building up of a fiscal-military state on the basis of taxation during the seventeenth and eighteenth centuries. Pressure on the country's resources was exerted in two ways: directly, through state consumption of resources, and indirectly, through the effects of the taxes imposed to finance state consumption.

State consumption, which began to increase rapidly at the beginning of the seventeenth century, was both civilian and military. Apart from expenses connected with the Danish court and with the growing corps of government officials, civilian consumption included splendid and prestigious building projects, among them a number of royal palaces, the most prominent being Frederiksborg Palace (1600–20) and Christiansborg Palace (1731–45). The consumption of timber and bricks for these buildings was considerable and made inroads into the country's forests. Some ten thousand beech trunks were required for the foundations alone of Christiansborg Palace, and the firing of the bricks used for this one project – at least thirty million – required close to ten thousand tons of wood as fuel.[18]

Wood was also used extensively for other purposes. One measure introduced for the benefit of both domestic and international shipping was the setting up of a lighthouse authority in 1560. The first lighthouses were built at The Skaw, on the island of Anholt in the Kattegat, and at Kullen. The original intention was to operate the lighthouses using local fuel; but after 1600 this plan had to be abandoned, and pit coal, which had just appeared on the market,

---

[17] Erik Arup 1925–55, I, p. 45.

[18] Carl Bruun 1887–90, II, pp. 672–90. Jan Steenberg 1950, p. 154 and passim. Other palaces built during the period included those at Hirschholm, Frederiksberg, and Fredensborg. The firing of one brick weighing 2.5 kg consumed 0.33 kg of wood. Letter from Hans Rose 15 May 1990.

14   Denmark, 1500–1750

was used instead. Before things had gone this far, however, considerable damage had been done to the forests at The Skaw and on the island of Anholt.[19] The price paid for improving the safety of national and international shipping in Danish waters during the seventeenth and eighteenth centuries was the deterioration of the Danish environment.

All in all, however, and measured by an international yardstick, state consumption in Denmark for civilian purposes during the seventeenth and eighteenth centuries was moderate.[20] The same could not be said of consumption for military purposes. During the seventeenth century, Denmark became the strongest militarized nation in Europe with military commitments extending from the North Cape to Hamburg.[21] The fleet, and therefore the building of naval vessels, played a central role in the forced pace of armament. On the basis of the research conducted so far, it is difficult to determine how much pressure was imposed on Danish forests by the building of naval vessels.[22] A calculation on the basis of figures for the second half of the eighteenth century, years during which the fleet was no longer expanded but merely maintained, shows that at this time the Danish navy required a quantity of timber corresponding to growth on about 120 square kilometres of oak forest, an area just under 0.5 percent of the area of the entire kingdom.[23] This may not sound very great. However, it must be borne in mind that what was involved here was solely the upkeep of a complete fleet in peacetime. The actual expansion of the modern naval fleet that was carried out during the seventeenth century and the early decades of the eighteenth century – a period of many wars and frequent loss of naval supplies – called for the use of considerably more timber, an amount affected also

[19] Henning Henningsen 1960, pp. 6, 12–17; Erik Pontoppidan 1763–81, V, 1, p. 230; Palle Friis 1967, p. 15, and C. Weismann 1931, p. 66.
[20] Cf. Edvard Holm 1891–1912, II, pp. 587–8.   [21] Gunner Lind 1986a, pp. 28–32.
[22] Oak was mainly used for the naval vessels, which meant that the Dano-Norwegian fleet was largely dependent on the Danish forests. However, see Alexander Bugge 1925–33, II, p. 357 and passim. Just how the union with Norway (which was rich in forests) affected the exchange of resources between Denmark and Norway still needs to be clarified.
[23] P. Christian Nielsen 1960, pp. 181 and 193, where annual consumption for the upkeep of the fleet is estimated at 4,500 m³. Calculation of equivalent areas: 4,500 m³ oak timber = 9,000 m³ standing timber = 1,800 fully grown oak trees = 36 ha fully grown, present-day oak forest; with the less dense forests of the day at least the double (cf. A. Howard Grøn 1955–61, suppl. p. 15), in other words, hardly less than 80 ha of fully grown oak forest per annum for the fleet. Setting the growth period for oak forests at 150 years (cf. Gregers Begtrup 1803–12, III, p. 435), it means that the Danish navy's requirements amounted to 150 × 80 = 120 km² of oak forest. Size of the fleet unaltered during the last half of the eighteenth century: Ole Feldbæk 1982, p. 100.

Road to Crisis 15

by the waste that took place during shipbuilding in the seventeenth century.[24]

Added to this was the pressure exerted on timber resources by military land forces. Unfortunately, existing research on this type of consumption has even less to relate than research about consumption for naval purposes.[25] Examples reveal, nevertheless, that the army was also a large consumer of timber.[26] All in all it may therefore be assumed that the reduction of Danish forests, from 20–25 percent of the total area around 1600 to 8–10 percent one hundred fifty years later,[27] was to a significant degree due to Denmark's position in the international armament race. The price for maintaining Europe's most powerful army – seen in relation to the size of the country's population – as well as the fleet, "the nation's pride and joy,"[28] was high, namely, ecological destruction and the undermining of the country's primary resources.

All of this does not fully answer the question of state influence on events. Another aspect, no less important, was the influence that the financing of state consumption for civilian, military, and naval purposes exercised on society. In the course of the seventeenth century, the state's economy became taxation based. Income derived from sources other than taxes decreased in importance, particularly after major disposals of Crown lands during the 1660s. Military and naval expenditures, which, at the beginning of the eighteenth century, swallowed up two-thirds of the national budget,[29] had, along with other public tasks, to be financed largely by taxation, and because Denmark's military expenditure was the highest in Europe, such taxation had to be correspondingly severe.[30]

---

[24] The increase in timber consumption for the fleet during the seventeenth century was caused partly by ship losses in battle and the squandering of timber and partly by the greater number of increasingly larger ships. Intensive building activity in the navy during the last decades of the seventeenth century and the first decades of the eighteenth century compared with the end of the eighteenth century: H G. Garde 1832–5, IV, pp. 575–629. Size of ships: A ship of the line in the time of Christian IV required 2–3,000 m³ of oak timber; a ship of the line in the time of Frederik IV 5–6,000 m³. A. Howard Grøn 1955–61, suppl. p. 15. See also A. F. Bergsøe 1837, II, p. 145, and Hugo Matthiessen 1942, p. 33. Squandering of timber: A. Howard Grøn 1955–61, I, pp. 30–1.
[25] K. C. Rockstroh does not touch on the question of the consumption of resources in his three-volume account of the history of the Danish army.
[26] A. Howard Grøn 1955–61, I, p. 31. Cf. Esaias Fleischer 1779, pp. 404–5.
[27] Extent of forests in 1750: Around 1800 the forests covered about 4% of the area (P. Christian Nielsen 1979–82, p. 50), which was just under half their extent 50 years earlier, cf. A. F. Bergsøe 1844–53, II, p. 204.
[28] Edvard Holm 1885–6, I, p. 464.   [29] Ibid., II, p. 256.
[30] Taxation level as one of the highest in Europe: Gunner Lind 1986a, p. 29.

16   Denmark, 1500–1750

Taxation demands made it necessary to force production, first and foremost in agriculture, which experienced a doubling of taxes between 1663 and 1720.[31] In contrast to what is generally assumed, this would appear to have occurred to an astonishing degree.[32] Never satisfactorily explained, a paradoxical factor in the economic development of Denmark after 1660 is that agricultural prices remained stable right up to the 1740s, despite a population increase of almost 30 percent that in turn led to a corresponding – or rather, if one considers sales to Norway and exports – to an even greater increase in demand (fig. 3). Under such circumstances one might expect food prices to rise, but they did not do so. On the contrary, the period was marked by slack agricultural prices, reaching an all-time low during the severe agricultural depression of the 1730s. A likely explanation for this peculiar phenomenon is that agriculture, because of the pressure of taxes, was pushed to such a high level of production that the bottom was knocked out of the foodstuff market – in other words, an overproduction crisis occurred in spite of increasing demand.[33]

The period 1660–1740 was one during which innumerable large estates found themselves in financial difficulties,[34] that led in many cases to bankruptcy. Such circumstances caused the collapse of the financier Henrik Müller's huge estates in 1682–3 and of the Gråsten-Tranekær estates in northern Schleswig and on the island of Langeland – the largest group at the time – in 1722. In other cases it proved possible for the owners to save the situation at the last moment by selling off parts of the forests and sowing corn on the cleared land.[35]

But this recession, which was due to forced production in agriculture and forestry without technological innovation, took its toll. Not only did the bottom fall out of the foodstuffs market – it also fell out of the ecological system.

---

[31] Claus Rafner 1986, p. 93. Cf. also Finn Stendal Pedersen 1982–3, p. 384.
[32] See, for example, Erling Ladewig Petersen: "The Government's financial requirements and activity increased much faster after 1630 than society's productivity (if this ever expanded at all)." (1980, p. 424).
[33] Jens Holmgaard 1977–8, p. 40. Cf. Niels Steensgaard 1969–70, pp. 501–4, especially p. 504.
[34] Fridlev Skrubbeltrang 1978, pp. 125–8.
[35] Among the estates that were saved at the last moment was Skaføgård Manor in East Jutland. In the 1710s, 260 *tønder* of forest were felled to raise money. The cleared land was then brought under the plough. Knud J. V. Jespersen 1975, pp. 44–5.

Road to Crisis

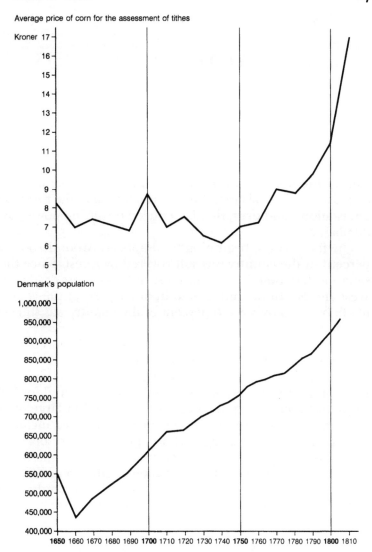

Figure 3. Agricultural prices and population, 1650–1800.

2

THE ANATOMY OF THE CRISIS

During the first half of the eighteenth century Denmark experienced an ecological crisis. Problems piled up in the form of forest devastation, sand drift, floods, reduced fertilizing power, and cattle plague.

The forests were beginning to disappear. Around 1600, 20–25 percent of the country was still covered by forest. Since then the situation had deteriorated in most districts, most dramatically in West and North Jutland, less so in other parts of the country. All in all, by 1750 only 8–10 percent of the country was still covered with forest.[1]

Wood, the most important raw material and source of energy, was fundamental to the economy of the time. It was used as fuel in households and in all kinds of industries, such as saltworks, iron foundries, and brickyards. Timber was required for building ships and houses and, furthermore, was used in large quantities throughout society for the most varied of purposes, including, for example, for fencing in agriculture. Pressure on resources was so great that instead of drawing only on growth in the forests, inroads also were made into forest capital. Observers could see the day approaching when society would grind to a standstill for lack of timber.[2] Furthermore, hunting, which in Frederik II's day was

---

[1] The extent of the forests around 1600: See Chapter 1, incl. n. 1; around 1750: See Chapter 1, n. 27. Innumerable examples of the decline of forests during the seventeenth and eighteenth centuries are in Erik Pontoppidan 1763–81, e.g., III, pp. 129, 146, 463; IV, pp. 26, 200, 307–8, 312, 426, 468, 476, 481, 488, 500, 504, 552, 591, 660, 668, 670, 772; V, 1, pp. 96, 103, 196, 334, 337, 522, 533; VI, pp. 54, 467, 518–19, 547, 680, 747. See also Christian Vaupell 1862, pp. 400–17, Trap Danmark 1953 72, 9, p. 911 (South Zealand); 14, pp. 31–2 (Northern Jutland); P. E. Jensen 1902, pp. 269, 282, 287; Elers Koch 1892, pp. 95–103; Fritz Jacobsen 1940, pp. 48, 54, 58; Frits Hastrup 1970–3, p. 87, and Bo Fritzbøger 1989a, pp. 62, 79–91.

[2] N. Hurtigkarl 1757, p. 58; Anon. 1758a, p. 313 and elsewhere; cf. C. Christensen (Hørsholm) 1886–91, II, pp. 115–18; O. D. Lütken 1762, p. 261.

Anatomy of Crisis   19

still an important supplementary source of meat, disappeared with the forests; by the eighteenth century it was insignificant.[3]

Another urgent problem in the eighteenth century was the drifting of sand and mould. Sand drift, which had started as early as the beginning of the sixteenth century, had spread slowly during the seventeenth century, from isolated peripheral regions to deeper into the countryside (fig. 4), and, at the beginning of the eighteenth century, it was rife along the North Sea coast, in Central Jutland, on the Djursland peninsula, and on the islands of Læsø and Anholt. It spread in North and East Zealand and on the island of Bornholm. Even on the island of Funen, where today the memory of sand drift seems to have completely disappeared, there were areas with considerable erosion. Since the beginning of the sixteenth century, large expanses that were formerly forests or fertile arable land had been transformed into sandy deserts or windswept surfaces almost devoid of topsoil.[4]

Sand drift and mould drift were caused either by overexploitation of the soil by forestry, as was the case, for example, on the islands of Læsø and Anholt,[5] or by agricultural overexploitation, particularly overgrazing, or by a combination of the two.[6] Around

---

[3] C. Weismann 1931, p. 66; V. J. Brøndegaard 1985–6, III, pp. 137–41, 212–13, 227; C. F. Bricka 1870–2.

[4] A differentiation is made in specialized literature between sand drift in the narrow sense, which is when sea sand and sand from inland dunes moves, and mould drift, which is when the topsoil (tilth) is blown off. Viggo Hansen 1964, pp. 76–7. Sand drift in general: E. Viborg 1795, pp. 4–14; V. Falbe-Hansen and William Scharling 1885–91, I, pp. 134–65; Palle Friis 1967 and 1970; Axel Steensberg 1969, pp. 509–13. On sand drift in various localities: J. Brüel 1918; Viggo Hansen 1957, 1964 (esp. pp. 70–8), and 1976; Holger Rasmussen 1970, p. 147. Especially about Funen: G. L. Wad 1921, pp. 115–22 (1743, Dreslette); Erik Pontoppidan 1763–81, VI, p. 640 (the parish of Ørslev); Gregers Begtrup 1803–12, III, p. 235 (about Helnæs: "one hopes it [sand drift] will not spread further"); and Jens Holmgaard 1962, p. 116. See also Rtk. 2484, Landvæsenskontorernes sandflugtssager 1793–1840, Danish National Archives.

[5] The island of Læsø: sand drift from the sixteenth century on account of forest felling to obtain fuel for boiling salt; from the 1680s no more trees on the island, after which sand drift got the upper hand. Bjarne Stoklund 1965 and 1969a, p. 12. The island of Anholt: tree felling for boiling tar and (1561–4) for the Lighthouse Authority; sand drift got the upper hand as from the 1640s. *Trap Danmark* 1953–72, 18, pp. 950–1; Vrads Sande, Central Jutland: all wood used as fuel when smelting iron, after which sand drift gathered momentum in the seventeenth century. Hans de Hofman 1758, pp. 23–4; cf. Robert Thomsen 1975, pp. 151–6. Other examples of sand drift as a consequence of the disappearance of forests: Hårup Sande, which arose around 1750. *Trap Danmark* 1953–72, 20, pp. 522–3.

[6] Madum parish, Western Jutland: Poul Hansen 1942, p. 12. Ansager parish, Western Jutland: H. K. Kristensen 1944, p. 11. Several parishes in Thy: Erik Pontoppidan 1763–81, V, 1, p. 409. The Skaw and the stretch from here to Hjørring: ibid., pp. 197, 221–2. The island of Bornholm: *Trap Danmark* 1953–72, 10, p. 393. Overgrazing as a cause of desert formation can be observed today in many places in Africa, cf. R. D. Mann 1990, p. 52.

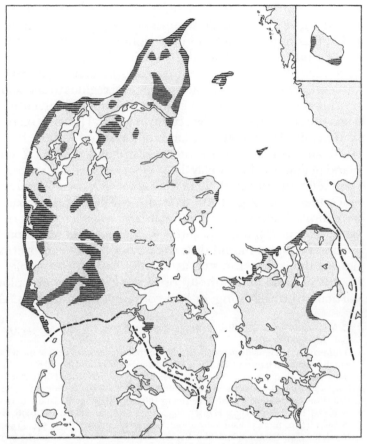

Figure 4.   Areas afflicted by sand drift in the eighteenth century.

1750 as much as 5 percent of the total area of Jutland was no longer cultivated owing to sand drift and mould drift, and the same applied to considerable areas on the islands of Zealand and Bornholm.[7]

Other areas were affected, sometimes through slow drifting, sometimes after terrible sandstorms during which the sand rose so high that it "hid the sun in the middle of the day," so that "one could not see one's hand in front of one's face." Erik Viborg, a civil servant responsible for inspecting sand dunes, described a sandstorm over Nørlund Sande in West Jutland around 1790 as follows:

[7] Viggo Hansen 1976, p. 56.

Anatomy of Crisis

> From several miles distant it appeared like a heath fire, way up in the air. The inhabitants came towards me, weeping, showing me how their properties had been destroyed. A strong northwesterly wind was blowing, so they durst not take me into the sand drift lest we should get lost. I proceeded, notwithstanding, and on entering this stretch of shifting sand could scarce open an eye. All objects disappeared. Nought was visible but smoke and sand, causing the sun to appear copper-coloured.

During such storms, nothing could stop the sand. It forced its way into the eyes, nose, and throat and into houses, and it spread itself in layers several feet thick on what previously had been fertile arable land.[8] Just as in the American Dust Bowl in the 1930s and in our own times in Africa and the Amazon Basin, deserts followed in the wake of agriculture and forestry.[9]

Not only in Denmark did drifting sands spread from the end of the seventeenth century onwards. Sand drift occurred throughout most of Europe: in Hungary, Prussia, Sweden, England, and Holland and along the Atlantic coast in France. Europe's largest contiguous sand drift region was Kurische Nehrung, in what was then East Prussia, with its enormous shifting dunes up to 70 metres high.[10]

A third problem for Danish society in the time of Frederik IV and Christian VI was the water level. Tree felling and soil erosion disturbed hydrological conditions. Lakes, rivers, streams, marshes, and meadows became swollen, and as a consequence fields were flooded for large parts of the year. The results were acidification of the soil, an increased tendency to peat formation, and a shortened growth season.[11] In the eighteenth century, because the soil was so wet in the spring, the growth season was only about 100 days as compared with about 125 today; with the relatively weak implements and tractive forces of the day the soil was not accessible until several weeks later than it is now.[12]

[8] Viborg's description of a sandstorm quoted by V. Halskov-Hansen 1968–9, pp. 320–1. See also Erik Viborg 1795, pp. 6–7. Viborg's description of Danish sandstorms in the eighteenth century corresponds precisely to those we have of sandstorms in the United States in the 1930s. See Donald Worster 1979, pp. 14–25.

[9] Donald Worster 1979, pp. 240–1; R. D. Mann 1990; Harald Sioli 1987.

[10] Hungary: V. Halskov-Hansen 1968–9, p. 319. Prussia: C. C. Andresen 1861, pp. 273–9; Bernhard Buderath and Henry Makowski 1986, pp. 209–10. Sweden: Arent Berntsen 1650–6, I, pp. 84–5; Enoch Ingers and Sten Carlssson 1943–56, II, p. 15; Carl von Linné 1874, pp. 242–3, 254–60. England: Viggo Hansen 1957, p. 81. Holland: C. C. Andresen 1861, pp. 262–73; Jan de Vries 1974, p. 196. France: C. C. Andresen 1861, p. 262; Gregers Begtrup 1803–12, VII, p. 198.

[11] S. P. Jensen 1987, pp. 88–9, 96–9.

[12] Fridlev Skrubbeltrang 1972–3, p. 263 (sowing and harvesting periods for a farmer named Chr. Andersen, who had a tenant farm at Nr. Tulstrup, near Viborg, 1786–97).

22 Denmark, 1500–1750

Finally, there was the difficulty of maintaining the fertility of arable land. An early recognition of this can be detected in a despondent sigh recorded by some anonymous hand in the records of the district of Øster Flakkebjerg in 1647:

> It hath been ascertained from the old record book of the diocese [of Zealand in 1567] that in former times the vicarage's crop was in sooth larger and finer than the last one; but whence it cameth, God wot.[13]

The situation was particularly critical with regard to nitrogen (N), which, in the form assimilable by plants, is relatively nonpersistent. Nitrogen was at a minimum practically everywhere and thus became the plant nutrient that determined the ultimate limit of the yield.[14] The annual nitrogen supplement received by cultivated (ploughed) land, some 500,000 hectares, where stable manure was used, was about 30 kilogrammes per hectare, corresponding to 10–15 percent of the average N-supplement given to Danish arable land during the 1980s. The grazing lands, which were very large (ca. 1.9 million hectares) compared to the ploughed areas, received no N-supplement in the form of stable manure – nor did the moorlands. On the contrary, these areas supplied a nutrient supplement to ploughed land through grazing, the gathering of hay and heather, and regular removal of the surface. Nitrogen supply to grazing areas was about 20 kilogrammes per annum per hectare, derived from the atmosphere (nitrogen in a form that can be assimilated by plants is released in small quantities in various ways, for example, by lightning), from free-living nitrogen-forming organisms, and from N-fixation through spontaneously growing leguminous plants.[15]

The interaction between these conditions meant that agricultural production was low by modern standards: on cultivated land about 800 Scandinavian feed units per hectare, on grazing areas even less, only about 450 feed units per hectare, which was 10 per-

---

[13] Svend Gissel 1956, p. 1.
[14] Johannes Dons Christensen 1952, p. 104. The amount of nitrogen assimilable by plants as a major determinant for agricultural yield applies with a few exceptions to agriculture throughout the world. See, for example, C. P. H. Chorley 1981 (Europe), Joseph Needham 1984, pp. 25–6 (China), and Flemming Juncker 1985, p. 81.
[15] The annual N-supplement to cultivated land in the eighteenth century has been estimated by S. P. Jensen (on the basis of calculations by R. S. Loomis in 1978) at between 21 and 36 kg per ha (1987, p. 93). I myself have reached (Thorkild Kjærgaard 1985b) a corresponding result (30 kg per ha); cf. C. P. H. Chorley 1981. In 1984 the average N-supplement per ha of arable land in Denmark was 220 kg. Thorkild Kjærgaard 1985b. Size of grazing areas: S. P. Jensen 1987, pp. 108–9.

Anatomy of Crisis

cent of what could be grown on a medium-quality Danish field of clover in the 1930s.[16] Even worse, production was unsustainable because it was ecologically self-destructive. The four big problems – devastation of the forests, sand drift, water level conditions, and the difficulty of maintaining the fertilizing power of the soil – not only exercised their individual effects but also entered into a negative, destructive interaction. An example of this was the use of cattle fodder and manure as fuel, which became widespread from the end of the seventeenth century onwards.

The reason why straw, sheep manure, turf, dried cowpats, and other valuable forms of feed or fertilizer were used as fuel was the lack of wood, not only in particularly severely stricken areas, such as the peripheral islands of Læsø, Anholt, and Rømø, but also in central parts of the country, such the larger islands of Zealand, Lolland, Falster, and Funen. As early as 1672 the farmers of Gedesby on the island of Falster wrote to the Dowager Queen Sophie Amalie at Nykøbing Palace, under whose jurisdiction they fell, saying that due to the shortage of forests, "we poor men have to burn fodder which our cattle and beasts should eat."[17] From Særslev, in North Funen, we learn of that town's consumption in 1682 that there was "no cutting of wood or turf for burning, nor of timber for building, and in respect of the cutting of hedge stakes such a very small quantity as scarce can be assessed."[18] At the beginning of the eighteenth century, straw was used at Antvorskov Manor[19] in Central Zealand as fuel for baking and brewing.

The consequences of using cattle fodder and manure as fuel proved fatal, for it was the following year's harvest and the following year's beef and milch cattle that were sacrificed as a result. As the agronomist Gregers Begtrup laconically put it, it was "in sooth,

---

[16] S. P. Jensen 1987, pp. 109–10. The yield in the 1930s is on the basis of Helge Drewsen et al., 1943, p. 283; cf. *Landbrugets Ordbog* 1937–8, 1, p. 484.

[17] Bo Fritzbøger 1989b, p. 18.

[18] Henrik Larsen 1937–8, pp. 33–4. Cf. Fritz Jacobsen 1940, pp. 41–2.

[19] Fritz Jacobsen 1940, pp. 41–2. See also Bjarne Stoklund 1965 (on the islands of Læsø and Rømø and the Harboør peninsula, where Limfjorden and the North Sea meet); Erik Pontoppidan 1763–81, IV, p. 707 (Læsø), and August F. Schmidt 1939, p. 649, and 1948, p. 109. Gregers Begtrup mentions corresponding examples from several of the country's districts. In the area between Roskilde, Køge, and Copenhagen, straw was used for heating ovens for baking, also on the island of Strynø. It is told that fruit trees were torn up and burnt on the island of Lolland "due to the dearness of firewood" (1803–12, II, p. 317; III, p. 533; IV, p. 707). Concerning the island of Lolland, also P. Rhode 1776–94, I, pp. 16–17. See also Christian H. Brasch 1859–63, II, p. 77; cf. Edvard Holm 1885–6, II, p. 265.

24   Denmark, 1500–1750

poor husbandry."[20] In 1698 the Zealand parson and poet Jørgen Sorterup described in a poem the destructive mechanisms in a society that lacked the barest minimum of energy resources for cooking and heating:

> But what stirs in me the greatest wrath
> Where'er I chance to come:
> The peasant from his humble hearth
> His pea straw ne'er doth spare.
> What shall you then, say I, you dupe
> Give your poor sheep to eat,
> When of your fodder you do burn
> One sheaf after the other.
> Your cattle die, no dung you spread
> Upon your fields; what you then plough
> Affords scant yield; and thus in time
> Dire poverty your fate shall be.
> Well, Master George, quoth he,
> Worse luck, unfortunately.
> A poor man can but listen to
> Such counsel folk will give him.
> . . . .
>
> My wife must do her washing
> Should I now dare to tell the truth:
> I have two sickly children.
> They needs must have a little warmth
> To help restore their fragile health.[21]

Another aspect of the self-destructive cycle that embedded itself in the primary production sector was the hydrological disturbances caused by sand drift. For example, at Arresø (Lake Arre), discharge into the Kattegat was stopped at the beginning of the eighteenth century as a result of sand drift in North Zealand. The result was flooding and stagnation to the detriment of agriculture around Denmark's largest lake.[22] Jutland provides corresponding examples. The seaward approach to the town of Ribe was closed by sand

---

[20]   Gregers Begtrup 1803–12, II, p. 317.

[21]   ("Men det giør mig dend største harm, / Jeg over alt erfarer: / Hvor bonden fra sin ild-sted-arm / Dend ertehalm ey sparer. / Hvad skal du, siger jeg din giek, / Gii dine taar for tanden, / Naar du af foeret brender vek / Een rulte efter anden. / Dit qvæg døer bort, din ager og / Ey giødis, det du pløyer, / Dig lidet giir: omsider nok / Sig armod til dig føyer, / Ja, Mester Jørgen, svarer hand, / Gud bedre det, disvære, / Jeg griber til jeg fattig mand / De raad, her er paa fære. . . . Vor moder skulle byge, / Og skal jeg skrifte sanden frit, / Jeg har toe børn er syge. / De skulle ha' lidt varme, at / De sig lidt kunde komme.") Jørgen Sorterup 1698, p. 115.

[22]   K. C. Rockstroh 1911, pp. 40–2, 46.

Anatomy of Crisis

at the end of the seventeenth century,[23] and the southern part of Ringkøbing Fjord (Ringkøbing Inlet) was filled with sand around the year 1700, "so that one now rides in the inlet where previously one could but sail and fish." The result was that drainage from the large meadows to the south of the inlet was blocked, leaving them under water. This was not all. Continued sand drift caused the meadows that had been flooded in 1714 to become covered with sand, and within five years "a great many thousand swaths of meadow" had disappeared.[24] The same thing happened in many other places, where the drifting sand filled lakes and blocked one drain after another, resulting in uncontrollable floodings, acidification, and the formation of bogs and peat.[25]

From an agricultural point of view, the felling of forests might at first appear favourable. The forest grazing for pigs and cattle that had been lost was replaced by open grazing areas, and the land could be cultivated, which indeed was done on a large scale. The topographer Erik Pontoppidan expressed the view in 1759 that the agricultural area since the land register of 1688 had been increased by what corresponded to about 60,000 *tønder hartkorn*, that is, by about one-sixth.[26] This estimate has aroused scepticism, but is fully confirmed by the latest research.[27]

The former forestland, which supplied the principal contingent of the 60,000 new *tønder hartkorn*,[28] initially provided excellent farmland, primarily because of its high content of humus, which is

---

[23] Erik Pontopiddan 1763–81, V, 2, pp. 649–52. Cf. Ludvig Holberg 1913–63, XVI, p. 10.

[24] Erik Viborg 1795, pp. 9–10; H. K. Kristensen 1975, pp. 172–3.

[25] Erik Pontoppidan 1763–81, IV, p. 22; V, 1, pp. 313, 381, 410, 454. See also Palle Friis 1967, p. 12, and 1970.

[26] Erik Pontoppidan 1759, p. 41.

[27] Karl-Erik Frandsen 1984, pp. 20–3 (expansion of the cultivated area in the village of Barup, Zealand, by 88% between 1682 and 1795), and Jens Larsen (II) 1983 (corresponding reclamation in the Vordingborg military district). C. Rise Hansen and Axel Steensberg demonstrated cultivation expansion of 9%, 13%, and 25% in the villages of Snekkerup, Hejninge, and Grøfte (all in Zealand), respectively, between 1682 and 1770 (1951, p. 240); Poul Rasmussen and A. F. Schmidt an increase of 50–100% of the cultivated area in the parishes of Frøslev and Mollerup on the island of Mors between 1683 and 1793 (1955, pp. 86, 130–1). On the 1730s Birgit Løgstrup 1983, p. 66; cf. Kai C. Uldall 1913–16, p. 559. See also Rtk. 434.10: A. C. Teilmann, "Erindringer ved det mig tilsendte Forslag on Hoverie [1788]," Danish National Archives. Reclamation was not an isolated Danish phenomenon, but can be observed elsewhere both within and beyond the borders of the Dano-Norwegian-Schleswig-Holstein monarchy. In Schleswig-Holstein expansion of arable land between 1710 and 1765 was typically 30–80%. Wolfgang Prange 1971, pp. 349–51.

[28] That it was to a large extent former forestland that was cultivated is apparent from, for example, Fridlev Skrubbeltrang 1978, pp. 91, 113; Hugo Matthiessen 1942, p. 79; P. E. Jensen 1902, pp. 362, 387; T. Thaulow 1957, p. 45; and Knud J. V. Jespersen 1975, pp. 44–5. Much information in Erik Pontopiddan (1763–81) about reclaimed forestland, e.g., III, p. 484; IV, pp. 258, 416, 660; V, 1, p. 85.

26   Denmark, 1500–1750

nitrogenous.[29] In the long run, however, the accounts that could be drawn up after forest clearance proved to be less attractive. The newly reclaimed forestland's addition to the total amount of nutrients in the agricultural area – and thus to agricultural productivity – disappeared rapidly. In particular, this applied to the nitrogen assimilable by plants; this nutrient disappeared solely because of the effect of light and air on the exposed forestland.[30] In the course of just a few years the nutrient content in the newly cleared land was stabilized at the low level predominating in the remaining agricultural area. Instead of having good forestland available, with a high N-content and stable production of wood and forest grazing, the farmer, after a short period of unusually high income (first from the felled timber and then from a couple of good crops on the nutritious soil) found himself left with yet another piece of low-yielding agricultural land. In certain districts, furthermore, this land was exposed to a high risk either of being covered with heather or of falling victim to sand drift.

There were also other negative, long-term effects of forest clearance. Forest is of considerable importance to hydrological conditions, not only because forestland retains rainwater better than unforested land but also because far larger quantities of water evaporate from a forest-clad area than from a corresponding open area.[31] Removal of forest initiates a chain reaction: More rainwater is released into the watercourses because there is less evaporation, and the bare soil's inferior water-binding ability results in the water so released reaching the watercourses faster. These consequently become more violent and carry large quantities of sediment, which, further along in the water system, where the flow becomes gentler, sinks to the bottom as deposit. The result is that the watercourses become blocked and choked with vegetation, the level of groundwater rises, and flooding occurs. The consequences of this are acidification and peat formation, resulting in a reduction of the agricultural area, inferior grass growth, a shorter growth season, and generally more difficult working conditions in agriculture.[32]

---

[29] The content of humus in forestland is partly due to the ability to assimilate nitrogen possessed by certain deciduous and coniferous trees. Eiler Worsøe 1979, p. 19; Carl Marius Møller 1950; Christian Kruse 1988, pp. 66–8; and Wendell Berry 1981, pp. 54–5, 61. See also S. P. Jensen 1987, p. 93. Description of the excellent qualities of newly reclaimed forestland: Gregers Begtrup 1803–12, IV, p. 724.

[30] S. P. Jensen 1987, p. 94.

[31] Niels Haarløv 1979–82, pp. 108–10; S. P. Jensen 1987, pp. 100–1; Steen B. Böcher 1942, p. 122.

[32] Niels Haarløv 1979–82, pp. 108–10; S. P. Jensen 1987, pp. 97–9; Fairfield Osborn 1948, pp. 49–50. Hans de Hofman observed in the 1750s that "grazing in meadows is

Anatomy of Crisis 27

In the Danish ecosystem the formation of low-level bogs and thus peat formation through the overgrowing of lakes is a natural but very slow process. What happened during the eighteenth century, therefore, was an acceleration of a process that otherwise takes place so slowly as to be invisible to humans.[33]

A dramatic intensification of these serious problems of maintaining overall ecological balance was cattle plague, which struck Denmark in the 1740s and in the course of a few years destroyed more than 200,000 head of cattle. For the individual farmer, who could use all the manure he could get hold of, and who needed to sell more and more meat and dairy products in order to pay his increasing taxes and to compensate for the persistently low agricultural prices paid between the 1660s and the 1740s, the obvious step had been to increase his herds. Cattle numbers did indeed increase after 1680 concurrently with forest clearance, soil cultivation, and the expansion of grazing land, until, during the 1740s, the figure reached was about 270,000 milch cows plus young stock, in all probably around 350,000–400,000, almost double the cattle population of the 1680s.[34]

This increase in cattle numbers produced an acute crisis in the ecologically weakened production system. Sufficient fodder could not be produced, and the standard of nutrition of the cattle dete-

decreasing considerably on account of the moss that grows on them, and because the water cannot be drained off in time" (1757, pp. 5–6). A detailed description of the growing over of watercourses and the consequences of this: Gregers Begtrup 1803–12, V, pp. 43–5. The claims made here about the influence on the environment of forest clearance are confirmed not only by modern experiences in the tropics but also by the massive forest clearances in the temperate zones of North America in the nineteenth century. For a dramatic account of the environmental consequences of forest clearance in the northwestern United States, see Henrik Cavling 1897, I, pp. 409–10.

[33] Elisabeth Munksgaard and J. Troels-Smith 1968, pp. 8–17.

[34] Doubling of the cattle population since 1862: Tue Axelgaard 1922–5, p. 272. Holberg was of the opinion in 1746 that cattle herds had doubled within the last fifty years (1913–63, XV, p. 244). This is confirmed in respect of 90 farms on the island of Falster by Svend Jespersen, who in 1692 found 0.43 head of cattle per *tønde hartkorn* and in 1741 twice as many (0.85) (1961, p. 102). Uncertainty exists about the exact size of the cattle population in the 1740s (before the cattle plague): Edvard Holm estimates the stocks of cattle at one milch cow per *tønde hartkorn* (1891–1912, III, 1, p. 290). This gives a figure of about 358,000 milch cows in Denmark plus young stock. Ole Feldbæk gives a total figure of 500,000 and would appear to stick to Holm's figures (1982, p. 150). S. P. Jensen gives the following figures for 1745: milch cows 270,000, bullocks over three years old 40,000, and other cattle 270,000, which gives a total cattle population of 580,000 (1985, p. 282); S. P. Jensen, however, would appear to give a rather high figure for "other cattle." The figures given here, which harmonize with Svend Jespersen's observations on the island of Falster, are after Erik Helmer Pedersen 1988, p. 64.

28   Denmark, 1500–1750

riorated, resulting in the herds' reduced ability to resist disease.[35] Cattle plague, which had been in Central Europe since the beginning of the sixteenth century,[36] now forced its way up into Denmark and struck with such violence during the 1740s that some 250,000 head of cattle, or more than half the country's cattle population, died before the disease began to ebb in 1747.[37]

Cattle plague (*pestis bovina*) is a disease characterized by necrosis of the mucous membranes, especially in the alimentary canal, resulting in mucous secretion, diarrhoea, dehydration, and fever, and finally, in the majority of cases, death. The infection is usually alimentarily conditioned, that is, transferred through the mouth when the animals touch each other or eat the same grass. Obviously, conditions were optimal for an outbreak of cattle plague in the 1740s, when the ability of Danish cattle to resist disease was weakened and the animals were cramped too close together in the fields, competing for insufficient quantities of fodder.[38]

To sum up, Denmark's population increase and civilian and military development, financed through taxation, resulted in a shortage of forests, leading to a shortage of fuel and raw materials, overgrazing, sand migration, hydrological problems, and cattle disease. If we look at the weakest link in the Danish ecosystem of the period, sand drift, the problems can be traced all the way back to the first half of the sixteenth century. It was not until the end of the seventeenth century that these problems began to spread in earnest. By then, there was no longer any mistaking them, and if Wolfgang von Utenhof had visited Denmark at the beginning of the eighteenth century it is unlikely that he would have recognized – in the desertlike stretches of drifting sand, the extensive, inaccessible bogs, the large commons with scattered trees and bushes gnawed by cattle, and the flooded fields – the healthy, fertile country he was familiar with in the 1520s and 1530s.

In the middle of the eighteenth century, Denmark's prospects were not good. It became clear that if a combined energy, raw materials, and foodstuffs crisis of incalculable extent was to be avoided, drastic steps would have to be taken. Development in the primary production sector would have to be changed, and the negative, self-generating mechanisms would have to be stopped. The formation of deserts and poor hydrological conditions would have

[35] Cf. S. P. Jensen 1987, p. 89.   [36] Hans Christian Bendixen 1973, p. 32.
[37] The figure for dead cattle after Edvard Holm 1891–1912, III, 1, p. 398. See also Ole Feldbæk 1982, p. 150.
[38] Epidemiology of the cattle plague: Torben Geill 1972, p. 104.

Anatomy of Crisis

to be brought under control and agricultural yields increased, especially in the extensive, low-yielding grazing lands and moors. Finally, the country would have to be ensured a stable and adequate supply of energy and raw materials. How this revolutionary re-creation of Denmark took place – and what its consequences were – is the subject of the remainder of this book.

Part II

THE ECOLOGICAL REVOLUTION

3

THE GREEN REVOLUTION

Terra, la tua virtute
Non è del Mondo, e da la gente intesa;
Che d'ignoranza offesa
Segue suo danno, e fugge sua salute.
Ma, se tue lode faran conosciute
d'altrui, come da me; per cui risplende
D'essa virtute un raggio:
St'util *Ricordo,* e saggio
Prenderà 'l Mondo tosto: che se 'l prende,
Ritorneran con la prima bontade
Gli anni de l'oro, e la felice estade.

Camillo Tarello, 1567

Earth, thy virtue
Is not understood by this world, nor by people
Who, afflicted by ignorance
Pursue their undoing and flee their salvation.
But if thy praises were known
By others, as by me, for whom a ray
Of this virtue shines:
Be useful, *Memoir,* and wise,
Seize the world forthwith: for if it accept thee
The golden age will return,
With the first abundance and happy summers.

3.1 SAND DRIFT IS ARRESTED

The first area in which action had to be taken if the Danish community's headlong course towards an ecological catastrophe was to be averted was to prevent ever greater parts of the country from being converted into desert. Sand drift had been causing concern ever since the sixteenth century, as evidenced by the various decrees, already mentioned, prohibiting the rooting up of lyme grass and marram grass on the west coast of Jutland.[1] These regulations were later included in the Danish Law of 1683 (Book 6, Ch. 17, §29), but not much else was done. Locally, farmers made considerable efforts to stop sand drift by building wattle fences and plant-

---

[1] The 1539 ban on rooting up marram and other grasses (see Chapter 1) was subsequently defined by the recess of 13 Dec. 1558 (repeated 11 Dec. 1679) and by the decree of 29 Oct. 1570. In addition, a number of rescripts were sent to various parishes in West Jutland, e.g., on 8 Sept. 1569 to Vedersø, Sdr. Nissum, Husby, and Staby, whose inhabitants were thus instructed to combat sand drift. C. C. Andresen 1861, pp. 237–41.

34   The Ecological Revolution

ing lyme grass,[2] but these had little effect. In the course of the seventeenth century, the situation was continually aggravated, especially in North Jutland and North Zealand. In 1647, Ole Worm – the same person who twenty-five years earlier had praised Denmark for her inexhaustible wealth – presented a disturbing report about the enormous sand hills that had accumulated at Asserbo in North Zealand and slowly but surely were transforming fertile land into desert.[3]

At the beginning of the eighteenth century, the villages of Tibirke and Tisvilde in North Zealand had their manorial dues considerably reduced to help them take steps to stop the sand, but in vain. The sand swept over the fields and choked the seed, and the secondary consequences of sand drift – flooding and stagnation – followed in its wake. In 1706 it was only a question of time before the sand would completely close the northern outlet from Arresø, with serious consequences for several of the surrounding villages.[4] The situation was out of control, and it was estimated that before long sand drift in this district would swallow up at least an additional 1,000 tønder hartkorn, corresponding to a whole barony.[5]

Things looked no better in Jutland. The rescript of 4 October 1723, issued to the inhabitants of the parishes of Ål, Ho, and Oksby in Southwest Jutland and requiring them to arrest the progress of the sand, had no more effect than the previous ones, nor did it prove possible to turn the course of events at the southern end of Ringkøbing Fjord, despite the energetic attempts made by Christian Hansen Teilmann,[6] chief administrative officer of the district. The prefect in Ålborg, Christian Reitzer, did what he could in North Jutland in the same way as his colleague at Ringkøbing. But the situation seemed hopeless, and a mood of impending disaster spread. In 1726, Reitzer wrote: "It is to be feared that gradually the whole of North Jutland will be covered with sand and virtually laid waste."[7]

In 1723, an expert in arresting sand drift was summoned from Holland, the Danish-born Lars Thott. However, after inspecting the sand drift area at Tisvilde, which extended over several thousand tønder hartkorn, he declared there was nothing to be done and returned to Holland.[8] The next authority consulted was less pes-

---

[2] Gunnar Olsen 1961, p. 129; Edvard Holm 1907, pp. 6–7.
[3] Gunnar Olsen 1961, pp. 130–1.
[4] Including Ramløse, Huseby, and Annisse. Ibid., p. 165.
[5] Edvard Holm 1907, p. 10; Gunnar Olsen 1961, pp. 166–7.
[6] Erik Viborg 1795, p. 10; J. Brüel 1918, p. 110; H. K. Kristensen 1975, p. 173.
[7] C. Klitgaard 1933–4, p. 334.   [8] Gunnar Olsen 1961, pp. 164–6.

The Green Revolution

35

simistic. This was a German official, Johan Ulrich Røhl, who presented himself immediately after Thott's departure. Røhl drew up a comprehensive plan for halting sand drift in North Zealand by means of a series of coordinated measures: making wattle fences to stop the sand, spreading seaweed from the beaches and turf from the surrounding lands, and planting lyme grass, whose roots would help to bind the sand. The latter method had been used in Jutland for centuries, but not in Zealand, nor, for that matter, even further east, on the German Baltic coast, where sand drift had been a problem ever since the seventeenth century.[9] Final stabilization of the district was to be achieved by planting forests in areas where sand drift had been arrested. Røhl's plan was immediately accepted and put into practice.

By mustering a large amount of labour, materials, and money – the total outlay was close to 100,000 rix-dollars[10] – sand drift in North Zealand during the following decade was indeed brought under a certain degree of control. But victory was not complete. During the following years the sand regularly went on the move, and in 1792 a major effort once more became necessary.[11] It was not until this time that trees were planted in the district. It was given the name Tisvilde Hegn (Tisvilde Enclosure) and was Denmark's first dune plantation.

During the first years after the success in North Zealand, the central administration saw no reason to work as assiduously on the matter of sand drift as might have been expected. It merely issued an injunction on 25 August 1749 to the inhabitants of a number of parishes in West Jutland requiring them to restrain sand drift by means of embankments and plantations and not to allow cattle to graze in the dunes unless under strict surveillance; in its essentials, this was a repetition of the rescript of 4 October 1723 mentioned earlier.[12]

Røhl, the architect of the arrest of sand drift in North Zealand, had inspected the sand dunes in Jutland as early as 1734, after which he applied, first in 1736 and again in 1741, to be placed in charge of measures to combat sand drift in West Jutland and on the island of Læsø, but on both occasions in vain.[13] We can only guess why his offer was not accepted. The high cost of combating sand drift undoubtedly played a part, but the possibility cannot be dismissed that the rejection arose to a certain extent from bu-

---

[9] Edvard Holm 1907, pp. 9–11, 19.   [10] Erik Viborg 1795, p. 12.
[11] Edvard Holm 1907, p. 15; Gregers Begtrup 1803–12, I, p. 94.
[12] J. Brüel 1918, p. 110.   [13] P. Christian Nielsen 1982.

36   *The Ecological Revolution*

reaucratic antipathy towards Røhl himself. Røhl, though unusually competent, was at the same time, judging from all reports, quarrelsome, which had led to conflicts during his work in North Zealand. The fact remains that during the following years, although the situation in Denmark was deteriorating, Røhl worked abroad.[14] During the 1740s, much of the worst damage was still to come, including, for example, the complete burial in sand (as had long been feared) of Skagen Church and its surroundings during a storm early in the spring of 1775.[15]

In the 1740s, 1750s, and 1760s, halting sand drift was left to local initiative everywhere. Teilmann's work was continued at the southern end of Ringkøbing Fjord, but with limited success. In 1760 sand drift flared up again, and although several hundred men laboured to build dykes in accordance with Teilmann's instructions (he died in 1749), the sand could not be stopped. A large-scale private attempt was launched in North Jutland by Birkelse Manor, which in 1759 obtained a royal concession to call upon the farmers of thirteen parishes to make a coordinated effort. No lasting results were obtained here either.[16] On the other hand, success was achieved with control work carried out in Vridsted and Vroue and in several other parishes in the Fjends district of mid-Jutland, where lyme grass was planted before 1768.[17] Unfortunately, despite these and a few other positive results,[18] the situation, as already indicated, worsened steadily with every decade that passed.

A sudden glimpse of the violence of sand drift towards the end of the eighteenth century is given by a laconic diary entry for 15 May 1790 made by Christian Andersen, a tenant farmer who on this day drove from Randers westwards to his home in Nørre Tulstrup between Viborg and Randers: "Very strong wind and sand drift against us on the way home." The sand blowing in the faces of Andersen and his companion probably came either from Alheden, an expanse of heath between Viborg and Herning, or from

[14] Edvard Holm 1907, pp. 16–17. Røhl's subsequent career: P. Christian Nielsen 1982.
[15] Anthon Fuglsang 1947–9, pp. 162–72; J. Brüel 1918, pp. 72, 86, 91 and passim; R. Mortensen 1917, p. 15 (sand drift spread over 3,500 *tønder* at Kompedal in 1780); cf. also A. Ravnholt 1934, pp. 156–8; M. K. Zahrtmann 1917, pp. 31–2 (Bornholm). Warnings about developments at Skagen: Søren Abildgaard 1761, pp. 348–9. The fatal storm: J. Brüel 1918, p. 14. A literary treatment of sand drift in its last phase is given by Steen Steensen Blicher in his short story "Marie. En Erindring fra Vesterhavet" (Marie. A Memoir from the North Sea) (1836).
[16] H. K. Kristensen 1975, p. 173; Anthon Fuglsang 1947–9, pp. 174–5.
[17] Erik Pontoppidan 1763–81, IV, p. 591.   [18] J. Brüel 1919, p. 72.

The Green Revolution

Mønsted, between Viborg and Holstebro,[19] to which the two travellers from Randers never came closer than about 30 kilometres – the sand drifted far in Denmark in those years.

Not until thousands of acres of land had been converted into new desert did the central administration again do anything serious about sand drift. An initial step was the issuing of a temporary law, dated 19 April 1779, covering the controlling of sand drift and applying to most of what is now the county of Thisted in northwest Jutland, which was one of the most seriously afflicted areas.[20] In 1786 and the following years, the previously mentioned Erik Viborg, who in 1785 had inspected sand drift areas in Sweden, traveled through Jutland to study the situation.[21] In 1788 Viborg, largely remembered for his veterinary work but at the same time a knowledgeable botanist, published for the benefit of the inhabitants of dunelands a manual on halting sand drift entitled *Efterretning om Sandvexterne og deres Anvendelse til at dæmpe Sandflugten paa Vesterkanten af Jylland* (An account of sand plants and their use in restricting sand drift on the west side of Jutland). This manual was distributed by the authorities free of charge to the inhabitants of dunelands in Jutland and to other interested persons.[22]

On 19 September 1792 a general decree covering the prevention of sand drift was finally issued, drawn up mainly along the lines prescribed by Røhl almost seventy years earlier. Just as had been the case in North Zealand, the combating of sand drift was based on massive conscription of men and vehicles, that is to say, on public villeinage. Sand drift commissions and later, also, sand drift commissioners and duneland bailiffs and wardens, were appointed in the counties affected.

Work progressed according to plan. The Rentekammer (the Danish Treasury and Ministry of Finance from about 1550 to 1848), which supervised these matters, received reports during the ensuing years revealing that the situation was changing. In 1817, for example, the following statement about sand drift at Hårup in Central Jutland was received, signed by four elderly farmers from Voel:

[19] Jens Holmgaard 1969, p. 82. Sand drift on Alheden [a heath] and in Mønsted: Niels Windfeld Lund 1984, p. 6; Valdemar Andersen 1975, pp. 106–12; *Trap Danmark* 1953–72, 17, p. 250.
[20] C. C. Andresen 1861, p. 239.
[21] Erik Viborg 1795, foreword. Cf. J. Brüel 1918, p. 51. Erik Viborg in Sweden 1785: V. Halskov-Hansen 1968–9, p. 318.
[22] A. F. Bergsøe 1837, II, p. 7; Anthon Fuglsang 1947–9, pp. 176–7.

38   The Ecological Revolution

In former times and before sand drift at Hårup was brought under the surveillance and control of Sørensen, the chartered surveyor, the sand was moving violently, and in a west wind would blow over the heath and eastwards like a thick fog or snow drift and sweep over the fields and village of Woel, which lies between a quarter and half a [Danish] mile to the east of the sand drift. But during the last few years the sand has no longer swept in this fashion, and no inconvenience is felt due to sand drift, as it has been reduced by the trees Sørensen caused to be planted, and no longer drifts much.[23]

Now and then complaints were received about the burden of work imposed by combating sand drift, particularly in the counties along the west coast of Jutland[24] – and not without reason. Just as had been the case when sand drift was fought in North Zealand in the 1730s, the amount of labour required was enormous.[25] Routine restrictive work in the county of Thisted, calculated in terms of a day's work, called for 166 men and seven horsecarts per *tønde*.[26] By applying these figures to the whole of Jutland, where official measures were introduced between 1792 and 1807 to restrict sand drift in an area of some 17,000 *tønder*,[27] it means that during these fifteen years alone in Jutland the government conscripted about 2,750,000 working days and 115,000 carting days to impede sand drift. If this overall total of almost 3 million working days were distributed equally among the rural population in Jutland, which totalled about 220,000 people aged between fifteen and seventy,[28] it would amount to 13 days each. This means that on an average, restricting sand drift in Jutland increased the work burden in the agricultural sector by about one day a year for all adults.

To this must be added what was done privately during this phase by those who took matters into their own hands. These individuals include two Jutland parish bailiffs, Johannes Pedersen of Randbøl, who in 1794 was awarded a prize of 20 rix-dollars from the Agricultural Society for various improvements made on his land, including control of sand drift, and Christian Christensen of Madum, who in 1807 received the Agricultural Society's second Gold Medal for his activities in connection with sand drift prevention.[29]

---

[23]   Quoted by Anthon Fuglsang 1943, p. 63. Thanks to the Rentekammer's surveillance of measures to combat sand drift, a large amount of material on sand drift in its last phase is to be found in the Danish National Archives (Rtk. 2484, Landvæsenskontorernes sandflugtssager 1793–1840). Supplementary material is in local archives, e.g., those of Hesselmed Manor, Sandflugt og klitbeplantning 1749–1874, Provincial Archives of Northern Jutland.

[24]   Anthon Fuglsang 1947–9, pp. 187–94.   [25]   Steen B. Bôcher 1942, p. 189.

[26]   Anthon Fuglsang 1947–9, p. 180.   [27]   J. Brüel 1918, p. 55.

[28]   Aksel Lassen 1965, pp. 407–11.

[29]   Agricultural Society prizewinners in 1794 and 1807, Danish National Business History Archives.

The Green Revolution   39

The final – or to all intents and purposes final – sealing of sand-drift areas that could not be put into sufficiently good order to be used for cultivation again was completed by the dune plantations. With Tisvilde Hegn as a model, plantations were established in former sand-drift areas in Jutland and on the islands of Zealand, Falster, and Bornholm.[30] However, the former sand-drift areas are still, and no doubt always will be, a vulnerable part of the Danish landscape.[31]

3.2 LAND RECLAMATION

Once the formation of deserts had been halted, the process of reducing the country's productive area, which had been in progress since the sixteenth century, was terminated. But that was not all: New land was now reclaimed. The first land reclamation project we know of admittedly failed. It is the sad story of a customs official, Johan Madsen, who around 1670 built a dam for his own account across the shallow water between Over Kærby and Tårup, northwest of Kerteminde on the island of Funen. "The said customs official ploughed and sowed once within the dam, but did not harvest, because the dam burst, and he became a poor man."[32] Ten years later, however, in 1680, the marshland known as Nylandsmosen, which came under Gavnø Manor in the south of Zealand, was successfully reclaimed.[33]

The following century saw a great many reclamation projects. Some of them were successful, whereas others failed, or had to be rejected as technically impossible. Among the successful eighteenth-century damming projects was that undertaken by Councillor Lassen of Åkær Manor, near Gyllingnæs in East Jutland, around 1710. The size of the reclaimed area is stated to have been "3–400 cartloads of hay," probably about 100 hectares.[34] A smaller reclamation project, involving about "100 cartloads of hay," was carried out in 1743 by Niels Juel of Valdemar's Castle on the island of Tåsinge to the south of Funen.[35] In about 1780, 600 *tønder* were reclaimed at Einsidels-

---

[30] P. Christian Nielsen 1979–82, pp. 52–5; V. Halskov-Hansen 1968–9; R. Mortensen 1917, p. 15.
[31] Considerable unrest arose in the Tisvilde area in the 1960s. Action against sand drift had to be started all over again in many places, for example, by sowing marram grass (reported by Hans Kuhlman, Geographical Institute, University of Copenhagen). See also J. C. Hald 1833, pp. 33–5.
[32] Erik Pontoppidan 1776–81, VI, p. 566.   [33] Einar Storgaard 1952–3.
[34] Erik Pontoppidan 1763–81, IV, p. 250.   [35] Ibid., VI, p. 726.

40   The Ecological Revolution

borg in North Funen,[36] and a few years later, in 1785–6, 500 *tønder* were reclaimed by the farmers on the promontory of Helnæs, in West Funen.[37] That same year, in the parish of Sønderby, not far from Helnæs, Niels Ryberg, who owned Frederiksgave Manor, reclaimed 300 *tønder* of littoral marshland.[38]

On the other hand, the attempt made for many years near the end of the eighteenth century by Niels Ditlev Riegels to reclaim Bøtø Bay, which at that time covered a large part of the south of Falster with water, was a failure. Riegels, who even went so far as to initiate the work at his own expense, had a canal dug, almost 6 kilometres long, near the small town of Marrebæk, after which he had to abandon the project. A later generation was to succeed where he had failed, just as the project initiated in 1670 by the unfortunate customs official Johan Madsen, after yet another unsuccessful attempt in 1726, was finally completed in 1812.[39] The possibility of reclaiming Rødby Fjord (Rødby Inlet) on the island of Lolland was discussed in the 1760s, though no concrete steps were taken because at the time this project was still not technologically possible.[40] Like the reclamation of Lammefjorden (The Lamme Inlet) in the northwest of Zealand, Kolindsund in East Jutland, and the River Skjern area in West Jutland, it was not possible to drain Rødby Fjord until the nineteenth century. Arresting the progress of the sand in conjunction with reclamation of new land from the sea established the basic framework for an ecological recovery.

3.3 CONTROL OF THE WATER LEVEL

During the eighteenth and nineteenth centuries the farming landscape was characterized by a network of ditches and canals through which surplus water was led to inlets and the sea. If we go back to the sixteenth and seventeenth centuries, this network of ditches and canals disappears. The word *grøft* (ditch) is very seldom mentioned, and when used may mean dyke just as often as ditch.[41] The

---

[36]   Gregers Begtrup 1803–12, III, p. 273.
[37]   J. C. A. Carlsen-Skiødt 1931–6b, p. 188. Cf. Aage Rasch 1964, p. 295.
[38]   J. C. A. Carlsen-Skiødt 1931–6a, p. 15.
[39]   N. D. Riegels 1796; Gregers Begtrup 1803–12, IV, p. 783. Tårup Strand: V. Woll 1931–6.
[40]   Erik Pontoppidan 1763–81, III, pp. 236–7.
[41]   C. Rise Hansen 1968, p. 352; Ole Højrup 1961, p. 281. Extensive material in land registry documents published by the Agricultural History Society indicates how small a part was played by ditches and drainage systems at the beginning of the seventeenth century. Cf. Ole Fenger, C. Rise Hansen et al. 1979, p. 27; 1980, p. 107; 1985, p. 122. In his

The Green Revolution

explanation for the slight significance of ditches and canals in Danish agriculture of the sixteenth and seventeenth centuries is that excess water in the fields was not an urgent problem. Field drainage could usually be achieved by ploughing water furrows at right angles to the contour lines and letting gravity do the rest,[42] or simply by placing high-ridged fields at right angles to the contour lines. Such excess water as remained would then find its own way into the side furrows, the balks, and thence into the waterway system and away.[43]

Due to the many-sided, mutually reinforcing effects of sand drift and tree felling, the amount of surplus water began to rise during the seventeenth century. The water level rose, and marshlands and acidified areas spread throughout the landscape. This led to the need for water-regulation measures not unlike those undertaken in the Middle Ages, when the expansion of agriculture, forest clearance, and sand drift had also created disturbances in the hydrological system. From Italy,[44] intricate canal systems gradually spread into the fields of Western Europe during the seventeenth century. Denmark was no exception, for although the country's ecological degradation commenced relatively late, the decline, when it finally did start, was sharp. From the beginning of the eighteenth century, the need for water regulation became imperative.

The first two water-regulation projects to be carried out were directly prompted by sand drift. On the island of Zealand it was a matter of excavating a new outlet from Arresø. This project, which was completed in 1717–19 by the king (i.e., the state) as the principal landowner in North Zealand, became necessary because, since about 1700, the outlet from the north of Arresø into the Kattegat had been gradually closed by sand. After 1710 it was frequently possible to walk dryshod across this outlet, whereas the villages surrounding the lake that were not covered by sand were now flooded. It was obvious that a new outlet would have to be excavated to lead the water away from the lake if the villages that had been spared by the sand so far were not to be lost. Projects were drawn up, but the size of the task and the expense involved caused it to be postponed several times.

otherwise detailed examination of the agricultural work carried out in North Zealand in the course of a year around 1670, Henrik Gerner, a priest, makes no mention of either ditching or digging water furrows (1670). See also Karl-Erik Frandsen 1983, for example, pp. 56–7, 156.

[42] Cf. Axel Steensberg 1956, p. 45.
[43] Karl-Erik Frandsen 1983, p. 59, also maps pp. 54 and 62.
[44] Cf. Carlo Poni 1982, pp. 15–152; Francesco Mineccia 1982, pp. 20–38.

42   The Ecological Revolution

After violent floods in two successive winters, 1714 and 1715, however, there was no getting round it, and after a few more minor postponements because of wartime conditions during the Great Nordic War (1700–21), excavation work was commenced in 1717, the labour force being provided by soldiers and Swedish prisoners of war. The new, southwesterly outlet canal, around which the town of Frederiksværk was later founded, was completed in 1719, and farmers could begin to cultivate the fields that had not disappeared under the sand.[45] During these years a new outlet canal was dug for the meadowlands at the southern end of Ringkøbing Fjord, which in about 1700 had been submersed in water as a result of sand drift. This work, which was initiated by the already-mentioned Christian Hansen Teilmann, was also concluded in 1719. The following year Teilmann was able to report that "many hundreds of meadows, which for 16 years have been under water, are now dry throughout the summer."[46]

In Bishop Erik Pontoppidan's *Danske Atlas,* a large topographical work published in 1763–81, water-regulation work is mentioned occurring as far back as the beginning of the eighteenth century. On the island of Funen, a place called 'The Lake,' between Allese and Broby, was drained in 1712 by digging canals, which made it possible to make hay and cut peat.[47] At about the same time – and here again, Swedish prisoners of war were used for the work – Captain Peder Matthias von Buchwald, the owner of Gudumlund, south of Ålborg, had his meadows improved with the result that he could make considerably more hay than before.[48] This project, which necessitated the destruction of a number of ancient burial mounds and a big kitchen midden in order to obtain earth with which to fill some low-lying areas, was the start of one of the eighteenth century's most comprehensive water-regulation operations. When completed, just after the turn of the century, it included a main canal, several kilometres long and 5 metres wide, leading to Limfjorden (the Lim Inlet) in northern Jutland, 34 kilometres of ditches both large and small, and a dam, almost 11 metres wide, which protected 2,800 *tønder* of meadowland against flooding.[49]

---

[45] K. C. Rockstroh 1911, pp. 63–82. Flooding could not be completely prevented until sand drift – the chief cause of the problem – had been overcome, which it had still not been in North Zealand, cf. Chapter 3.1. After 1719 flooding took place locally on frequent occasions. In 1725 a small stream near Ramløse was almost completely choked by sand and the surrounding meadows were flooded and ruined. Gunnar Olsen 1961, p. 168.

[46] H. K. Kristensen 1975, p. 173.

[47] Erik Pontoppidan 1763–81, VI, p. 547.   [48] Ibid., V, pp. 69–70.

[49] Ibid., V, p. 69; *Trap Danmark* 1953–72, 16, p. 1022; Gregers Begtrup 1803–12, VI, pp. 246–8.

The Green Revolution

Gradually, as we approach the period during which the *Danske Atlas* came into being, there were more examples of water-regulation work, and they were more extensive. In reference to the old county of Kalø (now Djursland), it was stated in 1768 that

> it is being cultivated with much diligence. There are lakes, overgrown streams and bogs, formerly regarded as bottomless, and in which all manner of fish were caught, that have now been laid completely dry, either grown over by themselves or dug out to transform them into meadowland or peat bogs.[50]

The *Danske Atlas* emphasizes the "carving out" of Lille Vildmose (a bog), which came under Lindenborg Manor, near Ålborg. This excavation, involving more than 5,000 hectares, was started in 1760–1, and within only a few years had already provided so much fertile land and meadows that it was possible to establish a manor farm of 30 *tønder hartkorn*, Vildmosegård, on an area that earlier had been under water.[51] A number of smaller projects were also honourably mentioned, for example, Johan Frederik Vedel had made himself "a good meadow ground" by conducting water away from a bog on his manor, Nørre Vinkel in West Jutland.[52] Mention is made in Zealand of Benzonslund Manor, where Peder Willumsen – and from 1757 also Christian H. Selchau – worked on "cutting through the peat-bogs."[53]

The *Danske Atlas* by no means mentions all the work of this kind. On the Zealand estate of Knabstrup, "shallow water ditches" were dug in unusable meadows during the years after 1732 to convert large areas of quagmire into beautiful meadows and pastures.[54] During the period after 1750 a number of large water-regulation projects were carried out in Zealand, including a drainage canal, some 10 kilometres long, that Niels Ryberg caused to be dug at Øbjerggård Manor before 1787.[55] On the island of Lolland, the fields of Gammelgård Manor were renovated in the 1770s "by the excavation of bogs [and] the trimming and digging of ditches."[56] At Løvenholm Manor, in the county of Randers in Jutland, Hans Fønss carried out major drainage operations between 1750 and

---

[50] Erik Pontoppidan 1783–81, IV, p. 262.
[51] Ibid., V, 1, p. 80. On this drainage project, greatly admired at the time and linked with names like A. G. Moltke (the lord high steward) and, from 1762, H. C. Schimmelmann, see also Erik Pontoppidan 1762.
[52] Erik Potoppidan 1763–81, V, 2, p. 825.
[53] Ibid., II, p. 386.   [54] F. Lunn 1876, p. 79.
[55] Aage Rasch 1964, p. 326.
[56] Archives of Gammelgård Manor, Diverse dokumenter 1751–1849: Forvalterinstruks, 20. maj 1774, Provincial Archives of Zealand.

44 The Ecological Revolution

1760.[57] It is known that considerable ditching work was done on a nearby estate, Skaføgård Manor, during the period of Niels Behr's ownership (1749–78), when a whole lake, called Lake Skafø, was reclaimed.[58]

Other lakes were also attacked, for example, Lake Nørreøkse at Bratskov in South Jutland, which Captain Rudolf von Grabow was allowed to reclaim in 1753 on condition that he build a windmill to replace a watermill powered by water from the lake.[59] Lake Søborg in North Zealand, an area of 600 hectares, was reclaimed in 1794–8, and so were the Dons lakes near Kolding in Jutland,[60]

Water-regulation work did not end with the digging of big canals to drain lakes, bogs, and impassable meadows. The aim was to bring the water level under control throughout the entire agricultural area. These impressive excavation works were merely a necessary basis for this purpose. From the renovated main run-off system the work was continued in the fields themselves, where one ditch after another was dug.

The first use of ditches for draining fields can be traced back to shortly before the year 1700. The Danish legal historian Poul Meyer cites two cases, from 1678 and 1691, respectively. At all events the second of these clearly concerns a farmer who not only, as was usual, wished to make dykes round his land to mark his proprietary rights, but also wanted to ditch it in the modern sense.[61] Another recorded instance of the use of drainage ditches prior to 1700 is in East Lolland, where Jørgen Skeel, the owner of Krenkerup Manor, before his death in 1695 had drainage ditches dug round the fields of the main farm and also round the land of the village of Radsted.[62] Little is known about how fast field drainage progressed during the early eighteenth century, but from the 1730s onwards the main farms of manors, about which most information is available, reveal examples of large field-drainage systems.[63]

A weakness of the three-field system of agriculture, which dominated in large parts of Denmark,[64] was the difficulty in reinforcing the old surface draining, the water furrows, by permanently open ditches across the terrain without cutting through the fields. Cut-

---

[57] Gregers Begtrup 1803–12, VI, p. 37. [58] Knud J. V. Jespersen 1975, p. 33.
[59] Trap Danmark 1953–72, 14, p. 395.
[60] Lake Søborg: Gunnar Olsen 1961, pp. 202–3; Niels Amstrup 1955. Dons lakes: Gregers Begtrup 1803–12, V, p. 263; cf. Trap Danmark 1953–72, 21, p. 1202.
[61] Poul Meyer 1949, pp. 132–4. [62] Erik Pontoppidan 1763–81, VI, p. 504.
[63] Thorkild Kjærgaard 1980, p. 29 (also n. 63); Axel Linvald 1905–11, ([I]), pp. 248, 282–3.
[64] Karl-Erik Frandsen 1983, p. 259.

The Green Revolution

ting through the fields meant virtually destroying the three-field system, the whole idea of which was to farm large, unbroken expanses.

The three-field system involved the dividing of all the arable land of a village, or of the main farm of a manor, into three fields of equal size. These fields, which could often be of considerable extent, were bordered by hedges. In this traditional system the fields were sown, successively, either with winter corn (winter rye), or with spring corn (spring barley, sometimes spring rye), or were left fallow. The field that lay fallow was used for grazing and hay making. Surrounding the fields were meadows and outlying fields that were not ploughed but likewise used for grazing and hay making.

A solution to the drainage problems of the three-field system was the multiple-field system, which was known in districts to the south of Denmark from the beginning of the eighteenth century and introduced into Denmark towards the middle of the century.[65] The chief principle of this system was the dividing of large expanses of land into a number (usually between eight and eleven) of smaller units of equal size, around which ditches were dug.[66] These closely placed ditches could – possibly aided by the old water furrows, which had been excellent but were no longer an adequate means of surface draining[67] – lead surplus water away from the fields, especially from hollows, which as a result of the rising water level, showed up far more frequently than before as wet spots on the terrain.

The main reason for the success of the multiple-field system in eighteenth-century Denmark was that it activated stagnant, harmful water that had been dammed up for decades. This explanation of the system's success concurs with contemporary accounts of its advantages. The Danish statesman and landowner A. G. Moltke, for example, who was one of the pioneers of the multiple-field system, emphasized the effects of improved draining,[68] and in 1778, T. Thaning, steward of Vemmetofte Manor in Zealand, explained that "in this way the water is led away from the soil."[69]

---

[65] Aage Friis 1903–19, I, p. 277; *Trap Danmark* 1953–72, 9, p. 237 (Tybjerggård Manor); ibid., 9, p. 800 (Højbygård Manor); Jørgen Andersen Schiöt 1758, p. 137.
[66] Thorkild Kjærgaard 1980, pp. 205–6.
[67] The digging of water furrows was still an important routine task in agricultural work of the 1780s: Thorkild Kjærgaard 1980, pp. 114–15.
[68] Hans Jensen 1917, p. 100.
[69] Jens Holmgaard 1962, p. 42. See also Erik Pontoppidan 1763–81, VI, pp. 179, 197, 204.

46   *The Ecological Revolution*

As early as 1770, the multiple-field system was widely used on the main farms of Danish manors. In 1770, according to information covering 491 main farms, 137 of them, that is to say about 30 percent, had introduced the new system.[70] Assuming that the proportion was about the same for the roughly 300 other main farms concerning which no information is available, by 1770 at least 200 of the main farms of Danish manors had carried out water-regulation work in the twenty-year period during which the multiple-field system had been known in Denmark. This rapid readjustment continued for the rest of the century; by 1800 the three-field system was only rarely still in use on main manor farms.[71]

Some figures available from Korselitse Manor on the island of Falster will serve to give an idea of the extent of the work involved in the transition to the multiple-field system on main manor farms in Denmark. The multiple-field system was introduced on the main farm at Korselitse Manor during the years 1773–85. During this period, 30 kilometres of double main ditches were dug in the fields, and to this should be added the secondary ditches, whose total length exceeded by far the length of the main ones.[72] At Store Restrup Manor, in Jutland, almost 34 kilometres of double ditches were dug in about 1780.[73] The fields of Korselitse Manor's main farm totalled just under 90 *tønder hartkorn* and of Store Restrup Manor's main farm 107 *tønder hartkorn*, whereas the total size of the main farms of Denmark's manors was about 32,000 *tønder hartkorn*.[74] If we assume that ditching work was more or less equally intensive all over Denmark, this would mean that more than 10,000 kilometres of main ditches were dug on the main manor farms alone, in addition to which came secondary ditches, whose total length was at least two or three times greater. Water-regulation work on main manor farm fields during the eighteenth century assumed tremendous proportions and may well have amounted, all told, to almost 50,000 kilometres of excavated ditches and canals.

In addition, there was all the water-regulation work carried out on the farms of tenant farmers. Our knowledge in this area is more

[70] Fridlev Skrubbeltrang 1978, pp. 398–9.
[71] Ibid., p. 399. See also Jens Holmgaard 1962 and Arne Hentze 1974, pp. 68–75.
[72] Karl-Erik Frandsen 1988a, p. 47.
[73] Archives of Store Restrup Manor, Forskellige dokumenter 1674–1844: hoveriforening 27. april 1792, Provincial Archives of Northern Jutland.
[74] Korselitse Manor: Harald Jørgensen and Fridlev Skrubbeltrang 1942, p. 313. Store Restrup Manor: Henrik Pedersen 1928, p. 276. Total area covered by all Danish main manor farms: ibid., p. 365.

The Green Revolution 47

sporadic. However, among other sources, the award system introduced by the Agricultural Society reveals many examples of farmers who carried out water-regulation work. The Agricultural Society's prizes for drainage were motivated by explaining that the drainage of deleterious water from fields, meadows, bogs, and roads could be regarded as "one of the first and most important steps towards improved farming."[75] A total of 377 prizes were awarded during the period 1770–1832, and of these, by far the majority were given before 1800.[76] During the five-year period 1774–9, the total length of ditches for which prizes were awarded to tenant farmers was about 61 kilometres.[77] Reports to the Rentekammer (see Chapter 3.1) by landowners during the 1770s, 1780s, and 1790s are also full of information about drainage work on tenant farms. A report received from Bregentved Manor on the island of Zealand, for example, stated that in 1774 the twelve inhabitants of Høsten in the parish of Dalby had dug 2,358 *favne* of water ditches during the previous year, 1773, in other words almost 4.5 kilometres.[78] Another report, from the estate owned by the University of Copenhagen, stated that in 1805 the farmers had dug 120 kilometres of water ditches.[79] These ditches, amounting to just under 200 kilometres in length, represented only a very small part of the general achievement.

Furthermore, concealed behind the transition to the multiple-field system that was also carried out on tenant farms at the same time as the changeover was made on the main manor farms was major water-regulation work.[80] Tens of thousands of kilometres of ditches must have been dug on the thousands of tenant farms, whose combined size was about ten times that of the main farms.

Water-regulation work may have had two diametrically opposite purposes: a need to drain and a need to irrigate. Draining serves to keep the soil dry and prevent acidification and peat formation and in this way helps to give cultivated plants the best growth conditions. Irrigation serves to add water in periods of drought and also to conduct plant nutrients from elsewhere into the cultivated fields, as has been practised in Europe for more than a thousand years in Andalusia and in the Po Valley in North Italy.[81]

---

[75] Ole Degn 1969, p. 212.   [76] Ibid., p. 210 (table 2), 212.   [77] Ibid., p. 215.
[78] Rtk. 2485.21: Bregentved Manor 1774–1807, Indberetning af 24. marts 1774, Danish National Archives.
[79] Ejvind Slottved and Mogens Thøgersen 1980, p. 103.
[80] Arne Hentze 1974, pp. 68–75; Kjeld Flensburg 1969, cf. Fridlev Skrubbeltrang 1978, p. 234.
[81] E. Møller-Holst 1877–83, I, pp. 538–55 (article: "Engvanding").

48   *The Ecological Revolution*

The high-water level in eighteenth-century Denmark naturally resulted in priority being given to the drainage of fields, meadows, bogs, and lakes. It must be added, however, that irrigation also had some significance. The oldest known example is at Åtte in the parish of Føvling in the far south of Jutland, where irrigation was used as early as the 1760s.[82] Some of the water-regulation systems to which the Agricultural Society awarded prizes featured mechanisms that made it possible to use them for both drainage and irrigation. In 1779 a tenant farmer in East Jutland, Niels Stounberg of Torsted, in the parish of the same name, was given a prize for a reversible system of this kind, and in 1787 the same honour was bestowed upon ten tenant farmers in nearby Hesseballe, in the parish of Uldum.[83] In other cases prizes were awarded to systems developed solely for irrigation purposes. The farmers of Harritslev, in the parish of Skovby on the island of Funen, for example, were awarded 50 rix-dollars in 1789 for an irrigation system that could water a plot of 100 *tønder*.[84] According to the agronomist Gregers Begtrup, irrigation was widespread in Jutland at the beginning of the nineteenth century, particularly in the vicinity of Horsens, in the county of Hjørring and on the Dano-Schleswig border.[85]

The constant struggle against sand drift required a great deal of labour, and so did the efforts to bring the water level under control. Behind an observation made in autobiographical notes compiled by a Zealand farmer, Søren Pedersen, to the effect that the cleaning of old ditches and digging of a few hundred *favne* of new ones "has cost me many a tired arm,"[86] one senses the incredible, almost superhuman, amount of manual labour that went into digging all these ditches in the heavy, sopping wet mud and water.[87]

[82] Erik Pontoppidan 1763–81, V, 2, p. 692.
[83] In 1782–4 the farmers of Hesseballe had dug 4,500 *favne* of ditches, as a result of which their meadows and peat bogs were improved. They had arranged the ditches in such a way that the meadows could be flooded. Agricultural Society prizewinners in 1779 and 1787, Danish National Business History Archives.
[84] Agricultural Society prizewinners in 1789, Danish National Business History Archives. A tenant farmer named Michel Thomsen of the parish of Hornborg, Eastern Jutland, received 7 rix-dollars in 1787 "for in 1783 and 84 having dug 686 *favne* of ditches, after which a bog 256 *favne* long and 282 *favne* wide, together with 6 field ponds could be used for haymaking; [also] arranging flumes to make it possible to flood a meadow of some 9,025 square *favne*." Agricultural Society prizewinners in 1787, Danish National Business History Archives.
[85] Gregers Begtrup 1803–12, V, pp. 111–13, 398; VI, p. 472. On the Schleswig border, especially in the parishes of Folding, Lintrup, Rødding, and Føvling.
[86] Søren Pedersen 1983, p. 192.
[87] See, for example, the archives of Guldborgland Manor, Diverse 1792–1810: grøfteregnskab for Soesmarke by i Majbølle sogn ved den separate udskiftning 1798, Provincial Archives of Zealand.

The Green Revolution 49

Sometimes we hear of farmers who shrank from the task. For example, in 1791 the tenant farmers of Lund, which belonged to Vemmetofte Manor, Zealand, requested that their fields be divided so as to introduce the multiple-field system, but thought better of it the following year and submitted an application requesting that their "fields might be allowed to remain as they were, and that the tenant farmers might be spared all the digging." But it was only a brief hesitation prior to the inevitable: Four years later these farmers were also busy digging ditches.[88]

The campaign against the rising water level had been organized by 1770, and the long, straight lines of ditches and canals began to crisscross the Danish landscape. Fields were drained, and meadows and bogs that had been impassable – sometimes for only a few years, such as the meadows bordering Ringkøbing Fjord and the areas round Arresø, sometimes for decades, and sometimes for centuries, such as the two bogs called Store Vildmose and Lille Vildmose in North Jutland, whose ecological system had collapsed during the cultivation expansion that took place during the Iron Age – once more became useful meadows and fertile fields. Yet another important step had been taken in the process that was to halt the ecological decomposition of the country and force development in new directions.

3.4 CONTROL OF THE PH BALANCE OF THE SOIL: MARLING

Ordinary agricultural plants grow best in soil that is neutral, or almost neutral, that is to say, with a pH value of about 7. If the soil is acid the biological turnover will drop and hamper the plant's growth. A pH value of 4, which is found in crude moorland and bog soil, precludes the growth of nearly all cultivated plants, whereas a pH value of 2 and less prevents virtually every form of plant growth, because in the event of very low pH values other chemicals may be present, for example, sulphuric acid, which is a strong plant poison.

In countries like Denmark, with plenty of rain and relatively little evaporation, there is a natural tendency for the soil to become acidified; as the surplus water seeps down it washes away the lime and in this way will slowly – in the court of a few thousand years – cause the pH value to drop. This is one of the major reasons why the ecological system, even if human beings refrained from inter-

[88] Christian H. Brasch 1859–63, III, p. 192.

50 The Ecological Revolution

fering with it, would still not be completely stable.[89] With the advent of agriculture in about 4000 B.C., acidification processes were accelerated, partly on account of the reduced evaporation caused by forest clearance. Following the ecological regeneration of the late fourteenth and fifteenth centuries, when the forest area was increased, the problems recurred during the seventeenth and eighteenth centuries.

Acidification can be counteracted by drainage and by lime. Drainage serves to aerate the soil and remove the surplus water that is the main cause of acidification. The addition of lime causes the pH value to rise. Lime can be added in the form of pure calcium carbonate ($CaCO_3$); as a rule, however, it is added in the form of marl, a calciferous earth. In addition to raising the pH value, marl, on account of the other substances it contains, may produce significant side effects, especially on sandy soil where the clay improves its consistency and increases the absorption properties of the surface.[90]

The use of marl has been known for a long time and is mentioned by classical writers on agriculture such as Columella, Varro, and Pliny. Characteristically, it is mentioned mainly as something used in the rainy, transalpine districts on the Rhine, in Gaul, and in the British Isles, and not so much in Italy and Spain, where the higher average temperature and consequently greater evaporation reduces the tendency to acidification from forest clearance compared with in northern Europe. In the Middle Ages, marl was commonly used in France and England, and in the second half of the sixteenth century, also in Germany.[91]

Marl is to be found in deposits of various geological origin over most of Denmark,[92] but it is not known when it was first used here. Peder Hansen Resen's observation in 1686 to the effect that there was chalk at Ringsted of the type "that peasants in England and France use to fertilize their fields" does not suggest that marl was used in Denmark in Resen's time, probably because there was no

---

[89] *Landbrugets Ordbog* 1937–8, I, pp. 464–5 (article: "Giftstoffer i Jordbunden"); 691–2 (article: "Kalkens Betydning i Jordbunden"); II, pp. 288–9 (article: "Jordbundens Reaktion"). The phases of the Danish ecosystem: Kim Aaris-Sørensen 1988, pp. 206–7.

[90] *Landbrugets Ordbog* 1937–8, I, pp. 500–1 (article: "Gødningskalk"); II, p. 128 (article: "Mergel").

[91] E. Møller-Holst 1877–84, IV, pp. 342–5 (article: "Mergling"); G. E. Fussell 1972, pp. 27, 43; Michael Havinden 1974; Gertrud Schröder-Lembke 1953, p. 116. Cf. Søren Thestrup 1760, p. 64.

[92] *Landbrugets Ordbog* 1937–8, II, p. 128 (article: "Mergel").

The Green Revolution
51

need for it.[93] Whatever the case, it is certain that the need made itself felt at the beginning of the eighteenth century, when increasing acidification of the soil formed part of the self-intensifying syndrome of negative ecological processes described in the first part of this book.

The oldest known case of marling in Denmark is believed to date from the 1730s, when large quantities were found in Thy in northwestern Jutland. To begin with, marl was used as building mortar, but it was soon exploited in agriculture over most of Thy.[94] The effect on the outlying fields, which were usually sour heathlands, was astonishing: "The soil is made very fertile with marl, and gives just as good white oats and barley as on the fields close to the village."[95]

On the face of it, this description of the effect of marl seems incredible, but it is not necessarily exaggerated. The use of marl on soil with a very low pH value can be compared to detoxification, after which such nutrients as are bound in the soil, and which the plants hitherto have been unable to utilize, suddenly become accessible. These accounts of the miraculous effects of marl are confirmed by other sources. Around 1760, Andreas Charles Teilmann of Nørholm, son of Christian Hansen Teilmann, began to use marl in Southwest Jutland – he was the first to do so – on "marshland, stagnant ponds, bogs and other kinds of sour, green soil which, as long as the world has existed, have never been of any particular use." On such soil, by adding marl, one could

> grow as much spring corn, especially oats, as one likes [and] . . . after the use of marl, grass and clover will appear in great amounts; and the last-named without having been sown. Should one, after the last crop, [i.e., before the field is turned into pasture] also sow clover seed – which I have also tried – it is all the better that artifice should come to nature's aid. White clover is not regarded in these cases as being the most beneficial.[96]

The use of marl spread rapidly in West Jutland during these years. In the district of Øster Horne, where Andreas Charles Teilmann's manor was located, the use of marl became common among

[93] Ib Rønne Kejlbo 1974, p. 8. That marl was still not in use in Denmark in these years would also seem to be evidenced by the fact that Thomas Walgensten, in his *Bonde Practie* of 1664, encouraged Danish farmers to follow the example shown by England and France and use marl, noting, "It is so powerful it exceeds all manure" (pp. [14–16]). See also Karl-Erik Frandsen 1983, p. 34, and Søren Toftgaard Poulsen 1988, p. 199.

[94] Gregers Begtrup 1803–12, VII, p. 192; Erik Pontoppidan 1763–81, V, 1, pp. 408, 520.

[95] Ibid., p. 408.

[96] A. C. Teilmann 1772a, pp. 15–16. Søren Thestrup relates similarly that at Dons Mølle (in the parish of Almind, Jutland) wild clover ("vilde smærer") grew after the spreading of marl (1760, p. 69).

52   *The Ecological Revolution*

farmers during the 1760s.[97] Further to the north, Mads Lillelund of Sindinggård, near Herning, spread marl on "unused as well as on broken sour heathland, or else on ploughed up, lowlying bogland" around 1760,[98] and in the parish of Mejrup, near Holstebro, marl is said to have been used even before 1760.[99] On the islands of Venø and Mors, and in Salling, the influence of nearby Thy was felt at an early stage. Here, marl was used before the end of the 1760s.[100] The German moorland colonists on the Juliane moors in the interior of Jutland, who arrived in the country in 1760, used lime in the form of kiln waste, which they fetched from the lime pits at Daugbjerg and Mønsted, close to Viborg. In this case too, the acid-eliminating substances naturally did their duty, and the anticipated effect was obtained: Yields increased substantially.[101] At Herningholm Manor and other manors, the same results were obtained with kiln waste from the Mønsted lime pit.[102] In East Jutland, marl, "the material that serves to mix bogland, and transform it into rich and fertile marsh soil," was not used until the 1760s. At the end of the 1760s marl was in use in Djursland and in the vicinity of Randers.[103]

The successful use of marl did not pass unnoticed by the agricultural observers of the time. *Danmarks og Norges Oeconomiske Magazin* (Denmark's and Norway's Economic Magazine), the leading journal for agronomical debate during the 1750s, strongly advocated the use of marl. So did the *Danske Atlas*, which drew attention to places where marl was used "for the pronounced, immediate and incredible improvement of the soil,"[104] and encouraged its use wherever possible, for example, on the sandy soil in the districts of Skast and Lysgård in mid-Jutland.[105]

The Agricultural Society also gave its keen support. One of its first publications, in 1776, was a treatise on marl.[106] The author was a Danish artist, Søren Abildgaard, whose son, P. C. Abildgaard, a veterinary surgeon, was also to win acclaim for his services to agriculture. Later, the Agricultural Society tried to promote the use of marl by making awards. A freeholder named Niels Pedersen was given 10 rix-dollars in 1783

---

[97] Erik Pontoppidan 1763–81, V, 2, pp. 733–4; A. C. Teilmann 1789, p. 568.
[98] Søren Thestrup 1760, pp. 65–7.   [99] Ibid., p. 65.
[100] Erik Pontoppidan 1763–81, IV, pp. 752–5; V, 1, p. 520.
[101] Niels Windfeld Lund 1984, p. 7.   [102] Erik Pontoppidan 1763–81, IV, p. 591.
[103] Søren Thestrup 1760, p. 65; Erik Pontoppidan 1762 and 1763–81, IV, pp. 283, 314, 334, 356. See also Fridlev Skrubbeltrang 1961, p. 32.
[104] Erik Pontoppidan 1763–81, V, 2, p. 659.   [105] Ibid., IV, p. 468; V, 2, p. 659.
[106] Søren Abildgaard 1776.

The Green Revolution

53

for having marled a stretch of bogland and on it harvested 15 stooks of extraordinarily good barley; for digging up marl for the improvement of his lands, and also for the good example he thus gave to others.[107]

Awards were made in particular for finding marl. In 1785, G. H. Lund, the tutor at Harritslev Manor, who during these years drew attention to himself as a diligent agronomist, received the Agricultural Society's Silver Medal for having found marl on the island of Funen in 1784. The following year, another senior employee on this estate, the steward, Knud Pedersen, received 5 rix-dollars for having made supplementary finds both on the lands of the main farm and on those of the tenant farmers.[108] In 1787 Jens Olsen, a tenant farmer at Krollerup in the parish of Øster Snede in eastern Jutland, received 10 rix-dollars for a marl find estimated at about 60,000 cubic feet (just under 2,000 cubic metres). For this he had perhaps made use of one of the soil augers for finding marl constructed by Iver Pedersen, a tenant farmer in the neighbouring parish of Ølsted, who received a reward of 5 rix-dollars for his initiative.[109] An indication of the zeal displayed in looking for marl during these years is the proposal made by the Agrarian Commission of 1784 that the four district surveyors in the counties of Frederiksborg and Kronborg, North Zealand, should be supplied with soil augers so that wherever they went they would be able to look for marl (fig. 5).[110]

The efforts to encourage the use of marl were not in vain. Marl use spread further during the 1790s, particularly in Jutland, where it now penetrated up to the northern regions.[111] On the islands of Zealand, Lolland, and Falster, development was somewhat slower. The only part of Zealand where marl may have been used extensively before 1800 was the area between the towns of Kalundborg, Holbæk, Ringsted, and Korsør; here the use of marl appears to have gathered momentum from about 1780.[112]

---

[107] Agricultural Society prizewinners in 1783, Danish National Business History Archives. Niels Pedersen came from the parish of Lejrskov, Jutland. Other examples are Lauritz Andersen, a farmer in the parish of Jordrup, Jutland, who in 1790 received 8 rix-dollars for having made "a piece of bogland fit for ploughing by spreading marl on it." Three other farmers from the same parish were similarly rewarded. Agricultural Society prizewinners in 1790.

[108] Agricultural Society prizewinners in 1785, 1786.

[109] Agricultural Society prizewinners in 1786, 1787.   [110] W. A. Hansen 1790, p. 27.

[111] Gregers Begtrup 1803–12, VI, pp. 461–2.

[112] Karoline Graves 1921, p. 48, and Seyer Mahling Beyer 1791, pp. 9–13. This development continued during the nineteenth century and into the twentieth. By 1929 about 1.97 million hectares, slightly more than half Denmark's arable land, had been marled. A. F. Schmidt 1939, p. 712.

54   The Ecological Revolution

A feature common to the measures mentioned in the foregoing chapters – arresting the progress of the sand and controlling the water level – was the enormous amount of labour involved. In this respect, marling was no exception. In 1772, Andreas Charles Teilmann made the following calculation: To marl one *tønde* of land required 173 loads of marl, each weighing 3 *skippund*, that is, about 83 tonnes of marl per *tønde*. These 173 loads of marl – a more or less adequate dosage for treating a normal degree of lime deficiency, assuming that the marl used has a high lime content – had to be dug up and loaded on carts by manual labour. Afterwards, it had to be carted out to the fields, where it was unloaded in heaps. These, each representing one load, were deposited so that each heap, when spread, would cover about 32 square metres. Finally, a labourer would spread the marl with a fork. As a landowner, Teilmann does not appear to have spared his workers. He estimated that a day's work for an experienced labourer would be "to fill 30 cartloads from the ground, or toss up just as many loads from the bottom of the marl-pit, and also, while the horses are grazing, spread 10 loads."[113] A labourer was thus supposed to load about 14.5 tonnes of marl a day and also spread about 5 tonnes, all by hand.

Even with such an extraordinarily forced rate of labour, and assuming that the marl could be loaded directly onto the carts, it would take more than six days for a labourer to marl a *tønde* of land because, when the 173 loads, after six days' work, were carted out, he would still have 120 loads to spread. If the marl had to be shovelled out of the marl pit before it could be loaded, labour costs increased, and if the expenses involved in opening up the marl pit are included, the total cost increases accordingly. It was not possible to marl a *tønde* of land in fewer than ten days, even under favourable circumstances, that is to say, even when the marl pit was dry and regular, when the marl was of high quality, when the marl had to be transported only a short distance, and when the labourers were strong fellows who, without fainting from exhaustion, could load and spread marl for twelve hours or more a day.

Under less favourable, but probably more realistic, conditions – when the marl pit was deep, wet, and dangerous on account of continual collapses,[114] when the marl had to be transported on stiff,

---

[113] A. C. Teilmann 1772a, p. 13. On the dosage stated: *Landbrugets Ordbog* 1937–8, II, pp. 130–1 (article: "Mergling").

[114] E. Møller-Holst 1877–83, IV, pp. 341–2 (article: "Mergelgrav").

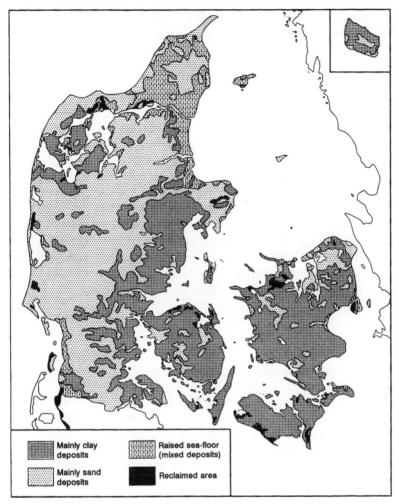

Figure 5. Soil map of Denmark.

rickety carts for miles in the rain and wind along miserable lanes,[115] and when the labourers were not unusually strong – labour costs soared. If decent results were to be obtained, 100 working days per *tønde* seems a likely figure.

[115] Fridlev Skrubbeltrang 1978, p. 358. See also Erik Pontoppidan 1763–81, IV, p. 520 (marl transported from Thy to the islands of Venø and Mors). On roads, especially those in West Jutland during the eighteenth century, see, for example, Jens Holmgaard 1986, pp. 54–6.

56   The Ecological Revolution

Just as was the case with arresting sand drift and water-regulation work, the number of working days that went into marling in the eighteenth century must be counted in millions. If no more than a twentieth part of the 9,490 square kilometres that together made up the three West Jutland counties of Thisted, Ringkøbing, and Ribe were marled between 1735 and 1800, and if the average amount of labour required is set at 50 days per *tønde* – which is a low estimate – the resultant figure is 4.5 million working days spent on marling alone in these three counties, 4.5 million days of hard, disagreeable, and often dangerous work distributed among a rural male population of just under thirty thousand.[116] If the struggle against sand drift had increased the working year by one day for the rural population, marling work certainly added a couple of more days.

Arresting the advance of the deserts and consequent reduction of the country's productive area was an entirely positive step. The same may be said of the water-regulation measures taken in the eighteenth century. As a rule, there was no risk of water shortage, or of large wetlands disappearing completely; these problems were not to arise until the twentieth century.[117]

Marling, however, is a different matter, for – as was discovered during the eighteenth century – it could have repercussions. The dangers associated with marling include not only overmarling but also deficiency diseases in plants that grow on marled soil. Overmarling, which means that the pH value is forced up too high and which is characterized by the soil becoming loose and ashlike, is just as destructive to plant life as acidification.[118] Overmarling seems to have taken place in several places in Thy in the eighteenth century.[119] One of the most serious of the deficiency diseases that may follow in the wake of marling is grey leaf, which is due to a lack of manganese, which in turn is a result of forced plant growth after successful marling. Unfortunately, manganese deficiency is particularly likely to occur in sandy soil, heathland, and bogland; in other words, in soils where marling is most necessary.[120] By all accounts, grey leaf was frequent in the eighteenth century in regions where fields had been marled. Already in the 1760s marling gave rise to the rather dismal saying that the process produces "a rich father but a poor son."[121]

[116] Aksel Lassen 1965, pp. 409–11.   [117] Kristian Dalsgaard 1984, pp. 296–9.
[118] *Landbrugets Ordbog* 1937–8, I, pp. 691–2 (article: "Kalkens Betydning i Jordbunden"); II, pp. 288–9 (article: "Jordbundens Reaktion").
[119] Erik Pontoppidan 1763–81, V, 1, p. 408.
[120] *Landbrugets Ordbog* 1937–8, II, pp. 99–100 (article: "Manganmangel").
[121] Søren Thestrup 1760, p. 74; Erik Pontoppidan 1763–81, V, 2, p. 734.

The Green Revolution

3.5 ADDITION OF PLANT NUTRIENTS THROUGH BETTER UTILIZATION OF EXISTING RESOURCES

Like marling, water regulation raised productivity in agricultural areas. The records of Agricultural Society prize citations include several examples of yields having been doubled or more after drainage. A farmer named Hans Christensen, for example, in the village of Ledøje on the island of Zealand, received in 1789 a Silver Medal and 10 rix-dollars for "in 1786 having dug 335 *favne* of water ditches in order to drain water away from a plot of land of 12 *tønder*, by means of which his hay harvest was increased from 8 to 20 cartloads." In another place a meadow had previously given 80 loads of "sour, poor hay" before drainage, but after drainage "147 loads of good hay at 50 *lispund* per load."[122]

Yield improvement was mainly due to two factors. The first was that drainage and marling provided better physical conditions for cultivated plants, that is to say, healthier and better aerated soil to grow in, and, in many cases also, a longer growth season because the seedbed became ready faster after draining. The other factor contributing to improved yields after water regulation was that plant nutrients already present in the soil but hitherto unutilized by plants on account of the slow biological turnover in sour, waterlogged earth, all at once became accessible. It has been asserted that the soil's "old power of fertilizing" became activated.[123] However, the soil's "old power" had its limitations. These were revealed most dramatically in cases when it was discovered that the yield increased miraculously after marling, only to drop after a while to a minimum.

As a general rule, it appeared that the "old power of fertilizing" was not equally distributed among all the necessary plant nutrients. Of the three main components in what is known today as NPK-fertilizer, there was normally no difficulty with the phosphoric acid and potash components (P and K), both of which are present in Danish soil in stable forms accessible to plants.[124] But the third component, nitrogen (N), was a different matter. The chemical forms in which nitrogen must be present if it is to be utilized by plants are nonstable, and in earlier times, the amount of nitrogen accessible to plants in agricultural soil tended to stabilize at a

---

[122] Agricultural Society prizewinners in 1789, Danish National Business History Archives; Gregers Begtrup 1803–12, V, p. 516, has yet another example.

[123] S. P. Jensen 1987, pp. 94–6.

[124] Johannes Dons Christensen 1952, pp. 34–5; C. P. H. Chorley 1981, p. 90.

58 *The Ecological Revolution*

low level.[125] Although it therefore made sense, in connection with phosphoric acid (P) and potash (K), as well as in connection with the great majority of micronutrients,[126] to speak of the earth's "old power of fertilization" as a form of saved-up capital that could be drawn on for a long time, this was not possible in the case of nitrogen (N). After a short period, during which possible reserves of humus[127] and accumulated remains of plants became decomposed, the soil's nitrogen content had to be constantly renewed. In other words, during the eighteenth century the plant nutrient problem was essentially identical with the problem of obtaining more nitrogen. Nitrogen was the nutrient most frequently at a minimum level, and therefore it was the one that nearly everywhere determined the limit of the yield.

In certain cases, the amount of nitrogen accessible to plants was automatically increased after draining and marling. This took place wherever clover and other plants of the pea family, which do not thrive on acid soil, sprouted spontaneously as soon as the pH value rose.[128] The increase in the quantity of nitrogen is due to the fact that clover grows in symbiosis with bacteria of the *Rhizobium* genus, which is able to fix the free nitrogen in the atmosphere so as to form nitrogen compounds assimilable by plants. Together with its relations in the pea family, such as peas, vetch, lentils, lucerne, and a few others, clover possesses the property – unique among plants that grow on open land – of being able to produce more nitrogen than it consumes.[129]

The scientific description of N-fixation is only about a hundred years old and was made by the German chemist H. Hellriegel.[130] Until then the question of establishing the precise nature of the special fertilizing properties of clover, peas, and so on, had been a controversial issue and one of the great riddles of agronomics.[131] The same applied to the related question of the role played by nitrogen in plant nutrition, which was first

---

[125] See Chapter 2; Johannes Dons Christensen 1952, pp. 28–34.
[126] But on manganese, see Chapter 3.4.   [127] See Chapter 2.
[128] See quotation from A. C. Teilmann, Chapter 3.4. The same report from Herningholm Manor, Western Jutland: A couple of years after lime had been spread on the fields, grass sprouted intermingled with red and white clover. Hans de Hofman 1758, pp 37–8. Parallel examples from England: J. D. Chambers and G. E. Mingay 1966, p. 8. Clover's inability to thrive in soil with a lime deficiency: P. Nielsen 1879, p. 486; K. Gram, Hjalmar Jensen, and A. Mentz 1937, p. 474.
[129] Survey of the pea family in Northern Europe: Richard Fitter and Alstair Fitter 1974, pp. 116–31. N-fixation has been described in a great many works. See, for example, Johannes Dons Christensen 1952, pp. 29–30; K. Gram, Hjalmar Jensen, and A. Mentz 1937, p. 474 and Hans Doll et al. 1987, pp. 189–91.
[130] H. Schadewaldt 1972 (with bibliography).   [131] Gerd Malling 1982, pp. 30–1.

The Green Revolution

definitively demonstrated by J. B. Lawes and L. W. Gilbert in 1851, after having been contested by many scientists, including Justus von Liebig, the most renowned agrarian chemist of the nineteenth century.[132]

As will be apparent, uncertainty about the nature of the miraculous properties of the pea family and the role played by nitrogen in plant nutrition had not prevented N-fixation from being exploited in practical farming in increasingly sophisticated ways ever since antiquity. This is not a unique instance of manipulating complex biological processes for commercial reasons without possessing a thorough knowledge of them. A parallel is alcohol fermentation, which was utilized and refined for many centuries before it finally became possible, in the middle of the nineteenth century, to give a comprehensive chemobiological description of the fermentation process.[133]

Where wild clover burst forth, or grew better, as a result of marling and drainage, the amount of nitrogen assimilable by plants increased. However, there is no evidence to suggest that spontaneous wild clover increased during the eighteenth century to such an extent that it could meet the increased demands made by crops on the soil's supply of nitrogen, now that the formation of deserts, acidification, wet soil, and a shortened growth season were receding as yield-limiting factors. If the ecological recovery was to be consolidated definitively and the long-term tendency towards decreasing yields arrested, the addition of fertilizers would have to be increased. More precisely – and formulated with the hindsight of a later age – the amount of nitrogen assimilable by plants would have to be increased, whereas what happened to the other plant nutrients was of less importance.

The problem was where to obtain extra nitrogen. Natural nitrogen compounds that could be assimilated by plants existed in large quantities in the fabulous Chilean and Peruvian guano beds bordering on the Pacific, but quite apart from the fact that these beds were hardly known at this time, the limitations of eighteenth-century transport technology meant that they were much too far away to be within reach of European agriculture. For a few more decades, the use of guano was to remain the prerogative of local Indian peasants.[134] If the nitrogen problem was to be solved, Danish and other European farmers would have to find their own answer. An attempt could be made to make better use of existing resources, and if this should prove insufficient, one would have to

---

[132] C. P. H. Chorley 1981, p. 71.   [133] Kristof Glamann 1962, pp. 201–8.
[134] Leslie Bethell 1984–6, II, p. 207; IV, pp. 17, 84, 601.

60   The Ecological Revolution

turn to the sea, because marine plants contain nitrogen, or to the atmosphere, exploiting the ability of plants of the pea family to fix nitrogen. All three possibilities were explored. Let us first examine what was done to make better use of existing resources.

A clear tendency can be observed in the eighteenth century to exploit and preserve existing fertilizing resources with greater care than formerly. As *Danmarks og Norges Oeconomiske Magazin* claimed in 1758, manure was "as precious as gold,"[135] a view certainly reflected in the prices asked. Around 1700, a load of manure cost 6 *skilling;* in 1759 it cost 32 *skilling,* in other words an increase of almost 500 percent, which was in striking contrast to the slow rise in prices for agricultural products in general.[136]

An indication of the efforts made by villages to retain such manure resources as they happened to have was the ban on selling manure introduced in the bylaws of more and more villages in the course of the eighteenth century.[137] Altercations as to who owned the right to the manure could arise even within the boundaries of the individual village. The restrictions on the rights of smallholders to let their cattle graze on commons, which turn up in village bylaws in the course of the eighteenth century, should also be seen in this context.[138] So too should the otherwise mysterious struggle against *lønnesæd* (literally, 'wage seed,' a term used for the practice of paying wages to farmhands in the form of a quantity of seed corn and the right to cultivate a prescribed patch of land), which represented one of the eighteenth century's great conflicts in the agricultural community. The *lønnesæd* system implicitly recognized the rights of persons other than farmers to use manure. With the increased demand for manure, the system came into conflict with the farmers' wish to monopolize manure reserves.[139] In these cases, the struggle for the distribution of manure reserves became a factor in the increasingly sharper social conflict in village life during the

[135]   N. Randulff With 1758, p. 129.
[136]   Erik Pontoppidan 1759, pp. 47–8. J. N. Wilse provides the information that a load of manure in Fredericia cost 24 to 48 *skilling,* and, "as manure is both costly and necessary it is not surprising that here a case about a dung-heap has been heard in court" (1767, p. 207). Price development for agricultural produce: Chapter 1.2.
[137]   August F. Schmidt 1939, p. 648. Market towns also introduced a ban on the sale of manure: Århus 1760; Skive 1769; Randers 1772. Ibid., pp. 646–7.
[138]   Cf. Birgit Løgstrup 1986, pp. 58–60.
[139]   All forms of payment in kind were permitted in the seventeenth century. *Lønnesæd* was forbidden for the first time by a decree of 23 Mar. 1701 and subsequently tightened by the decrees of 1 July 1746, §3, and 23 Mar. 1770, §7, cf. Fridlev Skrubbeltrang 1940, pp. 173–7, 233–8, and 1978, pp. 145, 196, 250.

The Green Revolution 61

eighteenth century, a conflict between farmers on the one side and cottagers and farm labourers on the other.

The wish to exploit existing reserves of manure better than had been done before also made itself felt very clearly in the efforts to avoid waste of manure in the pastures. The most important ways in which such waste was avoided were by movable fences and summer stall feeding. Movable fences – that is, movable pens – were used to round up grazing cattle at night or at certain times during the day. The aim was to collect some of the manure that would otherwise be spread over the entire pasture.[140]

Indoor feeding during the summer was an expansion of the movable fence principle, because by keeping the cattle in stalls throughout the summer, or during part of it, it was possible to collect all the manure and use it on the cornfields.[141] Stall feeding during the summer had been practised abroad since the beginning of the eighteenth century. In Denmark it was first practised during the 1750s and soon found many keen supporters.[142] Sources dating from the end of the eighteenth century reveal that stall feeding was widely employed by landowners, tenant farmers, and cottagers.[143] Stall feeding was easiest when the grass available was thick, grew evenly, and could be mowed with a scythe. In practice, therefore, it was often linked to clover growing. Basically, however, stall feeding had nothing to do with clover, for any form of feed could be used. By 1800, the Reverend Christian Jacob Boserup, vicar of the parishes of Terslev and Ørslev in the Ringsted district in Zealand, had been stall feeding his cattle dur-

---

[140] Movable pens were already being used at Vemmetofte Manor in 1720. Christian H. Brasch 1859–63, II, p. 73. Early mention of movable fences also in Povel Juel 1721, p. 11. Movable fences common in the county of Århus in the 1750s: Hans de Hofman 1757, p. 5. See also Thorkild Kjærgaard 1980, p. 237 (n. 420). Movable fences are also known in other countries, e.g., England: J. D. Chambers and G. E. Mingay 1966, pp. 63–4.

[141] "Only by means of this arrangement [stall feeding] can the manure, for whose sake the cattle are primarily kept, be fully exploited." Christian Olufsen 1809, p. 237. See also H. Hertel 1919–20, I, pp. 122–3; W. A. Hansen 1790, pp. 67–8; Gregers Begtrup 1803–12, II, p. 251; August F. Schmidt 1939, p. 653.

[142] Around 1715, stall feeding was common in Saxony and Thüringen and in certain parts of "the imperial countries." Gertrud Schröder-Lembke 1978, p. 140. In Denmark the question of stall feeding in the summer was raised in the *Oeconomisk Journal* in 1758; at the end of the January issue the editor requested "knowledgeable compatriots to submit their observations to the proprietress." In 1771, Hans Jensen Bjerregaard, a well-known farmer, recommended stall feeding in the summer "which would ensure that much good manure could be collected" (1771, p. 30). In 1782 stall feeding was so widely recognized that proposals concerning the practice found their way into the almanac. H. Hertel 1919–20, I, p. 122.

[143] W. A. Hansen 1790, pp. 9, 68; Gregers Begtrup 1803–12, II, pp. 249–68; Hans-Berner-Schilden-Holsten and Albert Fabritius 1940–70, I, 2, p. 193.

62   The Ecological Revolution

ing the summer for twenty years, not only with clover but also with dock leaves, hemlock, and nettles.[144]

A way of stretching stall manure was to mix it with peat, turf, leaves, and waste of every sort, from sweepings to fish waste.[145] Mixing manure with other substances was not in itself anything new – it had been used in the North Sea region since at least the pre-Roman Iron Age.[146] What was new, however, was the proportions assumed by this practice in the course of the eighteenth century. In many places in Jutland, composting with peaty soil accounted for a considerable part of the total amount of agricultural labour performed.[147]

Finally, there was night soil manure. The utilization of urban night soil would appear to have commenced in the years around 1650.[148] Night soil was to prove of particular importance in the environs of Copenhagen. The Danish capital underwent a considerable increase in population during the seventeenth and eighteenth centuries, primarily as a result of the increase in official appointments under absolutism and the consequent increase in secondary employment within the service sector. In the 1750s, Copenhagen, with its population of eighty-five thousand, had become Denmark's first big city.[149] The annual content of nitrogen in night soil in a form assimilable by plants amounted at this time to about 450 tonnes, which was enough to supply the environs of Copenhagen within a radius of about 10 kilometres with about 20 kilogrammes of nitrogen per hectare, a considerable increase of the standard dosage of 20 to 30 kilogrammes [150] – and the trend was increasing, because Copenhagen continued to grow throughout the eighteenth century, and by the year 1800 had a population of one hundred thousand. The possibilities of obtaining more manure for agriculture in this way were exploited very carefully. This explains to a considerable extent the high level of agricultural production during the eighteenth century on the island of Amager, close to Copenhagen, and in the villages to the west and north of the capital.[151]

---

[144] Gregers Begtrup 1803–12, II, pp. 267, 274.

[145] Thorkild Kjægaard 1991b; Caspar Schade 1811, p. 279.

[146] Bjarne Stoklund 1986, p. 53; G. E. Fussell 1958, p. 182.

[147] Bjarne Stoklund 1986. N. Hurtigkarl mentions as an example a bog from which "many thousands of loads of soil for mixture . . . have been removed for fertilizing" (1762, p. 422). See also Claus Bjørn 1979–81, pp. 17–18.

[148] Peter Riismøller 1972, p. 97.   [149] Poul Thestrup 1971, p. 132.

[150] Standard dosage of nitrogen in the eighteenth century: see Chapter 2.

[151] Erik Pontoppidan 1763–81, II, pp. 33, 63–4; VI, p. 2. On the hereditary leaseholders of Bernstorff Manor (Gentofte), in particular: C. W. von Munthe af Morgenstierne 1783, pp. 36–7. See also Gerd Malling 1982, p. 39.

The Green Revolution
63

Night soil amounts to about 500 kilogrammes per person per year and contains not only 5.3 kilogrammes of nitrogen but also phosphorus, potassium, and other plant nutrients.[152] With a population of eighty-five thousand, this resulted in 450 tonnes of nitrogen per annum. The manure from Copenhagen was used on the island of Amager and in the villages of Zealand within a radius of 10 kilometres from the city.[153] This area comprised in all about 24,000 hectares. Night soil also played a similar role in the environs of most other European cities. Goethe, who made many observations on agriculture during his Italian journey of 1786–8, was delighted to see hard-working donkeys carrying the excrement of Naples to the surrounding fields and gardens.[154]

Regardless of how much such transactions with manure served to benefit individual districts and individual farms, they still failed to improve the country's overall fertilizing accounts. It was a zero-sum game, because for every winner there was a loser. Prohibition of the sale of manure from one village to another improved the manure balance of the village that had previously sold manure, but at the expense of the neighbouring village, which previously had been able to buy. In the worst instances, the conflict over manure could mean that an otherwise efficient distribution of manure resources would be discontinued.

Similarly, redistribution of manure resources between farmers and other social groups in a village community for the benefit of the farmers failed to benefit the country's manure acounts as a whole. Movable fences and stall feeding also became a zero-sum game in the long run. The manure that was collected within a movable fence or in a stall and then brought out to a cornfield would otherwise have fallen on a pasture, where it would also have proven beneficial. Stall feeding and movable fences could actually worsen the imbalance between grazing areas and corn areas, which, as already indicated, represented the crux of the structural difficulties troubling early eighteenth-century agriculture. The mixing of peaty soil with manure to eke it out exercised a similar effect. In this case fertility was created in a small area by depriving and impoverishing a much larger outlying area within a system that has been appositely referred to as "concentration agriculture."[155]

The use of night soil from Copenhagen was also a zero-sum game in that the country's resources were concentrated around Copenhagen at the expense of the districts from which the city ob-

---

[152] K. Hansen 1920, p. 526.   [153] Gregers Begtrup 1803–12, I, p. 224.
[154] Johan Wolfgang von Goethe 1962, p. 258.   [155] Bjarne Stoklund 1986, pp. 53–4.

64 *The Ecological Revolution*

tained its supplies, first and foremost the remainder of Zealand, but also other parts of the country. The fertility of Copenhagen's environs thus was achieved by an uneven distribution of the country's resources. Here we are faced with one of the centralized state's many indirect offshoots that left their imprint throughout society in the most unexpected and peculiar ways. Hardly anyone can have wished, let alone foreseen, that the creation of a civil servant class in Copenhagen, financed by taxation, would contribute to a concentration of the country's available resources of nitrogen assimilable by plants on the island of Amager and in the eastern corner of Zealand at the expense of the rest of the country. And yet this is what happened.

Eighteenth-century Denmark was unable to solve the lack of nitrogen problem merely by improved exploitation of existing resources. What the country needed was an increase in the absolute amount of nitrogen at the disposal of plants. Other ways would have to be sought instead of just moving supplies from one place to another. Nitrogen would have to be brought into the agricultural system from outside, either from the surrounding sea or from the atmosphere's supply of free nitrogen, which, although inexhaustible, was not easily accessible.

3.6 NITROGEN FROM THE SEA

Throughout Denmark's inner territorial waters there were large amounts of seaweed, some of which was washed up on the beaches. In 1878 it was estimated that every year so much seaweed drifted ashore that it corresponded to a 10- to 12-foot-wide, 6-inch-thick carpet along the inner coastlines, and that annually it would be possible to recover 50,000 tonnes of dry seaweed, containing a total of 600 tonnes of pure nitrogen.[156] The amount of seaweed is unlikely to have been very different during the eighteenth century.

There is evidence that the use of seaweed as a fertilizer and composting element increased rapidly during the eighteenth century (fig. 6);[157] assuming that at least half the available seaweed was utilized at the end of the century, it would correspond to an improvement in the nitrogen balance of the Danish soil of about 300 tonnes of pure nitrogen annually. This may not sound like very much, but it was nevertheless enough to double the standard dosage of about 25 kilogrammes of nitrogen per hectare on an area

[156] Thorvald Schmidt 1878, pp. 492–3.   [157] Holger Rasmussen 1974, p. 395.

The Green Revolution

corresponding to half the island of Langeland, that is to say, about 140 square kilometres. And in this case it was not a question of a zero-sum game, but of a net profit for the country's nitrogen balance. The occurrence of seaweed on the shores of Denmark was irregular. Most of it was to be found in Limfjorden and in the Funen archipelago. Especially in the latter region, where there are a great many small islands and a long coastline, seen in proportion to the agricultural area, seaweed was of importance to the agricultural yield.[158] This is one of the reasons for the high level of agricultural production in this region during the eighteenth century. But seaweed was not the only explanation. It so happens that the southern part of Funen, as will be discussed, was also at the forefront in cultivating nitrogen-fixing crops, which was the other main road to improving Denmark's net nitrogen balance.

3.7 NITROGEN FROM THE AIR

For the country as a whole, the only way of obtaining more nitrogen was to cultivate plants capable of fixing nitrogen from the air. Essentially this was nothing new. The botanists and agricultural writers of antiquity, such as Theophrastus, Varro, Cato, Columella, Palladius, and Virgil (who wrote the *Georgics; or, The Art of Husbandry*), had recommended the use of plants from the pea family,[159] especially vetch, lupins, lucerne, broad beans,[160] lentils, and peas, all of which had the property of improving the soil while at the same time being very good forage plants; moreover, peas, lentils, and broad beans were excellent for human consumption.

Lentils, peas, and vetch had been cultivated since the beginning of agriculture. Together with one-grained wheat and emmer (both primitive species of wheat) and barley, they belong to the so-called Neolithic Near East crop assembly, the oldest group of domesticated plants in the Old World.[161] There are many unclear points in the history of the cultivation of the pea family. However, there seems to be no doubt that this special group of cultivated plants, after a considerable distribution in the Mediterranean area during

---

[158] K. von Essen 1807, pp. 174–84 (the island of Drejø); Gregers Begtrup 1803–12, III, pp. 527–35 (the island of Strynø).

[159] K. D. White 1970, pp. 189–91, 214–19 (references to the most important relevant places in the classics); Lucie Bolens 1981, pp. 129–35.

[160] Present-day ordinary beans are an American plant and were therefore unknown in European antiquity and the Middle Ages, when 'beans' meant what we now call 'broad beans.'

[161] Daniel Zohary and Maria Hopf 1988, p. 207.

The Ecological Revolution

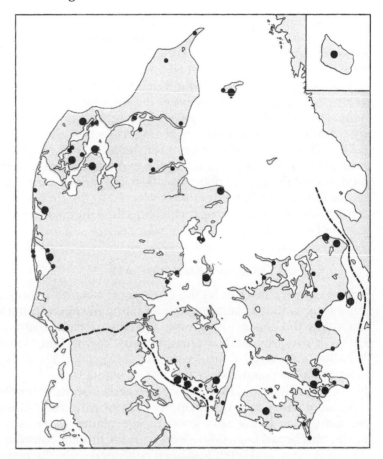

Figure 6. Use of seaweed as fertilizer in Denmark.

antiquity, declined during the second half of the first millennium of the Christian Era. The expansion of agriculture during the Middle Ages resulted in new progress,[162] which was succeeded in the late Middle Ages by another decline. But in the sixteenth century, cultivated plants capable of assimilating nitrogen were once more

---

[162] Pietro de' Crescenzi 1305, Book III, Chap. XIIII; Michael Nordberg 1987, p. 60. The ability of the plants of the pea family to improve the soil was also understood in the Middle Ages. Among others, de' Crescenzi wrote on the subject of lupins: "... sisemini ... per ingrassare e feconde fare [they are sown ... to make the soil rich and fertile]." Cf. Lucie Bolens 1981, pp. 129–39.

The Green Revolution 67

gaining ground and came to play a far more important role in agriculture than ever before.

When the pea family once more advanced in the fields of Europe, the team had been reinforced by a new member, which rapidly was to play a leading role as one of the most important cultivated plants not only in Europe but indeed in the whole world. This new plant was clover, of which it has been said that it "has had a greater influence on civilization than the potato, and much greater than any other forage plant."[163]

a. Cultivated Clover's Early History, Its Domestication, and Its Distribution in Europe

Cultivated clover is mentioned even as early as in the *Iliad*, but, during antiquity, it would appear to have been overshadowed by lucerne, vetch, lupins, and broad beans.[164] The reason why clover held such a humble position in the agriculture of antiquity was undoubtedly that it remained wild or only partially domesticated.[165] The competitive relationship between clover and other members of the pea family was not to change until much later, when clover became fully domesticated, in other words, after it had undergone a series of mutations that transformed it from a wild, or semiwild, plant into a cultivated plant. It then took the characteristic properties of all cultivated plants compared with their wild antecedents, including stronger and more luxuriant growth and a greater degree of climatic tolerance.[166]

There are several controversial issues in connection with the domestication of various cultivated plants, not only with regard to where but also to when and how domestication took place. Clover is no exception.[167] It has recently been asserted that the domestication of clover did not take place until the eighteenth century.[168] This is quite definitely several centuries too late. In Flanders, domesticated clover was mentioned in 1563, by the botanist Rembert

---

[163] N. L. Taylor 1985, p. 4. Taylor states that in the United States alone there is an annual production of 20 million tons of nitrogen through N-fixation. Clover contributes to the greater part of this. The other major producers of nitrogen are alfalfa and two non-European members of the pea family, soya beans and groundnuts. See also G. E. Fussell 1972, p. 150.

[164] F. Orth 1921, pp. 585–6.   [165] Ludvig W. Medicus 1829, pp. 20–31.

[166] A. J. Kupzow 1980.

[167] Daniel Zohary and Maria Hopf 1988. Particular references to the domestication of clover and the history of its early cultivation: Ludvig W. Medicus 1829, and Gertrud Schröder-Lembke 1978, pp. 133–4. See also N. L. Taylor 1985, pp. 2–4.

[168] A. J. Kupzow 1980, p. 65.

68   *The Ecological Revolution*

Dodoens (Dodonæus), who in his *Crûÿde-boeck* distinguishes clearly between cultivated clover, "Ghemeyn Claueren, Trifolium pratense," and wild clover, "Steenclaueren oft wilden Claueren."[169]

In northern Italy, two prominent agrarian writers, Agostino Gallo and Camillo Tarello, both from Brescia in Lombardy, started a campaign simultaneously, just after 1550, for the use of clover as a forage crop; Gallo in his best-seller *Le vinti giornate della vera agricoltura e piaceri della villa* and Tarello in his *Ricordo d'agricoltura.*[170] In his book Tarello declared that

> clover is an excellent fodder, not just as Pliny says, but as experience shows. Its roots benefit the soil by making it rich no less than grass benefits animals by nourishing them. That is why people from Brescia sow clover where they later intend to grow flax, which exhausts the soil a great deal.[171]

That Tarello is expressly thinking of domesticated clover is also evidenced by the emphasis he places on using the right seed:

> If one wishes to sow this crop, one should initially buy the seed in Brescia or some other place where it is to be found [after which one should produce one's own seed].[172]

Whereas clover had been a matter of secondary importance to the agronomists of antiquity, after domestication it became the focus of attention.

It is not from Dodonæus, Gallo, and Tarello, however, that we have the first evidence of domesticated clover. The evidence lies another three hundred years further back, in the work of the great medieval botanist Albertus Magnus, who in *De vegetabilibus,* from no later than 1270, describes a field of clover in such a fashion that there can be no doubt that what he had seen was domesticated clover.[173] Unfortunately Albertus does not tell us where he saw this field. But as he is known for having introduced Arabian

---

[169] Rembert Dodoens 1563, pp. 422–5; cf. Ludvig W. Medicus 1829, pp. 38–9, and Gertrud Schröder-Lembke 1978, pp. 137, 143.

[170] For a bibliography of the many editions of Gallo's *Vinti giornate* and Tarello's *Ricordo,* see Francesco Grasso Caprioli 1982. See also Carlo Poni 1989.

[171] "Trifolglio è ottimo cibo per gli animali, non solo come dice Plinio ma, come distra l'esperienza. Le radice delqua le giouano non meno alla terra ingrassandola, che gioui il feno a'bestiami, nutrendoli. Il perchè i Bresciani seminano del trifoglio, dove essi vogliono seminare poco dapoi del lino, che molto dimagra le terra."

[172] "Volendo adunque seminare de questo seme . . . bisogna mandare a comprarne per la prima volta, a su'l Bresciano, o altrove, dove ne sarà." Camillo Tarello 1567, p. 55r-v; cf. pp. 10v–11r.

[173] Albertus Magnus 1867, p. 633; cf. Knud Jessen and Jens Lind 1922–3, p. 90. On the dating of Albertus' treatise: James A. Weisheipl 1980, p. 572.

The Green Revolution   69

science to Europe, the trail leads to Spain, or more precisely, to Moorish Andalusia. Pointing in the same direction is that during the seventeenth century, and even in the early eighteenth, domesticated clover in Denmark and elsewhere was frequently referred to as "Spanish clover."[174]

A difficulty in establishing southern Spain as the original area for domesticated clover is that it has not been possible to procure positive evidence of domesticated clover in Spain earlier than in the seventeenth century, or long after the existence of evidence about domesticated clover in northern Italy and Flanders. However, it seems that this difficulty can be overcome. Assistance comes from Mexico and Peru. In America, where the flora and fauna of the New and the Old World met five hundred years ago, after having remained unconnected for millions of years, the most remarkable things took place.[175] For example, in the completely foreign biological environment presented by the New World there were European cultivated plants that found areas where apparently nothing could stop them. Cultivated plants that were delicate and required special care in Europe developed in the New World an aggressive, 'imperialistic' behaviour otherwise known only in weeds.

Examples were orange and peach trees, which successfully pushed their way through Central America until the new biological environment eventually developed defence mechanisms that restricted these conquests.[176] Another European plant to enjoy extraordinary success was domesticated clover, which in America advanced like wildfire: As early as the 1550s, only fifty years after the discovery of the American continents, it had spread all over the highland plains of Mexico and Peru.[177] Because clover did not exist in the pre-Columbian American plant world, and because all transference of plants and animals from Europe to the latter during the first years after the discovery of the New World took place from the Iberian peninsula,[178] there can be no doubt that clover came from Spain. Spain is thus the country where we find the earliest evidence of domesticated clover. As the other clues also point to Spain and more specifically to medieval Moorish Andalusia, there would appear to be the greatest likelihood that this is where cultivated clover originated. The theory that Andalusia was the

---

[174] As was the case with the first verified occurrence of cultivated clover in Denmark (1732). Gunnar Olsen 1961, p. 169. See also Johan Lange 1959–61 (index).
[175] Alfred W. Crosby 1986.   [176] Ibid., p. 151.   [177] Ibid., pp. 152–5.
[178] Alfred W. Crosby 1972, pp. 64–121; Leslie Bethell 1984–6, II, p. 204.

70   *The Ecological Revolution*

original domicile of cultivated clover is further strengthened by two circumstances: (1) Moorish agricultural science in Andalusia, which had upheld the tradition from antiquity, experienced a unique period of prosperity between 1000 and 1200; and (2) Andalusia was in every way the most important centre of agricultural innovation during the Middle Ages.[179]

Thus the history of European cultivated clover can be outlined briefly as follows. From Moorish Andalusia, where it was developed, and where Albertus Magnus probably saw it prior to 1270, cultivated clover was bequeathed to Christian Spain, a rapidly expanding power whose fortunes clover then followed to America, where we encounter clover early in the sixteenth century, and up through Europe, where our first evidence of domesticated clover is in two regions under Spanish rule: Lombardy, which was under Spain from 1535, and the Netherlands, which were part of the Spanish empire from the beginning of the sixteenth century.

The difference between domesticated and wild clover was striking. This is known, for example, from Denmark, where, because domesticated clover was introduced relatively late, the new, cultivated clover and the old, well-known wild clover could still be seen side by side during the second half of the eighteenth century. Philip Ernst Lüders, founder of the Royal Danish Agricultural Academy in Glücksburg, in what is now northern Germany, wrote in 1760:

> There are two kinds of clover, domestic,[i.e. wild] and foreign,[i.e. domesticated]. The domestic cannot be compared to the Spanish . . . . It is 1) of a species that grows more slowly, [and] 2) does not grow so high. From this follows 3) that neither its inherent urge to shoot up, nor its strength, can be as good and robust as in the foreign species.[180]

The same point was stressed in an article on clover, published in *Danmarks og Norges Oeconomiske Magazin* in 1763, in which the anonymous author compares the wild forms and the new, domesticated clover. Special emphasis is placed on the fact that the domesticated forms are stronger than the wild ones, and that they grow

> thickly and evenly, whereas [wild clover] since ancient times appears only in bushes here and there, and most places not at all, [and] that it [domesticated clover] yields more milk and butter than other grass; proof of which we have three times a day.[181]

[179] Lucie Bolens 1981, especially pp. 129–37.   [180] P. E. Lüders 1760, p. 82.
[181] W. E. 1763, p. 363.

The Green Revolution   71

Finally, there is the documentation provided by H. J. Trojel of Vissenbjerg, who in 1770 compiled a description of the flora of his home district in western Funen. In this he distinguishes between "the wild red clover" and "the red Dutch clover which is sown here in this country in many places, and which differs from the wild clover by virtue of its greater luxuriance."[182]

The tremendous amount of tree felling that took place between 1500 and 1800 turned large parts of Europe into a cultivated plain. As the forests gradually disappeared, difficulty was experienced in meeting demands in agriculture for nitrogen fertilizer and forage crops. Because domesticated clover was superior to the pea family's other cultivated plants (with the possible exception of lucerne and sainfoin), both as a forage crop and a producer of nitrogen, there were good reasons for following the suggestion to cultivate domesticated clover put forward by both Gallo and Tarello. From the close of the sixteenth century, the new crop began to take a firm foothold in Europe, first in Spain, Italy,[183] and the Netherlands (fig. 7); the latter were already suffering seriously from a shortage of forests during the sixteenth century.[184] Domesticated clover then moved to Henri IV's France, whose condition with respect to forests was summed up by Sully in the well-known words "La France périra faute des bois."[185] In France, cultivated clover, documented from 1583 onwards, had already achieved wide distribution in the seventeenth century.[186] In terms of forest shortage, England was not far behind the Continent,[187] and therefore it was not long before cultivated clover crossed the Channel. Around 1620 clover seed was exported from the Netherlands to England,[188] and with Sir Richard Weston's *Discours of Husbandrie used in Brabant and Flanders,* a description of the miraculous Flemish clover farming with which he had become acquainted during a sojourn in Ghent, Bruges, and Antwerp in 1644, a wave of en-

---

[182] Frederik Heide 1913–16, p. 603. See also *Avis for Bønder* 1780, p. 68, where a comparison of "foreign" (domesticated) with "domestic" (wild) red clover proved to be to the advantage of the foreign clover. The foreign domesticated clover grows faster and taller and is more nourishing than the local wild clover.

[183] Emilio Sereni 1958.

[184] Ferdnand Braudel 1949, pp. 109–10; Ester Boserup 1981, pp. 106–9. See also Chapter 4.1.

[185] Quoted by A. Howard Grøn 1959; Michel Devèze 1961.

[186] Antoine Furetière 1690 (article: "Trèfle"); N. L. Taylor 1985, p. 3; Bernard Garnier 1975; Ludvig W. Medicus 1829, p. 74. Cf. Michel Augé-Laribé 1955, pp. 7–8.

[187] John U. Nef 1932, I, pp. 156–64.

[188] J. D. Chambers and G. E. Mingay 1966, p. 8; Jan de Vries 1974, p. 141.

72   The Ecological Revolution

thusiasm for clover arose in the British Isles.[189] At the close of the seventeenth century, cultivated clover had spread over most of England.[190] In Germany, domesticated clover is documented from around 1645, when clover seed was offered for sale in Mainz. Before another hundred years had passed, clover was known throughout the German-speaking countries.[191]

b. The Pea Family, Especially Clover, in Denmark

The only cultivated plants of the pea family to reach Denmark from the Mediterranean area during antiquity and then be cultivated here were peas and broad beans, both of which have been known since the Bronze Age.[192] Vetch, which had been an important crop in the Roman Empire, did not reach northern Europe until after the Middle Ages. Vetch is mentioned in Holland for the first time in 1480,[193] and in Denmark in 1546.[194] Lupins took even longer to travel to northern Europe – they were not cultivated in Denmark until the nineteenth century.[195] Lucerne and its close relation sainfoin, which had played major roles in the agriculture of antiquity, and which in southern Europe continued to be (and still are) two of clover's important competitors, reached Denmark in the eighteenth century. They have never really become established here, however, primarily for climatic reasons.[196] Of all the cultivated plants of the pea family, the one to reach Denmark fastest was clover. In the year 1710, no more than one hundred and fifty years after the first word was heard of domesticated clover in northern Italy and in the Netherlands, the new crop reached what was then the Danish island of Fehmarn and thus came within the borders of the united monarchy of Denmark, Norway, Schleswig, and Holstein. This initial attempt to gain a foothold was shortlived. But in 1730 clover was back in Fehmarn, this time for good.[197] In the meantime, cultivated clover had reached the north of Schleswig-Holstein, where it has been grown since the mid-1720s.[198]

---

[189]   Sir Richard Weston's treatise was first published in 1650 by Samuel Hartlib. On this treatise's remarkable publishing history, as well as its author and his importance to the spread of clover: A. R. Michell 1974. Another treatise of the period advocating the use of clover was Andrew Yarranton's *The Great Improvement of Lands by Clover* (1663).
[190]   Eric Kerridge 1967, especially pp. 280–8.
[191]   Gertrud Schröder-Lembke 1978, pp. 145–68.
[192]   Johan Lange 1961 and 1976.   [193]   B. H. Slicher van Bath 1960a, p. 130.
[194]   V. J. Brøndegaard 1978–80, III, p. 233.   [195]   Ibid., p. 224.
[196]   Anon. 1747; *Landbrugets Ordbog* 1937–8, I, pp. 299–300 (article: "Esparsette"); II, pp. 58–60 (article: "Lucerne").
[197]   Karl A. Jørgensen 1930, p. 369.
[198]   P. E. Lüders 1758a, p. 302 (the years 1725–30 are said to have been particularly good clover years).

The Green Revolution

Figure 7. The expansion of cultivated clover in Europe, ca. 1250–ca. 1750.

In Denmark proper the first certain evidence of domesticated clover dates from 1732, when Johan Ulrich Røhl, the architect behind the halting of sand drift in North Zealand, wanted to sow "Spanish clover" – probably brought from Holland – in Tisvilde, so that cows and sheep might graze where a few years previously sand drift had prevailed. This was wholly in accordance with the optimistic theories of the day to the effect that "if one would only sow this seed [Spanish clover] in the poorest fields and deserts, . . . then one would discover that henceforward no complaints would ever be heard about the impossibility of breeding cattle."[199]

It was not that simple, however. Røhl's attempts with clover would appear to have failed – at all events, we hear no more of them. Not until 1786 and later is there certain evidence that clover was cultivated continuously in Tisvilde.[200] But it was not long before

---

[199] Gunnar Olsen 1961, p. 169; cf. Edvard Holm 1907, p. 11; Anon. 1747, p. 55 (quotation).
[200] Archives of the Agricultural Society, Landhusholdningsselskabets præmileprotokol 1789, no. 89, Danish National Business History Archives.

74   *The Ecological Revolution*

cultivated clover made its appearance in other parts of Denmark, and this time the plant took a firm hold. At a rate without parallel in Danish agricultural history, the new crop spread over the fields of Denmark from the end of the 1740s onwards.

Around 1900, the Danish folklorist Evald Tang Kristensen recorded a legend about the introduction of cultivated clover to Denmark. According to this tale, clover was supposed to have come to Denmark "more or less some 400 years ago," or, in other words, around 1500.[201] Because at this time clover had been common in Denmark for only a little more than one hundred years, the case serves to demonstrate how imprecise oral traditions can be as a historical source.

When Denmark became acquainted, during the 1740s and 1750s, with the new, successful crop from the south of Europe, the principle of cultivating soil-improving (that is to say, nitrogen-fixing) crops was already familiar. Peas and broad beans, which had long been grown, gained particular favour during the seventeenth century and the early eighteenth century. Peas especially were popular. "Peas that grow on fields are known to everyone," wrote the botanist Simon Paulli in 1648;[202] the pea harvests on the islands of Lolland and Falster were very important.[203] In Jutland there are examples of broad beans taking their place in crop rotation.[204] Vetch, which, as already mentioned, did not reach Denmark until the middle of the sixteenth century, also gained popularity and would appear to have had a not inconsiderable distribution during the seventeenth century, especially on the islands of Funen and Langeland.[205]

In practice this "proto-nitrogen revolution" [206] would appear to have taken place in the simplest possible way, namely, by introducing a crop of peas, or perhaps of vetch or broad beans, into the crop rotation system. On the islands of Lolland and Falster, where

---

[201] Evald Tang Kristensen 1928, p. 275.   [202] Simon Paulli 1648, p. 320.
[203] Arent Berntsen 1650–6, I, pp. 105–14; Henrik Pedersen 1907–8, pp. 131–2; Lars Rumar 1966–7, XVIII, p. 50; Fridlev Skrubbeltrang 1978, p. 119; Erik Pontoppidan 1763–81, III, pp. 248–9. At Orupgård Manor, Korselitse Manor, and Vesterborg Manor the amount of seed peas used rose 261% during the years 1718–51, reported by Bo Johansen. At Juellinge Manor pea breeding was stimulated in the 1730s and 1740s by distributing seed peas to the farmers. Archives of Juellinge Manor, Godsforvalter Chr. Sørensens arkiv, 1728–43, Provincial Archives of Zealand.
[204] J. G. Villadsen and Villads Villadsen 1941, p. 154.
[205] Vilh. Lütken 1909–10, p. 155; Karl-Erik Frandsen 1977–8, p. 29.
[206] After C. P. H. Chorley 1981, p. 73.

The Green Revolution 75

pea growing was particularly prominent, room was often made in the crop rotation system by converting a three-course system into a four-course one, after which the new field entered the rotation as a pea crop.[207] This means that 25 percent of the cultivated land was continually covered by a nitrogen-fixing crop.

During the seventeenth century, Lolland and Falster emerged not only as pea-producing but also as wheat-growing regions. As wheat is a demanding crop with a large consumption of nitrogen, there is probably a connection between the new position held by the two southern islands as wheat growers and the contemporary "proto-nitrogen revolution." This is supported by the fact that during the period 1718–51, on three estates, Orupgård, Korselitse, and Vesterborg, the sowing of peas increased by 261 percent and that of wheat by 182 percent.[208] According to tradition, one man alone, the Dowager Queen Sophie's chief administrator, lord lieutenant of Nykøbing, Joachim von Barnewitz, was responsible for encouraging so successfully the growing of both peas and wheat on the islands of Lolland and Falster.[209]

Not until the eighteenth century, however, did the method of improving the soil by the systematic use of nitrogen-fixing crops prove its true worth. Because the new cultivated clover – undoubtedly the most important agricultural innovation since antiquity – was available at this time, it naturally became the preferred crop for this purpose. The introduction of clover called for no major technical changes because clover crops could be included in the crop rotation in the same way that peas, broad beans, and vetches had long been used. With regard to the sowing of clover seed, the still customary procedure was quickly adopted, namely, sowing clover seed together with a grain crop – in the eighteenth century, usually oats. By the time the cover crop was harvested, what emerged was a growing field of clover that would have time to thicken during the autumn. The following year the clover field was usually used for hay, after which it could be grazed for two to four years.[210]

A survey of the introduction of domesticated clover into Denmark between 1732 (the year for which we have the first evidence

[207] Lars Rumar 1966–7, XVIII, p. 50.
[208] Reported by Bo Johansen. Additional evidence of the special importance of pea breeding on the island of Lolland is that from 1668 tithes were paid on this crop. Gerd Malling 1982, pp. 39–40.
[209] C. Christensen (Hørsholm) 1886–91, II, p. 33.
[210] See fig. 12. Numerous examples of slightly different crop rotation are given on pp. 269–336 of the Danish edition of the present book.

76   The Ecological Revolution

of cultivated clover) and 1805 is given in Figures 8 to 11. The four distribution maps show the status in 1775, 1785, 1795, and 1805, respectively.[211]

It is not easy to convert the clover-distribution maps and the information upon which they are based to absolute figures for the development of the clover areas during the last half of the eighteenth century. One important area of uncertainty is that in the case of villages not all records show how many of the farmers grew clover. Equally uncertain is the size of the clover fields. In the beginning, when clover was still a new crop, only small, experimental areas were sown, among other reasons because the seed was expensive and bought in small portions and often had to be procured from afar.

A letter dated 8 December 1760 from burgomaster Junghans in Kolding to the agricultural innovator Hans de Hofman hints at the modest scale on which a start was made: "Pray be so gracious towards a poor man as to let me have 3 or 4 pounds of clover seed in the spring with a little instruction as to how it is to be handled."[212] The reason the burgomaster of Kolding chose to approach Hofman to buy seed was undoubtedly because Hofman's clover enjoyed the best reputation. It was "the red, genuine, Dutch clover preferred throughout Europe to all other clover; even in France the Dutch clover is preferred to that which is grown in Normandy."[213]

The sources of the domesticated kinds of clover used in Denmark in the eighteenth century were principally the island of Fehmarn and Holland. Evidence of this is provided by, for example, the numerous purchases of seed made by the manors of Bregentved, Valdemar's Castle, and Frederiksgave as far back as the 1750s.[214] In the advertisements for clover seed frequently carried in newspapers from the 1760s onwards, the varieties of seed offered were mainly from Holland (Brabant) and Fehmarn, though occasionally also from Holstein.[215] But Danish clover breeders also had contacts elsewhere. For example, in the town of Erfurt, in Saxony, seed for Denmark was bought from an alderman, Christian Reichardt, "at the

---

[211] References for individual instances of the use of clover on which figs. 8–11 are based are given on pp. 269–336 of the Danish edition of the present book.
[212] P. Eliassen 1906, p. 103.   [213] J. N. Wilse 1767, pp. 221–2.
[214] Collection of unpublished documents for a history of prices, University of Copenhagen, Department of History.
[215] See, for example, *Kiøbenhavns Kongelige allene priviligerede Adresse-Contoirs Efterretninger* 8 Jan. 1762; *Odense Adresse-Contoirs Efterretninger* 1774, nos. 10–12; *De til Forsendelse med Posten allene priviligerede Kiøbenhavnske Tidende* (now *Berlingske Tidende*) 14 Oct. 1799.

The Green Revolution

Figure 8. Domesticated clover in Denmark, 1775.

present time one of the most renowned merchants dealing in those kinds of foreign seeds for *prairies artificielles*, or artificial meadows."[216]

It took only a few years to work up local clover-seed production on the basis of a small portion of foundation stock,[217] and as clover rapidly proved to have an extremely high-yielding capacity (provided the soil did not need to be marled or that it was not too wet and that no attempt was made to sow the clover in pure sand, which was what Røhl had done) greater boldness was displayed, and the clover area was expanded. On the small island of Strynø that lies between Funen and Langeland, clover was being grown on a large scale by 1754 at the latest. Here, one field would be sown with clover and some peas, and because the three-field system was practised on the island, the result was close to 33 percent clover in

[216] D. Schiöth 1760, p. 238; cf. Gertrud Schröder-Lembke 1978, pp. 166, 168. On the term 'prairie artificielle' (artificial meadow): Gerd Malling 1982, pp. 26–7 (incl. n. 21).
[217] See Danish edition of the present book, p. 281.

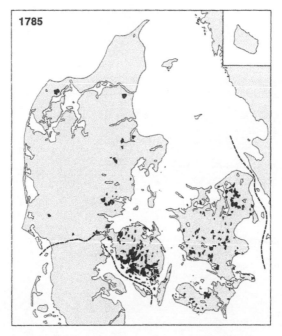

Figure 9. Domesticated clover in Denmark, 1785.

the crop rotation.[218] But this was by no means the limit. In 1775 the main farms of manors like Vemmetofte (Zealand), Korselitse (Falster), and Sæbyholm (Lolland) had crop rotations with 45 percent clover, excluding the year of sowing.[219] In 1778 the farmers of Køng in South Zealand followed suit by introducing a crop rotation with 45 percent clover (fig. 12).

Within a few years, experimental areas no bigger than gardens had turned into huge expanses of clover. In 1779 the farmers of Nybølle in the parish of Hillerslev on the island of Funen received a prize of 20 rix-dollars for having sown no less than 100 tønder with red clover seed.[220] At the big main farm at Gjorslev Manor on the Stevns peninsula in Southeast Zealand, scepticism about introducing clover prevailed for a long time, but finally, in May 1794, it was decided to give clover a try, and 50 kilogrammes of red and white clover seed were bought on the island of Funen. The result was apparently most satisfactory, for the very next year Gjorslev

[218] Ibid., pp. 270–1; Gregers Begtrup 1803–12, III, p. 530.
[219] Danish edition of the present book, pp. 273–4.   [220] Ibid., p. 277.

The Green Revolution

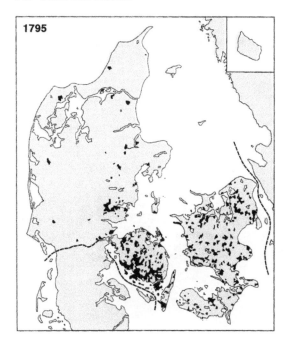

Figure 10. Domesticated clover in Denmark, 1795.

bought almost 750 kilogrammes of red clover seed from Funen, enough to sow 100 *tønder*.[221] In the 1780s and 1790s, clover fields covering 30 to 50 percent of the cultivated land became a matter of course, and in many cases the percentage was even higher.[222] The official agronomical view of the matter was formulated by the agricultural writer H. J. C. Høegh. In his *Anviisning til et velindrettet Jordbrug for Gaardmænd og Huusmænd paa Landet* (Directions for well-appointed husbandry for farmers and cottagers) of 1795, which was sponsored by the Agricultural Society, crop rotation was recommended in which almost 60 percent of the soil, excluding the year of sowing, was covered with clover.[223]

The question of the size of the clover area is rendered even more complicated by the fact that its extent was not merely a consequence of the confidence of clover growers in their crops but also formed part of a complex interaction with the areas outside the crop rotation and with the fallows within the rotation. The use of clover meant that forage production was moved to an increasing

[221] Ibid., pp. 307–8   [222] Ibid., pp. 277–317.   [223] H. J. C. Høegh 1795, p. 313.

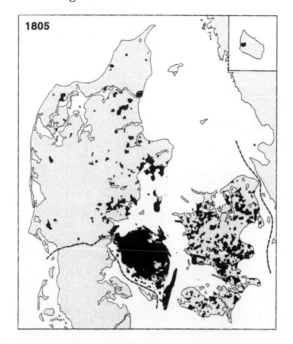

Figure 11. Domesticated clover in Denmark, 1805.

extent into the new 'artificial meadows,' and that the outlying areas – where large parts of forage production previously had taken place – gradually became superfluous and could be drawn into the cultivated area, which in turn served to increase the size of the clover areas. The hitherto prevailing and increasingly critical disproportion between grazing areas and cultivated areas (in that the size of the outlying areas had to be continually increased merely to keep the yield constant) was reversed.[224]

The gradual disappearance of the outlying fields after 1760 was a feature noted by several contemporary observers.[225] Elimination of the commons has usually been regarded as being connected with the enclosure movement. It has not been understood that because these areas were a symptom of an ecological crisis, they could be removed only in the course of ecological recovery.[226]

[224] Yield per cultivated unit of area does not fall regardless of putting outlying grazing commons under the plough. Erland Porsmose 1987, p. 262.
[225] See, for example, Jacob Mandix 1830, p. 15.
[226] For example, Lotte Dombernowsky 1988, pp. 381–2.

The Green Revolution

	No. 1	No. 2	No. 3	No. 4	No. 5	No. 6	No. 7	No. 8	No. 9
1780	Clover	Clover	Oats with clover	Peas and oats or barley	Barley	Rye and wheat	Barley	Clover and lie fallow	Clover
1781	Clover	Clover	Clover	Oats with clover	Peas and oats or barley	Barley	Rye and wheat	Barley	Clover and lie fallow
1782	Clover and lie fallow	Clover	Clover	Clover	Oats with clover	Peas and oats or barley	Barley	Rye and wheat	Barley
1783	Barley	Clover and lie fallow	Clover	Clover	Clover	Oats with clover	Peas and oats or barley	Barley	Rye and wheat
1784	Rye and wheat	Barley	Clover and lie fallow	Clover	Clover	Clover	Oats with clover	Peas and oats or barley	Barley
1785	Barley	Rye and wheat	Barley	Clover and lie fallow	Clover	Clover	Clover	Oats with clover	Peas and oats or barley
1786	Peas and oats or barley	Barley	Rye and wheat	Barley	Clover and lie fallow	Clover	Clover	Clover	Oats with clover
1787	Oats with clover	Peas and oats or barley	Barley	Rye and wheat	Barley	Clover and lie fallow	Clover	Clover	Clover
1788	Clover	Oats with clover	Peas and oats or barley	Barley	Rye and wheat	Barley	Clover and lie fallow	Clover	Clover

Figure 12. Crop rotation in the village of Køng, Zealand, 1780–8.

The amount of fallow land, that is to say, the unsown fields within the crop rotation, also began to diminish with the progress of clover. The principal motive for letting a piece of land lie fallow is usually that the fertilizing capacity is insufficient to keep the entire arable area under cultivation. The introduction of fallows in the twelfth century is one of the clearest signs of the intensifying ecological crisis, which culminated at the end of the thirteenth century and the beginning of the fourteenth. Conversely, the decrease in fallows at the end of the eighteenth century is evidence of a retreat from the brink of disaster. This favourable development, which later resulted in the complete disappearance of fallow land, necessitated an expansion of the clover areas.

In 1783, the landowner C. W. von Munthe af Morgenstierne declared that he had abandoned the policy of letting fields lie fallow and instead had sown legumes, presumably clover:

> I have never been able to comprehend the sense in using expensive labour [on cleaning a fallow field] . . . only to derive no income from it for a whole year. I have given up fallowing, and sow legumes in the soil.

82   *The Ecological Revolution*

.... England's best cultivated regions have abandoned fallowing. No doubt Denmark will follow this example some time.[227]

On the island of Als in Schleswig, where a large degree of clover growing had already been introduced by the 1760s, fallowing was fully abandoned in the 1770s. After a visit to the island in 1773, the Norwegian priest Hans Mossin wrote: "One can hardly find anywhere a patch of land big enough to sit on without its having been put to some useful purpose."[228] In Normandy, the gradual abolition of fallowing as a consequence of nitrogen-fixing crops can be traced from the seventeenth century "where the natural fertility of the soil is beginning to be maintained by a progressive replacement of bare fallow by green fallow, that is to say, legumes."[229] In other places too, including the Netherlands, the abandonment of fallowing can be observed as a consequence of the advance of nitrogen-fixing crops.[230]

It emerges clearly from the distribution maps (figs. 8–11) that during the period 1750–1805 clover spread not only fastest but also furthest on the island of Funen and the smaller neighbouring islands. However, Zealand, Lolland, and Falster soon followed suit. H. J. C. Høegh, who apart from his activities as an agricultural writer also had an incumbency to look after in Gentofte, near Copenhagen, had good reason for declaring in 1795 that "with every year we are approaching the point when a farmer cannot avoid its being a disgrace . . . not to sow clover."[231] Clover also became well established in East Jutland. Only in West and North Jutland was virtually no clover grown by the beginning of the nineteenth century.

On the Funen group of islands, where in 1805 clover was to be found more or less everywhere,[232] the amount of clover in the crop rotation was between 30 and 50 percent. Because the commons had nearly all disappeared, a clover coverage of about 20 to 25 percent of the whole area is likely. the annual amount of nitrogen received on Funen and adjacent islands from clover dur-

---

[227] C. W. von Munthe af Morgenstierne 1783, p. 16. Some twenty years later Gregers Begtrup declared, in the selfsame spirit as Morgenstierne: "On a well-run farm, no land should be allowed to lie fallow except with clover" (1803–12, V, pp. 481–2).

[228] Hans Mossin 1773, pp. 17–18.

[229] " . . . où la fertilité naturelle du sol commence a être soutenue par un remplacement progressif de la jachère nue par la jachère verte, entendez les léguminieuses." Bernard Garnier 1975, pp. 175–6.

[230] B. H. Slicher van Bath 1955, pp. 179–80. See also Wilhelm Abel 1967, p. 168, and Gertrud Schröder-Lembke 1978, p. 175.

[231] H. J. C. Høegh 1795, p. 119. Cf. Ingrid Markussen 1988, p. 212.

[232] Cf. Gregers Begtrup 1803–12, III, p. 113: "Everywhere [on the island of Funen] the land is sown with clover."

The Green Revolution

ing these years was about 15,000 tonnes, corresponding to as much as 50 kilogrammes of nitrogen per hectare of arable land, in other words, more than double the standard amount added under the old system.[233] It is not possible to quantify so precisely in the rest of the country. It is beyond question, however, that throughout Denmark, apart from West and North Jutland, clover influenced the nitrogen balance appreciably.

Clover's invasion of Danish fields greatly reduced the importance of the other nitrogen-fixing crops, which previously had reigned supreme. But this does not mean that peas, vetch, and beans disappeared. On the contrary, these crops continued to gain ground, although at a slower rate than formerly. Even when the clover-dominated crop rotations at the end of the eighteenth century and the beginning of the nineteenth were at their zenith, it was often decided to sow peas one year.[234] The special circumstance connected with peas was that right up to the close of the eighteenth century they still had no serious competition from the potato and therefore played an important role in feeding the population. This was not the case with vetch, which nevertheless made progress in

---

[233] The cultivated area for the Funen group of islands has been set at 321,033 ha (the area of Funen itself and adjacent islands). Allowance has been made for forest (5%) and for water areas. No allowance has been made for roads and market town buildings, nor for reclamation work carried out after 1805. The addition of nitrogen in a form assimilable by plants by growing clover has been set at 215 kilogrammes per hectare, corresponding to what is known from modern clover breeding (Kristian Ilsøe 1975, p. 563). The reason for regarding domesticated clover of the eighteenth century as having at least as high a yielding capacity as present-day clover is given in *Note on the yielding capacity of clover in the eighteenth century*, at the end of this chapter.

[234] On peas in general in the last half of the eighteenth century: Erik Pontoppidan 1763–81, I, p. 541; III, pp. 83, 248–9; V, 1, pp. 407, 524; VI, pp. 200, 453, 537, 564; Niels Siggaard 1945, pp. 161–2; Seyer Mahling Beyer 1791, pp. 71–2; S. P. Jensen 1986, p. 48. The importance of peas also emerges from the frequency with which they are mentioned in tenancy contracts, see, for example, the archives of Giesegård Manor, Forpagtningskontrakter vedrørende Spanager 1720–1879: 24. oktober 1763, Provincial Archives of Zealand; archives of Vedelslund Manor, Diverse dokumenter 1767–1826: forpagtningskontrakt 16. Marts 1779, Provincial Archives of Northern Jutland; archives of Marselisborg Manor, Forskellige sager 1662–1851: forpagtningskontrakt af 13. januar 1796, Provincial Archives of Northern Jutland. Peas in clover-dominated crop rotations: Gregers Begtrup 1803–12, V, table facing p. 612; VI, pp. 69–70, 240. See also fig. 12.

[235] Erik Pontoppidan 1763–81, III, pp. 145, 337, 382; IV, pp. 40, 166; VI, pp. 640, 669, 822; archives of Gjorslev Manor, Kasseekstrakt over indtægter og udgifter 1795–1802, april 1797, item 10 (the estate buys vetch seed from farmers), Provincial Archives of Zealand; J. P. Prahl 1777, pp. 30–1 ("The farmers of [the island of] Bornholm, who do little hay-making, sow all the more vetch, with which they feed their horses"). Archives af Gammelgård Manor, Diverse dokumenter 1751–1849: taksationsforretning 1774 (50% of the land sown with vetch in 1774), Provincial Archives of Zealand; Hans Mossin 1773, pp. 21–2. On the islands of Funen and Langeland: G. L. Wad 1916–24, III,

84   The Ecological Revolution

many places.[235] Nor were beans forgotten; evidence exists from mid-Zealand, for example, of efforts having been made to improve the cultivation of broad beans at the end of the eighteenth century.[236]

The historian C. P. H. Chorley has estimated that at the end of the eighteenth century peas and vetch together covered 4 percent of the sown area in northwestern Europe.[237] In Denmark, peas and vetch may well have covered even more sown land, perhaps 5 or 6 percent. In 1771, the production of peas accounted for just over 2 percent of the total cereal harvest in Denmark.[238] Assuming that the proportion of yields of peas and cereal was (just as it is today) about 1:2,[239] peas alone must have covered 4 percent of the sown area at the beginning of the 1770s. To this must be added the not inconsiderable areas that were covered with vetch.

The very large amounts of nitrogen that clover bound in the soil year after year, supplemented with increased amounts of nitrogen from seaweed, peas, vetch, and broad beans, presumably would provide (together with the greatly increased production of forage, estimated to have quadrupled where clover was used)[240] the basis for a considerable increase in agricultural production during the last half of the eighteenth century, most pronounced on the island of Funen and the neighbouring smaller islands but also considerable in the rest of the country. All in all production was likely to double. And this is precisely what happened, according to the calculations available from other quarters concerning the development of agricultural production. The cattle population is estimated to have increased by one-third during the period 1770–1805: from about 450,000 to about 600,000,[241] and without detriment to the standard of nutrition, which, on the contrary, was better than ever before; this in turn meant that the production of butter and milk was able to increase considerably. Grain production is estimated to have almost doubled in the course of the thirty-

---

pp. 115, 122, 124, 169; Vilhelm Lütken 1909–10, p. 399. On Jutland: J. N. Wilse 1767, p. 206. Vetch in clover-dominated crop rotations: Gregers Begtrup 1803–12, III, pp. 219 (table), 231–3, 299–300, 555–7; VI, p. 240; in 1793, the hereditary tenant Frederik Artzt of Glumsø, Zealand, was rewarded for a farm with 12 *tønder* of clover and 5 *tønder* of grass, peas, and vetch. Agricultural Society prizewinners in 1793, Danish National Business History Archives.

[236] Seyer Mahling Beyer 1791, pp. 72–3.   [237] C. P. H. Chorley 1981, p. 73.

[238] J. A. Fridericia 1888, p. 10.

[239] *Landbrugets Ordbog* 1951–2, I, pp. 714–16 (article: "Høstudbytte"); II, pp. 840–2 (article: "Ært").

[240] Lago Mathias Wedel 1792–6, III, pp. 268–9.

[241] Fridlev Skrubbeltrang 1978, p. 406; Gregers Begtrup 1803–12, II, p. 275. Cf. Bent Schiermer Andersen 1986, pp. 76–7.

The Green Revolution   85

five years between 1770 and 1805, from 4 or 5 million *tønder* to 8 or 9 million per annum.[242] This huge increase in production would not have been possible without domesticated clover, and the ecological recovery would have produced far more modest results.

The many difficulties that undermined Denmark's agriculture and threatened food production during the first half of the eighteenth century were overcome by a series of coordinated activities. The destruction and decomposition of the countryside by sand drift, flooding, and acidification had been halted by arresting sand drift, by reclamation work, by drainage, and by marling. The wasting away of the soil's fertility through exhaustion of its nitrogen resources had ceased and been replaced by a gradual building up of large new resources. Whereas previously, statistical graphs had revealed only threatening, downward curves, the new curves were both sustainable and rising, and agricultural production was greater than ever before in the country's history. A green revolution had been carried through.

Note on the yielding capacity of clover in the eighteenth century, 'clover fatigue,' and Danish historiography. Eighteenth-century observers were effusive in their praise of the new fields of clover. For example, the "red, genuine Dutch clover" cultivated in the Kolding region in eastern Jutland from the 1760s could be mown four or five times every summer and grew well for five years.[243] Nowadays, a field of clover cannot be mown more than twice in a season, and its lifetime will not exceed three years. If the report on clover in the district of Kolding were the only one of its kind it would have to be dismissed as pure fantasy engendered by contemporary awe of the fantastic new plant. But it is not the only one.

The clover on the island of Strynø stood "two feet high,"[244] and clover on the island of Als "grows to the height of two feet in such abundance as may be found on earth."[245] P. E. Lüders was of the opinion that clover, thanks to its incredible properties, would transform "this region into a new Canaan in which milk and honey will flow."[246] In 1815, the industrialist J. C. Drewsen, owner of Strandmøllen (The Strand Mill), north of Copenhagen, recalled how his father "often told me about his clover crops, which, when compared with those now obtained by me, on the same land, seem to border on the miraculous."[247]

[242] For 1770: H. C. Johansen 1979, p. 25. For 1805: Fridlev Skrubbeltrang 1978, p. 406; S. P. Jensen 1985, p. 275. A downward correction to 7 million *tønder* as suggested by S. P. Jensen is not supported by the empirical material.
[243] J. N. Wilse 1767, p. 221; P. Eliassen 1906, p. 103.
[244] Gregers Begtrup 1803–12, III, p. 530; R. Nielsen-Kold 1932, p. 4.
[245] Hans Mossin 1773, p. 19.
[246] P. E. Lüders 1761, p. 22, and 1758b, p. 312. For Lago Mathias Wedel, clover breeding was "the *lapis philosophorum* of modern economy" (1792–6, II, p. 175; III, pp. 268–93).
[247] J. C. Drewsen 1815, pp. 176–7.

86   *The Ecological Revolution*

In the 1790s, using Dutch seed, clover was grown in the district of Merløse in mid-Zealand, its "main flower . . . the size of [a] smallish hen's
egg."[248] There would thus appear to be so many independent reports
about the fabulous clover fields of the eighteenth century that there is
reason to believe that the first fifty or sixty generations of cultivated clover
must have represented a golden age.

The unique success of cultivated clover was also, however, the source of
its own decline. Its success led to very intensive cultivation, in the process
of which 40, 50, 60, and even 70 percent of the land within the crop rotation system could be covered by clover. This was too much, and after a
number of local outbursts,[249] serious crop rotation diseases, which were
called 'clover fatigue,' broke out in many parts of the country towards the
late 1790s.[250] These diseases were probably stem eelworm and sclero-
tinia.[251] Such attacks of disease prompted the uneasiness that can be
sensed in several agricultural writers around 1800, including Gregers
Begtrup. Begtrup, while emphasizing on the one hand clover's admirable
properties, did not fail to draw attention to the fact that in recent years
clover unfortunately had shown a hitherto unknown tendency to fail.[252]

After 1805 a difficult period began for cultivated clover.[253] In many
places the use of clover declined, and all over the country clover had to
be adapted to what from this time onwards were latent diseases. This was
effected by reducing the clover percentage and, at the same time, initi-
ating a search for alternative forage crops, such as sainfoin, lucerne,
bird's-foot trefoil, medick, rye grass, timothy grass, cocksfoot grass, tall
meadow oats, tufted hair grass, and many others.[254] Whereas previously it
had been possible to have 50 percent clover or more in a crop rotation,
a limit now had to be placed at 10 to 15 percent.[255]

It was not until the 1830s and 1840s that clover prospered anew, by this
time no longer alone but surrounded by a veritable army of subsidiary

---

[248]   C. Bech 1817, p. 71.

[249]   Gregers Begtrup 1803–12, III, pp. 530–1; R. Nielsen-Kold 1932, p. 4.

[250]   A typical example of clover fatigue is described in the Danish edition of the present
book, p. 281 (Ingslev Kro, Funen).

[251]   Frede Jensen 1941, p. 12; *Landbrugets Ordbog* 1951–2, I, pp. 858–60 (article: "Knold-
bægersvamp"); II, pp. 592–4 (article: "Stængelålen").

[252]   Gregers Begtrup 1803–12, II, pp. 229, 234, 236, 249–52, 271–2; III, p. 208, 532; IV,
p. 691. As early as 1797 another influential observer of agriculture, Christian Olufsen,
wrote that red clover, "despite everything the German stall-feeding windbags may say,"
was disturbingly unreliable and that "this forage plant has so many shortcomings that
nothing – apart from the circumstance that most and perhaps all the other forage plants
proposed have even more – could place it in the first rank" (pp. 42–3).

[253]   N. Jensen: *Agerdyrkningslære opskrevet paa Tune Landboskole* (The Theory of Farming
recorded at Tune Agricultural School) 1873 (Manuscript Collection, Royal Veterinary
and Agricultural College, Copenhagen); K. Hansen 1924–45, II, p. 281.

[254]   Material on the cultivation history of individual plants in V. J. Brøndegaard 1978–80,
especially I, pp. 88–164 and III, pp. 206–52.

[255]   Johan Paludan 1822–4, II, p. 218.

The Green Revolution

plants.[256] In the course of the 1850s and 1860s it recovered the position it had held in the last half of the eighteenth century as the highly praised key crop in Danish agriculture. Peter Nielsen, a leading authority on plant breeding during the nineteenth century, declared that "no forage plant has helped our farming to the same extent as red clover,"[257] and a plant breeder named Karl A. Jørgensen praised clover as "a blessed gift, one of Denmark's greatest benefactors, . . . that transformed our farming class into prosperous people in their own small way."[258]

Eighteenth-century conditions never returned, however. Crop rotations in which half the land was sown with clover that prospered for five years, and in addition with a pea crop here and a vetch crop there, were no longer possible, and for a present-day farmer belong to the world of fantasy. But the clover crisis at the beginning of the nineteenth century did not result in its beneficial effects disappearing overnight. A property peculiar to nitrogen combinations left by clover and other members of the pea family is that the nitrogen does not become available to plants until it has been broken down by the micro-organisms in the soil to NH_4^+-N and NO_3^--N, which takes place gradually over a period of twenty years.[259] At the beginning of the nineteenth century, when 'clover fatigue' became frequent, large reserves of nitrogen were stored up in the soil – the largest since the Renaissance – from the clover growing of the previous years, only to be liberated during the ensuing years. This explains why harvest yields did not diminish in the first decades of the nineteenth century.[260]

Danish historians who have not been aware of the phenomenal progress of clover during the last decades of the eighteenth century have seen the surprisingly high degree of fertility at the beginning of the nineteenth century as an indication of the beneficial effects of the agricultural reforms at the end of the eighteenth century. What else could be responsible for the big crops than the soil's 'inherent power,' which it had not been possible to activate under the earlier lethargic and inefficient agricultural system, but which now, at last, with fresh winds blowing, was liberated and began to prove beneficial?[261]

---

[256] "Red clover . . . is spreading more and more," writes S. Drejer in his guide to Danish forage plants from 1837 (p. 187). The same book, which lists about 350 different species and kinds of forage crops (including 35 different kinds of clover) gives an excellent impression of the myriad of forage plants that were now used together with clover and/or kept in readiness if the clover should fail. Growth of the clover area after 1838: Jens Christensen 1985, pp. 49–51; J. B. Krarup and S. C. A. Tuxen 1895–1912, I, pp. 198–215; II, pp. 108–35; III, pp. 128–53; IV, pp. 98–116; V, pp. 270–5; VI, pp. 223–8.

[257] P. Nielsen 1879, p. 473

[258] Karl A. Jørgensen 1921, p. 29; 1930, p. 371.

[259] C. P. H. Chorley 1981, p. 77; letter from Finn Eiland 10 August 1990.

[260] During the first three or four decades of the nineteenth century, agricultural production would seem to have been almost constant. Around 1835, grain production was between 9 and 10 million *tønder*, in other words practically unchanged since 1805. Only after this date did agriculture production begin to rise appreciably again. S. P. Jensen 1985, p. 275.

[261] S. P. Jensen 1987, p. 105–7. Cf. Thorkild Kjærgaard 1985a.

4

THE ENERGY AND RAW
MATERIALS REVOLUTION

4.1 THE ENERGY AND RAW MATERIALS CRISIS

Ever since agriculture was introduced into Denmark the forest-clad landscape had been under attack. Occasionally the forest recovered some of the ground it had lost, but in the long run the clearing of land always proved victorious. At the beginning of the eighteenth century Denmark was an open, cultivated plain with few forests; it was plagued by serious ecological problems and had a production apparatus that could be sustained only at the expense of ecological balance.

By mobilizing the country's inner resources, and by utilizing the great agricultural innovation of the period, domesticated clover, the course of events was successfully changed during the eighteenth century. Towards the end of the century, sand drift, stagnation, and acidification were brought under control, and the content of plant nutrients in agricultural soil began to increase. In contrast to earlier times, this meant that food production could be augmented without releasing self-destructive mechanisms into the ecosystem.

There remained, however, the serious problem of energy resources and raw materials. Formerly, it had been possible to turn to the extensive and seemingly inexhaustible forests, which had supplied not only energy in the form of firewood and charcoal for domestic purposes but also timber for houses, ships, and tools. In addition, the forests had provided fuel for smelting iron, making glass, evaporating salt, and so on. This system, which depended upon wood to provide both energy and raw materials, had long been ailing. With the continued depletion of the forests during the eighteenth century the situation became increasingly critical;[1] complaints about the lack of fuel and timber were common from

[1] Cf. Chapter 2.

Energy and Raw Materials Revolution 89

the end of the seventeenth century, and during the eighteenth century they overtook complaints of every other kind.

Advances in agriculture often went hand in hand with problems involving energy and raw materials. An example is the island of Strynø, a pioneer area for clover growing, whose agricultural yield and population density – 100 persons per square kilometre – at the end of the eighteenth century were on levels otherwise encountered only in the twentieth century. At the close of the eighteenth century, there was not so much as a tree or even any brushwood to be found on this island.[2] Just outside Copenhagen, on the island of Amager, where some of Denmark's finest agriculture was also to be found, there were only "a few small groves, a couple of dozen trees and some undergrowth."[3] In the region between Copenhagen, Roskilde, and Køge,[4] on the islands of Lolland and Falster,[5] and in large parts of the island of Funen[6] – all regions undergoing rapid agricultural development – difficulties in obtaining fuel and timber were encountered everywhere. Yet this does not make it possible to draw the converse conclusion that low agricultural production provided a guarantee of plentiful supplies of raw materials and energy. Thus the ecologically exhausted western part of the Jutland peninsula, from The Skaw in the north to Ribe in the south, suffered from a calamitous lack of forests without being able to demonstrate a correspondingly high level of agricultural production. The same applied to the islands of Læsø and Bornholm.

During the 1780s, at Borreby Manor in Zealand, farmers had to fetch their firewood from a point 15 to 20 kilometres away, and the timber situation was so precarious that the landowner was obliged to deny the farmers any form of assistance "be it as little as a plough-peg."[7] On the island of Lolland "one did not ask the price of firewood, here one asks only: is there any to be had?"[8] A report from the island of Funen in 1769 ran: "Year by year fuel becomes more costly and more difficult to obtain from elsewhere."[9]

In Jutland, although energy prices rose, this circumstance in itself was not enough to prevent the continued depletion of the forests.[10] Numer-

[2] Gregers Begtrup 1804, pp. 307–9.
[3] Erik Pontoppidan 1763–81, II, p. 64; cf. VI, p. 2.
[4] Margit Mogensen and Poul Erik Olsen 1984, pp. 17–18.
[5] Erik Pontoppidan 1763–81, VI, pp. 467, 471–2, 474; P. Rohde 1776–94, I, pp. 9, 16–17.
[6] Erik Pontoppidan 1763–81, VI, pp. 565, 615; Gregers Begtrup 1803–12, III, pp. 159, 270, 285, 323.
[7] August Fjelstrup 1909, p. 85.   [8] Gregers Begtrup 1803–12, IV, p. 738.
[9] Ludvig Boesen 1769, pp. 18, 41.
[10] Erik Pontoppidan 1763–81, IV, p. 95. See also ibid., pp. 395, 643–4, 720–1; V, 2, p. 749.

90 The Ecological Revolution

ous industrial enterprises, such as lime burning at Mariager, were in difficulties due to lack of fuel;[11] exploitation of the large reserves of lime around Limfjorden became impossible for the same reason.[12] Along the North Sea coast the lack of timber was more extreme than anywhere else:

> Now [in the 1760s] all the forests [in Thy], just as in all the western parts of Jutland, are quite destroyed, and there remains no trace of either forest or undergrowth in human memory. Moreover, the inhabitants suffer greatly not only from a lack of useful timber for carts, ploughs and building but also wood for fuel, fencing materials and all other kinds of domestic purposes; they must obtain everything from elsewhere, even wooden clogs and spoons.[13]

Broadly speaking, oak timbers were seen in Jutland only when there had been a shipwreck.[14]

A cross section of the country's energy situation as it appeared at the end of the 1770s is provided by information about grain cultivation and proposals to improve it collected by the Rentekammer in 1778. Amongst other questions, the Rentekammer had asked whether it would be a good idea to set up drying ovens for grain. This proposal met with scepticism throughout the country because of the shortage of firewood.[15] The conjunction noticeable in Denmark – on the islands of Strynø and Amager, for example – of hyperintensive agriculture on the one hand and a lack of energy and raw materials on the other could also be observed in other parts of Europe. In Sicily, "the granary of Europe," where at this time "an endless wealth of fertility" met the eye, there was not a tree to be seen in the 1780s along the 70-kilometre stretch between Agrigento and Caltanisetta.[16]

In the mid-eighteenth century, anyone who attempted to visualize what the situation would be in the course of a few decades would have had every reason to fear that society must be doomed within the none too distant future to come to a standstill. An entropic condition was likely to develop in which it would no longer be possible to procure as much as a hot meal, and in which the lack of raw materials would be so total that even manufacture of the simplest tools would be rendered impossible.

In 1757 Hans de Hofman warned against allowing food production to take up all the country's soil, for in this case "our descendants will suffer from the greatest shortage of wood, more than anyone who does not know the character of the country can

---

[11] Ibid., IV, p. 518.

[12] Ibid., V, 1, pp. 19, 30, 198, 544.

[13] Ibid., V, 1, p. 407.

[14] Anon. 1798, p. 42.

[15] Jens Holmgaard 1962, pp. 10, 55, 59, 78, 87, 100, 105, 125.

[16] Johan Wolfgang von Goethe 1962, p. 308.

Energy and Raw Materials Revolution

imagine."[17] The agronomist J. D. W. Westenholz voiced a similar complaint in 1772:

> In this way, everything is being exterminated in Denmark that stands in the way of the plough, all forests, bushes, undergrowth, all streams, rivers and bogs, all ponds and meadows, in short, everything must be ploughed, as if no land were needed for human life but arable land.[18]

In Spain, also, the writing could be seen on the wall:

> Who cannot speak of her [Spain's] glories in bygone times of the Romans? Who has read their writings and not learned from them not only how fertile and populous she had once been and how many wonderful mines she had had, but also how many splendid forests with which to work them? But what has become of it all? One can no longer find traces of the existence of these mines, and a Spaniard must make do with a few coals in his *brasero* to keep himself and his entire family warm, for the whole country is devoid of forests with the exception of the stretch along the mountains of the Pyrenees extending from the Atlantic to the Mediterranean. It seems . . . that the world's great housekeeper created these mountains and the trees that grow on them solely in order that this kingdom might obtain aid from them in time of need, when all other forests were destroyed, and in this wise avoid final destruction.[19]

The crisis was experienced throughout Europe. Everywhere, even in Russia, in Sweden, and in Norway, which still had immense reserves of forests, misgivings arose.[20] Great demands were made on these reserves, amongst other reasons because during the seventeenth and eighteenth centuries the manufacture of key products like iron and glass, both of which require large amounts of energy, began to move in a northeasterly direction, towards the forests of Scandinavia and Russia. This was of benefit to the economies and international positions of Norway, Sweden, and Russia, but not to their forests, which disappeared at a speed the world would not witness again until the 1860s, when the huge forests of Wisconsin and Minnesota were cut down.[21] As Werner Sombart wrote under the heading "The End of Capitalism," the threatening lack of energy was "*the* European culture question,

---

[17] Hans de Hofman 1757, p. 67. Cf. Otto Diderik Lütken 1762, p. 254.

[18] J. W. D. Westenholz 1772, p. 160. [19] Esaias Fleischer 1779, pp. xxv–xxvi.

[20] Ibid., pp. xi–xxviii with references to a number of contemporary writers; Werner Sombart 1916–27, II, 2, pp. 1143–55; Joachim Radkau 1986, p. 8 (n. 27). Fears that the Norwegian forests would be destroyed prompted the government to initiate a search for coal in Norway during the 1750s: Edvard Holm 1891–1912, III, 2, p. 156.

[21] Also of importance to the exhaustion of forest resources was the export of timber from the northwest of Europe to the west and south of Europe. The export of sawn timber from Sweden, Finland, and the eastern part of the Baltic increased more than sixtyfold between 1670 and 1805. Antoni Maczak and William N. Parker 1978, p. 45.

92   The Ecological Revolution

the outcome of which was perhaps more important than the other concern at the time, whether Napoleon or the united European powers would emerge victorious."[22]

What was imminent, however, was not the downfall of capitalism in an entropic nightmare, but a revitalized, energy-intensive capitalism. The gloomy predictions proved ill-founded. That the energy and raw materials crisis passed was to some extent due to untiring efforts made in many quarters to exploit existing possibilities, with the aim of rectifying the situation by dint of individual effort. What decided the matter, however, was that the declining stock of forests was gradually supplemented, after the beginning of the eighteenth century, by increasing quantities of wood alternatives, the most important of which were coal and iron.

Europe began to liberate itself from its dependence on forests and set a course towards a new point of balance, that of the industrial world. In this world the task of the living biosphere was restricted to functioning as a supplier of foodstuffs, and the supplying of energy and raw materials became a task left mainly to coal strata formed by subterranean, prehistoric forests and to ore deposits stemming from an even more distant geological past. When the forests of the carboniferous age were burned off, these ore deposits would be smelted and converted into metal, with which it would be possible to make tools, machines, and transport systems.

4.2 RELIEVING THE ENERGY AND RAW MATERIALS CRISIS BY ECONOMIZING

The simplest way of confronting the energy and raw materials crisis was to economize on the use of available resources.

a. Buildings and the Heating of Dwellings

The most usual way of dealing with the history of Danish building culture is to approach it in terms of architecture and the history of styles. But other approaches are possible. One of them is to examine the various kinds of building materials that have been used in the course of time. Seen from this angle, the most striking feature about the period 1500–1800 is the decline in the use of timber. If we disregard the churches, most of which were built during the twelfth and thirteenth centuries, that is to say, during a period

[22] Werner Sombart 1916–27, II, 2, p. 1153. Cf. Joachim Radkau 1983, pp. 530–2; R. P. Sieferle 1982, pp. 106–7, A. Oppermann 1887–9, p. 1.

Energy and Raw Materials Revolution

93

when timber became scarce on account of the medieval expansion of agriculture, a considerable number of the buildings in Denmark around 1500 were built of wood.[23] In this respect they resembled the log cabins built by pioneers in America during the nineteenth century.

From the sixteenth century onwards, it is possible to observe attempts to save timber by using half-timbered constructions. The supporting framework of the wooden house was retained, but the intervening space was filled with clay instead of oak planks.[24] This development, which culminated in houses made of bricks (or, when money was short, of turf), began in the market towns, where timber was particularly hard to obtain. After the middle of the sixteenth century, the half-timbered house and the brick-built house spread from the market towns out to rural districts.[25] As might be expected, development was most pronounced in districts where the forests had first begun to disappear. In Southwest Jutland, brick-built farms and turf-built houses and huts took precedence during the eighteenth century.[26] In parts of East Jutland, where forests were more abundant, wooden houses were still occasionally being built in the eighteenth century and could still be seen in the nineteenth century.[27]

The almost automatic connection between changes in building construction and timber supplies is reflected by the fact that the strength of the wooden framework of a half-timbered construction depended on whether the house was close to, or far away from, forest districts.[28] Roof constructions were also altered to meet a demand to economize on wood. Roofs made of strips of wood would appear to have almost disappeared in the course of the seventeenth century in favour of more economical open frameworks onto which roofing material – straw, later tiles – was fastened.[29]

In many cases, the fires of varying degrees of seriousness that time and again ravaged both town and country during the sixteenth,

[23] Harald Langberg 1955, I, pp. 110–20.
[24] Mogens Clemmensen 1937, I, pp. 250–69 and passim; Axel Steensberg 1974, p. 93; P. Christian Nielsen 1979–82, p. 17; Grith Lerche 1987; Harald Langberg 1955, I, pp. 192–4.
[25] Mogens Clemmensen 1937, I, pp. 250–2; Troels-Lund 1879–1901, I, p. 336.
[26] H. Zangenberg 1935, pp. 227–31; Axel Steensberg 1974, pp. 121–2; Grith Lerche 1969, pp. 564–5.
[27] Mogens Clemmensen 1937, I, p. 36; Troels-Lund 1879–1901, I, p. 211; Grith Lerche 1969, p. 565.
[28] Bjarne Stoklund 1969b, p. 35. Cf. Svend Gissel 1968, p. 239.
[29] Axel Steensberg 1974, p. 123.

94   *The Ecological Revolution*

seventeenth, and eighteenth centuries provided the immediate reason for building new houses.[30] In some cases, the wish to reduce the risk of fire may have accelerated the changeover to half-timbered and brick-built houses, which were less prone to destruction by fire (especially when roofed with tiles instead of straw) than were the old log-built constructions. But on the whole, the changeover from warm, well-insulated wooden houses to thin-walled, poorly insulated half-timbered houses was not advantageous.

The motive behind the switch to new materials should not be seen as a general wish to reduce the risk of fire, and even less as an effort to improve dwelling-house standards, but was quite simply the need to reduce timber consumption. This is confirmed, for example, by the fact that Norway and Sweden, apart from the densely populated and poorly wooded province of Skåne, did not follow Denmark's example but continued, despite the greater risk of fire, to build wooden houses. This characteristic difference between Denmark and Skåne on the one hand and the rest of Scandinavia on the other, which was immediately noticed by travellers in the nineteenth century[31] (and which still persists to some extent) arose during the sixteenth and seventeenth centuries and can be traced back to the need in the south of Scandinavia during these years to economize on the use of timber for building purposes. The development in Denmark corresponds exactly to what in England has been called 'the great rebuilding' between 1500 and 1800.[32]

Parallel with the change in building customs, buildings became larger and more impressive, especially in the country, where, in the seventeenth and eighteenth centuries,[33] enormous half-timbered manor barns and large farmhouses built round a quadrangle became common. This increase in the size of farm buildings was prompted by the need for additional space for increasing agricultural production and larger herds of cattle.

In 1692, the buildings on twenty-seven farms in the villages of Væggerløse and Hasselø on the island of Falster had a total of 776 bays; in 1751 the number of bays on the same twenty-seven farms had increased to 1,111 and in 1805 to 1,345.[34] At Frederiksgave Manor on the island of Funen, a new brick cow house was erected in 1778, and the barn was extended by almost 25 metres; a grain loft was also included above the

[30] Fires also played a role in rural districts. Axel Steensberg 1974, p. 90.
[31] Troels-Lund 1879–1901, I, p. 209.
[32] W. G. Hoskins's expression. Quoted by C. W. Chalklin and M. A. Havinden 1974, p. 345.
[33] Fridlev Skrubbeltrang 1978, pp. 212–13.
[34] Calculated on the basis of Svend Jespersen 1961, pp. 103–7.

Energy and Raw Materials Revolution

95

new cow house.[35] At Clausholm Manor in Jutland, a huge new barn was built in 1731.[36] In the middle of the eighteenth century, the barn at Tjele Manor, Jutland, was a colossal, three-aisled building almost 100 metres in length that completely dwarfed the main building, which dated from 1585.[37] At Østergård Manor in the parish of Fjellerup, also in Jutland, the barns were extended in the eighteenth century. There are numerous similar records.[38]

On average, it would appear that the size of farm buildings doubled between the end of the seventeenth century and the end of the eighteenth, precisely as claimed by A. C. Teilmann in 1771:

> We need but compare the tithe registers and taxes of a hundred years ago with those of today, and examine how many extra bays have been added during the past fifty years to granaries at manor houses, vicarages and farms, to discover that more than twice as much grain is harvested in the country than before.[39]

The changes in Denmark's overall stock of buildings between 1500 and 1800 represented a huge collective effort to save timber, and so did the changes that took place in methods of heating buildings. During the sixteenth century it was still the custom to have a fireplace in the middle of the floor and an opening, a so-called louver, in the roof.[40] The open fire has not enjoyed a good reputation. Writing in the late 1870s, the Danish social historian Troels-Lund explained the drawbacks:

> The fire had to be constantly fed with new logs and a door had to be opened just as frequently to create the necessary draught and force the choking smoke to find its way out through the louver. . . . The inhabitants lived in an eternal mixture of smoke and draught.[41]

On the other hand, an open fire of this kind was apparently not always intolerable. A description of conditions prevailing in the south of Sweden in the 1590s stated that farm people, children, and servants walked around indoors wearing nothing but a shift or a shirt throughout the winter, even though it was bitterly cold outdoors.[42]

---

[35] Aage Rasch 1964, p. 306.
[36] Hans Berner-Schilden-Holsten and Albert Fabritius 1940–70, III, 2, p. 104; 3, p. 28.
[37] H. H. Engqvist 1974, pp. 92–3.
[38] Mette Skougaard and Karl-Erik Frandsen 1988, p. 120; Tove Clemmensen 1942, p. 14; Hakon Lund 1980, pp. 136–7.
[39] A. C. Teilmann 1771, p. 66.   [40] Harald Langberg 1955, I, p. 121.
[41] Troels-Lund 1879–1901, I, p. 230.
[42] Axel Steensberg 1974, pp. 100–2, and 1940, pp. 118–19.

96   *The Ecological Revolution*

The open fire was dependent upon a plentiful supply of firewood, however, and therefore had to be abandoned.[43] As the price of firewood was rising while that of iron, relatively speaking, was falling,[44] fuel-saving measures such as chimneys and stoves began to win favour towards the end of the seventeenth century. Around 1750 more than half of all the farms in Zealand had iron stoves, in addition to which a great many stoves were built of clay. Stoves were also commonplace in the towns. A property in Copenhagen acquired in 1756 by the firm of Ryberg & Thygesen, for example, had fourteen stoves.[45]

The new systems of heating houses economized on fuel. Nevertheless, the average room temperature seems to have fallen. This was certainly the case on the island of Fanø, just off the west coast of Jutland, where the islanders gave up heating completely and lit fires only to cook food.[46] In general, the cold is a constantly recurring theme in letters from the close of the eighteenth century. On 24 March 1788 the Danish author Charlotta Dorothea Biehl complained to Johan Bülow in one of her numerous missives that

> those who receive a load of firewood every day for every stove cannot know how it feels to wait for a fortnight and more for a little fuel with which to warm oneself; hunger can be allayed with a piece of bread, but banishing the cold requires 7 or 8 rix-dollars, and my body, exhausted as it is by illness, is thus so deprived of its natural warmth that I now have to buy my ninth *favn* of firewood this winter and yet never have I been so cold in all my life.[47]

The eighteenth century had many faces. One of them is that the inhabitants of Denmark learned what it meant to feel cold.

In 1759 Erik Pontoppidan felt prompted to assure his readers that scarcely anybody ever died of cold in Denmark.[48] Regardless of how he may have reached this conclusion, it can hardly be de-

---

[43] Troels-Lund 1879–1901, I, pp. 229–30.
[44] Astrid Friis and Kristof Glamann 1958, pp. 322–50. During the forty years between 1760 and 1800 the price of firewood in Copenhagen trebled. The price of iron was almost constant throughout the eighteenth century.
[45] Peter Michelsen 1968; Lars Friis 1968, pp. 92, 94; Aage Rasch 1964, p. 26. In 1771, twenty years later, 57 out of 80 tenant farmers on manorial farms under Ringsted Convent had iron stoves. Archives of Ringsted Convent, Godsbeskrivelse og synsforretning 1769–1817: beskrivning holden 1769, 1770, and 1771, Provincial Archives of Zealand. See also S. P. Jensen 1984, p. 16. Jutland: Erik Pontoppidan 1763–81, V, p. 519. The open hearth has never been forbidden in Denmark, though it was elsewhere, for example, in Mecklenburg in 1562, because it consumed too much firewood. Axel Steensberg 1974, p. 104.
[46] Gregers Begtrup 1803–12, V, p. 194.
[47] Quoted by Svend Cedergreen Bech 1975, p. 56.   [48] Erik Pontoppidan 1759, p. 3.

Energy and Raw Materials Revolution   97

nied that the Danish population has never in historic times suffered as much from the cold as it did during the last five or six decades of the eighteenth century and the first three or four decades of the nineteenth – even though people kept their hats, their coats, and their boots on indoors and sometimes even in bed. At no other time in Denmark have there been so many indoor walls glistening with frost, so many draughty floors, so many dripping noses, and so many people suffering from the cold and rheumatism as there were during those endless years, with the result that tuberculosis – that ever-faithful attendant of unhealthy, cold dwellings – spread.

Not until later in the nineteenth century, when energy became more plentiful, did the cold, rheumatism, and tuberculosis gradually relax their grips and allow people to remove, even if hesitantly, some of their outdoor garments when they came indoors.[49] In our own century, we have once again returned to the point where, like the country people in Skåne in the sixteenth century, we can walk around indoors in relatively light clothing, no matter how cold it is outside.

The savings in firewood consumption effected between 1500 and 1800 cannot be established with accuracy, although it is possible to form an idea of their extent. Keeping an open fire going required an average of about one cubic metre of beech firewood a week throughout the year. On the basis of 100,000 households averaging five persons each at the beginning of the sixteenth century, this means that the annual consumption of fuel for heating and cooking was about 5,000,000 cubic metres, corresponding to about 2,250,000 Danish *favne* of beech firewood.[50] This figure can be compared with the estimate made by the economist Christian Olufsen, in a treatise of 1811 entitled *Danmarks Brændselsvæsen, physikalskt, cameralistiskt og oeconomiskt betragtet* (Fuel in Denmark, considered physically, administratively and economically), to the effect that at the beginning of the nineteenth century fuel consumption in Denmark, converted into beechwood equivalents, was about 1,720,000 *favne*.[51] If these figures are more or less correct, fuel consumption on a nationwide basis fell by 20 to 25 percent between 1500 and 1800, the three centuries during which the population doubled. Between 1500 and 1800 this will have meant

[49] A. F. Schmidt 1948, pp. 11–13.
[50] Letter from Axel Steensberg 2 Jan. 1989. See also Axel Steensberg 1974, p. 104. Number of inhabitants: Chapter 1.1. In Kärnten, Austria, 30,000 private households used more than 1 million cubic metres in 1768. R. P. Sieferle 1982, p. 90.
[51] Christian Olufsen 1811, p. 251.

98   *The Ecological Revolution*

a reduction for the individual person of more than 50 percent in energy consumption for heating and cooking.

b. Fences

Within living memory, plaited or stacked fences, mostly of alder branches and sometimes combined with low earth embankments, had been the commonest form of cattle fence in all parts of Denmark. In order to renew and maintain all these fences – which were not particularly durable – large quantities of fencing materials had to be cut every year. As a result of agricultural expansion and the depletion of the forests in the seventeenth and eighteenth centuries, the consumption of fencing materials represented an increasingly heavy strain on the forests. Erik Pontoppidan estimated in 1763, by which time the erection of alternative, permanent fences was already well advanced, that every year, in Zealand alone, at least a million cartloads of fencing materials were used, that is to say, an average of 60 to 70 loads per farm; it may therefore be assumed that consumption on a national scale would have been between 3 and 4 million loads a year.[52]

There were two ways of reducing this consumption: either abolish the fences or replace perishable brushwood fences with earthfast fences. The first alternative was used to a certain extent; it has been believed, for example, that the culmination of the so-called intercommoning system at the beginning of the eighteenth century should be apprised in this connection. Intercommoning was an ingenious system of coordinating the field cultivation of several villages, often across the boundary lines of several parishes, with the result that fields used for grazing adjoined one another. This in turn meant that fences between individual villages could be abolished.[53] Taken as a whole, however, the expansion of the intercommoning system and the resultant reinforcement of mutual cooperation between villages conflicted with the major trend of the eighteenth century, which was to separate and enclose the rights of the individual villages and plot owners.[54] So the other

---

[52] Erik Pontoppidan 1763–81, I, pp. 420–1. According to L. M. Wedel, one load of fencing material was enough for 15 *favne* of fence; he estimated that a fence might last two years (1792–6, I, p. 87). An annual average consumption of 60 to 70 loads of fencing material per farm, corresponding to 1.5 to 2 kilometres of newly erected fencing every year, would not appear to be unreasonable.

[53] Karl-Erik Frandsen 18 Feb. 1988; Frits Hastrup 1970–3.

[54] Ordinance of 29 Dec. 1758, "Angaaende Land-Vaesenets Forbedring ved at faae det derudi værende Fælledskab, for det første, saavidt Sædland, samt Møen og Amager er betreffende, ophævet med videre (Concerning the Improvement of Agriculture by having

Energy and Raw Materials Revolution   99

course had to be pursued: Perishable fences had to be replaced with permanent, earthfast fences. This presented interesting possibilities. If all the alderwood and other kinds of wood hitherto being used for fences could now be used for firewood instead, "it should be possible to spare the harder species of forest trees and considerably reduce the price of fuel."[55]

Various types of earthfast fences could be made. If there were many stones in a field, stone walls of various kinds were recommended, with or without ditches on either side. If such stone walls were established with an inner filling of earth it would be possible to plant willow or hawthorn along the top. In this way not only would a saving in wood be achieved, but new reserves of timber and firewood could be built up. If there were no stones on the surrounding fields, quickset hedges could be planted, possibly on an embankment, with or without ditches on either side. In moorlands and along the coasts, fences could by made of heather turf or of seaweed.[56]

One disadvantage of earthfast fences was the amount of space they took up, which meant sacrificing valuable arable land. The clearing of the stones from the fields represented a certain form of compensation. To the east of the main standstill line of the last Ice Age (which passed from the north to the south of central Jutland), millions upon millions of stones, when the ice had withdrawn, lay on the surface of the earth, both small stones and huge boulders weighing several tons and lodged several feet deep in the ground.[57] Some of these stones had been used in the course of millennia for erecting dolmens and making passage graves. Others had been used for building churches, and there is scattered evidence that stone walls had already been built as fences in the Middle Ages.[58] But at the beginning of the eighteenth century, most of these stones were still on the ground, impeding agricultural work on thousands of acres of arable land – and, as soon as the forests were felled, more stones came to light.

the present Commons, firstly as regards Zealand, likewise the islands of Møn and Amager, abolished, etc.) of 28 Dec. 1759 (concerning Funen, etc.), and of 8 Mar. 1760 (concerning Jutland). Cf. Hans Jensen 1936–45, I, pp. 37–8, and Chapter 6.2, section b.

[55] Erik Pontoppidan 1763–81, I, p. 421.

[56] A survey of various types of fences is given in F. W. Trojel 1784; cf. L. M. Wedel 1792–6, I, pp. 83–169, and A. F. Schmidt 1953. Illustrations of various types of fences are given in Thorkild Kjærgaard 1980, pp. 126–7. Fences of heath turf: Axel Steensberg 1969, p. 497; Ole Højrup 1961, p. 280. Seaweed fences: Holger Rasmussen 1974, pp. 393–5; Erik Pontoppidan 1763–81, VI, p. 564, and P. Rhode 1776–94, I, p. 17.

[57] Gregers Begtrup 1803–12, III, pp. 470–1; Christian H. Brasch 1859–63, III, p. 189; Hugo Matthiessen 1942, pp. 143–4.

[58] Ole Højrup 1961, pp. 279–80.

100   *The Ecological Revolution*

Permanent fences are mentioned as early as the last half of the sixteenth century as a way of saving timber. On 28 July 1562 the farmers in North Zealand were ordered to build stone walls and earth dykes in order to spare the forests belonging to the Crown.[59] It is not known to how great an extent this order was obeyed. Conclusive evidence exists that some walls were built at Glorup Manor on the island of Funen in the sixteenth century. Nevertheless, earthfast fences were still rather unusual, for we discover that the owner of the manor, Christoffer Valkendorf, counted the building of these stone walls among his most splendid achievements. In 1599 he had a plaque mounted on a wall in Svindinge Church, recording the following three highlights of his career:

> I have built both Glorup Manor and [this] Church.
> I have brought all the parish of Svinninge under Glorup Manor.
> I have built all the stone walls round Glorup Fang.[60]

Scattered examples of stone walls can be traced to the seventeenth century,[61] and continued legislative interest in the matter is proved by the fact that the injunction to build stone walls and other forms of earthfast fences issued to the farmers of North Zealand in 1562 was repeated in 1623 and now applied to the whole of Zealand.[62] The forest regulations of 13 September 1687, §17, stated:

> and since it has been found that the undergrowth has been much harmed by heavy felling for the many fences found everywhere, no fences shall be erected where the soil is clayey and suitable for dykes, but dykes shall be built, and this shall also be done in places with marshy ground on which willow, hawthorn, hazel, alder and the like may be planted.[63]

A special ordinance dated 17 August 1695 covering stone walls was issued and subsequently repeated with increasing strictness in the forest regulations of 21 January 1710, §17, 26 January 1737, §20, and 18 April 1781, §3; it was finally separated from these by the ordinance 29 October 1794, §3, 16.

---

[59]   A. F. Schmidt 1953, p. 110; Ole Højrup 1961, p. 281.
[60]   Quoted by Erik Pontoppidan 1763–81, II, p. 556. [Glorup Fang was the main farm of the manor]
[61]   Ole Karup Pedersen and Karen Marie Olsen 1958–74, I, p. 63; IV, p. 224; Viggo Petersen 1967, pp. 314–15.
[62]   A. F. Schmidt 1953, p. 110.
[63]   The forest laws referred to throughout the text are collected in L. S. Fallesen 1836, passim.

Energy and Raw Materials Revolution

The breakthrough for permanent fences came during the eighteenth century, when the ecological crisis called for widespread action. A start on building stone walls all over the island of Bornholm was made around 1730, and in 1777 it was reported that "now there are stone walls almost everywhere.... Here probably... some hundred thousand *favne* of stone fences have been built over the past 50 years."

The stones that previously "were strewn all over the fields" and impeded cultivation were far fewer in number than before "seeing that now efforts are made everywhere to make better use of them for walls."[64] In Zealand in 1741, on Crown lands alone, almost 200,000 *favne* of stone walls were built in addition to a number of other earthfast fences.[65] Thousands of *favne* of walls were built during the years prior to 1750, for example, at the manors of Egeskov and Hvidkilde; a report on Lykkesholm Manor written in 1769 stated that "so many stone walls have been built around the main farm that no more are to be expected, for all the usable stones in the fields have been cleared."[66] Stone walls made their appearance in Jutland wherever stones were available. In the county of Koldinghus alone, a survey revealed that 55 kilometres of new stone walls had been built in 1730.[67]

During the 1750s the fencing question became a matter for agronomical debate. In 1757 the *Oeconomisk Journal* published the first printed "Anviisning til Steen-Diiger at sætte" (Instructions for building stone dykes), and before long a whole range of specialist literature covering this subject became available. In 1803 Gregers Begtrup was able to declare that "no branch of our economic literature is better or more comprehensively covered than that which concerns fences and their various advantages and uses."[68]

Like marling and clover cultivation, the fencing question was one of the subjects on which the Agricultural Society focused after its foundation in 1768 by making awards, first for dissertations on fencing and second to farmers who had established earthfast fences "to spare the forests."[69] A monograph that won an award in 1784 was F. W. Trojel's *Fuldstændig Afhandling om alle Slags Indhegninger omkring Marker, Haver og Plantager, som kan anvendes i disse*

[64] Jacob Peter Prahl 1777, pp. 94–6; Erik Pontoppidan 1763–81, III, p. 168.
[65] Viggo Petersen 1967, p. 316.
[66] Erik Pontoppidan 1763–81, III, pp. 552, 565, 572.
[67] Ibid., IV, p. 332; Viggo Petersen 1967, p. 315.
[68] Gregers Begtrup, 1803–12, I, p. 322; Ole Karup Petersen 1958, nos. 3848–3872.
[69] Ole Degn 1969, p. 212.

102   *The Ecological Revolution*

Lande (Comprehensive treatise on all kinds of fencing around fields, gardens and plantations that can be used in these provinces). In no other area were so many prizes awarded between 1770 and 1800 as for the building of stone walls and the planting of hedgerows.

We find on page after page of *Adresseavisen's* annual reports covering the Agricultural Society's awards ceremonies almost identically worded citations of farmers who were rewarded for having put up fences: the farmers of Viby, "who are 21 villeins under Viby Manor, are awarded 50 rix-dollars for having been an example to many others here in Zealand by building, during the years 1779 and 1780, 1,637 *favne* of single stone walls, provided with proper embankments, and furthermore having dug some 1,000 *favne* of water ditches, etc." Hans Pedersen, a cottager in Asminderød, north of Copenhagen, was awarded 5 rix-dollars for having set up "102 *favne* of single stone walls made of quarried stones and in some cases stones split by fire." Lars Mortensen, a tenant farmer of the parish of Gudbjerg on the island of Funen, was awarded 4 rix-dollars "for [having] built, during a period of 6 years, 503 *favne* of stone walls; fenced and cleared, 10 years ago, 4 *tønder*, on which he now harvests 8 to 10 loads of hay. Furthermore, in 1782, he cleared six-eighths of a *tønde*, and used the stones he dug up for building stone walls." And so the reports continue, endlessly; almost one thousand awards were made.[70]

It was not only reasonable but necessary to coordinate the erection of permanent fences with the other changes taking place during the eighteenth century. These changes, primarily drainage work and the consequent transition to the multiple-field system, involved a tremendous increase in the length of field demarcation lines and therefore also of fences. The shortage of fencing materials meant that a switchover to the multiple-field system could seldom even be contemplated unless brushwood fences were abolished. The individual enclosures (to establish compact holdings) that gained favour in the course of the 1780s and 1790s resulted in an additional increase in the length of field borderlines. If a farmer wished to have a fence round his holding (and he was virtually obliged to have one, particularly after the special fencing ordinance of 29 October 1794, which made strict demands on each individual farmer to keep his cattle fenced in), the only answer was

[70] *Kiøbenhavns Kongelig allene priviligerede Adresse-Contoirs Efterretninger* 1782, no. 66; 1784, no. 107; Ole Degn 1969, p. 215.

Energy and Raw Materials Revolution   103

permanent fences. The lack of fencing materials meant that brush-wood fences, as Begtrup expressed it, "were out of the question."[71]

It is therefore idle to suggest, as has been done, that it was the pleasure of the new state of farm ownership, of "setting up house for oneself and one's descendants,"[72] that gave farmers the courage and strength to undertake the enormous amount of work they performed around 1800 in order to establish permanent fences. They acted quite simply under compulsion. It is hardly surprising that newly established freeholders proceeded, with the same diligence as displayed by the foregoing three or four generations of tenant farmers, to perform a task that they would have been obliged to undertake in any case.[73]

About a hundred years ago the historian Povl Hansen felt it was time somebody wrote the history of agricultural fencing.[74] As yet, no one has taken up the challenge, and in the meantime only approximate figures can be given for the lengths of permanent fences that were set up in Denmark during the eighteenth century.

A considerable amount of information is available about the extent of permanent fencing established prior to 1790 in the area on either side of Roskilde Fjord (Roskilde Inlet), north of the line Copenhagen – Roskilde – Kalundborg. Already before 1741, more than 130,000 *favne* of earthfast fences were erected on the Crown lands in this area.[75] F. W. Trojel, who was inspector of the Crown lands in Odsherred, stated in his previously mentioned dissertation of 1784 that he himself had caused 50,000 *favne* of earthfast fences to be built.[76] From the other side of Roskilde Fjord information is available to the effect that before the end of 1789 some 158,000 *favne* of fences had been erected on the Crown lands, and among them a considerable number of stone walls.[77] Furthermore, on two estates alone, those of Torbenfeld[78] and Jægerspris, 20,000 and 22,359 *favne* of stone walls respectively were built in addition to other forms of earthfast fences.[79] It is thus evident that prior to 1790 at least 750 kilometres of earthfast fences had been established on this part of Zealand, which represented barely 10 percent of Denmark's total area.

If we apply this figure (which is a minimum) to the whole country, we come to the result that prior to 1790 more than 7,500

[71] Gregers Begtrup 1803–12, V, p. 384.   [72] Erland Porsmose 1987, p. 263.
[73] Viggo Petersen 1967, pp. 318–19; Erik Pontoppidan 1763–82, III, p. 84.
[74] Povl Hansen 1900, p. 163.   [75] Viggo Petersen 1967, p. 316.
[76] F. W. Trojel 1784, preface.   [77] W. A. Hansen 1790, p. 39.
[78] Ibid.   [79] C. F. Wegener 1855–6, II, pp. 164–6.

104 *The Ecological Revolution*

kilometres of permanent fencing must have been established.[80] Erection of permanent fences continued at the same rate throughout the 1790s and for some time into the nineteenth century under the compulsion not only of agricultural and ecological demands but also as a result of the individualization of farming activities brought about by enclosure and fencing legislation.

Not only the loose stones in the fields but also a considerable part of the country's ancient monuments were swallowed up by the stone walls of the eighteenth century. This occurred at such a rate that even an otherwise uncompromising advocate of the new agricultural methods and their demands as the South Zealand priest Lago M. Wedel had his misgivings. In 1792 he declared that it was "desirable that some of the old burial mounds and heathen places of sacrifice should be saved as monuments to the art, strength and customs of our forefathers."[81]

A substitute for permanent, earthfast fences appeared at the end of the nineeenth century, when barbed wire – and later electrified smooth-wire fencing – provided a flexible and less bulky alternative to the fencing of former periods, which has since declined. Nearly all the stone walls have ended as filling for building roads and railways. The willow hedges and other quickset hedges have been ploughed away.

As already mentioned, the amount of labour used in establishing permanent fencing was considerable. Between 1798 and 1804, on a piece of land of 97 *tønder* (i.e., less than 1.5 square kilometres) belonging to the main farm of Skjoldemose Manor on the island of Funen, 10,000 loads of stones were collected, that is to say, about 100 loads per *tønde*. The stones were enough to build just under 3 kilometres of stone walls.[82] Simple multiplication reveals that if more than 3,000 loads of stones were required for one kilometre of wall, millions of loads of stones must have been collected and used in the eighteenth century and the first decades of the nineteenth century to build stone walls. A particular problem was presented by the big boulders, weighing several tons, of which only a small part protruded, like an iceberg, above the surface. Some of

---

[80] The figures given here are probably too low rather than too high. By way of comparison it may be noted that in Schleswig-Holstein, during the major fence-building period, 1650–1800, it is estimated that some 40,000 kilometres of fences were erected. Bernhard Buderath and Henry Makowski 1986, p. 76. Further information about fencing in the various districts of the country: H. Hertel 1919–20, I, pp. 106–10.

[81] L. M. Wedel 1792–6, I, pp. 90–1. See also L. Boesen 1769, p. 41; Ruth Tanderup and Klaus Ebbesen 1979, pp. 29, 49, 73–4; Kristian Kristiansen 1979–80. As from 1793, Denmark's road-building authorities also took a keen interest in acquiring stones from ancient stone constructions. Palle Eriksen 1987, p. 20.

[82] Gregers Begtrup 1803–12, III, p. 470.

Energy and Raw Materials Revolution
105

the boulders had to be left, but most of them were attacked time and again with spades and chisels, with fire and gunpowder, first to make them brittle and then to blast them.[83]

Building a stone wall was no task for weaklings, and many workers overstrained themselves. One of them was Hans Hansen, formerly a forester in the parish of Åkirkeby on the island of Bornholm, who in 1779 was awarded the Agricultural Society's Small Silver Medal for

> [building] 706 *favne* of single stone walls, for which he has cleared the stones from the land he had previously had officially assigned to him, and by dint of this arduous work he has impaired his health to such an extent that he has had to retire and consequently cannot reap the fruits of his labour.[84]

No wonder the tenant farmers of the 1750s occasionally kicked against the traces before setting about this overwhelming task. This was the case, for example, with the farmers on the Funen estate of a Danish courtier named Holst, who at first had to be ordered to build stone walls round their fields. But this situation was not to continue for very long. As soon as the farmers "had become accustomed to it, and saw its advantages, they proceeded with enthusiasm until they had completed their walls."[85] There was a great deal to be done in the eighteenth century, so of course it was all to the good that Denmark's farmers developed a taste for hard work.

c. Shipbuilding and Road Surfacing

Efforts to economize on the use of energy and raw materials can also be observed in other areas. Even the Danish navy, a major consumer of timber, had to bow to the demands of necessity. The earlier squandering of timber that had contributed to the ecological crisis of the eighteenth century was less pronounced towards the end of the century.[86] From about 1800 detailed instructions were given as to how timber consumption could be reduced in shipbuilding, not merely by utilizing the natural shapes of branches better than previously, but also by training a tree during its growth with the aim of obtaining timbers of the desired shapes (fig. 13).

---

[83] A detailed description of the heavy and dangerous work involved in the digging up, splitting, and carting away of boulders is given in L. M. Wedel 1792–6, I, pp. 88–100. Blasting of boulders with the help of gunpowder would appear to have started in the 1780s. Christian H. Brasch 1859–63, III, p. 191.

[84] Agricultural Society prizewinners in 1779, Danish National Business History Archives.

[85] D. H. 1758, p. 410.   [86] Cf. Chapter 1.2.

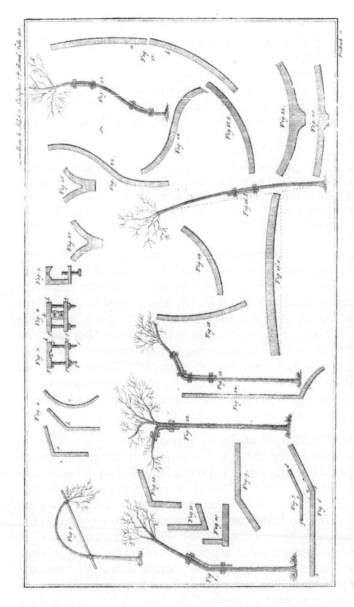

Figure 13. Instructions for training tree growth according to the needs of the shipbuilding industry.

Energy and Raw Materials Revolution 107

Rising timber prices also resulted in urban decisions to go ahead with the major task of surfacing roads using stone instead of planks as had been used hitherto. Great progress was made in this area in the eighteenth century, especially in Copenhagen, and it proved to be beneficial, not only to the forests but also, presumably, to public hygiene.[87]

4.3 INCREASED PRODUCTION OF ENERGY AND RAW MATERIALS

In addition to economizing, it was also possible to augment domestic production of energy and raw materials, primarily by making forestry more efficient. There were also the possibilities presented by peat deposits and wind power.

a. Expansion of Forestry Production

At the beginning of the eighteenth century, the yield per unit of area in Danish forests was low. There were various reasons for this, including the widespread and still increasing practice of allowing cattle to graze in them, which kept the forests open and impeded the growth of new, sprouting plants. As the Danish playwright Ludvig Holberg expressed it in 1746: "Within half an hour a bullock or cow can gobble up what otherwise might have become a few thousand cartloads."[88] Or, in the words of the forestry expert Esaias Fleischer: "To him who would await the growth of forest in such places [one should put the question] how can one expect the population to grow in a country where nearly all children are smothered in their cradles?"[89]

Forestry people were agreed that the first prerequisite for increased production of wood was that the growth of new trees should not be impeded by cattle. Permitting natural growth was justifiably regarded as more important than replanting. Denmark was, and still is, a latent forest country, with billions of seeds in the soil; if the land were left in peace, forests would shoot up on their own. Furthermore, it was recommended that forestry operations should be made systematic, including the dividing up of a given area of forest into a number of plots corresponding to the average growth period of the trees. In the case of oaks, for example, a type

---

[87] Carl Bruun 1887–90, III, pp. 114–15, 306–7, 419–20, 753–4; cf. "Forordning angaaende de Kgl. Skove og Tørvemoser udi Danmark" (Ordinance concerning the royal forests and peat bogs in Denmark) of 18 April 1781, §2.

[88] Ludvig Holberg 1913–63, XV, p. 244.   [89] Esaias Fleischer 1779, p. 398.

108   *The Ecological Revolution*

of tree whose growth period was calculated at one hundred and fifty years, the forest should be divided into 150 plots, of which one would be ready for felling every year and another for replanting. Felling trees at random without any overall felling plan (and therefore without consideration for future production and rejuvenation of the forest) should be abandoned.

The main features of this rotation system, which was first discussed in Denmark during the 1660s, met with general approval.[90] On the other hand, the details, including the question of how often thinning out should be done to reach the point where the trees' competition for light and nutrients would result in optimal wood production, was the subject of extensive experimentation and the cause of silvicultural controversies that continued into the nineteenth century.[91]

The difference in yield between an ordinary open forest in which cattle were allowed to graze and a forest run on silvicultural principles was estimated to be 1:4. In the event of clear felling of an ordinary, open forest one could expect a yield of 50 *favne* per *tønde*. Clear felling of a well-run, first-rate forest would yield four times as much, in other words, about 200 *favne*.[92]

The major ordinances by means of which the government tried to control forestry in 1670, 1680, 1687, 1710, and 1737 were all individually admirable attempts to convert the new silvicultural principles covering maintenance and improvement of forests into practical policies.[93] However, despite these ordinances, and despite the financial encouragement of those who planted new forests and severe punishment of forest thieves,[94] it proved impossible to sustain the forests, which continued to decline decade by decade. Contrary to what is commonly believed, this decline was hardly due to "ignorance, incompetence and fraudulence."[95] The Department of Forestry and Game as well as many private forest owners made excellent and doubtless unappreciated endeavours to ensure the survival of the forests.[96] That these endeavours should have failed

---

[90] A. Oppermann 1929, pp. 7–8. An account of the principles of regular rotation forestry: Esaias Fleischer 1779, pp. 447–94.

[91] One of the major works in Danish silviculture, Prime Minister C. D. Reventlow's *Forslag til en forbedret Skovdrift, grundet paa en Undersøgelse over Træernes Vegetation i Danmarks og Slesvigs Skove*, written around 1820, deals with this question. English translation *A Treatise on Forestry*, Hørsholm 1960.

[92] Christian Olufsen 1811, pp. 130–2. Cf. Gregers Begtrup 1803–12, III, p. 25.

[93] A. Oppermann 1929, pp. 1–20; P. Christian Nielsen 1979–82, pp. 27–32.

[94] Hugo Matthiessen 1942, p. 37.   [95] A. Oppermann 1929, p. 12.

[95] Viggo Petersen 1967 and 1969; Bo Fritzbøger 1989b, pp. 13–21; P. Christian Nielsen 1979–82, pp. 31–2; cf. Christian H. Brasch 1859–63, II, p. 73; Erik Pontoppidan

Energy and Raw Materials Revolution 109

to produce the desired results is another matter and due not so much to ignorance, incompetence, and fraudulence as to the fact that the task was insoluble in the face of the enormous and complex economical and ecological pressures exerted on the forests by population growth and huge state consumption.[97]

Financial encouragement in the form of tax relief for those who set aside land for planting new forest was given for the first time in an "Ordinance Covering the Planting of Young Forest" dated 13 October 1693 and repeated almost unaltered in the forest ordinances of the eighteenth century. Furthermore, in accordance with the ordinance of 21 January 1710, §2, a remuneration of 8 *skilling* per tree was paid to all men over the age of fifteen who planted oak trees and helped them to grow. The reward was paid in a lump sum if and when the man got married.

In 1762 Christian Gram, head of the Department of Forestry and Game, drew the government's attention to the "stream of gold" that was flowing out of the country to buy firewood, especially to meet the demands of the capital. It should be possible, Gram believed, to produce this firewood in the country's own forests – provided they were properly run.[98]

This was to be the beginning of the Gram-Langen forestry system of 1763, so named after its two originators, Christian Gram and the prominent German-born forester J. G. von Langen. In this way, the royal forests in North Zealand entered a period of strictly regular operation. They were divided into portions entailing one hundred annual fellings, and fences were built round the young plantations. These fences were only temporary, and they were removed as soon as the trees were big enough to permit forest grazing when the cattle could do no harm. However, this laborious principle,[99] basically admirable as it may have been, still meant that the Gram-Langen system became inordinately expensive, which was the main reason why it had to be rescinded in its original form as early as 1776.

But the rescindment was nominal rather than actual, for the principles were continued in the ordinance of 18 April 1781 covering

1763–81, IV, pp. 26, 304 (with special mention of three private forest owners in Jutland: Iver Rosenkrantz of Rosenholm, died 1745; Jakob Severin of Dronninglund, died 1753; and Councillor Peder Fogh, owner of Ryomgaard, 1713–50).

[97] Holberg, who found the main cause of the depletion of the forests to be the excessive number of grazing animals, i.e., ecological destabilization, was closer to the truth than A. Oppermann (1913–63, XV, p. 244).

[98] E. Laumann Jørgensen and P. Christian Nielsen 1964, p. 27.

[99] A. Oppermann 1923, pp. 55–73.

110   *The Ecological Revolution*

"Denmark's Royal Forests and Peat-Bogs." The most important change in relation to the Gram-Langen system was that agricultural grazing rights in forests were now decided by separating a part of the forest corresponding to the estimated value of the grazing. This rendered superfluous the difficult temporary fencing off of young trees in the remainder of the forest, which was now largely left in peace.[100] The Gram-Langen system continued in this modified form, which, despite a shaky start, proved a success in the long run. Progress was made during the years after 1760, not only by state-owned forests but also by a number of privately owned forests. For the first time since the sixteenth century, Danish forests showed signs of recovering.[101]

It was not possible to protect the forests everywhere. The tax burden on agriculture, which previously had been a seriously destabilizing factor, decreased from the 1730s onwards.[102] On the other hand, rising fuel prices and the selling of land to freeholders (which had commenced with the privatization of Crown lands during the 1760s) led to a wave of buying up of land by speculators with a view to realizing the locked-up capital that lay in the value of its forests.[103] In the same way that the navy had prospered at the expense of ecological balance, so too did the developing owner-occupier system prosper in agriculture.

Hereditary holding was also frequently financed at the expense of ecological balance. Thus the most highly praised hereditary tenure reform of the times, carried out by the agricultural reform hero J. L. Reventlow in 1788 at Brahetrolleborg Manor on the island of Funen, was financed in this way. After 1788 Brahetrolleborg ran into serious financial diffi-

[100]   E. Laumann Jørgensen and P. Christian Nielsen 1964, pp. 111–12 and passim; A. Oppermann 1923, pp. 54–60.
[101]   Erik Pontoppidan 1761–83, III, pp. 114, 166, 563, 609; IV, pp. 264, 440; V, 1, pp. 398, 440; VI, pp. 19, 62, 96, 817. See also Gregers Begtrup 1801, p. 211; P. Christian Nielsen 1979–82, pp. 40–2; Hans Berner-Schilden-Holsten and Albert Fabritius 1940–70, I, 2, pp. 193, 216; Holger Munk 1962, p. 146 (forest at Jægerspris Palace, in North Zealand, laid out by Esaias Fleischer); Fridlev Skrubbeltrang 1973, pp. 60 (Rosenfelt Manor's tenant farm forests, Zealand), pp. 66, 86.
[102]   Claus Rafner 1986, p. 93. Cf. Chapter 1.2.
[103]   Esaias Fleischer 1779, p. 410; Erik Pontoppidan 1763–81, VI, pp. 615, 633; C. W. von Munthe af Morgenstierne 1783, pp. 37–9; Gregers Begtrup 1803–12, III, p. 302; V, p. 179; A. F. Bergsøe 1837, II, pp. 135–6; Christian Vaupell 1862, pp. 426–32; A. Oppermann 1887–9, pp. 89–90; H. Hertel 1919–20, I, p. 115; Jens Holmgaard 1970, p. 129; P. Christian Nielsen 1979–82, pp. 38–9; Lotte Dombernowsky 1988, pp. 359, 382. Cf. Ove Høegh-Guldberg's observation to P. Christian Schumacher on 18 Sept. 1798: "Here, manors are continually being bought with a view to parcelling out and profit; forests close enough to the sea are clear felled and wiped out." J. O. Bro Jørgensen 1972, p. 530.

Energy and Raw Materials Revolution

culties that were partly due to the hereditary tenure reform. The storm was weathered by massive felling in the estate's age-old forests.[104] J. L. Reventlow's brother, C. D. Reventlow, who had introduced similar reforms on his lands on the island of Lolland, also ran into financial difficulties and also was obliged to resort to felling trees to deal with the situation. In a letter of 29 November 1800, C. D. Reventlow's wife wrote:

> Alas, what we are suffering from is not just a temporary embarrassment but a balloon of debt that has become larger with every year – if only it would melt like snow! These years serve rather to increase than diminish it. However, my husband is felling vigorously in his forests; perhaps this can save us, if God be willing! Whatever is felled is bought by the Admiralty as timber for shipbuilding.... For the time being, despite owning a countship, we are in truth poor.[105]

The difficulties of the Reventlow brothers were basically bound up with the fact that hereditary tenure implied fixed payments from farmers, preventing the landowners from continuously adapting their income from tenant holdings to meet varying financial situations and production conditions. During the last half of the eighteenth century, which was marked by increasing production and rising prices, this was particularly unfortunate.[106] Landowners who had introduced hereditary tenure very easily found themselves forced to choose between bankruptcy and tree felling that was not only ecologically but also, sometimes, economically questionable.

Irrespective of how serious these new setbacks might appear, the general picture was positive. In any event, the problems were largely solved by the Forest Reserve Act of 1805, a result of which was that fundamental silvicultural principles of preservation and replanting, already applied in Crown forests, became compulsory throughout the country.

Along the same lines as for the Crown forests, agricultural rights to private forests were to be terminated permanently by the separation of areas representing the current value of cattle grazing. The duty to preserve a forest could no longer be abolished in the remaining area, which was to be fenced in; the forest was to be a reserve. A stipulation that a forest could not be felled until it had been the property of a new owner for at least ten years restrained the

---

[104] Elers Koch 1892, pp. 116–22. In 1810 Brahetrolleborg's forests were evaluated as being among the poorest of the island of Funen. Ibid., p. 122.

[105] Christian B. Reventlow 1902–3, I, p. 213.

[106] Hans Berner-Schilden-Holsten and Albert Fabritius 1940–70, I, 2 p. 194 (A. C. Holsten to Christian Martfelt on 11 and 22 Aug. 1781). Cf. Thorkild Kjærgaard 1980, pp. 45, 215.

112   *The Ecological Revolution*

speculative clear fellings that had provided part of the financial basis for the selling of land to freeholders ever since the 1760s.[107]

Broadly speaking, the law enacted in 1805 was implemented, with the result that high forest grew during the following years on the 4 percent of Denmark's soil that had survived the forest reductions of previous centuries. Timber production, which had probably (despite the continued reduction of the overall forest area) been stabilized as early as the 1780s, as a result of the positive development in Crown and private forests, has risen without interruption since 1805. Why the forest laws of the last half of the eighteenth century and the Forest Reserve Act of 1805 could be implemented – unlike earlier forest legislation – will be examined at the end of this chapter.

b. Peat

The gradual disappearance of the forests caused the water level to rise, resulting in stagnation and sometimes even in floods. This was bad for the entire country, both in itself and as a symptom of profound ecological crisis. Nevertheless, as the saying goes, 'tis an ill wind that blows nobody any good, and this also applied to stagnation, which furthered the process of peat formation and in this way augmented disposable peat resources.

Bog peat is formed in either low water or soaking-wet earth. It is an accumulation of dead plants that have been more or less preserved by lack of air, in other words, their carbon content has been only partially oxidized, which is what gives peat its value.[108]

Together with heath peat, which had been forming on the surface of the gradually spreading heather moors – also a result of ecological degradation – since the sixteenth century,[109] bog peat represented a large reserve of fuel. A cautious estimate indicates that the total area covered by bog and heather moors in the eighteenth century was close to a million hectares, in other words, between one-fifth and one-fourth of the country's total extent.[110] Throughout this large area, peat could be found almost everywhere, though of widely varying quality. Only a fraction of the peat was of a consistency that complied with the definition of a

[107] Niels K. Hermansen 1955; A. Oppermann 1887–9, pp. 90–8.
[108] A. F. Schmidt 1948, p. 9.
[109] Cf. Chapter 2. On the use of heath turf for making fertilizer and fencing, Chapter 3.5 and Chapter 4.2, section b.
[110] Viggo Hansen 1979–82, pp. 12–15; A. F. Schmidt 1948, pp. 8–9.

Energy and Raw Materials Revolution

peat deposit as "a natural deposit, whose thickness is at least one-third of a metre and whose ash content as a rule does not exceed 30 per cent of the dry material."[111]

Peat from a good peat bog is excellent fuel. One reason peat was not used until there was no longer free access to wood was that it was difficult to dig. However, the energy and raw materials situation developed during the seventeenth and eighteenth centuries in such a way that it became obvious that attention should be focused on peat, not only where the peat was of good quality but even where it failed to meet minimum definitions. Heather peat, for example, seldom did. As a rule it was a thin layer that often contained a lot of sand and therefore burnt slowly and poorly, with an ash content far higher than 30 percent.[112]

The earliest use of peat on a large scale was in West Jutland, where the fuel shortage was first felt. This took place in the sixteenth century.[113] From here the use of peat spread eastwards, and in the seventeenth century it became common to dig peat on the main Danish island.[114] Of importance to peat production were the major drainage operations initiated in the course of the eighteenth century. The primary aim of these was to lower the water level, but they had the additional advantage of exposing the peat and making it accessible. In some places, peat became a major economic factor. The reclamation of Lille Vildmose in North Jutland[115] marked the commencement, at the beginning of the nineteenth century, of a peat industry that provided work for five hundred men during the summer season.[116]

The demand for peat was enormous. At brickworks alone, millions upon millions of pieces of peat were used. At the Gudumlund lime pits and brickworks, which mainly used peat from Lille Vildmose, 14 million pieces of peat were used in 1798.[117] According to a 1771 source, farmers on the island of Zealand were "forever carting loads of peat."[118] The authorities encouraged the use of peat, for it was seen as a way of saving wood. This is why in eighteenth-century forestry legislation provisions covering peat bogs were

---

[111] A. Mentz 1912, p. 5.   [112] Ole Højrup 1979–82, pp. 84–7.

[113] T. T. Hove 1983, pp. 13–14. On sporadic use of peat during the Iron Age and the Middle Ages: ibid. p. 10. Cf. A. F. Schmidt 1948, pp. 17–25.

[114] Ole Fenger, C. Rise Hansen et al. 1979 and 1985 (group 328): digging for peat already common in the district of Sokkelund, north of Copenhagen, in the 1620s but not as yet in the Næstved area. North Zealand: Henrick Gerner 1670, p. 46; cf. "Forordning om Tørveskjæring for Helsingøer" (Ordinance on the cutting of peat for Elsinore) of 26 May 1688. Bornholm: A. F. Schmidt 1948, pp. 26–7.

[115] Chapter 3.3.   [116] Gregers Begtrup 1803–12, VI, p. 246.

[117] Steen Bo Frandsen 1984, pp. 9–10.   [118] Anon. 1771, pp. 22–3.

114   *The Ecological Revolution*

included; in the forestry ordinance of 1710, §37, it was decreed for the first time that wherever peat was available it was to be used as fuel instead of wood. But supplies of peat were not unlimited either, and attempts to increase peat consumption had to be counteracted time and again by restrictive regulations covering peat digging. Strict rules covering the regulation of peat digging are also to be found in local legislation applicable to market towns and villages.[119]

The importance of peat as a source of fuel increased with the gradual disappearance of the forests and the rise of firewood prices. The long-term development in the changeover from wood to peat can be traced in the assignments of firewood received from Crown forests by the market town of Skanderborg in Jutland. In 1648 the town was assigned 200 cartloads of firewood from the surrounding forests. Around 1770, these 200 cartloads had shrunk to 25 cartloads, which were now supplemented by 50 cartloads of peat.[120] During the 120-year period from 1648 to 1770 it is possible to observe a double movement in the fuel supplies to Skanderborg that no doubt applied to the country as a whole. For one thing, the total consumption of energy was considerably reduced, and for another, peat was used more and more instead of wood; in 1770 it accounted for a significant part of the total energy consumption.

Digging peat was unpleasant work. First the peats had to be dug out of the peat beds, which were difficult to keep dry with the technical resources of the day. Afterwards they had to be stacked prior to undergoing a lengthy and difficult drying process that had to be kept under continual surveillance. Originally, peats were cut with a spade. Later, new methods were found. Kneading the turf mass by hand and casting the peat in moulds resulted in better utilization of the material but also meant that labour consumption soared.[121] Here we find once more a feature that was characteristic of all the measures taken to counteract both ecological degradation and the energy and raw materials crisis: They demanded an enormous amount of labour. In order to procure the same amount of heating energy as could formerly be obtained by spending a winter's day or two in the forest engaged in brisk, healthy work, it was now necessary to toil for days on the moors and in wet,

[119] A. F. Schmidt 1948, pp. 33–4.
[120] Erik Pontoppidan 1763–81, IV, pp. 189–90; letter from Jagt- og Skovbrugsmuseet, Hørsholm, 4 Sept. 1990.
[121] T. T. Hove 1983, pp. 17–19.

Energy and Raw Materials Revolution

unhealthy peat bogs, finally to be left with dirty peat that burned badly instead of good beechwood, at whose flames and steady heat many Danes were still warming themselves at the end of the seventeenth century. One of the few positive things the then English ambassador to Denmark, Sir Robert Molesworth, could find to say about Denmark and the Danes in his report *An Account of Denmark as it was in the Year 1692* was to remark on "the pureness of their firing, which is Beech-wood."[122]

c. Renewable Sources of Energy: Water-power and Wind-power

Water-power had traditionally played an important role in Denmark's energy supplies. A very large number of the country's corn mills were driven by water-power.[123] Water-power was favoured by the rise of the water level during the seventeenth century and at the beginning of the eighteenth century, but on the other hand, it was by no means plentiful. On the contrary, an investigation carried out by the Rentekammer in 1761 revealed that Denmark's water mill capacity was insufficient to meet requirements.[124] An important feature of the green revolution of the eighteenth century was a lowering of the water level. This created an extremely unpleasant conflict between two of the country's requirements that had the highest priority: the need for energy and the need for a stable, preferably rising, agricultural production. As Denmark has few watercourses with a powerful head, it had often been necessary to build dams in order to exploit the water-power. In order to lower the water level and prevent stagnation it was necessary to take steps in the opposite direction and remove as many as possible of the dams that impeded the water's free course.[125]

Even though the freer flow of water could sometimes be an advantage to the mills,[126] the only tenable way out of the dilemma was to increase the use of wind power and in so doing render some of the water mills superfluous. This is the reason for the the increasing number of already numerous windmills at the end of the eighteenth century.[127] Cases are known of permission being given to undertake major drainage work solely on condition that windmills be built to replace the loss of water-power.[128]

---

[122] Robert Molesworth 1694, pp. 8–9.   [123] Steen B. Böcher 1942.
[124] Holger Rasmussen 1970, p. 143.
[125] Steen B. Böcher 1942, pp. 132–4, 182.   [126] Ibid., pp. 210–11.
[127] Holger Rasmussen 1970, p. 143; Johannes Olsen 1937, pp. 15–23; Gregers Begtrup 1801, p. 286; Torben Ejlersen 1990, pp. 41–2.
[128] Steen B. Böcher 1942 , pp. 192–3. Cf. Chapter 3.3

116   *The Ecological Revolution*

4.4 USE OF WOOD SUBSTITUTES

Since the seventeenth century, Denmark's imports of the two most important substitutes for wood – iron and coal – had been increasing. A modest start was made with imports for special purposes, for example, coal for the Lighthouse Authority.[129] But before the eighteenth century was over, iron and coal had become indispensable features of the Danish economy.

a. Iron

The first area in which iron assumed a prominent and indispensable role was in the heating of dwelling houses, where iron stoves became a major factor in the transition towards the more economic forms of heating that won favour during the seventeenth and eighteenth centuries.[130] At the end of the seventeenth century the use of iron spread from the heating of houses to the agricultural sector. Torquato Recchia had observed during his visit to Denmark in the late 1620s that farmers had carts without iron on their wheels.[131] A few years later it was different. In 1698 Jørgen Sorterup, the poet-priest of Stevns, wrote that

> He who hath not bands of iron
> Must needs use wheels of wood.[132]

In 1717, about every fifth farm belonging to Vemmetofte Manor in Zealand had a cart with iron fittings. In 1742, twenty-five years later, carts with iron fittings were to be found on seven out of ten farms at this manor. A new stocktaking, dating from 1754, shows that during the intervening twelve-years iron had made even further advances. Nearly all farms, nine out of ten, now had a cart with iron fittings.[133] Around 1800 "carts with iron fittings were now the most commonly seen" in the eastern part of the country.[134]

During the 1750s, carts with iron fittings were to be found on the tenant farms belonging to Løvenholm Manor in Jutland,[135] and during the last three decades of the eighteenth century such carts became common throughout this part of the country. Gregers

---

[129] Chapter 1.2.   [130] Chapter 4.2, section a.
[131] Johannes Lindbæk 1909–13, p. 364; cf. p. 361.   [132] Jørgen Sorterup 1698, p. 109.
[133] Carl-Johan Bryld and Harry Haue 1982, p. 81.
[134] Gregers Begtrup 1803–12, IV, p. 668; cf. III, p. 478; S. P. Jensen 1986, p. 49; Jens Østergaard 1956, p. 35.
[135] Gregers Begtrup 1803–12, VI, p. 37.

Energy and Raw Materials Revolution 117

Begtrup reported from West Jutland, shortly after the turn of the century, that

> carts are now much bigger, probably half as big again as they were 30 years ago [1770–80]. Most farms have three carts, one of which will have iron fittings. These are particularly strong, because wood is expensive and hard to come by. Such fittings usually amount to 10 *lispund* of iron per cart.[136]

Correspondingly, in the country of Hjørring in North Jutland, "every farmer now has at least one cart with iron fittings, which was not the case thirty years ago."[137] The same applied to the counties of Ålborg, Randers, and Århus, where "carts with iron fittings are to found on every farm, whereas 30 years ago they were rarely seen."[138]

The use of iron spread even more rapidly to harrows, whose weak and ineffective wooden teeth were exchanged as soon as possible for iron ones. By 1717, four out of five farms on Vemmetofte Manor had an "iron harrow," by which was meant a harrow with a wooden frame and iron teeth. In 1742, all the farms on the estate had iron harrows.[139] By all accounts, virtually every farm in Denmark was equipped with an iron harrow by the end of the eighteenth century.[140] In hand tools, iron became increasingly common towards the year 1800:

> A shovel is now tipped with iron, because a wooden blade soon gets blunt. A blade with an iron tip is also thinner and thus easier to push under whatever has to be lifted. Finally, it saves wood . . . forks of all sizes are found, some with wooden prongs, some with thin, flat iron prongs.[141]

By the turn of the century, iron bought for making tools and fittings in smithies was, understandably, a fixed item in the accounts of many of the country's estates.[142]

Since the Middle Ages, iron had been used in ploughs for the coulter – the part that makes the vertical cut of the furrow – and

---

[136] Ibid., VII, pp. 58–9.   [137] Ibid., VI, p. 445.

[138] Ibid., V, p. 467; VI, p. 196.

[139] Carl-Johan Bryld and Harry Haue 1982, p. 81.

[140] Gregers Begtrup 1803–12, V, p. 467 (East Jutland); Bo Johansen 1987, I, p. 122 (on the increased use of iron harrows on the island of Falster, 1755–1809); S. P. Jensen 1986, p. 49; archives of Ringsted Convent, Godsbeskrivelser og synsforretninger 1769–1817, Provincial Archives of Zealand.

[141] Gregers Begtrup 1803–12, VII, p. 58.

[142] See, for example, archives of Gjorslev Manor, Kasseekstrakter over indtægter og udgifter 1803–8/1819–24; december 1803, post 13; november 1804, Provincial Archives of Zealand.

118   *The Ecological Revolution*

for the actual ploughshare. The rest of the plough was made of wood, sometimes reinforced at particularly exposed points.[143] There was no question of the mouldboard – the part that receives the soil cut loose and turns it over – and other large parts of the plough being made of iron. In the 1680s the use of iron components in ploughs would appear to have been slightly more general.[144] At all events, iron became popular in the ploughs of the eighteenth century.[145] In 1774 Martin Hübner, vice-president of the Agricultural Society, asserted in his farewell speech to its members that no less than twenty-five thousand ploughs, corresponding to between a third and a half of all the ploughs in the country, had been changed "to save time and better cultivate the soil"; in other words, they had been given iron fittings and equipped with iron mouldboards, [146] which turned the wheel plough into an excellent tool.

Once the wheel plough had been riveted and reinforced with iron at its most exposed points, it was broadly speaking, as good as the plough made entirely of iron. In conjunction with its relatively low cost, this explains why the modified wheel plough remained in use in Denmark until the end of the nineteenth century.[147] The main problem about the classical wheel plough was not, as often was claimed, that it was 'clumsy,' but was that few of the cutting and movable parts were made of iron. This made the frictional resistance extremely high while at the same time reducing the quality of the ploughing and making the plough fragile despite its large dead weight.

At the end of the eighteenth century there would appear to have been iron ploughs on at least two-thirds of all Danish farms:

> Nearly everywhere there are now iron ploughs, which ease the work, being judged better than those of wood, as formerly used. . . . On account of the iron ploughs that can now be used it is less common to plough with four horses; many have only two to a plough, others three, walking beside each other.[148]

[143]   Axel Steensberg 1968; Grith Lerche 1985, p. 96.
[144]   Henrik Vensild 1985, pp. 121–2.
[145]   Bjarne Stoklund 1985, p. 106; Henrik Vensild 1985, pp. 121–2; J. N. Wilse 1767, p. 212.
[146]   Martin Hübner 1774, p. 63.
[147]   Jens Østergaard 1956, p. 38; Henrik Vensild 1985, p. 128 and passim.
[148]   Gregers Begtrup 1803–12, V, p. 466; Martin Hübner 1774, p. 63. A striking example of the inverse ratio between the amount of iron in the ploughs and the size of the team of horses is provided by developments on the island of Læsø in the eighteenth century. Bjarne Stoklund 1985, p. 106.

Energy and Raw Materials Revolution 119

The teams of two or three horses known from the agriculture of later periods were appearing. A detail of great importance to this development was the horseshoe. In about 1730 the shoeing of carthorses was still a rarity.[149] Seventy years later it had become common.[150]

Shoeing meant that horses could pull better. At the same time, thanks to iron, larger, more effective, and more durable implements were made whose cutting and moving components offered less frictional resistance. This coincided with a general improvement of conditions in agriculture, thanks to the lowering of the water level. The significance of these mutually reinforcing improvements can hardly be overestimated.

The remarkable circumstance – seen from the viewpoint of a later age – that the number of horses kept on a average farm at the beginning of the eighteenth century was just as large, if not larger, than its herd of cattle and occasionally even larger than its flock of sheep,[151] was not due, as generally assumed, to an excessive degree of villeinage, but, first and foremost, to the small amount of iron used in agricultural implements and the poor tractive power of unshod horses. The fact that the number of horses did not, contrary to what might be expected, increase throughout the eighteenth century, despite agricultural expansion and increasing villeinage, but rather would appear to have slightly decreased,[152] was above all due to the advance of iron in agriculture.

Gradually, as production rose thanks to ecological stabilization and cultivated clover, room was found during the last half of the eighteenth century for more domestic animals, none of which needed to be horses. The increase therefore affected cattle and other domestic animals, especially sheep. The relative number of horses compared with the numbers of other domestic animals shifted towards the situation familiar in the nineteenth and twentieth centuries, when cattle and sheep far outnumbered horses. Around 1800 there were 30 to 50 percent more cows than horses

---

[149] Holger Munk 1951, pp. 38–9.
[150] P. Grunth 1928, pp. 57–94. Cf. archives of Gjorslev Manor, Kasseekstrakter over indtagter og udgifter 1803–8/1819–24: juni 1805, post 8, Provincial Archives of Zealand.
[151] Fridlev Skrubbeltrang 1978, pp. 244–5.
[152] Fridlev Skrubbeltrang 1978, p. 407; Bo Johansen 1987, I, p. 89 (a slightly decreasing tendency over the period 1775–1805 is revealed in the number of horses kept on farms on the island of Falster). A report from Vierne in the parish of Hårslev on the island of Funen dated Jan. 1786 reads: "Superfluous beasts disposed of and instead more cattle kept to the advantage of the farmer." Hans Berner-Schilden-Holsten and A. Fabritius 1940–70, I, 2, p. 193. Increasing villeinage in the last half of the eighteenth century: Thorkild Kjærgaard 1980, pp. 25–42.

120   The Ecological Revolution

and almost twice as many sheep as horses.[153] Because of iron the production increase made possible by the green revolution could be diverted into corn production for both human consumption and the feeding of milch cows and animals for slaughter. Had it not been possible to increase the draught power of horses and the size and efficiency of farm implements, the cultivation expansion of the eighteenth century would have necessitated the keeping of far more horses, which, in turn, would have detracted considerably from the level of the production increase.[154]

It was not only in the agrarian sector that iron began to take precedence over wood, for it applied just as much to the urban sector.[155] Despite the abolition in 1794 of the Norwegian iron monopoly in Denmark, iron was in short supply in Copenhagen during these years.[156]

b. Coal

Coal was used as a substitute for wood by the Lighthouse Authority from the seventeenth century. In the 1730s, coal must have been a recognized form of fuel in Copenhagen – otherwise, it would be difficult to understand why, in 1739–40, selling cheap coal from the royal stocks could be a form of social relief.[157] During the ensuing years, mention of English coal becomes increasingly frequent in Copenhagen records. In the 1740s the city's big merchant houses began to take an interest in coal.[158] Of the sixty-six ships that arrived in Copenhagen from Great Britain in the course of one year during the 1760s, nearly all carried cargoes of coal.[159] By the 1780s, coal had become commonplace in the Danish capital; together with lime, stone, and sand, such large quantities of coal were dropped from ships during loading and unloading that these materials threatened to fill up the entrance to the harbour as well as the various small canals.[160]

[153] Fridlev Skrubbeltrang 1978, p. 407.
[154] Carl-Johan Gadd has made a detailed study of the county of Skaraborg in the Swedish province of Västergötland that includes an examination of the advance of iron in the agricultural sector. Parallels can be drawn in many ways between Gadd's results and those given here (1983, especially, pp. 145–95. For a European perspective on the importance of the introduction of iron in agriculture: Jean Meuvret 1955, pp. 159–61.
[155] Astrid Paludan-Müller 1923, pp. 14–52; J. O. Bro Jørgensen 1943, pp. 171–99; Jens Vibæk 1964, p. 456; Axel Nielsen 1944, p. 408.
[156] Aage Rasch 1964, p. 117, and 1955, p. 262.
[157] Edvard Holm 1891–1912, II, p. 558.
[158] Collection of unpublished documents for a history of prices, University of Copenhagen, Department of History. Cf. Edvard Holm 1891–1912, II, p. 540.
[159] Edvard Holm 1891–1912, III, 2, p. 291. Cf. Aage Rasch 1964, p. 116.
[160] "Placat angaaende adskillige Foranstaltninger til at forekomme Canalernes og Havnens Formuddring i og omkring København" (Proclamation covering various means of pre-

Energy and Raw Materials Revolution

Coal played an important role as fuel for the industry of the capital from the 1760s at the latest.[161] During the 1770s, for example, the energy-intensive and rapidly expanding sugar refineries used coal.[162] Evidence of the importance of coal as fuel in private households at the end of the eighteenth century is provided by a proclamation, dated 21 November 1787, issued by the Town Hall of Copenhagen, concerning trading in coal in small portions, "The Purchase and Sale of Coal in Copenhagen in smaller Quantities than whole *tønder*." This poster proclaimed that

> for the general convenience of tradesmen and the public . . . we have . . . so arranged that the Department of Weights & Measures here in the capital shall make, and hereinafter sell to all concerned, verified weights of 25, 50 and 100 pounds, also half and quarter *tønder*, for the measurement of coal, which, in order to distinguish them from the ordinary corn measures, are stamped with the royal cipher and the letters: St[een].K[ul]. [pit coal].

A gold medal that the Agricultural Society awarded Captain Philip Lange for a model of a baking oven employing coal as fuel is further proof of the interest in developing the use of coal in households.[163]

In the provinces, the use of coal had been known since the 1730s. Støvringgård Manor, near Randers, started to use coal in 1734, and in the next few years many of the other big estates followed suit, including, for example, Lindenborg Manor near Ålborg, Frijsenborg Manor near Århus, and Holsteinborg Manor near Skælskør on the island of Zealand. At the last-named manor a start was made with the purchase of 5 *skæpper* of coal in 1755, after which consumption increased decade by decade. In 1797, 10 *tønder* of Newcastle coal was bought for Holsteinborg;[164] in 1803, 36 *tønder* of coal arrived at Gjorslev Manor.[165] Little is known, however, about the use of coal by tenant farmers and other people in rural districts. Coal is said to have been sold in the 1760s to farmers around Nykøbing on the island of Mors in Limfjorden.[166] Coal

---

venting the muddifying of the canals and the harbour in and around Copenhagen) of 2 May 1788, §2.

[161] Edvard Holm 1891–1912, III, 2, p. 291.

[162] P. P. Sveistrup and Richard Willerslev 1945, p. 81; Aage Rasch 1955, p. 150.

[163] Agricultural Society prizewinners in 1792, Danish National Business History Archives. See also Else Mølgaard and Old Schou Vesterbæk 1987, pp. 76–7.

[164] Collection of unpublished documents for a history of prices, University of Copenhagen, Department of History.

[165] Archives of Gjorslev Manor, Kasseekstrakter over indtægter og udgifter 1803–8/ 1819–24; december 1803, post 13, Provincial Archives of Zealand.

[166] Erik Pontoppidan 1763–81, V, 1, p. 552.

122   *The Ecological Revolution*

had been heard of in Djursland at this time, but it was not used.[167] Still, only thirty or forty years were to pass before many village blacksmiths were dependent upon coal.[168]

Coal was used in the provinces in industrial production before 1750. At a brickworks in Thy, where no local fuel was to be had, the kilns were fired with "coal and wood, brought hither from outside."[169] From 1765 there was "a fine sugar factory" at Roskilde that used coal, and this fuel was also used at the Classen Foundry in Frederiksværk; in the year 1798 about a dozen loads of coal were cleared through customs in the little North Zealand port of Rørvig, destined for Frederiksværk.[170] In 1785 steps were taken to introduce coal firing at the Kastrup Faïence Manufactory on the island of Amager, near Copenhagen.[171] Elsewhere, plans were made: For example, in the mid-1760s there was talk of reviving saltworks on the island of Læsø with the help of coal from England.[172] Nothing came of this, but the major fact remains that not only iron but also coal acquired an important position in the housekeeping of the Danish community in the course of the eighteenth century.

c. The Importance of Imported Energy

From the middle of the eighteenth century until some way into the nineteenth, Denmark's energy situation was the subject of extensive public debate.[173] Among the many contributions to this discussion was the excellent book, mentioned earlier, *Danmarks Brændselsvæsen, physikalskt, cameralistiskt og oeconomiskt betragtet,* published by Christian Olufsen in 1811.

Olufsen calculated the annual Danish consumption of fuel at 1,720,000 *favne* of firewood (wood and other fuel, converted to wood equivalents). According to Olufsen, because the import of coal amounted to only 9,000 *læster*, corresponding to about 50,000 *favne* of beechwood, Denmark supplied almost all its own energy. If one made do with an average annual consumption of four-fifths of a *favn* of beech firewood per individual "or its effectual equivalent in other forms of fuel" (which, in the case of sensible and economical use of fuel, would be sufficient to meet all the country's

---

[167] N. Lund 1809, p. 5.
[168] Gregers Begtrup, 1803–12, VII, p. 104. Cf. Sven Henningsen 1944, p. 159.
[169] Erik Pontoppidan 1763–81, V, 1, p. 411.
[170] Ibid., VI, p. 155; Astrid Paludan-Müller 1923, p. 243; cf. Laurits Engelstoft 1961, pp. 89–92; Anders Monrad Møller 1981, p. 151.
[171] Jørgen Ahlefeldt-Laurvig and Anne-Mari Steimle 1977, p. 54.
[172] Gregers Begtrup 1803–12, VI, p. 576.
[173] Cf. A. Oppermann and V. Grundtvig 1931–5, pp. 466–7.

Energy and Raw Materials Revolution   123

needs, private as well as industrial), no further problems in connection with energy supplies would arise within the foreseeable future.[174] The lack of fuel was only apparent, and the widespread concern for Denmark's future energy supplies was, in Olufsen's opinion, exaggerated.

By the standards of the 1990s, four-fifths of a *favn* per individual, corresponding to an annual consumption of less than one million *favne* of beechwood for the whole country, was a scanty fuel ration. Per individual it would represent an annual gross energy consumption of 3.85 gigacalories (Gcal). In comparison, the average annual consumption per individual in 1989 was 38.2 Gcal, in other words, nearly ten times as much.[175] For Danish society as a whole, the amount of energy stated by Olufsen to be sufficient corresponds to about one-fiftieth (2 percent) of present-day consumption, because the population of Denmark today is five times greater than it was in Olufsen's time.

A significant deficiency in Olufsen's analysis of Denmark's energy situation was that he disregarded the hidden imports of energy bound up with imported raw materials, the most important of which were iron, salt, glass,[176] and timber. Iron, for example, was indispensable. It played a vital role in carrying through Denmark's program for economizing on energy, but it also occupied a key position in the primary production sector. In particular, agriculture's favourable structural development during the eighteenth century was dependent upon large and continually increasing supplies of iron. In addition to noting the direct import of energy products, first and foremost coal, a complete evaluation of Denmark's energy situation at the time should also take into account the energy content in imported raw materials (less the energy content in exports).[177]

---

[174] Christian Olufsen 1811, p. 118, 124.

[175] Letters from Laboratory for Energy Technology, Technical University of Denmark, 9 Feb. 1989, and from Michael Bræstrup, 27 July 1990.

[176] The manufacture of glass required large amounts of energy. The manufacture of 1 kilogramme of glass required 2,400 kilogrammes of firewood. R. H. Sieferle 1982, p. 84. Domestic glass production using wood as fuel was forbidden in 1707 (Harald Roesdahl 1977, p. 15); the eighteenth century's sharply increasing consumption of glass was therefore based entirely on imported energy. Evaporation of salt: 1 cubic metre of firewood produced between 15 and 100 kilogrammes of salt. R. H. Sieferle 1982, p. 85.

[177] From this point onwards only iron and coal will be considered. A number of smaller, but far from inconsiderable, items such as salt, glass, timber, and bricks, as well as secondary raw materials like copper, silver, lead, and so on, will be omitted. It is estimated that the total energy content of these items more than compensates for the energy content in Danish exports, which consisted mainly of agricultural products and therefore had a low energy content per unit.

124   *The Ecological Revolution*

If hidden imports of energy are taken into account it immediately becomes clear that Denmark's energy problems were indeed genuine. Denmark's iron production came to a standstill at the very beginning of the seventeenth century, although there was no shortage of iron ore. Bog iron ore reserves in Jutland, which were exploited later (for example, during the Second World War) amounted to several million tonnes and therefore would have been quite sufficient to meet Denmark's iron requirements during the seventeenth and eighteenth centuries.[178] The reason why domestic iron production was abandoned was that Denmark lacked the energy resources necessary to smelt bog iron ore.[179] Shortly after iron production had to be given up, it also became necessary to discontinue even the resmelting of old iron in Zealand for want of charcoal.[180]

In the eighteenth century it was a plain fact that iron extraction could not be carried out in Denmark. In Pontoppidan's *Danske Atlas*, after a description of bog iron ore deposits in the Ribe district, a routine note is added to the effect that "it would not be worth while building a factory because of the lack of furnace fuel."[181] Iron had to be obtained from elsewhere, mainly from Norway, which throughout most of the eighteenth century had a monopoly of the Danish market.

Vain attempts were made to find domestic coal to relieve this unpleasant energy deficit, which caused the government concern, partly on account of the uncertainty of supplies and partly because of its effects on the balance of payments. Lignite deposits on the island of Bornholm had been known since the beginning of the seventeenth century, and an attempt to exploit them had been made even at that time, but without success. During the second half of the eighteenth century, however, interest in exploiting these deposits flared up again.

In 1769 the Agricultural Society, which took an interest in social economy as a whole and displayed understanding for the connection between agriculture and energy, sent Christian Martfelt, who had previously travelled through the English coal districts, and the mining expert Henrik Blichfeldt to Bornholm to examine the coal deposits. Their account, *Beretning om Steenkul* (Report on pit coal), was published in 1770 by the Agricultural Society. Their report was optimistic, and Martfelt felt so con-

---

[178]   Johannes Humlun 1943, pp. 173–4; Niels Nielsen 1928, pp. 266–76.
[179]   Erik Pontoppidan 1763–81, IV, p. 24; Johannes Humlun 1943, p. 173.
[180]   Aksel E. Christensen 1943, p. 148.
[181]   Erik Pontoppidan 1763–81, V, 2, p. 664. See also Gregers Begtrup 1803–12, VI, p. x: "Jutland contains much bog iron ore, which was used in olden times, when firewood was more plentiful."

Energy and Raw Materials Revolution 125

fident about a breakthrough for the Danish coal industry that he translated de Tilly's *Mémoire sur l'utilité, la nature et l'exploitation du charbon minerale* of 1758 into Danish and published it in Copenhagen in 1770; it is one of the few books on mining available in Danish.

Extraction of the deep-seated, partially submarine deposits of Bornholm coal however, involved such considerable technical difficulties that attempts to start up production also failed on this occasion.[182] It was not only on the island of Bornholm that a search for coal was made. During the years 1808–11, trial borings were made for example, in Jutland, on the Limfjorden islands of Fur and Mors, and near Århus, and on the island of Funen.[183]

Figure 14, a survey of Denmark's energy situation in the eighteenth century, shows the amount of imported iron and coal converted to forest equivalents, that is, the amount of good beechwood necessary to supply continuously, year after year, the equivalent of the amount of energy represented by imported iron and coal. These figures have been continued up to the present day in order to place them in a clearer perspective.

It is apparent that although much was done within the framework of the combined energy-saving and energy-developing programmes drawn up in the sixteenth, seventeenth, and eighteenth centuries, this represented only a partial solution to Denmark's energy problems. Already before 1750, supplies of energy and raw materials and thus also, indirectly, the green revolution, were dependent on the ability of the coal and iron industry to counteract the ever-increasing shortage of energy and timber resulting from the gradual removal of the forests. Otherwise, the Danes (and also the entire European community which also experienced forest decline) would have come to a halt in an entropic nightmare: People might have wandered about, shivering with cold and searching for dried cowpats to provide a little heat and, with which to cook, and there might not have been enough wood to make as much as a spade handle. Ecological chaos would have reigned, marked by hitherto unknown degrees of sand drift, increasingly violent hydrological disturbances, and unmercifully decreasing agricultural production. Precisely these conditions can be observed now, at the close of the twentieth century, in several parts of Africa, in South America, and on the Indian subcontinent.

Denmark was faced with this catastrophic situation in the eighteenth century. But after long teetering on a knife's edge, the Dan-

[182] M. K. Zahrtmann 1934–5, I, p. 228; II, pp. 127–32.
[183] Petrine Sand 1945; Gregers Begtrup 1803–12, VI, pp. vii, xii–xvi; VII, p. 272.

	Coal (tønder)	Wood equivalent (favne beechwood)[a]	Iron (tonnes)	Wood equivalent (favne beechwood)[b]	Total wood equivalent for coal and iron (favne beechwood)	Forest equivalent (ha. good beech forest)[c]
1722–4 (average)	10,832[d]	3,385	—	—	23,769	6,548
1731	—	—	1,325[e]	20,384		
1752–4 (average)	31,674[d]	9,898	—	—	—	—
1760	—	—	1,950[f]	30,000	43,114	11,877
1762–4 (average)	41,964[d]	13,114	—	—		
1772–4 (average)	58,582[d]	18,307	—	—	—	—
1782–4	91,001[d]	28,438	—	—	—	—
1792–4	105,801[d]	33,063	2,340[g]	36,000	69,063	19,026
1811	162,000	50,625[h]	—	—	—	—
1832–4 (average)	—	—	5,062[i]	77,854	—	
1842–4 (average)	398,971[j]	124,678	10,104[j]	155,446	280,124	77,179
ca. 1870	4,500,000[f]	1,406,250	45,000[f]	692,308	2,098,558	578,115
1986	—	—[k]	669,000[l]	10,291,963		22,150,000 (about 5 times the area of Denmark)[m]

Figure 14. Coal and iron imported into Denmark during the period 1722–1986, converted into forest equivalents.

Notes to Figure 14:

[a]1 *favn* beechwood = 3.2 Danish *tønder* Newcastle coal. E. Møller-Holst 1877–83, I, p. 316. Corresponding figures in R. P. Sieferle 1982, p. 136.

[b]During the eighteenth century, between 18 and 23 weight units of wood went into the production of 1 weight unit of iron, J. H. L. Vogt 1908, p. 48, and (for conversion ratio between wood and charcoal) E. Møller-Holst 1877–83, VI. p. 73. A ratio of 1:20 has been used here as an average. Corresponding figures in Wilhelm Abel 1972, p. 68.

[c]Annual production per ha. of good beech forest around 1800: 3.63 *favne*. Christian Olufsen 1811, pp. 130–2 (a fully grown, first-class beech forest when clear felled yields 200 *favne* per *tønde*; as a beech tree takes about 100 years to grow, the average annual growth is 2 *favne* per *tønde* equal to 3.63 *favne* per ha.). The figures used here for forest growth are slightly higher than the 5m^3 per ha. given in R. P. Sieferle 1982, pp. 76–7.

[d]Birgit Nüchel Thomsen et al. 1965, p. 65, from English customs administration accounts. That during the eighteenth century Denmark also imported a small amount of coal from Germany has not been taken into consideration (V. Falbe-Hansen and William Scharling 1885–91, III, p. 375). Conversion from nominal values in sterling in English customs administration accounts to *tønder* of coal on the basis of J. U. Nef 1932, II, p. 370, and Elizabeth B. Schumpeter 1960, Table XLVII (£5 = 1 Newcastle chaldron = 53 cwt. = 2,692 kg), also E. Møller-Holst 1877–93, I, p. 316 (300 Danish *pund* Newcastle coal = 1 *tønde* coal). Until 1814 English customs administration accounts regarded Denmark and Norway as a single unit for customs administration purposes. However, as it is unlikely that much coal was exported to Norway, which still had plenty of wood, Denmark-Norway's imports of coal during the eighteenth century may be equated, without risk of significant error, with Denmark's imports of coal.

[e]Albert Olsen 1936, p. 35.

[f]Falbe-Hansen and William Scharling 1885–91, III, pp. 375–6.

[g]Denmark's consumption of iron had corresponded during the foregoing decades to about a quarter of Norway's total production of iron, cf. J. H. L. Vogt 1908, p. 27, and sources of documentation given in nn. e and f. The figure given here corresponds to a quarter of Norway's average production of iron in the 1790s (J. H. L. Vogt, loc. cit.).

[h]Christian Olufsen 1811, p. 124.

[i]Axel Nielsen 1944, p. 361.

[j]A. F. Bergsøe 1844–53, II, p. 575 (coal) and 571 (iron). Cf. Anders Monrad Møller 1988, pp. 194–6.

[k]The forest equivalent of Denmark's total fuel consumption is 4 1/2 times the area of the country. Anders Evald 1989.

[l] *Statistisk Årbog* 1989.

[m]Cf. R. P. Sieferle 1982, p. 138.

128   The Ecological Revolution

ish energy balance was saved by ever-larger supplies of energy from Europe's subterranean forests of coal. These deposits provided energy either directly as coal or indirectly in the form of iron smelted with the help of coal. As a result, the nineteenth century was marked, not by an increasing shortage of energy, but, on the contrary, by a decreasing shortage of energy. Houses no longer grew colder, but warmer. Danish glass production, which had ceased in 1707 for want of fuel, was revived. The same applied to iron production. By constructing railways and steel steamships, gigantic energy-consuming transport and communication systems were established – built and operated with the help of coal. Among other things, during the 1830s and 1840s, they brought the tremendous, hitherto inaccessible, nitrogen reserves from the guano beds of South America within the reach of European agriculture.

Yet if the green revolution was dependent on the energy and raw materials revolution, the converse was also the case. Without ecological stabilization and the nitrogen revolution it would have been impossible to sustain, let alone increase, agricultural production to the extent demanded by the population growth rate. The green revolution and the energy and raw materials revolution (the latter corresponding broadly to the Industrial Revolution) were, therefore, two sides of the same complex. They developed not as two more or less independent albeit parallel processes, but in mutual interdependence.

Thanks to coal and iron, the energy and raw materials crisis was overcome, and the sword of Damocles hanging over Denmark and the whole of Europe was removed. The pessimists, who had preached that Denmark would freeze to death and that the country would have to be abandoned as uninhabitable, were put to shame,[184] as were those who, like Otto Diderik Lütken, had doubted that coal could be a subsitute for wood on a large scale.[185] In the 1820s, the gloomy prophecies abounding in books and periodicals vanished like the morning dew. Even the memories of the energy and raw materials crisis that had threatened society with slow strangulation disappeared. It is

---

[184] Frederik Høegh-Guldberg, quoted by P. W. Lütken 1808, p. 38. The Lolland priest Daniel Huusfeld was of the same opinion and called Luther to witness: "Our blessed and – in his time – perspicacious Lutherus has foreseen that a shortage of wood would lead to the end of the world, and no doubt cause great suffering to the human race, mostly towards the globe's North Pole" (1771, p. 30).

[185] "By the word *brændsel* [fuel] I [O. D. Lütken] understand solely wood or peat, for coal cannot be said to be common in this world, and from the discoveries made so far one cannot promise the Danish State any particular relief." O. D. Lütken 1762, p. 252.

Energy and Raw Materials Revolution 129

strange how few traces of the energy crisis of the eighteenth century exist in the abundant Danish literature about the period.

4.5 STABILIZATION OF THE FORESTS, 1763–1805

It is generally agreed that the Forest Reserve Act of 1805 was a milestone in the history of Danish forestry.[186] In contrast to the major forestry ordinances dating from the end of the seventeenth century and the beginning of the eighteenth, the Forest Reserve Act and its precursor, the Gram-Langen forestry system of 1763, were, broadly speaking, observed,[187] and they remained in force for more than a hundred years. The forest area, which by 1805 was the smallest in Denmark's history, gradually increased, and today about 10 percent of Denmark is again forest clad – about the same area as in the middle of the eighteenth century. Present-day forests, however, unlike those of the eighteenth century, are closed and dense. The amount of timber in today's forests is considerably greater than it was in forests about 1750. In terms of amounts of timber, present-day Danish forests should be compared with forests in the year 1650 rather than with those in 1750.

Quite another matter is why it proved possible, in contrast to the experience with earlier forest legislation, to implement the forest acts of the last half of the eighteenth century and the Forest Reserve Act of 1805. Analysis of the ecological revolution outlined above will help to provide an explanation. The success was a result of the complicated interaction between the main lines of development within the ecological revolution and not of the agrarian reforms, which here, as elsewhere, have been regarded as an immediate solution to all the problems of the eighteenth century.[188] The green revolution and the energy and raw materials revolution contributed jointly to the success of the Forest Reserve Act. Three major factors served to ease the formerly irresistible pressure on the forests and helped them to grow again:

1. *Ecological stabilization of agriculture and the nitrogen revolution.* The ecological stabilization of agriculture and the nitrogen revolution caused the pressure hitherto exercised on the forests by

---

[186] A. F. Bergsøe 1837, II, pp. 143–7; A. Oppermann 1887–9, pp. 96–108; Niels K. Hermansen 1955, p. 93 and passim; P. Christian Nielsen 1979–82, pp. 48–51.
[187] A. F. Bergsøe 1837, II, p. 144.
[188] A. Oppermann 1887–9, p. 127; Hans Jensen 1936–45, I, p. 230; Niels K. Hermansen 1955; P. Christian Nielsen 1979–82, p. 48–51; Claus Bjørn 1990, p. 17.

130   The Ecological Revolution

agriculture to diminish and finally cease altogether. Ecological stabilization meant that agriculture's need to compensate for declining yields on old arable land by taking over forest land came to an end. At the same time, after the appearance of clover, forest grazing, despite increased numbers of domestic animals, was no longer necessary.

2. *Programmes for saving and developing energy, 1500–1800.* The introduction of new building materials, iron stoves, earthfast fences, economical use of materials in shipbuilding, and so on, all represented savings in wood. At the same time, forestry was rationalized, which increased the yield of the forests (fig. 15). Furthermore, the plantations established on the former sand drift areas helped to augment supplies of wood.[189] Presumably it was also of some significance that the Danish population learned to accept feeling cold as part of life and so made do with less fuel, which in turn reduced pressure on the forests.

3. *Coal and iron.* In the long run, the most important factor contributing to the success of the Forest Reserve Act was the use of wood substitutes, coal and iron. Already by the middle of the eighteenth century, iron and coal were relieving the heaviest pressures on the forests, and during the ensuing decades the situation slowly improved. This provided the opportunity that made it possible to stick to the Gram-Langen forestry system and later – with decreasing difficulty – the Forest Reserve Act. In the course of the nineteenth century, the use of iron and coal spread so much that the country's forests were almost forgotten in many sectors of society. This applied, for example, to the navy and to the shipbuilding industry, which formerly had been amongst the forests' most demanding and impatient customers. After the transition from wood to iron as the dominating material for building ships during the decade 1845–55,[190] the shipyard sector lost virtually all interest in the forests. Under the shelter of this development the forests were permitted, not merely to exist, but even to grow.

The pressure on peat resources diminished in a similar fashion. In 1798, as already mentioned, 14 million pieces of peat had been used at the Gudumlund brickworks. Fifty years later this figure had dropped by almost a third to 10.5 million.[191] In the same way, the introduction of coal meant a falling demand

---

[189] Chapter 3.1; R. Mortensen 1917.
[190] I. C. Weber 1919, pp. 78–85. Cf. P. Christian Nielsen 1979–82, pp. 45–6.

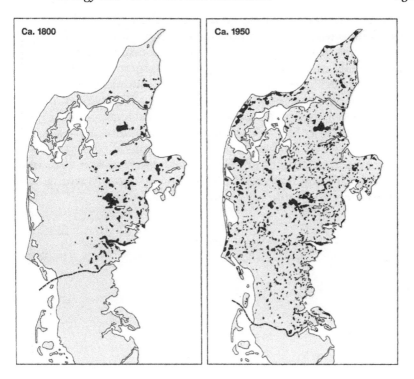

Figure 15. Areas covered by forest in Jutland, ca. 1800 and ca. 1950.

for waterpower as a source of energy, which in turn served to resolve the old conflict between waterpower and agriculture.[191] The abundant and increasingly larger supply of energy from sources outside the living biosphere now left the way clear for unilateral favouring of the demands of agriculture,[192] which in turn, along with the augmentation of technological possibilities, led to the implementation of huge drainage projects in the nineteenth and twentieth centuries. These were to bring about considerable changes in Denmark's physical outline.

Thanks to the green revolution and the energy and raw materials revolution, agricultural production, the forest area, and the consumption of energy and raw materials have all been able to

[191] Steen Bo Frandsen 1984, p. 10.
[192] Chapter 4.3, section c.
[193] Steen B. Böcher 1942, pp. 219–20; Johannes Olsen 1937, p. 4.

132   *The Ecological Revolution*

increase concurrently in Denmark since the eighteenth century. This would have been an impossible combination in the society of former times, when wood was the only important source of both raw materials and energy: The agricultural sector and the energy and raw materials sector were constantly hindering each other. Seen in this context, the success of the Forest Reserve Act of 1805 bears witness to one of the most striking characteristics of the modern world, namely, the restriction of the living biosphere's task to that of supplier of foodstuffs, while the supply of energy and raw materials is now left almost entirely to the forests that were here 300 or 400 million years ago and to iron ore deposits dating back to when the Earth came into being as a planet.

Part III

THE NEW DENMARK

5

LANDSCAPE

Through a series of spontaneous, self-intensifying, unforeseen, and unforeseeable nonlinear processes, the ecological revolution reshaped the nation's landscape, working conditions, social structure, disease pattern, and political life. In the course of this process, a new Denmark was created. Let us begin with what was immediately visible, the new landscape.

5.1 THE DENMARK FACING EAST

Where in the past there had been barren, cropped, greyish, scentless, silent outlying areas and poor pastures of self-sown couch grass, the countryside now became full of life, colours, scents, and sounds. Clover provided not only the soft, cool "clover-field for noonday peace" that Poul Martin Møller, the Lolland vicar's son, dreamed about when he lay beneath the burning tropical sun in the South China Sea, but also several new colours. From the end of the eighteenth century, fields of red, white, and green clover appeared between the cornfields, creating the yellow-and-green and red-and-white patterns that have characterized the Danish agrarian landscape ever since. Finally, the clover also brought new scents. As P. E. Lüders wrote as early as 1758

> it is incredible how much superfluous sweetness is generally to be found in these clover-flowers when the summer weather duly alternates between dew and warmth; when walking in the fields the sweetest smells often linger in one's nostrils.[1]

The new fences also introduced scents and colours: Stone walls had willow and hawthorn planted on them, and hedges of poplar, bullace, and elder were planted.

[1] P. E. Lüders 1758a, p. 302.

135

136 The New Denmark

Weed flora, which is closely linked to agricultural technology and cultivation patterns, also changed and thus helped to transform the landscape. Marling resulted in the retreat of one of Denmark's commonest
weeds, corn marigold, which grows best in lime-deficient, that is to say,
unmarled soil, but its place was soon taken by coltsfoot, which prefers cal-
careous soil. The opportunity to sow at an earlier date – made possible,
among other things, by water level regulation – meant that new species
of weed, such as navew, charlock, and wild radish, soon spread; they
sprout in April and had previously been destroyed by the final treatment
of the soil in the spring.[2]

The ecological revolution introduced not only new colours and
scents into the landscape, but also the life and sounds produced
by large herds of cattle. By about 1800 cattle were wading in clover
up to their bellies in the same fields as those in which, only a few
decades earlier, poorly nourished animals had succumbed to cattle disease. Innumerable small birds discovered new ecological
niches in the woodland fringes and hedges of the now parklike
landscape.[3] Birdsong rose over Denmark to the accompaniment
of eagerly buzzing bees, which previously had found little of interest in the meagre pastures and cropped commons but were now
fully occupied gathering clover pollen. Everything became as the
nineteenth-century poet Holger Drachmann described it:

> Look, the meadow is humming with sunshine
>   honey bees are filling their hives
> And the humblest siskins and sparrows
>   are living their own little lives:
> and there's rejoicing throughout the day,
> but at nightfall everything's quiet.[4]

Clover needs insects to secure reproduction: without bees (bumblebees
and honeybees) no clover. One of the many positive effects of clover
growing was the increase in beekeeping and thus of honey production.[5]
The importance of this, however, was reduced by the arrival of West
Indian cane sugar, which already by the end of the eighteenth century
had become the dominating sweetener in Danish households.[6] The rule
about no clover without bees was most convincingly demonstrated in

[2] Thorkild Kjærgaard 1991a.   [3] Helge Volsøe 1797–82, p. 427.
[4] Quoted by F. J. Billeskov Jansen 1985–7, IV, p. 16.
[5] H. Hertel 1919–20, I, pp. 159–60.
[6] Esaias Fleischer 1777, pp. 15–16. The average consumption of refined sugar and syrup
per inhabitant increased fifteenfold between 1745 and 1798 from 1/6 of a pound to 2
1/2 pounds per inhabitant. P. P. Sveistrup and Richard Willerslev 1945, p. 364.

Landscape 137

New Zealand in the Pacific Ocean during the nineteenth century. Here, attempts to grow clover were made repeatedly early in the century but in vain, because although the clover grew extraordinary well it was impossible to get it to produce seed capable of germinating. This continued until 1839, when bees, which did not form part of the original fauna of the islands, were introduced. Since then, clover crops of considerable importance have been grown in New Zealand, and there is a large production of honey.[7]

The new, parklike landscape, with its innumerable, richly varied little biotopes, was also a paradise for butterflies – which are nearly all linked to the open countryside – and for a large number of other insects. A great many small animals, such as hares, partridges, and pheasants, found protection in the hedges and forest fringes and plentiful food in the new pastures. Larger, dangerous wild animals, such as wolves and wild boars, had been forced out, as a result of which the Danish landscape became tamed and idyllized. However, this is not to say that nature's general wealth had in any way deteriorated. On the contrary, it is estimated that the total number of species of flora and fauna increased from the middle of the eighteenth century, culminating during the 1820s, 1830s and 1840s, by which time the new landscape was fully grown and in its prime. After a long period characterized by ecological disintegration, the countryside became green, bringing to a halt the negative ecological process that had started in the sixteenth century. Since the middle of the twentieth century, however, the total number of species has been decreasing with great rapidity and is now estimated to be reduced to the same level as at the beginning of the Christian Era.[8]

In combination with the abundance of animals, the new colours, sounds, and scents imbued the landscape with an increasing wealth and variety, balanced in other respects by a new atmosphere of order and stability. This was primarily due to the fences. Whereas the old landscape had been characterized by borders winding in various directions and by soft transitions between fields, outlying areas, and open forests, the new fences now extended through the landscape in regular, military lines, dividing not merely forest from field, but also field from field.

Tumuli, field stones, and wetlands disappeared beneath straight, clean-cut plough furrows, turned by new, strong ploughs rein-

---

[7] Alfred W. Crosby 1986, pp. 239–40; K. Gram and Knud Jessen 1957–9, III, pp. 785–6.
[8] Bernhard Buderath and Henry Makowski 1986, p. 84.

138   *The New Denmark*

forced with iron, and gave way to dense fields of corn and clover. No irregularities were permitted, not even in human dwellings. The village of closely built houses that had characterized eastern Denmark since the beginning of the early Middle Ages fell into discredit. Furthermore, larger crops and herds of cattle demanded larger buildings, for which there was no room in the closely huddled villages. A certain amount of thinning out became necessary, and a newly built farm in the middle of recently enclosed lands became the ideal of the period. In the same way that fields were now strictly fields, forests were now strictly forests, and cattle were no longer allowed to graze in them – after all, cattle were now being fed on new forage crops. As the vegetation gradually became denser, the beech ousted the oak except in regions where naval considerations made it necessary to maintain large stands of oak for a few more decades.

The typical tree in the open forests of the seventeenth and eighteenth centuries was the oak. Unlike the beech, the oak can tolerate having its top shoot bitten off – as inevitably happens to many young trees growing in forests where domestic animals graze. When the forests were turned into reserves and forest grazing ceased, the competitive relationship between the oak and the beech changed to the advantage of the beech. The oak is a tree that does not cast a dense shadow and therefore permits other trees, for example, beeches, to grow up beneath it. The beech, on the other hand, casts a dense shadow, which prevents other trees – young oaks, for example – from growing beneath it. The beech will therefore normally oust the oak, and if Denmark's forests were left in peace, beechwoods would gradually be formed over most of the country.[9]

People and poets alike took the beech to their hearts as Denmark's national tree, which can be confirmed by comparing references to the beech with those to the oak in seventeenth- and eighteenth-century literature. Ludvig Holberg (1684–1754) mentions the beech 4 times, but the oak 18 times.[10] The beech is mentioned in all 19 times in Danish poetry between 1690 and 1750, whereas the oak is mentioned no less than 63 times, nearly four times as frequently as the beech. During the last half of the eighteenth century, the beech catches up with the oak: In poems published between 1750 and 1800, the beech appears 78 times, whereas the oak is now mentioned only somewhat more than twice

[9] Christian Vaupell 1863, pp. 199–218.   [10] *Holberg-Ordbog* 1981–8.

Landscape 139

as often, namely, 184 times.[11] During the nineteenth century, the picture becomes the complete opposite of the one that prevailed in the seventeenth and early eighteenth centuries: The beech becomes unrivalled as the most frequently mentioned tree in Danish poetry and, like clover, becomes a symbol of Denmark and of the Danish landscape.[12]

Nobody could foresee that the reign of the beech in Denmark's forests was to be shorter than that of the oak. Within a period of barely two hundred years, the beech was overtaken by exotic trees like spruce and fir, which were introduced into Denmark at the end of the eighteenth century and planted experimentally in the forests of North Zealand, on sand drift areas at Tisvilde, and on the Jutland moors. Now, towards the close of the twentieth century, beech trees represent only 15 percent of the Danish forest stand.

The ecological revolution transformed the landscape into a garden in which soon not even the smallest patch of land was permitted to remain uncultivated. This development coincided with the breakthrough of the English landscape garden,[13] and there might be a connection between these two contemporary trends. The baroque demand for symmetry and order, which had hitherto proven realizable only on the microscale of the garden, now became the basic principle for the organization of the macrolandscape. One could say that the garden and the open landscape exchanged roles.

Previously it had been the task of the garden to uphold a dream of order, of keeping nature under control (fig. 16). Now that this control had been virtually achieved, the new purpose of the garden was to preserve the memory of free, uncontrolled nature in a countryside that had been harnessed (fig. 17), and which, as the hedgerows and drainage ditches drew their straight lines in all directions, was itself beginning to look like a well-trimmed baroque garden.[14] The building of roads intensified the picture of a well-regulated landscape. The proud manorial avenues of the 1740s[15] were reduced to miniature layouts compared with the achieve-

---

[11] C. Raunkiær, Samlinger vedrørende Planterne i dansk Poesi, XI, Royal Library, Copenhagen, Manuscript Collection, NKS 3446 4°.

[12] C. Raunkiær 1930, p. 58.

[13] Christian Elling 1942, p. 44. See also Christian Elling 1939, pp. 28–32, and Hakon Lund 1963, p. 30. On the first attempts at landscape gardening in the 1770s: Hanne Raabyemagle 1988, p. 119.

[14] Hugo Matthiessen 1942, pp. 175–6.

[15] Hakon Lund 1963, p. 22, and 1980, pp. 147–8.

Figure 16. Change in garden styles, 1740–1820. The garden as an image of cultivated nature: Ledreborg Park, Zealand, as it was laid out in the 1740s.

Figure 17. Change in garden styles, 1740–1820. The garden as an image of free, unregulated nature: Ledreborg Park, Zealand, in the 1820s.

142   *The New Denmark*

ments of the road engineers whose new highways would, by the end of the eighteenth century, form long, straight lines across the landscape. Perspectives and views were created on the stretch from Køge to Vordingborg that surpassed even the wildest dreams of the baroque landscape gardener Le Nôtre and his Danish pupils.[16]

Sometimes it is suggested that the transition from the baroque garden to the landscape garden was prompted by financial considerations. Upkeep of a baroque garden, with its clipped hedges in complicated shapes, was expensive, whereas the 'natural' landscape garden might have "almost emerged by itself."[17] Closer examination disproves this theory. Establishing a 'natural' hill in a park, trimming a 'natural' lawn with a pair of clippers, and maintaining a 'natural' little river with a few islands in the middle, complete with leafy arbours worthy of Robinson Crusoe, was obviously just as expensive and extravagant as maintaining a baroque garden.[18] Both the baroque garden and the English landscape garden required an enormous amount of labour, not only to create but also to maintain.

5.2 THE DENMARK FACING WEST

Only in West and Central Jutland did the new times fail to assert themselves fully. The advance of the desert was halted, and a considerable amount of marling was done, but afterwards development almost ceased. During the 1750s and 1760s, great expectations had accompanied the introduction of clover on the moors of Jutland. It was hoped that it would be possible, "by means of artificial meadows, to solve the main problem, to wit, that of finding finds ways of making hay on Alheden when all other difficulties had been overcome."[19] But these expectations were disappointed by harsh reality; early attempts to sow clover here failed completely.[20]

Sandswept heather moors, underlying layers of hard, impermeable pan, strongly acidified areas, and a harsh climate made the recovery of western Denmark in the wake of severe ecological deterioration a task of such magnitude that it could not be handled all at once. Despite intensive efforts to reestablish the soil's pH balance by marling, western Denmark was still further from

[16]   Cf. Christian Elling 1942, p. 24.
[17]   Margit Mogensen and Poul Erik Olsen 1984, p. 183.
[18]   Christian Elling 1942, pp. 24–43. Cf. Hanne Raabyemagle 1988, pp. 119–23.
[19]   D. Schiöth 1760, pp. 237–8. Cf. Hans de Hofman 1757, p. 9.
[20]   N. Hurtigkarl 1757, p. 57; Valdemar Andersen 1953, p. 48; Erik Pontoppidan 1762, p. [7].

Landscape 143

achieving this goal than anywhere else in the country.[21] Whenever hard pan occurred, the breaking up of the heath with the implements available in the eighteenth century was almost impossible. Instead of sowing clover it became necessary to pursue a less ambitious line of development in which an attempt was made to increase forage production with the help of hardy plants such as spurrey,[22] buckwheat, and knotgrass. During the nineteenth century these were gradually supplemented with some of the lower yielding but also less demanding nitrogen-assimilating crops, such as bird's-foot trefoil, tufted vetch, yellow melilot, and hop medic.[23]

Knotgrass, spurrey, and buckwheat can all be used both as forage and as edible crops. Knotgrass, which to this day is a common weed, has been utilized in Denmark since antiquity, and so has spurrey. Buckwheat, which like spurrey resembles knotgrass, came to Denmark in the Middle Ages and seems to have had a considerable distribution during the sixteenth and seventeenth centuries. The cultivation of knotgrass ceased at a very early stage in eastern Denmark, and in the course of the eighteenth century, the cultivation of both spurrey and buckwheat decreased, ousted by the nitrogen-fixing crops. On the other hand, knotgrass, buckwheat, and spurrey advanced in the western part of Jutland, where in some places cultivation continued into the twentieth century. Not even in this century has knotgrass lacked its advocates. Jens Nielsen, a spokesman for smallholders and himself a plant breeder, was enthusiastically supporting the use of knotgrass in the infertile districts of Jutland during the years around the First World War.[24]

Many years were still to pass before the great dream of the 1750s about "artificial meadows" on the cultivated Jutland heather moors could be realized: They came eventually, but not until late in the nineteenth century, when the improved situation in regard to energy and raw materials made it possible to lay out lines for marl trolleys[25] and use the powerful machinery that was necessary

[21] Fridlev Skrubbeltrang 1966, p. 305 and elsewhere.
[22] Gregers Begtrup 1803–12, VII, pp. 79, 130.
[23] Cf. P. Nielsen 1878, p. 435.
[24] V. J. Brøndegaard 1978–80, II, pp. 131–45, 146–9; Svend Gissel 1956 (index); Karl-Erik Frandsen 1977–8, pp. 25–32; Johan Lange 1959–61 (index), and 1966, pp. 205–6; Gregers Begtrup 1803–12, V, pp. 88, 120, 314; VII, pp. 79, 130; Johan Paludan 1822–4, II, p. 220; A. Ravnholt 1934, p. 14. Buckwheat was often introduced into crop rotation in the same way as clover. See, for example, archives of Vedø Manor, Forskellige sager 1691–1822; hoveriforening af 6. juni 1792 §1, Provincial Archives of Northern Jutland, and archives of Volstrup Manor, Forskelligt 1530, 1753–1872: forpagtningskontrakt 23. januar 1795, Provincial Archives of Northern Jutland. On Jens Nielsen and knotgrass: Fridlev Skrubbeltrang 1954, II, p. 92.
[25] Svend Jørgensen 1984, pp. 34–81.

144   *The New Denmark*

in order to attack the heath. The dune plantations that had been established in the meantime – and were now beginning to close up – also proved beneficial. They created a milder local climate in western Denmark, which meant that cultivated clover was no longer so exposed to the risk of being destroyed by frost as it had been in the past.[26] Not until about 1900 did clover take a firm hold in Central and West Jutland.[27]

As a result of this slower development, the western part of the country was left to its own devices at the end of the eighteenth century – at least for the time being. Whereas the landscape in the eastern part of Denmark became ever greener, and the birdsong filled the air, large parts of the region to the west and north of the line from Skagen via Viborg to Kolding remained primitive, immovable expanses, unaffected by time, with open, silent skies and with barren stretches of brown moors where ancient burial mounds, by now removed in most of eastern Denmark, were allowed for a while longer to remain undisturbed as they had lain for thousands of years. This was the Jutland that took its place in literature, in art, and in the public mind alongside the image of the fertile, smiling, eastern Danish landscape, with its clover fields, beech forests and warbling birdlife.[28]

[26] Fridlev Skrubbeltrang 1966. On improvement of the microclimate in particular: *Trap Danmark* 1953–72, 22, p. 22. Peter Riismøller 1972, p. 108. Complaints that clover was destroyed by frost in West Jutland: Danish edition of the present book, p. 331 (the parish of Torning).

[27] A. F. Schmidt 1949, pp. 165–73; H. P. Hansen 1959, p. 196; Aage J. Kjærgaard 1987. Cf. Karen Thuborg 1928, p. 124.

[28] Danish writers and artists who helped to create this picture of Jutland as being primitive and old-fashioned included Steen Steensen Blicher, Hans Christian Andersen, Martinus Rørbye, and Frederik Vermehren.

6

LABOUR BURDEN AND SOCIAL STRUCTURE

The clover-fields increase the work greedily.

M. H. Løvenskiold, 1796

Toil – persisting, unending and fundamentally at odds with human-kind's propensities as shaped by the hunting experience – was the lot of all farming populations.

William H. McNeill, 1977

6.1 LABOUR BURDEN AND WORKING HOURS, 1500–1800

In *The Conditions of Agricultural Growth* (1965), the Danish economist Ester Boserup formulated the general thesis that growth in agriculture is inextricably bound up with (1) an increasing use of labour and (2) a decreasing yield per working hour.[1] In other words, growth in agriculture is achieved only through increasingly labour-intensive forms of farming in the course of which the yield from every extra hour of labour gradually decreases.

The optimal ratio between labour and yield is achieved by the slash-and-burn method in which, after burning off a forest, two or three crops are cultivated in the weed-free, nutrient-rich ash, whereupon the area is abandoned for twenty or thirty years until the forest has grown and is ready to be burned off again. Working days of two or three hours and long periods during which there is nothing to do is the rule in societies that live on the slash-and-burn method. It is unlikely that this privileged form of farming has been used in Denmark since the Stone Age, and today it is practised only in a rapidly diminishing number of areas in the tropics.[2]

The slash-and-burn method can support only a small population. As the population gradually increases – which it invariably does, because Homo sapiens as the dominating species has a bio-

---

[1] Ester Boserup 1965.   [2] Axel Steensberg 1980.

145

146   *The New Denmark*

logical advantage that is converted sooner or later into imperialism in relation to other species[3] – societies are forced to employ increasingly labour-intensive methods of agriculture in order to survive. The period of fallow – which when using the slash-and-burn method is so long that a forest has time to grow and permit a spontaneous reestablishment of nitrogen reserves before the land is cultivated again – is reduced. Via a series of intermediary stages, a form of agriculture is achieved in which fallow periods virtually disappear, the land is ploughed and fertilized, comprehensive water level regulation systems are established and maintained, and nitrogen-fixing plants are cultivated in order to provide forage for animals and ensure the necessary reserves of plant nutrients in the soil.

The advantage of the more intensive forms of agriculture is that they increase overall production and make it possible to provide food for ever-increasing populations, which in turn are a prerequisite for providing the necessary labour. A disadvantage is that production does not increase at the same rate as the consumption of labour. If a water level regulation project combined with the introduction of nitrogen-fixing forage crops increases production by, say, 50 percent, the extra labour connected with the digging and maintaining of ditches, marling, ploughing, sowing, and harvesting of the larger crops will be even greater, perhaps 100 percent or more.

In other words, the price of growth in agricultural production is a lowering of living standards for society as a whole. The lowering of living standards is revealed in various ways, such as longer working hours, reduced nutrition, poorer housing standards, and a greater degree of ill-health. Theoretically, a lowering of living standards can be distributed evenly among all levels of society, but in practice it will always be unfairly distributed. According to Boserup, growth in agriculture is therefore inextricably linked to rising social inequality and more sharply defined confrontations in society.

Ester Boserup's theories can be used to advantage in an analysis of the development of Danish society between 1500 and 1800. A considerable intensification of agriculture took place, but not without an accelerating consumption of labour, partly for measures designed to increase production, such as water level regulation, marling, and – not least – cultivation of forage crops where previously one had made do with what Boserup called "the free gift of nature," and partly for preventive measures, for example, the

[3] Mark Cohen 1977, pp. 42–70.

Labour Burden and Social Structure 147

combating of sand drift. Finally, an increase in labour consumption took place within the energy and raw materials area. From the close of the seventeenth century onwards, the forests, which, like the pastures, had been previously regarded as "the free gift of nature," were gradually subjected to rational handling. Similarly, both rising peat production and the establishment of fences represented increases in the burden of labour. Furthermore, it should be borne in mind that the harvesting of larger crops and the milking and feeding of an increasing number of cattle, particularly when summer stall feeding was practised, also augmented the amount of labour required.

Although it may be easy to establish that the use of labour rose in Denmark as a result of the intensification of agriculture during the period 1500–1800, the extent to which it did increase is not as simple to determine. The length of working days and their number are seldom noted in agricultural records, and in contrast to what present-day social researchers have done in India and elsewhere,[4] historians are unable to create their own source material by making comparative studies of working hours in places where agricultural methods are undergoing change.

There is some evidence, however, of the development of daily working hours and the number of annual working days between 1500 and 1800. In terms of the villeins who were given food at Ringsted Convent during the 1570s, records would appear to show that a number of the working days discharged at the monastery were actually only 'half' days.[5] This means that a working day for a villein lasted only until noon, that is, for five to seven hours, eight at most during the summer months, when it was possible to work from four o'clock in the morning until noon. A working day of this length during the 1570s and 1580s tallies with slightly older records; for example, there are English records in which a 'working day' also took up half the day, or until noon.[6]

If this interpretation of the Ringsted material is correct, it may be concluded at the same time that during this period, at the end of the sixteenth century, the short working day was gradually being abandoned and perhaps in reality survived only in special situations such as villeinage. As early as in 1570s day labourers on the convent's main farm received, unlike the villeins, three meals

---

[4] Ester Boserup 1965, pp. 30, 39–40.
[5] Fridlev Skrubbeltrang 1969–70, pp. 230, 232.
[6] B. H. Slicher van Bath 1960b, pp. 203–4, 400 (n. 150).

148   *The New Denmark*

a day and undoubtedly worked from morn till night.[7] Before long this probably also became the lot of the villeins. An extension of the working day by 50 percent or more seems to be the explanation of the otherwise inexplicable and highly paradoxical fact that the number of villeinage days discharged at Ringsted Convent during the half century between 1570 and 1620 – a period during which villeinage, according to all other available sources, increased considerably – fell by almost 20 percent, from just under eleven thousand days to nine thousand days per year. If this was the case, rather than a decrease in villeinage it would indicate an increase, masked by a slight drop in the number of working days.[8]

Hardly anything is known about the length of a working day during the seventeenth century. However, there are reasons for assuming that it became appreciably longer. Fencing work became more extensive,[9] and finds of datable potsherds around market towns make it possible to determine that a labour-intensive measure such as the carting of night soil from market towns to the surrounding villages started around 1650.[10] We do have precise information about the length of working days during the second half of the eighteenth century. According to the villeinage ordinance of 20 February 1771, villeins were obliged, in the absence of other arrangements, to present themselves for work during the months of

> November, December, January and February at 8 o'clock in the morning; they are granted in all one hour's break in the middle of the day and may leave at 4 o'clock in the afternoon. During the months of March, April, September and October they are to present themselves at 7 o'clock; they may reset for two hours and leave at 6 o'clock in the evening. In May, June, July and August they are to present themselves at 6 o'clock; rest for two hours and leave at 7 o'clock in the evening.

By now an effective working day was eleven hours, slightly shorter during the winter. The last drop had still not been squeezed out, but it soon would be, as becomes apparent from many of the villeinage agreements at Danish manors during the 1790s. In the case of Gerdrup-Lyngbygård Manor on the island of Zealand, for example, it was agreed in 1792 that during the winter villeins were

[7] Fridlev Skrubbeltrang 1969–70, p. 230; C. Rise Hansen 196, pp. xxiii–xxviii.
[8] C. Rise Hansen 1968, pp. lix–lx.   [9] Chapter 4.2, section b.
[10] Peter Riismøller 1972, p. 97.

Labour Burden and Social Structure 149

to work from sunrise until sunset, and in the summer from five o'clock in the morning until seven o'clock in the evening.[11] And, also in 1792, at the other end of the country, the following rules concerning hours to be worked by villeins at Glomstrup Manor on the island of Mors were agreed upon:

> In the months of May, June, July and August, from 5 o'clock in the morning until noon, then two hours' rest, thereafter work again until the sun sets. In September from 6 o'clock in the morning until 6 o'clock in the evening. In October, from 7 o'clock in the morning and home at 4 o'clock. In November, from 8 o'clock in the morning and home at 3 o'clock. In December, from 9 o'clock in the morning and home at 3 o'clock. In January, from 9 o'clock in the morning and home at half-past 3. In February, from 8 o'clock in the morning and home at 5 o'clock. In March, from 7 o'clock in the morning and home at 7 o'clock. In April, from 5 o'clock in the morning and home at 8 o'clock.

From September to April there was no break in the middle of the day except when the villein brought horses, in which case, out of consideration for the horses, an hour's rest was permitted.[12] Similar rules applied on another Jutland estate, Boddum Bisgård Manor, where, with special reference to threshing, villeins were to present themselves for work at six o'clock in the morning and, thereafter, "continue to work steadily until evening, without spending time on smoking tobacco."[13]

As these rules show, working hours during the winters in the 1790s corresponded more or less to the hours of daylight. During the summers the effective working day was about twelve hours, but the gross working period was fourteen hours or even more if the time it took to get to and from work is added. After this, little could be gained by extending the length of the working day any further.

There was, however, another way of increasing the number of hours worked, namely, by increasing the number of working days. Considerable change took place in this connection over the three hundred years from 1500 to 1800. Around the year 1500, the average working week was about four and one-half days, which cor-

---

[11] Archives of Gerdrup-Lyngbygård Manor, Diverse dokumenter 1725–1830: hoveriforening 24. oktober 1792, § 14, Provincial Archives of Zealand.

[12] Archives of Glomstrup Manor, Forskellige dokumenter 1653–1849: redegørelse af 17. november 1792 angående de under Glomstrup hørende bønders hoveri efter hoveriforeningen, Provincial Archives of Northern Jutland.

[13] Archives of Boddum Bisgård Manor, Hoveribestemmelse i henhold til forening af 16. april 1792, Provincial Archives of Northern Jutland.

150   *The New Denmark*

responded largely to what the church permitted if the various religious festivals were to be observed.[14]

After the Lutheran Reformation of 1536 a number of religious festivals were abolished by the church ordinance of 14 June 1539,[15] and from an ecclesiastical viewpoint there was no objection to increasing the length of the working week to more than five and one-half days. This protraction of the working week would appear to have been met with protests, for the Danes, as is the case with other 'primitive' societies, had a deeply rooted, instinctive 'preference for leisure.'[16] At all events, Bishop Peder Palladius felt prompted to embark on a campaign against 'day thieves':

> The day on which you work for your living is one of God's good holy days. Therefore you should also work on monks' days, which we no longer have to observe, so that you do not become thieves of God's holy days. . . . God has commanded you to work, you day-thief, not to sit down and drink ale![17]

Peder Palladius gradually got his way, perhaps not so much because the Danish people came to share his Protestant disdain for 'monks' days,' but because an extension of the working week was a macroeconomical necessity at the time.

It was then possible to continue to look for other holidays that were serving to reduce the length of the average working week in the same way as church holidays had done before many of them were abolished by the Reformation. In this connection, attention was focused primarily on what were known as *skulteuger* (literally, 'adjustable weeks'), amounting in all to two or three weeks around those days at Easter and in November when servants, farmhands, and the like traditionally were free to change their jobs and arrange their affairs in this connection. The first attempts to undermine the comprehensive system of holidays were indirect, concealed behind repeated prohibitions of *lønnesæd* from the beginning of the eighteenth century.[18] It so happened that the two phenomena – *lønnesæd* and *skulteuger* – were linked, to the extent

[14] Thomas Riis 1990, pp. 70–3 (Malmö, Skåne, now in Sweden, 1517–19). Sweden, in 1493, had an average of four work-free days a month apart from Sundays. Sigurd Kroon 1964, p. 201. The usual working week in Denmark and Sweden corresponded to what was common throughout Europe, including Turkey. Thomas Riis 1990.
[15] H. F. Rørdam 1883–9, I, pp. 66–7. In all, sixteen annual holidays were retained apart from Sundays, which reduced the average number of days off per month to one and one-third.
[16] Jesper Hoffmeyer 1985, p. 152. Cf. Ester Boserup 1965, p. 75.
[17] Peder Palladius 1872, pp. 106–7. Cf. Martin Schwarz Lausten 1987, p. 175.
[18] Chapter 3.5.

Labour Burden and Social Structure 151

that the granting of days off was motivated by the labourer's need for time first to sow the seed he had received in lieu of wages when he took on new employment and, subsequently, to thresh his corn and put his affairs in order before moving on to new employment in the autumn.

A decisive blow was dealt against the *skulteuger* in 1770, when the days on which farmhands and servants could change their jobs were switched to 31 December and 30 June (which, of course, did not coincide with the seasons for sowing and harvesting), whereupon the system crumbled.[19] That same year, on 26 October, an ordinance covering holidays was issued aimed at stopping "Indolence and Vice." This abolished an additional nine holidays, leaving only seven of the almost fifty on the calendar at the beginning of the sixteenth century. This law paved the way for a working week that averaged 5.9 days. At the same time, the length of a working day gradually increased and came close, on an annual basis, to averaging ten hours, the maximum that could be achieved prior to the advent of electric light.

All in all, the period 1500–1800 saw an increase in the length of the average working day by three or four hours and of the working week by one or two days. Whereas at the end of the fifteenth century a working week seldom exceeded thirty-five to forty-five hours, by the year 1800 it was almost sixty hours. On a rough average, working hours increased by about 50 percent during the three centuries. By the end of the eighteenth century, the farmhand who was picked out for military service and obliged, Sunday after Sunday, to report for training to a location often many miles away, was truly to be pitied. His life was no more than a treadmill.[20]

From the farmhand's point of view, another unfavourable development during the eighteenth century involved his working rhythm. The period's larger herds and larger milk yields represented permanent pressure of hitherto unknown dimensions, especially when summer stall feeding and other advanced methods were used. Furthermore, many of the labour functions that arose in connection with the green revolution were not strictly seasonal as they always had been in classical farmwork. Marling, ditch digging, peat digging, stone digging, and the like could to a large extent be done outside peak load periods.[21] Clover, which could be harvested several times during a season, also contributed to the

[19] Gunnar Olsen 1950–2, p. 200.   [20] Jens Holmgaard 1986, p. 61.
[21] See, for example, archives of Gjorslev Manor, Kasseekstrakter over indtægter og udgifter 1793–1802, Provincial Archives of Zealand.

152   *The New Denmark*

elimination of dead periods in agriculture. The days off that were cancelled were thus not wasted, as would inevitably have been the case within a less intensive agricultural system with a more fluctuating rhythm of labour.

Rural industry, so-called proto-industry, which made its appearance in several parts of Europe during the last half of the eighteenth century, also contributed to making the rhythm of labour more even. In Denmark, such industry covered mainly the manufacture of textiles and household articles, the best known examples being lace from North Schleswig and knitted stockings and pottery from the moorlands of Jutland. This form of activity could be taken up whenever there was any kind of pause in the farmwork.[22] Development in the towns took place along the same lines as it had in the country. During the eighteenth century the net tightened, particularly around journeymen, who, like farm labourers, had had a well-developed system of holidays.[23]

Between 1500 and 1800 the Danish people became accustomed, albeit unwillingly, to long, hard, and regular hours of work. During the sixteenth century, as already mentioned, those who drank ale instead of working were accused of 'day thieving,' and during the eighteenth century threshers were suspected of smoking tobacco instead of getting on with their threshing. In the 1730s there was still a tradition calling for a festival that might last two or three days celebrating the conclusion of any major piece of work (fig. 18). In 1732 a priest remarked disapprovingly that "peasants were hardly able to spread dung without a celebration; at mowing time many of them bring their fiddles or drums and celebrate for two or three days running."[24]

Several records exist of attempts to obstruct the new, labour-intensive agricultural methods. Farmers on the island of Lolland, for example, protested against the fact that grass was no longer to be 'nature's free gift' by throwing the first clover seeds they received from the landowner on to the midden.[25] Tenant farmers did the same at Tåsinge. There the sabotage was extended to include resistance to the attempt by the landowner, Niels Juel, to improve the farmers' fruit growing by ordering them to plant grafted fruit trees instead of continuing to make do with the ordinary wild fruit trees provided by nature; some of the farmers cut the roots of the fruit trees they had received from the landowner to prevent them

---

[22] Ove Hornby and Erik Oxenbøll 1982.   [23] Thomas Bloch Ravn 1983, pp. 8–10.
[24] Ibid., p. 10.
[25] J. B. Krarup and S. C. A. Tuxen 1895–1912, VI, p. 223.

Figure 18. Dancing and music during a haymaking festival in June.

154   *The New Denmark*

from growing.[26] This was effective, but only for a while. Some years later, Tåsinge became a centre not only for clover growing but also for fruit growing.[27]

Working morale improved, and when the Swiss preacher Johann Caspar Lavater visited Denmark at the end of the eighteenth century he was delighted to see so much diligence wherever he went: "Everybody works in the fields and on the roads. You will see no maid or farmer's wife who is not knitting. Even when carrying something on their heads they continue to work as they walk."[28]

Two Danish officials, J. Selmer and O. Kynde, who paid a visit in 1799 to Jutland, where a colony of mainly German immigrants was trying to cultivate the heath, were also most pleased by the splendid industry and diligence they observed: "One finds the immigrants, especially the Germans, at their work by 3 o'clock in the morning and continuing until past 10 o'clock at night, without devoting time to sleep or rest."[29]

At the end of the eighteenth century there were people here and there who worked nineteen or twenty hours a day, which from a biological viewpoint is probably the absolute maximum.

Between 1500 and 1800 the population of Denmark doubled. At the same time, working hours increased by about 50 percent. As the ratio between rural and urban populations remained more or less constant throughout the period, the total increase in labour consumption in Danish agriculture between 1500 and 1800 must be calculated at about 200 percent. A particular consequence of the growing use of labour was a considerable increase in villeinage during these three centuries, scarcely less than 200 percent, perhaps even more.[30] The demand for labour resulting from the new, intensive form of agriculture was insatiable.

The violently increasing pressure on labour during the period 1500–1800 was traumatic, not only for Denmark but also for the rest of Europe. It is against this background that a great many of the important intellectual and philosophical trends of the period should be appraised. This applies in particular to two major views of theoretical economics: populationism and the theory that work is the source of all wealth.

---

[26] Thorvald Hansen 1934, p. 22. Cf. T. C. Smout 1987, pp. 83–4. On wild apple trees: Hugo Matthiessen 1942, p. 29.
[27] Figures 8–11.   [28] Louis Bobé 1898, p. 16.
[29] Niels Windfeld Lund 1975, p. 59.
[30] Thomas Munch 1979, pp. 35–6; Thorkild Kjægaard 1980, pp. 27–35.

Labour Burden and Social Structure 155

Populationism was defended by nearly all eighteenth-century economists in Denmark and throughout Europe.[31] This theory would appear to be a reflection of the intense demand for labour that lay in the macroeconomical long-term development of the period. Until the publication in 1798 of Thomas Malthus's sensational *Essay on the Principle of Population*, few economists had demonstrated the necessary vision to realize that a larger population was only an apparent solution and that, on the contrary, the real problem was that the population had long since passed the limits of the optimal. Among them was a Dane, Otto Diderik Lütken, who observed as early as 1760 that

> since our globe has a certain circumference that does not increase according to the increasing number of its inhabitants, and that means of travelling to other planets deemed habitable have not yet been devised; since the fertility of the earth has a certain limit beyond which it cannot be brought; since human nature will no doubt continue unchanged, wherefore a certain number will need, for their sustenance, hereafter as now, the same quantity of the fruits of the earth, and that their individual portions cannot be reduced according to whim, it becomes clear that no general claim may be made that the greater the number of inhabitants in the world, the more blessed they shall be. For as soon as their numbers exceed the figure which our Earth, with all its fertility on land and in the oceans, is capable of sustaining, they must needs starve each other, quite apart from other incalculable difficulties, to wit a shortage of many of the other amenities of life such as wool, flax, timber, fuel, etc.[32]

In the same way, the theory that work is the source of all wealth (which can be traced back to the physiocrats of the eighteenth century and was finally expounded by Adam Smith, David Ricardo, and Karl Marx)[33] can be seen as an interpretation of the macroeconomic developments of the seventeenth and eighteenth centuries. What could be more natural than to single out work as the source of all wealth in an economy whose demand for labour appeared unbounded?

The harsh, censorious view that arose in the seventeenth and eighteenth centuries that poverty and beggary represented indolence[34] should no doubt also be seen in relation to the steadily increasing need for labour and the traumatic dislike for meeting this need. There is a striking contrast between the relative mildness with which poor people and beggars were regarded during the late Middle Ages and the Renaissance and the increasing harshness with which these groups were treated during the eighteenth century.

[31] H. L. Bisgaard 1902, pp. 140–67; Jørgen Estrup 1976, pp. 67–8. Cf. H. Christian Johansen 1968–80, I, pp. 218–19.
[32] O. D. Lütken 1760, I, p. 3.
[33] Joseph A. Schumpeter 1963, pp. 309–10; H. L. Bisgaard 1902, pp. 131, 146–9.
[34] Tyge Krogh 1987, pp. 52, 146, 172.

156   The New Denmark

Erasmus of Rotterdam, in his work on the education of a Christian prince, *Institutio principis Christiani* (1515), recommended that laws show special consideration for the poor and attempt to equalize such injuries or losses as citizens might have suffered at the hands of fortune ("in fortunae præsidiis").[35] A Danish cleric who opposed these views was the bishop of Zealand, Peder Hersleb (1689–1757). In his popular sermons, several collections of which were published, Bishop Hersleb advocated charity, declaring that it should be shown to all, both believers and nonbelievers, who, even if not precisely "God's children" were at least "God's domestics." But at the same time he warned against misunderstanding the Christian injunction to love one's neighbour. He felt one should not indiscriminately display love towards the beggars and idlers who were sorely plaguing the country and already abusing charitable foundations and institutions quite sufficiently.[36]

This pious man of God was not the only person to hold such views about the poor. On the contrary, similar pronouncements were repeatedly made by others, including Erik Pontoppidan, who complained of "the difficulty in suppressing beggary, because people in general are charitable and often display untimely mercy towards those who rightly should have no share of alms,"[37] and Gregers Begtrup, who launched a powerful attack against "the self-made poor." According to Begtrup, their numbers were proliferating day by day because excessive welfare work often made the poor disinclined to work. This meant not only that wage levels were forced up because of a shortage of workers but also that

> the industrious and good class of citizens, who themselves feel the pressure of the times and taxes, find it impossible in the future to support those who are indolent and indifferent to profit, home, clothing and thrift.[38]

Another manifestation of the harsher attitude towards the poor that arose after 1500 concerned ideas about education. The theory that schooling and education could lead to upward social mobility and that education was something to which the poor should be encouraged to aspire, was replaced by the view that the poor should be kept out of the schools, which they attended only to avoid 'fatiguing work' anyway.[39]

The chronological coincidence between the growth of Protestantism and the inevitable macroeconomical demand for people to work harder – as rationalized by Protestant leaders through a fanatical reappraisal of

[35] Aage Kragelund 1976, p. 99.
[36] P. G. Lindhardt 1939, pp. 163–4. On Lutheranism advocating a harsher view of the poor: Martin Schwarz Lausten 1987, pp. 174–85.
[37] Erik Pontoppidan 1763–81, III, p. 398. Cf. N. Rasmussen Søkilde 1888, p. 29–30.
[38] Gregers Begtrup 1803–12, V, pp. 572–3.
[39] Jette Hellesen and Ole Tuxen 1984, p. 323. Cf. Edvard Holm 1891–1912, III, 2, pp. 421–2.

Labour Burden and Social Structure 157

work, which they saw as moral and pleasing to God, whereas they saw indolence and idleness as the marks of Catholicism and the Devil – has given rise to a number of wide-ranging hypotheses within the social sciences about the connection between Protestantism and working morale. Particularly well-known is Max Weber's thesis on Protestant ethics. According to Weber, it is a characteristically Protestant notion to regard work as a vocation, and this created the basis for the hardworking capitalistic societies of northwestern Europe.[40] Weber's thesis, which is based on an analysis not of the objective, macroeconomic processes of development, but of 'attitudes' and 'moods,' turns things upside down. Instead of asserting that Protestantism created the new working morale and hence modern capitalism, it would seem more reasonable to claim that the objective macroeconomic processes of development forced the evolution of a work-oriented public attitude that Protestantism then eagerly adopted.

One senses in the thesis of a Protestant like Max Weber an extension of early Protestant propaganda against Catholicism mingled with the semi-despising, semi-envious notions held by Protestant northern Europe about the free, the slightly indolent, the idle, and the erotically coloured life of Catholic Italy. However, such notions do not harmonize very well with reality, which even in southern Europe meant an increasingly heavier work burden during the sixteenth, seventeenth, and eighteenth centuries. Carlo Levi had good reason to describe southern Italy as a region where "il tempo e il lavoro . . . non contano e non costano" (time and work count for nothing and cost nothing).[41]

6.2 FALLING MARGINAL PRODUCTION AND CHANGES IN THE SOCIAL STRUCTURE, 1500–1800

Despite occasional dramatic setbacks, for example, during the cattle plague wave of the 1740s, agricultural production rose considerably during the period 1500–1800. An appreciable rise in production during the last half of the seventeenth century and the beginning of the eighteenth was followed by a new rise during the last half of the eighteenth century.[42] Altogether, the increase in agricultural production was definitely far more than 100 percent during these three hundred years.

Not all of this agricultural growth was available for domestic consumption, however. The rise in production was based largely upon

[40] Max Weber 1920.   [41] Carlo Levi 1947, p. 77.
[42] Chapter 1.2 and 3.7; section b.

158   *The New Denmark*

steadily increasing imports from neighbouring regions of energy and raw materials in the form of iron and coal. Like Denmark's other imports, these were financed mainly by agricultural products, partly within the framework of a triangular trading pattern in which Danish corn was sent to Norway and Norwegian timber to England, accounts finally being settled by shipments of English coal to Denmark.[43]

At best, the disposable net production increase was on a level with the population increase during the period 1500–1800, in other words, about 100 percent, and thus considerably less than the increase in consumption of labour, which, as already indicated, was probably about 200 percent. From this it may be deduced that the average wage level decreased between 1500 and 1800 and that the Danish economy was consequently subjected to the law of falling marginal production. The standard of living – made up of components such as nutrition, housing conditions, health conditions, and leisure – was deteriorating, and there was no way of halting this process.

a. Danish Society during the First Period of Falling Marginal Production: Until about 1740

Heaping the burden on to the environment was the easiest solution and therefore the strategy largely followed until Denmark's ecological crisis during the first half of the eighteenth century. The government's extensive building activities and armament in connection with taxation policies exercised in their turn an influence on the social distribution of the burdens. Armament and impressive building projects ensured that a demand for labour was upheld in the building sector and in the urban trades as a whole. At the same time, agricultural prices were kept down as a result of the overproduction crisis provoked by an intensive taxation policy directed against the agricultural sector.

On the macroeconomic level this had the effect of a transfer of income from agricultural employers, landowners, and tenant farmers to wage earners, not only in the towns (where the bulk of government consumption was placed) but also in rural districts, where low prices for agricultural products and the demand for labour in the urban sector also had their impact. Regardless of the limitations that serfdom (*vornedskab*, a system of bondage in force on the eastern Danish islands until 1702) and, later, adscription

---

[43] Albert Olsen 1936, p. 11; Birgit Nüchel Thomsen et al. 1965, p. 51.

Labour Burden and Social Structure 159

imposed upon the free movement of labour, workers could always find their way to the towns if the real wage level in rural districts was appreciably lower than that in the urban sector.[44] The final result of this interplay between large public consumption and high taxes on agriculture was a society experiencing economic growth and with an agricultural sector in which costs were imposed, first upon the environment and thereafter upon its employers, whereas both urban and rural wage earners to quite a large extent remained unaffected. This may help to explain the frequently observed circumstance that wage earners at the end of the seventeenth century and early in the eighteenth were in a strong position to confront their financially hard-pressed employers.[45]

An impression of the attitude displayed by servants towards their employers is indicated by a diary entry for 27 April 1703 made by Bishop Jens Bircherod of Ålborg:

> Seeing that corn prices were now quite low ... vagrants and day-labourers became exceedingly indolent and reluctant. We were unable to find a woman in the whole of this town willing to weed our garden for payment. .... People who lived in the country voiced similar complaints, even more strongly indeed, about the recalcitrant pride displayed by day-labourers and farm-hands in these times; it seems that they hold bread or food in low esteem, but demand double wages for their services.[46]

Tenant farmers in particular were pressed from all sides: by farmhands, whose wages did not fall as fast as prices, and who therefore successfully defended their *skultedage* (see Chapter 6.1) and other privileges; by landowners, who tried to maintain rent levels for land leased to tenant farmers, because the expenses of the former were not being reduced at the same rate as agricultural prices;[47] and by the state, whose tax demands were continually increasing.

b. Danish Society during the Second Period of Falling Marginal Production: From about 1740

During the first decades of the eighteenth century, nature fought back so fiercely with sand drift, rising water level, cattle plague, and falling productive capacity in the primary sector that the

---

[44] Hans H. Fussing 1957, p. 89; Albert Olsen 1932, pp. 45–6.
[45] Gunnar Olsen 1950–2, pp. 199–200. [46] Christian Molbech 1846, pp. 422–3.
[47] Reductions in manorial dues were nevertheless common at the end of the seventeenth century. Thorkild Kjærgaard 1980, p. 25.

160   *The New Denmark*

costs of growth could no longer be heaped on to the environment. On the contrary, the accumulated environmental debt had to be paid off by measures to combat sand drift and by other forms of ecological recovery. At the same time, consumption of labour in the agricultural sector soared as a result of intensified exploitation. Like an irrepressible tidal wave, rising agricultural prices swept over the Danish community; from 1740 onwards, prices of agricultural products rose, decade by decade, and by the beginning of the following century had more than doubled (see fig. 3).[48]

Once again, the expenses were not divided equally among the various strata of the population. This time it was the turn of farmhands and servants, cottagers, and the urban population, whereas previously the sufferers were agricultural employers, landowners, and tenant farmers. Working hours were extended to the absolute maximum, and real wages fell, not just by the working hour but also in terms of overall purchasing power. Agricultural wage lists from the second half of the eighteenth century show more or less unaltered wage payments from 1750 up to the 1790s, after which some adjustments were eventually made. However, these by no means compensated for the price increases that had taken place since the 1740s.[49] A reduction of real wages by 50 percent, due also to the gradual abolition of various forms of payment in kind, first and foremost *lønnesæd*, (see Chapter 3.5) which compensated, as long as they existed, for rising prices, and an increase in working hours of 20 to 30 percent, would have represented a typical course of development for people working on the land during the second half of the eighteenth century.

For the cottagers, who, in contrast to farmhands and servants, were not compelled to accept employment, but were free to look for work wherever they liked – with the risk of not finding any – the development was similar. Just as farmhands no longer received *lønnesæd*, the cottagers lost rights that they had enjoyed for centuries, especially rights regarding utilization of village pastures for their cattle to graze on. The pressure on resources during the eigh-

[48] Erik Helmer Pedersen 1983, pp. 66–7.
[49] Hans Christian Johansen 1979, p. 194 (real wage index for farmhands, 1725–1868). Bent Schiermer Andersen 1986, p. 89. A very large number of wage lists from the 1730s and the rest of the century: collection of unpublished documents for a history of prices, University of Copenhagen, Department of History. Employment in the rural proto-industrialization sector as an attempt to compensate for falling real wages in agriculture: Peter Kriedte et al. 1978, pp. 41–6; Fridlev Skrubbeltrang 1940, p. 206.

Labour Burden and Social Structure 161

teenth century was considerable. For the farmers, who now quite definitely had the upper hand in the villages, the obvious course was to incorporate the struggle for grazing, manure, access to forests, firewood, and other resources in the overall social struggle by attempting to eliminate or limit the rights of cottagers to share these benefits. Individual enclosure arrangements soon became the preferred method of reorganizing the use of a village's basic resources in accordance with a formula that, to a greater degree than hitherto, recognized the farmers' wishes.

The predictable effects of enclosure were not slow to emerge. Cottagers in Seem, near Ribe, for example, where enclosure took place as early as the beginning of the 1770s, lodged a complaint in 1788 with the chief county administrative officer in Ribe:

> Some fifteen or sixteen years ago a redivision of land was completed in the village of Seem, and at the time cottagers were excluded from the division on the grounds that every farmer was to provide the cottagers on his land with grazing for 1 cow in return for a reasonable payment. Before the division took place a cottager paid 4 marks for grazing 1 cow and 8 *skillinge* for 1 sheep; there was no charge for calves and pigs. After the division, the farmers began to increase the tariff for grazing a cow; from that time until a twelvemonth or so ago up to 3 or 4 rixdollars, and at present many [of us] are unable to obtain grazing for any money at all.[50]

In the former Copenhagen military district, which was privatized in 1766 and where the new owner-occupier farmers in the ensuing years had arranged enclosures, an observer described the situation around 1780 as follows:

> The poor cottagers, whose numbers are six times greater than the farmers, have scarcely a single hen, whereas formerly [a cottager] would have 1 cow, 4 sheep, 1 sow, 2 geese (which produced 18 to 20 goslings every year); then it was a pleasure on a summer's evening to see any number of gambolling lambs, many advancing armies of geese and large herds of pigs galloping home; but now this pleasing sight has disappeared.[51]

Enclosure involved the abolition of communal cultivation principles and the division of the land into separate holdings for each individual farmer. Enclosures took place in most Danish villages at the end of the eighteenth century. Regulation of enclosures was introduced by a comprehensive ordinance dated 23 April 1781. This ordinance included a

---

[50] Søren Mulvad 1988, p. 223.   [51] Fridlev Skrubbeltrang 1940, p. 304.

162   The New Denmark

recommendation, but no injunction, to concede land to cottagers when carrying out an enclosure. As a result of this ordinance, an enclosure corresponded in reality to abolishing all the customary rights to communal village resources that cottagers might previously have enjoyed. If, as was often the case, the farmers failed to display the necessary 'willingness' nothing could be done for the cottagers. Later, supplementary legislation during the 1790s somewhat rectified the cottagers' complete lack of legal rights in connection with enclosure. Among other things, it was decided that in cases where a farm was closed down in connection with an enclosure, four smallholdings were to be set up instead.[52]

In older historical writings one quite frequently comes across the now abandoned view that the farmers were opposed to enclosure. On the contrary, it was the farmers, more than any other group, who pressed for enclosures because they stood to benefit from them.[53]

For urban communities, the rise of agricultural prices meant a depreciation in their terms of trade with the agricultural sector. Consequently, towards the end of the eighteenth century, the average standard of living was falling in Copenhagen as well as in the market towns.[54] The poorest group of city dwellers suffered especially from a considerable lowering of living standards.[55]

Pauperism became a feature of the eighteenth century and left its mark on all Western European societies.[56] Denmark was no exception. Here, between about 1740 and 1800 nutritional conditions deteriorated appreciably in the lower strata of society, which had managed to remain on an astonishingly high level during the first decades of the eighteenth century. Cheap vegetable foodstuffs gained ground at the expense of animal products, and undernourishment and/or malnutrition became an increasingly frequent phenomenon. An idea of the macroshifts in diet that took place between 1500 and 1800 is provided by the fact that around 1500 one ox was consumed per inhabitant per year,[57] whereas in 1800 the annual consumption of beef in Copenhagen amounted at most to fifteen thousand animals, in other words, less than one-sixth of an ox per inhabitant.[58]

---

[52] Claus Bjørn 1981a, pp. 20–1; Karl-Erik Frandsen 1988a, pp. 48–53; Lotte Dombernowsky 1988, pp. 311–31, especially pp. 321–3; Rita Holm 1983, p. 194.
[53] Claus Bjørn 1981a, pp. 16–19.
[54] Thorkild Kjærgaard 1977–8, pp. 425–6 (with references).
[55] Keld Mikkelsen 1989, pp. 21–38.
[56] Wilhelm Abel 1972, p. 69; Stuart Woolf 1986, pp. 50–60.
[57] Niels Siggaard 1945, p. 39. Cf. Knud Fabricius 1932–4, p. 542.
[58] Poul Thestrup 1971, pp. 208–17.

Labour Burden and Social Structure 163

In 1758, an anonymous observer from Zealand complained that in the homes of smallholders, "for want of a reasonable supply of victuals for a man and his family . . . a brood of puny, skinny youngsters is raised."[59] Matters did not improve during the following years. In 1772, A. C. Teilmann wrote from western Jutland that

> it is generally possible to tell at a glance a well-to-do farmer's son from a poor man's; the former usually looks so healthy compared with the latter, which is no wonder; for nature demonstrates in the same way, not only in dumb creatures but even in plants, what advantages may result from proper nourishment during upbringing.[60]

There is no shortage of appalling descriptions of the misery suffered by the common people during the second half of the eighteenth century. In 1786 the cleric and writer H. J. Birch asked:

> How far will 2 marks and 4 *skillinge* a week serve a thresher for food and clothing for his wife and children, for extra tax and house tax, for peat, straw, bedclothes, etc. when 1 *tønde* of rye costs 26 marks, 1 *tønde* of barley 19 or 20 marks and 1 *tønde* of butter 40 or 50 rix-dollars?

Hunger was inevitable. Birch continued:

> I can assure you that last year most of the cottagers in my parish [Glostrup, near Copenhagen] and in all the parishes around here were unable to buy themselves a bushel of malt to brew a little thin beer. But their wives and children have to make do with plain water throughout the year, and get no hot food other than breadcrusts boiled in water with a little syrup, or cabbage boiled in water without meat. . . . When enclosure is carried out and cottagers receive not the smallest patch of land or grazing for cows or sheep, and are not even entitled to keep as much as a couple of geese on the common . . . then poverty and need reach dire extremes; then cottagers begin to beg – people who have never begged before, and never thought of begging.[61]

Thomas Malthus also noted miserable conditions when he crossed Zealand in 1799: "The peasants had a greater appearance of poverty than any we had hitherto remarked."[62] Together with deteriorating housing conditions in respect of materials and heating, increasing overpopulation of houses and flats can be observed as a result of the demographic pressure. In Copenhagen the average dwelling area for the poorest third of the population in 1801 was down to 4.2 square metres per individual, corresponding to

---

[59] Anon. 1758 pp. 97–8.
[60] A. C. Teilmann 1772b, pp. 15–16. Cf. Fridlev Skrubbeltrang 1978, p. 428.
[61] H. J. Birch 1786, pp. 44–5.   [62] Thomas R. Malthus 1966, p. 52.

164   *The New Denmark*

the space taken up by a bed and a curtain.[63] It is unlikely that conditions were much better for the poorest groups of the rural population. Other manifestations of the spread of pauperism and proletarianization in the population included the increasing rate of theft. The Danish criminologist Flemming Balvig's simple thesis is that when the price of rye goes up, offences against property increase.[64] The price of rye rose towards the end of the eighteenth century, and although thorough studies have not as yet been made there is evidence to show that offences against property increased correspondingly.[65] The increasing number of children born out of wedlock[66] is probably also evidence of worsened conditions for large groups of the population.

The lowering of real wage levels caused large groups of society to come closer to experiencing poverty than before. It took less than ever for individuals to be brought down to where they could no longer manage on their own. As a consequence, beggary increased to the extent that "the eye of the patriot is blinded by tears . . . when he sees . . . how the streets in the towns and the roads in the countryside are practically swarming with poor people begging for bread."[67] A report from the parish of Lumby, to the north of Odense on the island of Funen, stated that every farmer was visited by about forty-five hundred beggars annually.[68]

Extant records leave no doubt that towards the end of the eighteenth century the lower classes differed from the more fortunate groups of society in being physically smaller and punier. It is not so easy to establish whether this proletarianization also influenced cerebral development in the lower classes. However, modern information from developing countries, where insufficient cerebral development and subsequent physical and mental deficiency occurs in millions of children due to lack of basic proteins in their food, makes it seem probable that this was indeed the case.[69]

As demonstrated by the previously mentioned information relating to diet in Denmark at the end of the eighteenth century, it was certainly not

[63] Richard Willerslev 1983, pp. 402, 406.   [64] Flemming Balvig 1987, pp. 22–8.
[65] Fridlev Skrubbeltrang 1940, pp. 262–3; S. P. Jensen 1986, p. 46; Jens Engberg 1973, pp. 77–85. Marked rises in offences against property at the end of the eighteenth century are known from other parts of Europe, for example, in Tuscany, where more detailed studies of criminal statistics have been made than in Denmark. Carla Nassini 1985, pp. 192–6.
[66] Hans Christian Johansen 1979, pp. 66–7.
[67] J. L. Lybecker 1772, p. 5; J. D. W. Westenholz 1772, pp. 49–50, 105–7 (a pitiful description of begging children); Fridlev Skrubbeltrang 1940, p. 260; Aage Rasch 1964, p. 233.
[68] Gregers Begtrup 1803–12, III, p. 287.   [69] René Dumont 1977, pp. 78–9.

Labour Burden and Social Structure 165

possible to give children everywhere, in all strata of society, sufficient quantities of foodstuffs with a high protein content, such as milk. The difficulty in obtaining fuel would also have played a part, as inadequate cooking of food impedes the process of absorbing protein. Insufficient cerebral development as a result of malnutrition or undernourishment in childhood, perhaps even during the embryonic stage, would seem to account for part of the large number of eccentrics and inadequate creatures in Danish society throughout the nineteenth century; now, towards the close of the twentieth century, seventy to eighty years after the entire Danish population rose above the subsistence minimum, these pitiful cases have almost entirely disappeared.

Compared with the conditions endured by the lower classes, the development during the second period of falling marginal production presents a less gloomy picture in respect of Denmark's approximately sixty thousand tenant farmers. There is hardly any doubt that working hours also increased for tenant farmers, and this was not always welcome. On the other hand, the farmer class managed to keep clear of the fall in real wages and even to fight successfully for a better financial and social position. Evidence of this has already been mentioned: Enclosure confirmed and strengthened the social and financial superiority of the farmer class in relation to cottagers. There are several other testimonials. One of the most important is the development of 'family tenancy' during the eighteenth century. Convincing statistical documentation of this development was presented by Fridlev Skrubbeltrang in 1978 after a lifetime of study in the social history of Danish agrarian society.[70]

The term 'family tenancy' applies to the situation when a close relative of a tenant farmer, as a rule a son or a son-in-law, takes over a farm when the farmer retires or dies. Thus the 'family tenancy percentage' in a given year means the percentage ratio between the number of instances in which a farm has been left by a previous tenant to a close relative and the total number of tenancies to have changed hands within the year in question. The family tenancy percentage illuminates the social position of the farmer class, for it demonstrates not only the degree of stability within the farmer group but also the influence exercised by this group in relation to other social groups, particularly the landowners.

A high family tenancy percentage is evidence of a marked degree of social stability in the farmer class. Furthermore, it indicates not only that the group as a whole had influence on decisions as to who was to take

[70] Fridlev Skrubbeltrang 1978, p. 464 and index.

166 *The New Denmark*

over a tenancy but also that taking over a tenancy was in itself an attractive proposition. Conversely, a low family tenancy percentage is a sure sign of social instability in the farmer group. It also indicates a dwindling interest on the part of the rising generation to take over a farm.[71]

The development of family tenancy provides a clear picture of the social position of tenant farmers from 1740 to 1800. Around 1740, the family tenancy percentage for the country as a whole was about 30, which implies that about 30 percent of all newly started tenant farmers were closely related to the retiring or deceased tenant. Thirty years later this figure had increased to 45 percent, and around 1800 it was as high as about 65 percent. From having been a group characterized by poor stability and many changeovers, tenant farmers developed in the course of just over half a century into a closely knit segment of society with few newcomers. Whereas the majority of Danish farms at the beginning of the eighteenth century were transferred from one family to another, by the end of the century a large number of them stayed within the same family, becoming "small entailed estates that always, according to the father's wishes, remained with one of the children, a son or a daughter." It had become a group in which children nearly always followed their parents as predictably as those brought up on big manorial estates.[72]

What must be added to the picture painted in the foregoing chapters of an extremely competent farmer class that proved itself, broadly speaking, to be keen on innovation, is that as a group it was definitely on the way up, both socially and economically. Or, in the words of C. W. von Munthe af Morgenstierne concerning the Danish farmer class in 1783:

> Most of them can pay their dues and have sufficient money for clothes and food, not like the German and Holstein peasant, who must needs live on carrots, turnips, apples and pears. No, thank heavens, in this country he who deserves his bread enjoys it, eats good rye bread, pork, cheese and butter, and drinks good beer.[73]

Many details support this picture and provide additional nuances. From the middle of the century, a number of observers noted the more elegant and cultivated lifestyle of the farmer class. The Reverend P. L. Hersleb, for example, writing of 'Brønshøj folk'

---

[71] Thorkild Kjærgaard 1981–2, p. 279.
[72] Erik Pontoppidan 1783–81, V, 2, p. 665; A. C. Teilmann 1772b, p. 31; Fridlev Skrubbeltrang 1961, p. 25.
[73] C. W. von Munthe af Morgenstierne 1783, p. 31.

Labour Burden and Social Structure

recorded that they had now "imperceptibly become so humanized that many people from Copenhagen visit the farmers in the summer and enjoy themselves for two or three days, and they avail themselves, without revulsion, of the farmer's bed and board, and milk."[74]

Progress was being made, not only in the village of Brønshøj near Copenhagen, but also by the farmers of Funen, of whom one Danish author and landowner, Tyge Rothe, wrote, "they lived splendidly," and "in their homes you will find a silver jug, a panelled living-room, a made-up bed, and even tea things."[75]

Tea things were not the only indication that the farmers on the island of Funen, like those on the outskirts of Copenhagen, were to an increasing degree adopting the lifestyle of the urban bourgeoisie. On the subject of the same Funen farmers, Pontoppidan wrote in 1767 that "nowadays tenant farmers everywhere have adopted town ways of dressing."[76]

On the island of Lolland, the farmers – nearly all "tenant farmers doing villeinage work" – at the end of the 1760s were "generally regarded as being by no means wanting, and sometimes affluent." Their style of living was in many cases "not far from sumptuous," displaying "fastidiousness" mainly in regard to their food, less in their clothing. The following description is given of the Lolland farmer's physique:

> The Lolland farmer is plump and of medium height, and he usually has rather fat legs, but with regard to strength he is generally somewhat superior, as one can often see him take a Danish barrel of wheat . . . and without difficulty carry it up to the second floor, and even to the third.

With becoming patriotic pride Pontoppidan adds: "Hardly one French or High German peasant in ten could emulate him, for the daily fare of Lollanders is what *they* have only on festive occasions."[77]

The clothing of Jutland farmers in the 1760s was modest, especially on "the moors and infertile districts," where the farmers

> wear black homespun trousers and stockings without feet, so that both summer and winter they walk barefoot, though they wear clogs in the winter. In other districts [of Jutland] they wear full stockings and clogs for daily purposes and boots when they go to church; leather shoes are not common among the farmers of Jutland.[78]

[74] Steffen Linvald 1962, p. 19. [75] Quoted by Edvard Holm 1888, p. 181.
[76] Erik Pontoppidan 1763–81, III, p. 397. [77] Ibid., pp. 253–4.
[78] Ibid., IV, p. 44.

168 The New Denmark

In the words of Hans de Hofman, however, it was possible to observe

> a kind of emulation of the customs of the middle classes, in which the farmers time and again seem to find something to their taste; moreover they display a kind of contempt for the inebriation and drunkenness that in former times gave rise to so much evil and so many misfortunes. ... In my youth [the 1730s] it was common for the farmers to lie sprawling around the town on every market day until late at night, whereas nowadays most of them leave at noon, 1 o'clock, or 2 o'clock, as soon as they have sold their produce and then bought whatever they need.[79]

An astonishing testimonial to the considerable cultural and social ambitions prevailing in the farmer class was to be found in Hjermind Church in the county of Viborg, where there was "a beautifully carved altar-piece" donated by a farmer.[80]

There was nothing wrong with their diet, not even in Jutland. In the county of Riberhus, in southwest Jutland, food was healthy and plentiful, and on festive occasions more than sumptuous. At weddings, five or six courses would be served, namely,

> meat broth, ham with stewed kale, *Bergfisk* [dried codfish steeped in a lye of potash], or fresh fish, poultry, mutton or beef, gruel or *Ægmelk* [egg yolks stirred with milk, sugar, and flour] with white bread in it, and the well-to-do [might even serve] plum tart or waffles.[81]

This was the state of affairs that prompted the government to issue an ordinance on 12 March 1783 "concerning restrictions on the lavishness prevailing among the farming classes in Denmark and Norway." It ran:

> As it has come to our knowledge that lavishness amongst the farming classes hath been increasing of late, in our kingdom of Denmark as well as in Norway, partly with respect to food and drink and partly with respect to clothing, with the result that farmers no longer rest content with such articles as our country can produce, but in some places display extravagance with wine and coffee, and garments made of foreign fabrics, thereby occasioning their impoverishment and causing money to pass out of the country and be paid to foreigners. ... In order to prevent such harmful prodigality in the farming classes we have therefore decided that henceforth wedding feasts shall be limited to 32 persons and last no longer than one day. No more than four courses shall be served. Neither wine nor coffee are permitted. The same rules shall apply to festivities in connection with childbirth, baptism, first churching

[79] Ibid., p. 177. Jutland farmers have money earning interest: C. W. von Munthe af Morgenstierne 1783, p. 31. Cf. Erik Pontoppidan 1763–81, IV, p. 392.
[80] Ibid., p. 659.   [81] Ibid., V, 2, p. 666.

Labour Burden and Social Structure

after childbirth, and also to funerals, special attention being drawn to the fact that nothing but food shall be served to those who come from afar; coffee-drinking amongst peasants in the country is forbidden.

This ordinance of 1783, issued one year before the appointment of the Agrarian Commission of 1784 and three years before the Greater Agrarian Commission of 1786, also included a number of rules concerning clothing that likewise indicate that whatever may have formed the background for the agricultural reforms of these years it certainly was not the poverty of the tenant farmers. Among other things it was deemed necessary to forbid the wearing of silken jackets and skirts. Henceforth, the only garment of silk that women in the farming community were permitted to wear was a cap. The responsibility for ensuring that these regulations were observed was placed in the hands of the local parish bailiff. In order to remind people of the ordinance it was decreed that it should be read out from church pulpits twice a year.

It is doubtful whether any purpose was served by these petty attempts to restrict the Danish farmers' right to enjoy, in all modesty, the fruits of their labours. Court cases involving assertions of sumptuousness at country weddings developed into pure parodies, with parish bailiffs displaying a certain inability to remember precisely what had been served and how many guests had been present at festivities in which they themselves had participated.[82]

If the ordinance had any effect at all, it certainly was not one of long duration. It is evident from Gregers Begtrup's report on the state of Danish agriculture as it appeared just after the year 1800 that the attempts during the 1780s to restrict luxury consumption in the farming classes were written in sand. Begtrup complains that the farmers around Copenhagen had far too large a consumption of "extravagant articles like coffee, tea, sugar, wine, schnapps, etc.,"[83] but at the same time he had to concede that things were not much better in the provinces. On the island of Falster, farmers let themselves be tempted by "coffee-beans, sugar and Flensburg rum,"[84] and if one attended a country wedding in the district of Vindinge in the east of the island of Funen (where nearly all the farmers were still tenant farmers doing villeinage service), one could not leave before three days had passed, nor before one had eaten one's way through oceans of soup and mountains of roast pork, beef, goose, and lamb, with which red wine, beer, and

---

[82] Vilhelm Lütken 1909–10, pp. 375–8. Cf. T. Bundgaard Lassen 1932.
[83] Gregers Begtrup 1803–12, I, p. 221.   [84] Ibid., IV, p. 762.

170   *The New Denmark*

schnapps would be served. Cakes and waffles would be served for dessert.[85]

In the district between Kolding and Fredericia there were farmers during these years who had their own barouche, sent their daughters to the market towns to learn to sew, engaged dancing tutors in the winter and gave little balls, drank wine, coffee, and tea, and wore exclusively "factory-made cloth." One could even come across instances, otherwise unheard of in farming circles, of children who did not go into service at all but stayed at home until they acquired a farm of their own.[86]

This information about the increasingly comfortable lifestyle of tenant farmers in the eighteenth century, for the most part drawn from contemporary observers, can be supplemented by the result of later research. The refinement of customs observed by the Reverend Hersleb at the beginning of the 1750s among the farmers in the vicinity of Copenhagen, which meant that people from Copenhagen were able to enjoy "without revulsion" the farmer's bed and board, and milk, is also noticeable in other parts of the country. In the Kolding district, wooden plates fell into disuse after the middle of the eighteenth century, and at the same time farmers began to hang pictures on their walls and curtains in their windows.[87]

The tea things Tyge Rothe mentioned were no rarity in the homes of these Funen farmers who "lived splendidly." Probate records covering the private estates of Funen farmers between 1730 and 1780 mention tea tables in no less than 14 percent of the cases.[88] Another indication of the financial capacity of the farmers of Funen during the 1750s is that the tenant farmers of the district appear as creditors in one-third of all loans registered in the market town of Odense.[89] Nor were tea tables found solely in farmers' homes on the island of Funen. On the islands of Zealand, Lolland, and Falster they are mentioned during the same period (1730–80) in 8 percent of farmers' probate records. Only in Jutland did tea drinking appear to have failed as yet to gain popularity, for tea tables are mentioned in only 3 percent of probate records in North Jutland and not at all in East and West Jutland.[90] Nevertheless, it may be asserted with considerable certainty that no small amount of the enormous quantities of tea

[85] Ibid., III, p. 383. The same all over Funen, see, for example, ibid., p. 330.
[86] Ibid., V, pp. 240–1.   [87] P. Eliassen 1923, p. 208.
[88] Hans Christian Johansen 1979, p. 224.   [89] Ibid. 1983, p. 158.
[90] Ibid. 1979, p. 224.

Labour Burden and Social Structure 171

brought to Denmark through trade with China during the eighteenth century[91] found its way into the homes of tenant farmers. This is a testimonial to the farmers' purchasing power and also a refutation of the often reiterated claim that Danish farmers of the eighteenth century were sluggish and unreceptive to cultural innovation.

Tea was first heard of in Denmark in the middle of the seventeenth century and even by the end of the century was known only in the most distinguished circles.[92]

Other glimpses of the sophisticated aspects of life on Denmark's tenant farms during the last third of the eighteenth century are provided by a few farmers' diaries from the end of the century that have been published in recent years. In 1786 a West Funen tenant farmer, Peder Madsen, acquired a pair of spectacles,[93] and from Nørre Tulstrup in Central Jutland we have a description penned by a tenant farmer himself, Christian Andersen, to the effect that during the 1780s and 1790s he bought large quantities of wine, silken garments, and gold braid; for example, in 1792 he bought twenty-one cotton and silk kerchiefs from a Jewish merchant. The year before he made this purchase he had celebrated his daughter's wedding, to which sixty guests were invited, almost twice as many as the number allowed in the ordinance of 1783 covering the restriction of lavishness among the farming community.[94] Clocks, which were rarely seen in farmers homes during the first half of the eighteenth century, became common towards the end of the century, and around the year 1800 were probably to be seen in the majority of Danish farmhouses.[95] The ability to read, which

[91] Kristof Glamann 1960, pp. 130–44. Aage Rasch and P. P. Sveistrup 1948, pp. 110–11. Cf. Aage Rasch 1964, p. 21.

[92] Tove Clemmensen and Mogens B. Mackeprang 1980, p. 47. Cf. Christian Molbech 1846, p. 313. On the procedure for serving tea during the eighteenth century, including use of the tea tables found in such large numbers among tenant farmers: Nina Fabricius 1975, p. 21.

[93] Karl Peder Pedersen 1985, p. 45.

[94] Jens Holmgaard 1969, pp. 88, 97, 105. Among the merchants who at an early stage perceived and managed to exploit the possibilities that lay in a growing market in rural districts was Niels Ryberg, the son of a farmer, who became one of the richest people in eighteenth-century Denmark. Aage Rasch 1964, pp. 20–1.

[95] Clocks as a rarity in farmers' homes at the beginning of the eighteenth century: Poul Halkjær Kristensen 1946, p. 139. Cf. Edvard Holm 1885–6, II, p. 286. The period after 1750 was a heyday for clockmakers in Denmark. On clockmakers and the widening distribution of clocks during these years: D. Yde-Andersen 1953, p. 23 and passim; P. Christensen 1962–3; Jens Lampe 1980 and 1982. See also Gregers Begtrup 1803–12, III, p. 229, and S. P. Jensen 1986, p. 49.

172   *The New Denmark*

was common among the farming community even in the seventeenth century,[96] increased with the ever-widening distribution of newspapers,[97] almanacs, and informative,[98] entertaining[99] and edifying books throughout the country. When Bishop Balle in 1797 published the first part of his *Bibelske Søn- og Helligdagslæsninger* (Bible readings for Sundays and church festivals) in a large edition, a great many of his 36,047 subscribers to the 384-page publication were farmers: "Subscribers have otherwise mainly been farmers and craftsmen. In some parishes twenty to thirty, in others sixty to eighty, and in yet others up to two hundred copies have been sold."[100] It is difficult to imagine that after 1770 there can have been tenant farmers in Denmark who were unable to read.[101]

If we turn from the farmers' bookshelves to their gardens, other clear signs of progress become visible. The farmer's garden of the day was most neatly arranged – a late, rural echo of the dying baroque.[102] All in all, there is no doubt that the years after 1740, though often represented as a period of hardship, were most favourable for Denmark's approximately sixty thousand tenant farmers.

Regarding the overall social development between 1500 and 1800 as it took shape under the yoke of falling marginal production, it can be seen that just as a new physical landscape was created, a new social pattern also emerged. A new, strong farmer class crystallized beneath the old upper class of landowners. This changed the balance of social power in rural districts to the advantage of the farmers. Its effect was intensified because at the same time cottagers and farmhands became socially weaker and proletarianized. Due to the agricultural sector's absolute dominance,[103] the situation in rural society was of decisive importance in establishing a new social and political centre of gravity in Danish society as a whole.

The new balance in rural society was stabilized by the circumstance that social dividing lines became strictly hereditary. For-

---

[96] Troels Dahlerup 1986; Robert Molesworth 1694, p. 257.
[97] Thorkild Kjærgaard 1989b, pp. 217–24.
[98] Lis Toft Andersen 1986; Gerd Malling 1982; Thorkild Kjærgaard 1986.
[99] Rasmus Nyerup 1816.   [100] Harald Ilsøe 1989, p. 20. Cf. Ingrid Markussen 1988.
[101] Cf. Daniel Roche 1981, pp. 206–7.   [102] Grethe Jørgensen 1986.
[103] In 1769 the rural sector accounted for 82% of the population and the urban sector for 18%. In 1845 the ratio between the two sectors remained more or less the same, namely 79:21. Throughout the eighteenth century and for some time into the nineteenth century, the rural sector was still four times as large as the urban sector.

Labour Burden and Social Structure 173

merly, before family tenancy had become established, upward social mobility had formed part of the social pattern of the rural community. Cottagers and cottagers' sons who took over the tenure of a farm were no rarity in the 1720s and 1730s. By the end of the eighteenth century this was virtually impossible. As the Reverend H. J. C. Høegh wrote in 1795: "No-one born into the cottager class can ever nurture the slightest hope of rising into the farmer class."[104] On the contrary, downward social mobility was stronger than ever, and with the exclusion of all hope of later revenge for the expelled, or at least for their children, this downward mobility became even more threatening and depressing.

The previously mentioned farmer in West Funen, Peder Madsen, had ten children, of whom eight reached adulthood – seven boys and one girl. Of these seven sons, four became cottagers. One obtained employment at a manor, one married the widow of a farmer, and one took over the family farm. The daughter was mentally deficient and an invalid. Only three of the eight siblings – seven if one disregards the invalid daughter – succeeded in staying on their father's social level. The remainder were pressed downwards in society. In recognition of the inevitability of this massive negative social mobility we find North Zealand farmers in the 1780s reserving smallholdings for their children.[105]

6.3 FACTORS BEHIND THE RISING INFLUENCE OF THE FARMER CLASS DURING THE LAST HALF OF THE EIGHTEENTH CENTURY

A detailed analysis of the development during the period 1500–1800 in its various phases reveals a series of individual problems, among them the question, already touched upon, of how it proved possible for the urban population as well as for the unpropertied rural classes – cottagers and servants – to maintain their relatively strong position for so long. At the close of the period, after 1740, we meet the opposite problem, namely, the question of why proletarianization of the wage-earning groups took place with such force as to result in their bearing virtually the entire burden imposed on society by the falling marginal production, while at the same time the development proved to be extremely favourable to the farmer class.

[104] H. J. C. Høegh, quoted by Fridlev Skrubbeltrang 1978, p. 410.
[105] Karl Peder Pedersen 1985, pp. 35–6; Fridlev Skrubbeltrang 1940, p. 302.

174   *The New Denmark*

Considering that there was a large and increasing demand for labour at the end of the eighteenth century, it is surprising that it was not possible for the workers (who supplied the indispensable labour) to keep their employers at bay – at least to some extent – in the same way as had been possible during the decades around 1700. There is no simple explanation of why this extraordinary social debilitation of the lower classes took place. However, a number of circumstances exercised an influence in the same direction; together, they contributed to the development of pronounced class divisions in Denmark at the end of the eighteenth century – divisions that were to have far-reaching consequences for the country's social and political future. Four such decisive factors were inflation, the farm tenancy system, population increase, and the public expenditure and taxation policy.

Inflation. Price increases for agricultural products during the last half of the eighteenth century released a mechanism well known in inflationary societies: Wages and manorial dues increased at a lower rate than prices in general. The social group that derived more benefit than any other from this development was the tenant farmers, who were not only producers of agricultural products and employers of farmhands, servants, and cottagers but also payers of manorial dues. Tenant farmers were able to sell their products for rising prices, and at the same time, in their capacity as employers, they derived benefit from the lower rate of increase in wages. As rent payers tenant farmers also had the upper hand in an inflationary society, because, like wages, their obligations – the villeinage work, manorial dues, and fees they paid at the commencement of their lease – increased at a lower rate than prices for agricultural products.[106] This threefold advantage helps explain why it was possible for the farmer class to steer clear of the burden imposed on society by falling marginal productivity.

The tenancy system. Another factor that protected the farmer class was the tenancy system as it had developed in Denmark since the fourteenth century; not merely in the way already mentioned, that is, by favouring tenants during an inflationary period, but quite fundamentally, by serving to keep farms intact. Tenant farms could not be closed down[107] and were divided only to a limited extent into smaller farms of a half or a third of the size of the original.

[106] Thorkild Kjærgaard 1980, pp. 25–42.   [107] Hans Jensen 1936–45, I, pp. 17–18.

Labour Burden and Social Structure 175

The prohibition against closing down farms was broadly respected. Despite the protracted crisis for farmers during the seventeenth century and at the beginning of the eighteenth century, the net closure of farms during the period 1525–1774 did not even amount to 5 percent of the total number of farms. Of this percentage that closed down during the roughly 250 years between 1625 and 1774, more than one-third disappeared during the fifty years between 1650 and 1700.[108]

As appears from extant tenancy registers and other eighteenth-century sources, most estates had instances of 'half-farms' and in some cases also of one-third, two-thirds, and quarter farms. No investigations are available of the pattern and character of these farm divisions. In a very large number of cases probably all that happened was that two or three farmers ran a farm together for some period of time. At all events, these 'part farms' were relatively few in number and do not alter the overall picture of eighteenth-century Danish farms as a more or less uniform block of large farms.

The prohibition against closing down farms prevented the otherwise almost inevitable splitting up of farms during the distribution of land among children, which is what took place in countries where the farmers themselves controlled the land, for example, in Ireland.[109] If the division of farms into increasingly smaller units had taken place, Denmark too would have ended up with the dwarf-farm system that developed during the eighteenth century in Ireland and elsewhere in Europe.[110] It would have meant a fairer distribution within the rural community of the burdens from falling marginal production and would have prevented the farmer class from developing into a very powerful social factor. The consequences of this in regard to politicosocial development right up to the present day can only be guessed at.

In order to avoid harsh and distressing differentiation between children – something that inevitably occurred in the Danish farming class during the eighteenth century, when those who were unable to take over a farm were banished into the class of cottagers and servants[111] – there will always be great pressure on farmers to divide their property more or less equally. This is indicated not only by many examples abroad but also by the numerous instances of farms in Denmark being split up during the nineteenth century, when the owner-occupier principle gradually gained

[108] Gunnar Olsen 1957, pp. 172–5.   [109] T. C. Smout 1987, pp. 89–91.
[110] George Rudé 1975, p. 72.   [111] Chapter 6.2, section b.

176   The New Denmark

popularity and farmers secured control of the land.[112] The real friends of the Danish farmer class were, paradoxically, those who defended the tenancy system and opposed freehold. One such true friend of the Danish farmers was the landowner who declared to the Agricultural Commission of 1757 that freehold farmers should be "exterminated like weeds," and that it was undesirable that any farmer should own land, for in the case of inheritance and distribution, increasing numbers of plot owners would emerge and cause confusion.[113]

Population increase. A third factor that protected the farmer class was the growth in population. In all European countries, populations increased rapidly during the eighteenth century, and although Denmark was not among those most severely affected, its growth was none the less considerable.[114] Because the ratio between the urban and rural sectors remained more or less unchanged at 1:4;[115] because the farmer class was of an unalterable size (a result of the tenancy system); and because furthermore, there was no possibility (as there would be in the following century) for mass emigration to America, just about the entire growth in population was channelled into the farmhand and cottager group. There was simply nowhere else to go. The effects of this are demonstrated by the changes in the composition of the rural population during the eighteenth century.

Around 1700, the ratio between cottager and farmer families on the islands of Zealand and Møn was about 3:4; in other words, for every three cottager families there were four farmer families. Seventy years later the picture was reversed. By this time there were three cottager families on these same islands for every two farmer families. On a national basis, the ratio between cottager and farmer families at this time, around 1770, was about 1:1, cottager families in the rest of the country being comparatively fewer in number than on the islands of Zealand and Møn. This development continued unabated, and thirty years later, around 1800, the cottager population on the island of Zealand accounted for about 50 percent of the total rural population. The remainder was made up of farmers (28 percent), farmhands and servants (just under 20 percent), and certain smaller groups. On a national level, cot-

---

[112] A comparison of a group of tenant farms with a corresponding group of owner-occupier farms during the period from 1800 to 1850 reveals a strong tendency to division into smaller plots as a result of the introduction of a freeholder system. In 1850 this development had already reduced the typical owner-occupier farm to half the size of the typical tenant farm. Erland Porsmose 1987, pp. 89–91.

[113] Edvard Holm 1891–1912, III, 2, p. 91.   [114] Chapter 1.1.   [115] See n. 103.

Labour Burden and Social Structure

tagers accounted, around 1800, for just under 42 percent of the total rural population and thus in the course of the eighteenth century had become its largest individual group.[116] The steady growth of the cottager and farmhand class resulted in a steady increase in the availability of labour. In this way, the tendency towards higher nominal wages, which the increased demand for labour would normally have promoted, was curbed and for several decades remained at a standstill. More and more labour was needed in agriculture; even so, the labour market remained a buyer's market.

Public expenditure and taxation policy. Finally, a slower rate of increase in government expenditures, in conjunction with tax relief for farmers and tax increases for the farmhand class, played its part in the agglomeration of factors that shifted the social balance in the rural community during the last half of the eighteenth century. The change in the taxation system can be traced to the early 1730s, when political pressure forced the government to impose lower taxes on farmers, who had been hit by a prolonged depression.[117] The first forms of relief were introduced in 1731, after which the taxes paid by farmers, after decades of steady augmentation, ceased to rise. In 1745 the *hartkorn* tax on land was fixed at 1.5 rix-dollars per *tønde hartkorn*, and it remained unchanged until after 1800.[118] Allowing for inflation, this meant that taxes on land for farmers fell throughout the rest of the century. Around 1731, this tax represented about 9 percent of the value of a *tønde hartkorn;* around 1800, it was only 2 percent.[119]

Part of the lost income from taxes was recovered through the so-called extra tax levied in 1762, after which it became permanent. However, in contrast to *hartkorn* taxation, the 'extra tax' was a personal tax imposed on everybody – farmers, farmhands, and cottagers alike – they all paid the same.[120] The final result of the taxation policy in the eighteenth century was thus a reduction in taxes for farmers; this tax relief was financed, broadly speaking, by shifting taxes on to the growing group of farmhands and cottagers.[121] In conjunction with a more moderate government ex-

---

[116] Thorkild Kjærgaard 1980, p. 217; T. C. Smout 1987, p. 89.
[117] Jens Holmgaard 1977–8, pp. 40–1.
[118] Kristof Glamann 1966, p. 34; Thorkild Kjærgaard 1980, p. 203.
[119] Axel Linvald 1942, p. 208. Cf. Claus Rafner 1986.
[120] Birgit Løgstrup 1983, pp. 108–31.
[121] The function of the 'extra tax' as an instrument for transferring taxation from one class of taxpayer to another has already been pointed out by the eighteenth-century Danish economist O. D. Lütken, cf. Fridlev Skrubbeltrang 1940, p. 138.

178   *The New Denmark*

penditure policy towards the end of the eighteenth century, this rearrangement of the tax structure represented a departure from the previously familiar mechanism, by means of which the increasing tax pressure on farmers had resulted in overproduction of agricultural products (which in turn kept prices down), whereas increasing public consumption intensified the demand for labour.[122]

The four factors just mentioned – inflation, the tenancy farm system, population increase, and public expenditure and taxation policy – share the main responsibility for the social development that took place during the last half of the eighteenth century and hence for the emergence of the class-divided, Danish society in which industrialism expanded during the following century.

There were other elements as well that contributed to the transformation of the social landscape. For example, it is likely that serfdom, which prevailed on the eastern Danish islands until 1702, and its immediate successor, adscription, which applied to the whole country, may have had a local wage-distorting effect with repercussions on the social structure of the rural community.[123] But compared with the massive weight of the other factors, serfdom and adscription have been of only marginal importance and have not deserved the attention traditionally accorded to these measures.

[122] See, however, Jens Holmgaard 1992, pp. 44–5.
[123] On the wage-distorting effect of restrictions on the free movement of labour: Johan Hvidtfeldt 1938, pp. 28–32. Adscription introduced immediately after the abolition of serfdom: Jens Holmgaard 1988. The viewpoint put forward by Holmgaard is not, as he himself emphasizes, new, but was voiced as early as at the end of the nineteenth century by O. F. C. Rasmussen. However, Rasmussen's view – which was correct – was smothered in an argument with Edvard Holm during which the latter violently defended the traditional belief that adscription was not introduced until 1733, almost thirty years after the abolition of serfdom.

7

THE DISEASE PATTERN

The ecological revolution influenced not only the landscape and the social structure but also the world that is only visible under a microscope, the infinite microworld of bacteria and parasites. Some of the diseases that had terrorized the population for centuries disappeared – plague was one of these. Others were forced back; malaria, for example, which by the year 1800 was on its way out of the disease pattern. On the other hand, tuberculosis emerged from relative obscurity and was ready to assume the role of great killer as soon as the last remaining competitor, smallpox, had been eliminated; after a long preliminary attempt, this was finally achieved just after 1800. The nineteenth century became the century of tuberculosis.

7.1 PLAGUE

Plague is caused by the bacillus *Pasteurella pestis*.[1] *Pasteurella pestis* has its ecological basis far from human beings, both geographically and biologically, and comes into contact with them only in exceptional circumstances. A modus vivendi has never been established between human beings and the plague bacillus as it has with most of the other infectious diseases, AIDS being the latest and perhaps most important exception. This explains the violence with which plague attacks, and still attacks, when it goes astray amongst human beings, as occasionally happens, for example, in the western United States and in parts of the former Soviet Union.[2]

The plague bacillus has its focus, or permanent base, amongst burrow-dwelling rodents such as squirrels and beavers. Here the disease (which is passed from individual to individual by fleas) is

---

[1] Where no other source is indicated, the following information about plague is based on William H. McNeill 1977 and John T. Alexander 1980, pp. 1–8.

[2] The Danish daily *Politiken* 31 July 1990; *Weekly Epidemiological Record/Relevé épidémiologique hebdomadaire*, vol. 65, pp. 321–3 (19 Oct. 1990).

180   *The New Denmark*

enzootic, which means that it occurs permanently in the animal populations in question, where it mainly strikes the young. Mortality is limited, and after recovering from the disease the animal will normally remain immune for the rest of its life, corresponding to the well-known pattern in endemic children's diseases.

Sometimes plague spreads beyond its focus and infects other rodents, primarily rats, which normally do not have the disease and therefore have no immune response. If the disease takes a real hold amongst rats it will develop epizootically, and mortality will be high. If diseased rats and their infected fleas stray into the vicinity of human beings, a transfer of the disease may take place as a result of these fleas moving, either from necessity because the host rat dies, or by accident, to human beings, who then become infected through flea bites. The course of the disease, which is characterized by pronounced swelling of the lymphatic glands and an attack on the blood circulation system and related organs, is frequently fatal. Within one to five days, 60 to 90 percent of diseased persons die. So, concurrent with a plague epizootic among rats, an epidemic of plague amongst humans may also arise. It should be noted that in practice the disease can only be conveyed via fleas, and that direct infection from rat to rat or from human being to human being hardly ever occurs.

In the course of an epidemic of plague, however, a variant of the disease may develop that affects the lungs, and this is transferable from one human being to another by coughing and spitting. This disease, lung plague, presents a pathological pattern that is different in important respects from common plague. Lung plague is one of the most lethal infectious diseases known to medical science; if it is not treated with antibiotics within a few hours of its outbreak the mortality rate of its victims is virtually 100 percent.[3]

It is believed that the original focus of plague was on the southern slopes of the Himalayas overlooking the Bay of Bengal, where the disease has probably existed among rodents for millions of years. Later, via trade routes, a number of new foci have arisen where there were large uncultivated areas with sufficiently large populations of rodent species among which the disease could adapt itself and become stabilized as enzootic. The most recent of these foci is in the Rocky Mountains in the United States; this focus has arisen in the twentieth century, the disease having been brought to California by ship.

[3] John T. Alexander 1980, p. 3.

The Disease Pattern 181

If we examine the occurrence of plague in Denmark and North-west Europe, interest centres primarily on the focus to be found in Central Asia. When at its zenith, its area extended from the Ukraine in the west to China in the east. From this focus, which is believed to have arisen at the beginning of the present millennium as a result of the increasing number of links between India, China, and regions in Central Asia, plague was able to penetrate into Europe, the first occasion being in 1347, in the south of Europe, after which it spread throughout the European world of the day under the name of the Black Death. It reached Denmark in 1349. For the next 350 years, plague was a frequent and greedy guest in our country. In all it came about forty times, on average once every nine years.[4]

Like all other biological mechanisms, however, plague was dependent upon a complicated ecological balance. As this balance gradually became distorted as a result of the major changes that took place between 1500 and 1800, the disease lost its basis for existence and disappeared just as spontaneously as it had arisen. A decisive factor was the shortage of timber in large parts of Europe from the end of the sixteenth century, to which European communities reacted by replacing old wooden houses with new types of houses built either wholly or partly of bricks or stone. The replacement of wooden houses with brick houses made human dwellings less attractive to rats – a virtual *cordon sanitaire* was set up between human beings and rats and thus between human beings and plague. At the same time, the wave of intensified agricultural cultivation – not merely a Danish but also a wider phenomenon, one that spread to the Ukraine and western Russia – meant that burrow-dwelling rodents and hence the Eurasian focus of plague were pressed eastwards. The disease's lines of communication to Europe became longer and thus more fragile. What may also have played a part is the so-called Little Ice Age during the sixteenth, seventeenth, and eighteenth centuries, which forced the rodents southwards, removing the focus of the disease even farther from Europe.[5]

Evidence demonstrates that from the middle of the seventeenth century as plague came to Western Europe less frequently its area of distribution was reduced. It reached London for the last time in 1665 and Denmark in 1710–11 after an interval of thirty-four years, the longest since 1349. On this occasion the disease broke

---

[4] Gunnar Olsen and Poul Alkærsig 1965, p. 32; F. V. Mansa 1873.
[5] William McNeill 1977, pp. 172, 326. On the possible importance of climatic changes: John T. Alexander 1986, p. 247.

182 *The New Denmark*

out in Elsinore and Copenhagen.[6] The Great Fire of Copenhagen a few years later (1728) and the subsequent rebuilding of the town without the thatched roofs that previously had been a favourite rat habitat and from which rats and their fleas could drop on to people's heads enabled Copenhagen to close its gates to plague. During the remainder of the eighteenth century, plague continued to withdraw towards the southeast. The last major outbreak in our part of the world was the epidemic in Moscow in 1772.[7]

One frequently comes across the presumption that the disappearance of plague from Europe was linked to the fact that the brown rat ousted the black rat, because unlike the black rat the brown rat was not supposed to be receptive to plague. However, it does not appear to have been established that the brown rat is any less suited to carrying plague than the black rat. Moreover, plague disappeared before the brown rat ousted the black rat.[8]

7.2 MALARIA

Malaria, which today is known only outside Europe, was one of the most prominent diseases in the ecological system prevailing in Denmark prior to the period of major changes. Malaria was common during the Middle Ages and the Renaissance; Christiern Pedersen, in his book of medicine of 1533, describes in detail daily, three-day, and four-day variants of the disease, and so does Henrik Smith in his manual of medicine of 1577. In the latter work mention is also made of a malaria epidemic in 1556, the earliest instance in Denmark about which we have any information.[9]

In F. V. Mansa's account of the history of common diseases in Denmark until the beginning of the eighteenth century, mention is made of malaria epidemics in 1629, 1652, 1678, and 1680. In addition, several of the fever epidemics placed by Mansa in the typhus class may well have been malaria, because during the outbreak phase the symptoms of both diseases bear a certain similarity, especially high fever and the shivers.[10] Malaria occurred all over Denmark, though with a certain preponderance in low-lying

---

[6] William McNeill 1977, p. 172; Gunnar Olsen and Poul Alkærsig 1965, p. 32; F. V. Mansa 1842.

[7] John T. Alexander 1980. [8] William McNeill 1977, pp. 172–3.

[9] Vilhelm Møller-Christensen 1959; Christiern Pedersen 1533, pp. 77r–78v; Henrick Smid 1577, I, pp. 162v–175v. Cf. Paul Horstmann 1986, p. 70.

[10] F. V. Mansa 1873, pp. 297, 384–5, 476, 478–9.

The Disease Pattern 183

regions, primarily Lolland, which is why malaria is also sometimes referred to in Denmark as "Lolland fever."[11] Like plague, malaria was unable to resist the changes brought about by the ecological revolution.

In order to understand this it is necessary to know the main characteristics in the epidemiology of malaria.[12] The malaria parasite, *Plasmodium*, is introduced into human beings by stings from infected malaria mosquitoes of the genus *Anopheles*, of which the species *A. atroparvus* is the most important in Denmark and throughout most of Western and Central Europe – apart from Italy. The sting of the malaria mosquito introduces the plasmodia into the blood. After propagation in the liver the parasites return to the blood, whereupon they attack the red blood corpuscles and develop explosively in an asexual series of propagation.

A remarkable characteristic of *Plasmodium* parasites is that, according to the type in question, they develop in a regular cycle, as a rule lasting two or three days. When a cycle is over, all the parasites simultaneously attack new red blood corpuscles instead of the old, destroyed ones, which are now abandoned. During an attack of this kind the number of red blood corpuscles in the body is violently decimated. The result is one of the periodic attacks of acute fever preceded by shivers that gave rise to the disease's former name, ague. When the invasion of the red blood corpuscles is over, the newly placed *Plasmodium* parasites leave the body in peace; the attack of fever ceases, reproduction of red blood corpuscles can recommence, and the patient feels well until the next attack comes.

If the patient does not die and the disease is not renewed by new stings, it will gradually burn itself out, because the malaria parasite's asexual propagation has a limited course. To conclude its life cycle the parasite has to return to the malaria mosquito. A number of the parasites develop into sexed forms (male and female gametocytes), which the malaria mosquito sucks up when it stings a malaria-infected person. Not until the plasmodia have been brought back to the malaria mosquito can sexual propagation take place, and new parasites be formed, in the malaria mosquito, which, through infecting human beings, can keep the disease going.

The weak link in the life cycle of the malaria parasite is its dependence upon the malaria mosquito, not only for it to be trans-

[11] Poul Horstmann 1986, pp. 76–7.
[12] The following is based on L. J. Bruce-Chwatt 1985, pp. 12–165 and passim.

184   *The New Denmark*

ferred to a human being but also, through renewed stings, for it to be brought back to the malaria mosquito. Observations made by the Danish zoologist C. Wesenberg-Lund and others have shown that certain malaria mosquitoes perform this role unwillingly. This applies, for example, precisely to *A. atroparvus,* the most widespread malaria mosquito in Denmark. *A. atroparvus* is zoophile and prefers to sting cattle and other domestic animals rather than human beings. The opportunities for its doing so increased during the last half of the eighteenth century, when the green revolution brought about a pronounced increase in the number of herds of domestic animals in Denmark. This proved fatal to the malaria parasite because cattle do not develop malaria, and the parasite's life cycle was therefore severed.[13]

The results of this decline in malaria gradually became visible. In 1776 Peder Rhode referred to malaria as still the most frequent disease on the islands of Lolland and Falster:

> Their [the inhabitants'] most common disease is fever (which both strangers to, and natives of these parts seldom escape), of all kinds, somewhat severe, but not dangerous and seldom lethal; the three-day kind usually keeps recurring for a year or two; I have fought with it for a year-and-a-half, and finally cured it with digestive powders and thereafter prepared quinine.[14]

During the years 1815–24 malaria is referred to as having disappeared from the county of Maribo on the island of Lolland,[15] though it had not done so entirely. During the following years it flared up from time to time, and even in the 1860s there were still four to five thousand cases, a considerable number of them in Lolland. However, attacks became increasingly milder, and by the turn of the century malaria virtually was no longer part of the Danish disease pattern.[16]

There would appear to be no doubt that the green revolution, which decade by decade from the latter half of the eighteenth century increased the numbers of domestic animals in Denmark, was responsible for the withdrawal of malaria. Whenever animals were kept in stalls, as was the case wherever summer stall feeding was introduced, the effect was particularly beneficial, because zoophile malaria mosquitoes collect in stalls. Not until late in the nineteenth century, by which time the disease had long since been

[13] L. J. Bruce-Chwatt and J. de Zulueta 1980, p. 25; cf. p. 118; C. Wesenberg-Lund 1921, pp. 237–9. Cf. Søren Mørch 1982, pp. 185–6 and Poul Horstmann 1986, pp. 86–7.
[14] P. Rhode 1776–94, I, p. 12. Cf. Christian B. Reventlow 1902–3, I, p. 89.
[15] A. F. Bremer 1848, p. 129.   [16] Paul Horstmann 1986, pp. 74–7, 80–2.

The Disease Pattern 185

on the retreat, did medical treatment of malaria with quinine, and later, after the Second World War, with chloroquine, become common.[17]

The popular notion that malaria is expelled by drainage, which destroys the breeding grounds of the malaria mosqito, does not apply to Denmark, where the malaria mosquito is still to be found in large numbers, especially in cowhouses. As Wesenberg-Lund expressed it, "there cannot be many cowstalls that do not have sufficient anopheline material with which to furnish the inhabitants of the farm with malaria."[18] Water level control was a central phase in the green revolution, and therefore there was a connection between drainage operations and the disappearance of malaria, but in Denmark it was indirect.

In respect of Italy, the picture is more complicated as this country has a number of anthropophile species of the malaria mosquito. Here, malaria continued to be a major disease until after the Second World War.[19] On account of the presence of anthropophile malaria mosquitoes it is not enough to explain the continued existence of malaria in Italy, as has been attempted by William McNeill, by the smallness of the cattle population, which in turn is supposed to be due to the fact that the new forage crops were not cultivated in Italy on account of the summer drought.[20] Incidentally, it is not correct that the new forage crops were not grown in Italy – on the contrary, Italy was an important centre for their development.[21] But if the area under examination is confined to Denmark and the remainder of northwestern Europe, where the most important insect vector for malaria was the zoophile *A. atroparvus*, it may be justifiable to regard the disappearance of malaria and the triumphal progress of cultivated clover as two sides of the same thing.

7.3 TUBERCULOSIS

Tuberculosis is one of the world's ancient diseases. Bone distortions that can probably be ascribed to tubercular infection have been observed in fossils originating from long-extinct Pleistocene animals, such as cave bears and cave lions.[22] Tuberculosis has fol-

---

[17] C. Wesenberg-Lund 1921. On the subject of medicine, especially the significance of quinine: C. Wesenberg-Lund 1921, p. 236; Svend Heinild 1979, p. 16 and 1989a; Jens Larsen (I) 1977, p. 26. Views differing in some respects from these are in Poul Horstmann 1986, pp. 89–92. On malaria's simultaneous withdrawal from England and the rest of northwest Europe: William McNeill 1977, pp. 246–7.

[18] C. Wesenberg-Lund 1921, p. 236. Cf. Jens Larsen (I) 1977, pp. 25–6.

[19] L. J. Bruce-Chwatt 1985, pp. 127–65.   [20] William McNeill 1977, p. 247.

[21] See Chapter 3.7, section a.

[22] Aidan Cockburn 1963, pp. 219–20; S. E. Bendix-Almgreen 1964, pp. 138–40.

186   *The New Denmark*

lowed humans since their beginnings, and it belongs to the small group of diseases that existed in both the New and the Old World prior to the discovery of America.[23]

Tuberculosis – also known as phthisis, consumption, scrofula, and pleuropneumonia – is an infectious ailment belonging to the group of diseases common to animals and human beings, so-called zoonoses. The infection can be passed from one human being to another and also from animals to human beings, especially from cattle via milk and other diary products, whereas it seems the infection does not pass from human beings to animals.[24] However, the outbreak of the infection would appear to depend on general social conditions. If living standards deteriorate, no matter whether as a result of poorer dwellings, reduced heating, malnutrition, longer working hours, or worsened working conditions, tuberculosis advances; in the same way, the disease will recede in societies where living conditions improve.[25]

The prevailing mood in society also seems to have an influence on tuberculosis. René Dubos, one of the best-known physicians of our century, expressed this as follows: "If hope flourishes in the hearts of men, tuberculosis will withdraw as it has always done, spontaneously, when life has become easier and happier."[26] Dubos was not the first to see this connection. As early as 1809 we find corresponding views expressed by Heinrich Callisen, Denmark's first public health physician. After referring to this "unfortunately so widespread and consuming disease of the chest organs that is to be found amongst people of all stations," he adds: "Perhaps in later years, poverty, fears about nutrition and dark prospects for the future could have contributed to increase this disease amongst us."[27]

As just demonstrated, the period between 1500 and 1800 was characterized by a number of factors that promote tuberculosis. A pronounced increase in human population and in the size of cattle herds increased the risk of infection.[28] In addition, living standards deteriorated in many respects, both objectively and subjectively. The objective deterioration is obvious: poorer dwellings, less heating, longer working hours, and inferior nutrition for the ma-

---

[23] Folke Henschen 1965, pp. 100–1.
[24] J. Arthur Myers and James H. Steele 1969, pp. 57–72; H. C. Bendixen 1944, pp. 338–42. There are two mycobacteria that can attack human beings: *M.hominis* (belonging to human beings) and *M.bovis* (belonging to cattle).
[25] René Dubos and Jean Dubos 1953, pp. vii, 208–28; Kjeld Tørning 1945, pp. 125–31.
[26] René Dubos and Jean Dubos 1953, p. 167. Cf. Svend Heinild 1989b, p. 1253.
[27] Henrich Callisen 1807–9, II, p. 543.   [28] H. C. Bendixen 1944, p. 279.

The Disease Pattern

187

jority of the population. The subjective deterioration of living conditions is represented by the despondency that must have been engendered, particularly in the young, by increasingly harder toil, deteriorating living standards and an ever-present fear of poverty and social degradation. Under these circumstances it was only to be expected that the position of tuberculosis in the Danish disease pattern would undergo major changes during the three-hundred years from 1500 to 1800 – and this, in fact, seems to have been the case.

During the sixteenth century and the beginning of the seventeenth century, tuberculosis was not unknown in Denmark. In his manual of medicine of 1577 Henrik Smith describes tuberculosis as "the disease through which man becomes dessicated and disappears, fades away, leaving no more than skin and bone."[29] But there is nothing to indicate that tuberculosis was particularly widespread in either the sixteenth or the seventeenth centuries, at all events, not among human beings. Tuberculosis is not even mentioned in F. V. Mansa's book on common Danish diseases, which covers the period up to the beginning of the eighteenth century. Not until the end of the seventeenth century are there indications that tuberculosis was beginning to attract attention in the very active and wideawake medical milieu in Copenhagen; a doctoral thesis on the subject was defended in 1688.[30]

During the seventeenth century, in England and France, where the ecological crisis and the social development connected with it were more advanced, tuberculosis undoubtedly played a more important role than it did in Denmark. The laying on of hands by the king, especially against scrofula, a type of tuberculosis that produces violent swellings on the neck, throat, and shoulders (*scrofa* is the Latin for sow), was much sought after in both England and France. One of the disadvantages that the Cromwellian period (1649–60) imposed upon the English people was that it was no longer possible to obtain "the king's touch." This was rectified with the ascension of Charles II, who during the ensuing twenty-two years performed the act one hundred thousand times.[31]

We have virtually no information about the development of tuberculosis in Denmark during the first half of the eighteenth century, but by about 1750 it had established itself as a common disease. In Heinrich Callisen's survey of the causes of mortality in

---

[29] Henrick Smid 1577, I, pp. 65v–67r.
[30] Nicolaus Erici 1688. This work was the beginning of a large body of Danish specialist literature on tuberculosis. Cf. *Biblioteca Danica* I, pp. 856–7.
[31] René Dubos and Jean Dubos 1953, pp. 6–8; Vilhelm Møller-Christensen 1963, pp. 92–3.

188   *The New Denmark*

Copenhagen, published in 1809 as the first attempt to compile Danish mortality statistics, tuberculosis, under various names, was responsible for 19.2 percent of all deaths in the decade 1749–58. During the ensuing years the incidence rose, and during the decade 1799–1808, the last covered by Callisen's statistics, 22.6 percent of all deaths in Copenhagen were attributed to tuberculosis.[32] At the end of the eighteenth century the annual mortality rate ascribed to tuberculosis in one form or another was more than 800 per 100,000 inhabitants.

Due to the almost inevitable gaps in the older material, Callisen may easily, in the course of extrapolating backwards from the better-recorded years after 1800, have been led to overrate tuberculosis frequency during the 1750s and 1760s. Accordingly, the rate of increase during the period 1749–1808 may in reality have been considerably greater than indicated by Callisen's figures.

Tuberculosis is a disease that generally emerges more strongly in large urban societies with massive conglomerations of human beings rather than in rural districts, where the paths of infection are longer and therefore weaker.[33] Taking the country as a whole, the mortality rate for tuberculosis around 1800 must therefore be estimated as having been somewhat lower than in Copenhagen.

Little is known about the causes of death in rural districts during the eighteenth century, though vicars would occasionally add relevant information in parish registers. The Vonsild parish register shows that tuberculosis, here referred to variously as inflammation of the chest, tightness of the chest, and consumption, was found in the vicinity of Kolding during the period 1659–1701.[34] The historian Hans Christian Johansen found a total of 246 cases in the various rural parishes during the 1740s and 1750s in which the cause of death is recorded. According to this material, 11 of these 246 deaths were caused by consumption or disease of the chest organs, that is, by tuberculosis. Adding dysentery and violent haemorrhage, which often were probably due to tubercular sufferings, we arrive at a figure of 20 out of 246 deaths that can be assumed with reasonable certainty to have been connected with tuberculosis, in other words, 8 percent.[35]

[32] Henrich Callisen 1807–9, II, pp. 656–9.
[33] The relatively more forceful appearance of tuberculosis in towns and urbanized societies can be observed all the way back to antiquity. H. S. Collins and D. Armstrong 1986, p. 193.
[34] Hans H. Worsøe 1982.   [35] Hans Christian Johansen 1975, pp. 124–5.

The Disease Pattern
189

The figures for the development of tuberculosis in Denmark correspond more or less with information available from Sweden and England. In Sweden, which in 1749 was the first country in the world to introduce death certificates stating the cause of death and therefore possesses the most dependable mortality statistics for the eighteenth century, tuberculosis increased greatly between 1750 and 1830. During the period 1750–70, deaths resulting from "lung disease," "consumption," and "disease of the chest organs" for the whole country amounted to about 475 per 100,000 inhabitants. Up to 1830, tuberculosis as a cause of death rose to almost 600 per 100,000 inhabitants. However, various changes in disease nomenclature make it impossible to establish a precise figure for the increase.[36] In England it is believed that tuberculosis was the cause of 13 percent of all deaths in 1715. Around the year 1800 this figure had more than doubled. Phthisis alone was estimated at this time to be the cause of 25 percent of all deaths in England.[37]

At the beginning of the nineteenth century tuberculosis reached the level that proved to be its maximum. Both the green revolution and the energy and raw materials revolution gradually prevailed over population growth. Living standards finally ceased to deteriorate in our part of the world, a fact that was to influence tuberculosis mortality. In England it is estimated that the mortality rate for tuberculosis began to fall just after 1800.[38] A parallel development may be assumed to have taken place in Denmark. In 1835 the mortality rate for phthisis in Copenhagen was 350 per 100,000 inhabitants. Even giving a broad margin to include deaths caused by other variants of tuberculosis there would appear to be no doubt that an improvement had taken place since the beginning of the nineteenth century.[39]

The theory that an all-time low in living standards was reached at the beginning of the nineteenth century, and that during the following decades there was a slight improvement in standards and thus probably a decline in tuberculosis, is supported by the fact that the average height of newly enrolled Danish conscripts dropped to its lowest point in 1815. Moreover, during the years up to 1848 a slight increase can be observed in the height of young men called up for military service.[40] By the 1870s the situation had

---

[36] Gustav Sundbärg 1905, pp. 169–70 and passim. Cf. Immanuel Ilmoni 1846–53, III, p. 588.
[37] René Dubos and Jean Dubos 1953, p. 9. Cf. Vilhelm Møller-Christensen 1963, p. 96.
[38] René Dubos and Jean Dubos 1953, p. 231.
[39] Knud Faber 1926, p. 49.
[40] L. G. W. Thune 1848. Cf. Peter Riismøller 1952, pp. 30–1.

190   *The New Denmark*

clearly improved. Only 12 to 14 percent of all deaths were due to tuberculosis, and measured in the number of deaths per 100,000 inhabitants the figure was now down to about 200, which was less than half the probable level sixty or seventy years earlier. It continued to drop during the ensuing years. In 1920 the mortality rate for tuberculosis in Denmark among the urban population was reduced to 105 per 100,000 inhabitants, and in recent years hardly anybody has died of the disease.[41]

It should be noted that the most pronounced decrease in mortality from tuberculosis took place before a systematic campaign against the disease was launched in Europe with the help of sanatoriums and other methods at the end of the nineteenth century. This confirms that tuberculosis is first and foremost a social disease. Its recrudescence during the eighteenth century and its gradual disappearance during the nineteenth century were to a large extent the result of the general social development. There is nothing to indicate that the tuberculosis mortality rate today would have been very much above zero even if the medical world had taken no action against the disease.[42] It was not medical science, but the ecological revolution (and, later, the welfare state's endeavours to bring about an acceptable distribution of the results) that forced tuberculosis to withdraw in Denmark almost to the point of extermination. For this reason, no physicians would be able to prevent tuberculosis from returning if the welfare state were to disappear. This is demonstrated by modern experiences in affluent societies with high levels of social inequality and violent social anxiety. In the United States, although more money is spent in the health sector per capita than in any other country, tuberculosis is increasing and is now killer No. 1 among the infectious diseases.[43]

Tuberculosis is closely related to leprosy, which is similarly an infectious disease whose impact depends upon social conditions.[44] The violent wave of leprosy that swept across Europe during the late Middle Ages – Denmark also suffered severely – was undoubtedly the outcome of the deterioration of social conditions that followed the agricultural expansion during the twelfth and thirteenth centuries. Correspondingly, the

---

[41] V. Falbe-Hansen and William Scharling 1885–91, I, p. 465; Knud Faber 1926, p. 35, states that tuberculosis mortality in the 1870s was 213 per 100,000 inhabitants in the urban population. Figures for the rural population are not known, but were undoubtedly lower. A tuberculosis mortality of 200 per 100,000 inhabitants for the entire population as suggested here seems probable; Svend Heinild 1979, p. 16.

[42] Cf. Svend Heinild 1989a–b.

[43] H. S. Collins and D. Armstrong 1986, p. 202; World Health Organization, press release No. 148, Oct. 1990: "World Tuberculosis Toll is Rising."

[44] Folke Henschen 1965, pp. 109–17, especially p. 117; Vilhelm Møller-Christensen 1961–2. Cf. Erik Mønster 1951–2 and René Dubos and Jean Dubos 1953, pp. 262–3.

The Disease Pattern 191

disappearance of leprosy during the fourteenth century is a significant (though seldom noticed) indication of the considerable improvement in social standards that arose after the Black Death had decimated the population to a size more in proportion to the resources available.

It is uncertain why it was tuberculosis and not leprosy that gained a foothold during the eighteenth century as the major social disease. A factor that may have played a part is that leprosy appears to be linked to comparatively warmer regions, as can be observed in modern times.[45] In other words, it is conceivable that the mild climate during the Middle Ages pushed the leprosy border further north in the same way that the colder climate during the Little Ice Age in the sixteenth, seventeenth, and eighteenth centuries may have pushed the disease further south again. However, this is still not a full explanation, for although leprosy disappeared completely from Denmark, and did not return during the eighteenth century, it continued to strike in Norway, where it had a considerable distribution until late in the nineteenth century. Other factors besides climate must therefore have influenced leprosy's geographical distribution.

That tuberculosis is a zoonotic disease may have played a part. The ever-growing herds of cattle, large numbers of which were probably already infected during the seventeenth century, provided tubercular infection with an increasingly wider basis and, consequently, an advantage over leprosy, which, being an exclusively human disease, was unable to take advantage of the new biological possibilities created by agricultural expansion in Denmark and in neighbouring countries to the south and west. It was different in Norway, where growth in the agricultural sector was more modest and the relative competitiveness of leprosy was accordingly better. A compromise between the two closely related diseases was not possible; they seem to exclude one another to the extent that the appearance of the one provides protection against the other.[46]

7.4 SMALLPOX

The disappearance of smallpox was the only major change in the disease pattern between 1500 and 1800 that was not due to the microlandscape's spontaneous and unpredictable reactions to the ecological revolution. It was due to medical science. The first step was inoculation, based on the controlled transfer of variola from one individual to another. Inoculation spread in Europe after 1710 and came to Denmark in the 1750s.[47] The second step was vacci-

---

[45] Vilhelm Møller-Christensen 1961–2, p. 20; Folke Henschen 1965, p. 117.
[46] R. Chaussinand 1948, pp. 431, 434, and passim; Folke Henschen 1965, p. 117; Aidan Cockburn 1963, pp. 220–3.
[47] Julius Petersen 1896, pp. 80–206.

192   *The New Denmark*

nation, which was far more reliable as it consisted of the controlled inoculation of the less virulent cowpox (the word 'vaccination' comes from the Latin for cow, *vacca*). Like tuberculosis, smallpox belongs to the diseases that are common to both human beings and animals.

The vaccination technique was developed at more or less the same time in several places in Europe – the rule rather than the exception in nearly all major scientific and technical advances since the Renaissance. Among others, the Holsteiner Peter Plett introduced the technique in 1791, a few years before the experiments made by the British physician Edward Jenner in 1796. It is Jenner's name, however, that came to be associated with the new vaccination technique. Jenner wrote a dissertation that, within a few years, made vaccination widely known in the world so that smallpox was eradicated with astonishing speed in many places, including Denmark. Plett gave up when he was ignored by the medical faculty in Kiel, to which he had submitted a report on his experiments.[48]

Inoculation and vaccination were the results of systematic medical science, which in turn had evolved from the scientific revolution of the sixteenth and seventeenth centuries. The same scientific revolution stimulated the mining and blast furnace technologies that had made the energy and raw materials revolution possible and the systematic botanical and agricultural sciences from which the green revolution derived nourishment.[49] Seen in this wider perspective, the disappearance of smallpox and the ecological revolution unite in the common European pool of knowledge that developed at an explosive rate from the middle of the fifteenth century with the invention of a new and highly efficient system for collecting, preserving, developing, and disseminating information: the printing press.[50]

7.5 THE CHANGING PATTERN OF DISEASE AND ITS IMPACT ON SOCIAL LIFE

The change in the disease pattern between 1500 and 1800 altered the character of human sufferings. One of the most famous passages about suffering during illness is to be found in Dante Alighieri's *Divina Commedia* and concerns malaria. It is in the "Inferno," Canto XXIX, where the Poet, close to the lowest circle of Hell, meets vari-

[48] Ibid., pp. 209–10; Erik Jacobsen 1987, p. 138.
[49] H. Butterfield 1957, pp. 185–6 and passim.
[50] Elizabeth L. Eisenstein 1979; Thorkild Kjærgaard 1986; Chapter 10.

The Disease Pattern 193

ous forgers. The wailing of these forgers, which is so terrible that Dante has to cover his ears with his hands, reminds him of the horrible sight that could meet one's eyes during the summer months in Italy's malaria regions:

> Qual dolor fora, se de li spedali
> di Valdichiana tra 'l luglio e 'l settembre
> e di Maremma e di Sardigna i mali
> fossero in una fossa tutti 'nsembre
>
> As were the torment, if each lazar-house
> Of Valdichiana, in the sultry time
> 'Twixt July and September, with the isle
> Sardinia and Maremma's pestilent fen,
> Had heaped their maladies all in one foss
> Together;[51]

Malaria disappeared, but other sufferings took its place. The Swedish poet Carl Michael Bellman's farewell poem "To Father Movitz, during his illness, consumption" paints unmercifully and in every detail, down to the unbearable stench, the pathological picture presented by a patient in the advanced stages of phthisis:

> Golden yellow skin, dully glowing small cheeks
> Sunken chest and flattened shoulder-blades
> Show me your hand; each vein, blue and plump,
> Lies damp and swollen, as in a bath
> Your hand is sweaty, the veins rigid.
>
> Heavens! You are dying, your cough scares me
> Emptiness, resonance, your bowels rumble.
> Your tongue is white, your anxious heart beats fast
> Soft as sponge your sinews, marrow and skin
> Breathe at me! Ye gods, the stench from your ashes.[52]

The gradual elimination of diseases like plague and smallpox, which time and again had caused demographic development to make sudden, violent spurts,[53] resulted in a more stable population curve and faster demographic growth.

The disappearance of plague would appear to have been of great importance to the public mood: Whereas the disease was still rag-

---

[51] The "Inferno," Canto XXIX, 46–49; this English rendering is from the 1805 translation by Henry Francis Cary.

[52] Carl Michael Bellman 1790 (Epistle No. 30).

[53] Eino Jutikkala has demonstrated by means of a late Finnish example the extent to which demographic havoc could be caused by an epidemic (1983).

194   *The New Denmark*

ing in the rest of the world, our part of it had become a safer place in which to live. This fostered European self-confidence and optimism. It was believed that the disappearance of plague was a result of strict quarantine regulations enforced since the seventeenth century. Contemporary European observers took this as evidence that Europe was superior to the rest of the world. Montesquieu, for example, heaped scorn upon the Turks because they had been unable to organize a proper quarantine system and were therefore unable keep the plague at bay.[54] This partly explains the light-hearted and cheerful mood, the lightness and bluffness of outlook, and the lively, critical, and ironical way of thinking so prominent during the first decades of the eighteenth century[55] and as represented so eminently by French writers like Montesquieu and Voltaire, and by Ludvig Holberg, who was the leading Enlightenment personality in Scandinavia. It is also tempting to see the bold and playful rococo style that characterized both art and architecture as a reflection of the changing pattern of disease.

The quarantine regulations introduced across Europe during the seventeenth century with the aim of preventing the plague from spreading did no more than control the movements of merchandise and people. Flea-infested rats, however, which came from towns and districts where the plague had broken out and were the real culprits, were largely free to leave, via mooring ropes, the hundreds of ships that constantly lay in quarantine, first in one port and then in another, all over Europe. In reality, the quarantine arrangements had no influence on plague whatsoever. It is strangely ironic that the European sense of self-confidence and optimism at the beginning of the eighteenth century, arising partly from the belief that it had been possible to 'drive out' the plague, was based on an illusion.

The elimination of plague made life less dangerous. Later in the eighteenth century the gradual decrease in the number of smallpox cases was probably one of the main reasons why child mortality was reduced throughout most of Europe, including Denmark.[56] One probable consequence of the improved chances of survival would appear to have been the strengthening of emotional ties, not only between spouses but also between parents and their children; this has been pointed out by historian Edward Shorter as one

[54] Montesquieu 1748, I, pp. 248–50.   [55] Paul Hazard 1939–40.
[56] Letter from Hans Christian Johansen 26 Sept. 1990. Cf. Edward Shorter 1975, pp. 201–2, and Lawrence Stone 1977, p. 69.

The Disease Pattern 195

of the characteristic features of mental development during the eighteenth century.[57]

As long as plague and smallpox were frequently returning guests there was good reason to warn spouses, as a seventeenth-century English moralist did, against loving each other "inordinately, because death will soon part you."[58] In a world free of these diseases it was more acceptable to give vent to one's emotions freely, as demonstrated by the deluge of best-selling novels, headed by Samuel Richardson's *Pamela; or Virtue Rewarded* (1740), that flowed over eighteenth-century Europe.[59] When the fear of a sudden death faded into the distance, a mother could also permit herself to display love for her child with a greater sense of security than before.[60]

Not all aspects of the change in the pattern of disease were positive, however. The demographic reverberations certainly disappeared, and children lived in greater security. On the other hand, mortality among young people increased. As the eighteenth century gradually drew to its close, tuberculosis, which often strikes young people in their twenties and thirties,[61] cast a dark shadow over social life. People became painfully aware that death could come unexpectedly. Death struck not only old people, as it should in the natural order of things, but also, most unreasonably, young people. In the very years when they were about to live their lives in earnest, they ran the risk of wasting away. No one could feel secure, for even though tuberculosis was a lower class disease, its focus of infection was so massive that it struck at all levels of society.

The elegiac mood so characteristic of the end of the eighteenth century undoubtedly stemmed in part from the advance of tuberculosis during these years. An early example of the melancholy that replaced the robust optimism of the Voltairian period is Edward Young's *The Complaint; or Night Thoughts on Life, Death and Immortality* (1742–5), which is full of nocturnal graveyard scenes and laments about early death. This doleful poem was a tremendous success all over Europe, including Denmark, where it was

[57] Edward Shorter 1975, pp. 168–204. Cf. Ib Olsen 1983, p. 173; Kirsten Nannestad 1990, p. 137; and Tyge Rothe 1795.

[58] Lawrence Stone 1977, p. 215.

[59] Cf. Hakon Stangerup 1936, pp. 207–411. In Denmark, the translation of *Pamela; or Virtue Rewarded* was a tremendous success.

[60] See, for example, Johannes Ewald's poem of 1769 "Tanker da Arveprinds Frederik giennemgik Smaa-Koppernes Indpodning" (Thoughts on the Occasion of Prince Frederik's Inoculation against Smallpox), Johannes Ewald 1969, I, pp. 266–7.

[61] René Dubos and Jean Dubos 1953, p. 237 (graph no. 10); Aidan Cockburn 1963, p. 224.

196   *The New Denmark*

translated twice within the space of a few years (1767 and 1783), an honour seldom accorded to a poem the length of a novel in a foreign language. Furthermore, Young's poem was imitated far and wide, for example, by the Danish poet Johannes Ewald in his "Natte-Tanker" (Night thoughts).[62]

Not only in late-eighteenth-century literature do we meet a pronounced tendency to cultivate melancholy and emphasize the transitoriness of life. It is also to be found in gardening. The new 'landscape garden' that emerged at the end of the eighteenth century, inspired by English models, not only reflected the longing for the 'unspoilt nature' that had now become inaccessible[63] but also became a way of expressing the elegiac mood of the times. The hermit's huts, artificially constructed ruins, and tombstones located at suitable points reminded the garden wanderer, lost in reveries about the relationship between culture and nature, that culture, no matter how powerful and impressive it might appear, still had its limits: Everything human, everything created by human hands, was perishable.

A correspondingly self-contradictory mood of *Weltschmerz*, in which culture, nature, and transitoriness were played against each other, is reflected in the interest in classical antiquity and its memorials, which enjoyed a tremendous revival at the end of the eighteenth century. On the one hand, the Greek and Roman societies of antiquity were ideals for art, architecture, and politics, proof that humans could achieve the sublime and that a better society was possible.[64] On the other hand, antique ruins were ominous reminders of the impermanence of all things. Where could one better or more poignantly comprehend not only life's rich possibilities but also its limitations, than in Rome, city of former glories, where nothing was now left but a miserable and corrupt papal state? The thirty-year-old Danish poet B. S. Ingemann, who had seen his mother, three brothers, and a niece carried off by pulmonary tuberculosis, was overcome by emotion at the sight of the Forum Romanum during his visit to Rome in 1818 and burst out:

> Behold a heap of ruins – yet thence did
> Cicero's speeches ring. Where men of power
> Did once debate is called the pasture[65] now.
> Are all these stones thy glory then? Rome![66]

---

[62] Johannes Ewald 1969, V, pp. 87–9.   [63] Chapter 5.1.
[64] Torben Damsholt 1972; Patrick Kragelund 1988 and 1989.
[65] Cattle grazed in the Forum until the beginning of the nineteenth century, hence the name "Campo Vaccino."
[66] Quoted in Louis Bobé 1935–7, II, p. 33.

The Disease Pattern

Those Danes who, unlike Ingemann, had no chance of visiting Rome, and who were unable to linger in precious landscape gardens with artificial ruins, had the possibility of cultivating an elegiac mood by going to Frederiksborg Castle in North Zealand. This old royal castle, by now almost abandoned, could arouse memories of former pomp and magnificence almost comparable with those of Rome. And although the castle was still not a ruin in the way of ancient Rome, one could always, as the Danish historian Christian Molbech did when he visited the castle in 1811, give oneself up to premonitions of its future ruined state.[67]

Famous exponents of the melancholy-cum-sentimental moods that arose in the shadow of tuberculosis were the three greatest heroes of European Romanticism – "the young dead" – Percy Bysshe Shelley, John Keats, and Lord Byron. The public reconciled itself to the objective realities of life in the short, hectic lives of these poets. One could even, by regarding tuberculosis as a variant of "the disease of love," idealize the disease and early death as expressions of a particularly rich emotional life. Lord Byron (about whom the Danish sculptor Bertel Thorvaldsen ironically remarked, "He always tried to be so unhappy!"[68]) is even said to have expressed the wish to die of consumption, for then all the ladies would say: "Look at that poor Byron, how interesting he looks in dying!"[69] Unlike Keats and Shelley, Byron had the misfortune not to suffer from tuberculosis.

Religious life too was influenced by the changing pattern of disease. Just as the Voltairian period's lighthearted flirtation with deistic ideas was supported by the less aggressive and changeable disease pattern that emerged from the end of the seventeenth century, the stricter religious outlook that made its appearance towards the end of the eighteenth century was probably influenced by the new, ominous characteristics of the disease pattern that presented themselves with the advance of tuberculosis. The revivalist movements that arose throughout Europe around 1800 may well have had some of their roots, as emphasized by the Danish ecclesiastical historian P. G. Lindhardt, in social developments,[70] but they also closely bound up with the changing pattern of disease.

---

[67] Mette Bligaard 1987, p. 10.   [68] Erik Lassen 1989, p. 137.
[69] Susan Sontag 1978, p. 31. Cf. H. D. Chalke 1962.   [70] P. G. Lindhardt 1978.

8

POWER

Parce que vous êtes un grand seigneur, vous vous
croyez un grand génie! . . . noblesse, fortune, un
rang, des places; tout cela rend si fier! qu'avez-vous
fait pour tant de bien? Vous vous êtes donné
la peine de naître, et rien de plus: du reste homme
assez ordinaire!

Beaumarchais, 1784

We both have – my friend! – the same goal: to overthrow
the power of the nobility and the despotism of privilege and
to consolidate the liberty of the people; . . . the Government
must be brought to the point where it feels that the Throne
has no other reliable support upon which to rest than
the productive classes, the prosperity and love of truly
active citizens.

Knud Lyne Rahbek to P. A. Heiberg, 1794

On the periphery of the complexity of nonlinear transformations
created by the ecological revolution lay a new and different power
structure. During the period 1500–1800 an intense struggle for
power took place between two important factions within the Danish elite: a decentralized, aristocratic faction whose origins were
lost in the tribal society of prehistory, and a new, rival faction gathered round the central royal power, whose existence cannot be
traced further back than to the ninth or tenth century. The ecological revolution became a factor of great importance to the outcome of this struggle.

8.1 THE DANISH POWER STRUCTURE
FROM THE VIKING AGE UNTIL 1766:
THE RULE OF THE ARISTOCRACY

As far back as records can be traced, the power structure in ancient
Danish society was decentralized, dominated by local and regional
chieftains and aristocrats against whom the central royal power
was incapable of asserting itself to any serious degree.[1] Canute the

---

[1] On the power struggle between the throne and the aristocracy in general during the Middle Ages: Aksel E. Christensen 1945. Christensen's thesis about a development marked
by breaches and mutations has been contested by John Danstrup (1947–9b) who stresses
the stable characteristics in medieval Danish society. Cf. Thomas Riis 1977.

198

Power   199

Holy's attempt to strengthen royal power after his accession to the throne in 1080 ended in open rebellion: He was murdered in 1086 in St. Alban's Church, Odense.[2]

During the following centuries, Danish monarchs made repeated attempts to consolidate the royal power. However, powerful landed magnates, together with the rival candidates for the throne who were associated with them, put up such overwhelming resistance that it proved impossible for the monarchs to do so. In 1282 the limited power of the throne compared with that of the aristocracy was codified by the coronation charter of Erik V (Klipping) and so became part of Denmark's political system. This charter obliged the king to respect the rights of the nobles and every year hold "that Parliament which is called Court."[3] During the next few years parliamentary intervention was used to restrict the royal government's legal and administrative powers even further. Finally, in 1286, Erik was murdered at Finderup Lade near Viborg, probably because he continued to pursue an independent royal policy that conflicted with the spirit of the coronation charter and with subsequent agreements made with the nobles – in other words, for reasons similar to those that precisely two hundred years earlier had led to the murder of Canute the Holy.

After Erik's murder the throne would appear to have largely acknowledged that its role was to establish a balance and mediate between the various aristocratic factions rather than to strive to be the kingdom's sovereign ruler. However, there were occasional spasms of resistance. Valdemar Atterdag (reigned 1340–75), for example, and, to an even greater extent, his daughter Margrethe I (reigned 1387–1412) nurtured strong feelings about the elevated state, dignity, and authority of the monarchy, and they both tried energetically, with the help of a royal chancellery staffed by loyal civil servants, to curb the aristocracy. Also, under Christian I (reigned 1448–81) there was a violent struggle for power between the king and the aristocracy that culminated in the 1460s. Like Margrethe, Christian I sought in the course of his conflict with the aristocracy not merely to play off the various dominating aristocratic families against each other but also to ally himself with the lesser nobility and the farming community.[4]

---

[2] Aksel E. Christensen 1977, pp. 247–8.
[3] Aksel E. Christensen 1945, pp. 87–97; Helge Paludan 1977, pp. 461–6.
[4] Troels Dahlerup 1971, p. 71, and 1989, pp. 213–20; Erik Ulsig 1985, p. 270; Kristian Erslev 1882; Stewart Oakley 1972, p. 81; Harry Christensen 1983, pp. 113–15.

200   *The New Denmark*

The endless trouble experienced by Denmark's medieval monarchs while trying to assert themselves over local centres of power was a problem they shared with other European rulers. Its cause no doubt lay in an all-important structural weakness, namely, the lack of an efficient and reliable means of communication between the throne and society, this being the essential cement needed to bind any political organizations together.[5] There was no way in which a medieval central power could maintain regular connections with all its subjects at once. Even though a few medieval monarchs, by making a special effort and under particularly favourable conditions, occasionally managed to establish strong positions for themselves, such positions were quickly eroded.[6] Power tended naturally to gravitate around small political units that made it possible to maintain stable and lasting internal lines of communication without exorbitant expense, which could not be met in the long run. During the Middle Ages, when communication was largely dependent upon word of mouth, these units were small, local communities dominated by 'feudal,' aristocratic, landowning families.[7]

The art of printing, introduced into Europe in the second half of the fifteenth century, spread with lightning speed, providing for the first time a mass communication system that made it possible for a single person to establish contact with an unlimited number of other people. In the hands of a monarch, this meant that royal ordinances, laws, and other announcements – for example, propaganda in the form of text and pictures – could be distributed throughout large areas with complete accuracy and at low cost.

In contrast to earlier times, by using printing as a connecting link it became possible to build efficient and stable political organizations over a wide geographical area. These new opportunities were seized upon by rulers throughout Europe,[8] including Denmark. However, this did not mean that the problems associated with wielding central power had been solved. In Denmark, three hundred years of laborious bureaucratic development and exhausting power struggles still lay ahead before the monarchy would finally subdue the decentralized forces. This took place around 1800. Contributory factors were the social, economic, and mental displacements brought about by the ecological revolution.

---

[5] Karl W. Deutsch 1966, p. 77.   [6] Aksel E. Christensen 1945, pp. 62–83.
[7] Harry Christensen 1983, pp. 53–73 and passim.
[8] See, for example, Sten Carlsson and Jerker Rosén 1961–2, I, pp. 322–6 (Sweden), and G. R. Elton 1953 (England).

Power 201

The new phase was initiated with Christian II (reigned 1513–23), who pursued an aggressive, anti-aristocratic, centralistic policy for which he and his government sought to create a power base by allying themselves with both the farming community and the market towns.[9] This in itself was not new, for, as we have already seen, elements in Christian's policy were to be found in the policies of several of his predecessors. The new aspect was that this time the defeat was not total. The movement towards a stronger and more effective central administration could be momentarily obstructed, as occurred with Christian II's fall and exile. But it did not permit itself to be halted (as had happened in the Middle Ages), and it was continued energetically by future kings. Christian III (reigned 1533–59), for example, reorganized the administrative system by expanding his control over the nobility and curbing the role played by his lords lieutenant, so that instead of being semi-independent political agents they became royal functionaries.[10]

Christian III's son Frederik II (reigned 1559–88) took an even firmer position against the nobility. One of his achievements was to impose a tax on them,[11] which was a triumph of great symbolic significance to the central administration. From the nobles' perspective, it was not fitting for them to pay taxes, for as the medieval Norwegian chieftain Asbjørn said: "We refuse to acknowledge taxes, but we have no objection to sending the king presents, as to a friend."[12] After 1570, in contravention of the coronation charter that he, like all other Danish kings since Erik V, had had to sign, Frederik II would appear to have come gradually closer to establishing a genuinely autocratic rule.[13]

Under Frederik II's successor, Christian IV (reigned 1588–1648), the lines of demarcation were drawn even more sharply. Among his entourage, the king came to be regarded as the vicar of Christ – as emerged, for example, from Bishop Peder Winstrup's speech at Christian IV's coronation in 1596. In this way, the ground was prepared for conflict between a powerful monarchy based on divine right – a revival of ideas that had circulated at the medieval court of Valdemar the Great – and an aristocratic constitutionalism supporting traditional decentralized government.[14]

---

[9] Erik Arup 1947, pp. 75–7; Kristian Erslev 1879, p. 209.
[10] Kristian Erslev 1879. Cf. Mikael Venge 1980, pp. 319–31, 351–2.
[11] Frede P. Jensen 1978, p. 74, cf. p. 55.   [12] Quoted in Viggo Starcke 1946, p. 194.
[13] Frede P. Jensen 1982, pp. 340–1.
[14] Steffen Heiberg 1988, pp. 36–7, 51–67. On kings as gods in the Middle Ages: Thomas Riis 1977, pp. 66–85.

202 *The New Denmark*

Art was also made to serve the new, strong monarchy by emphasizing the widening gap between royalty and the nobility. Frederik II decreed that the tombs of aristocrats were not to display any splendour that might outshine the tombs of monarchs.[15] Both Frederik II and Christian IV, through their many building projects, first and foremost being Kronborg Castle and Frederiksborg Castle (both in North Zealand), enlisted architecture to demonstrate their power to an extent never before seen in Scandinavia.

The real basis for the increase in royal power since the Renaissance was the strengthening of communications between the central government and society, which had been the weakest link during the Middle Ages. In this respect, progress continued uninterruptedly after 1500. Law texts – the concentrated expression of the monarch's will – were among the first and most frequently printed texts in Denmark. The Jutland Law of 1241 had already been printed by 1486, four years after the first Danish book. A deluge of editions of new and old law texts followed.[16] Together with religious treatises and almanacs, law texts were the most widespread printed matter in Denmark during the sixteenth and seventeenth centuries and as such emphasized the power of the central administration. A regular postal service – indispensable to the existence of an effective central administration – was organized in Denmark at the beginning of the seventeenth century.[17]

If we look at the number of royal bureaucratic transactions – which, like the distribution of law texts, is a manifestation of communication between the central power and society and hence of the amplitude of the governmental power structure – an explosive growth in the number of cases dealt with can be observed during the period after the Renaissance. Between 1570 and 1630 the number handled by the Danish chancellery rose by 400 percent.[18] Another yardstick by which to measure the degree of communication between the state and society is the work of the law courts. An equally explosive growth took place in this area during these years. Around the time of Christian IV's accession to the throne in 1588, one bound volume was sufficient to record four or five years of negotiations conducted by the King's Court. In 1640, just a single year's negotiations at the King's Court filled at least one thick volume.[19]

[15] Steffen Heiberg 1984, pp. 203–4. [16] Lauritz Nielsen 1935, p. 113.
[17] Fritz Olsen 1889, pp. 21–5.
[18] Jens Villiam Jensen 1983–5, p. 519. Cf. Ditlev Tamm 1988, p. 109.
[19] Reported by Jens Christian V. Johansen.

Power   203

Under Christian IV and Frederik III (reigned 1648–70) the growth of the central administration's power was like an unstoppable wave, and more and more Danes therefore chose to regard it as both inevitable and desirable. The aversion felt towards the aristocracy ever since the Middle Ages – expressed more or less openly by the central government and sometimes even by the king in person – spread throughout the clergy and the academic world, not only at the University of Copenhagen but also at Sorø Academy, an aristocratic seat of learning. Increasing numbers of people, including even members of the aristocracy, were beginning to feel that the best solution for Denmark would be a hereditary absolutist monarchy in which the nobility's immediate influence on the government was eliminated. Few, however, are likely to have approved of mathematician Christoffer Dybvad's proposal to make short shrift of the aristocrats: In his view, all that separated Denmark from a better government was a couple of cartloads of blood from the eight hundred nobles of any importance.[20]

The prevailing tendency during these decades to regard the strengthening of central government as an ideal led to absolutism, which emerged in Denmark in 1660. After almost 50 years of virtually uninterrupted war against Sweden resulting in large economic and territorial losses (the hitherto Danish provinces of Skåne, Halland, and Blekinge in the south of Sweden were lost in 1658), the country was in a state of extreme political stress – always an ideal situation for radical solutions. Danish absolutism was formalized by the Danish Royal Law of 1665, which turned Denmark into the most extreme absolutist state in Christendom, headed by a central government whose demands for power knew no bounds. However, it soon appeared that even though the country's internal communication system had been much improved since 1500, and the bureaucracy had increased considerably,[21] the government was quite unequal to its new task.

Absolutism proved to be more than the throne could handle. Just as the central administration had gradually undermined the aristocracy's time-honoured rights (behind its medieval form the rule had become increasingly centralized) in the course of the previous one hundred fifty years, developments now moved in the opposite direction, to such an extent that one could almost believe it was the nobility who, by dint of a brilliant political chess move, had introduced absolutism. Behind the glittering façade of the Royal Law of 1665, the decentralized forces began to undermine the ab-

[20]   Knud Fabricius 1920, pp. 78–9 and passim. Cf. Steffen Heiberg 1988, pp. 62–3.
[21]   Cf. Hans Christian Wolter 1982, pp. 82–3.

204   *The New Denmark*

solutist royal power. After the triumph in 1660, there followed a hundred years of darkness for the supporters of a strong and independent central administration – a long, frustrating period during which Denmark, behind an absolutist mask, found itself more and more under a rule of aristocratic constitutionalism.

One of the first areas in which the central power had to give way was at the same time one of the most important, namely, the imposing and collecting of taxes. A matter of major importance to the new absolutist government – from the perspective of finances as well as of prestige – had been the abolition of the old exemptions from taxes enjoyed by the main farms of manors and by tenant farms in the same parishes as the main farms. This form of tax exemption was abolished a few months after the introduction of absolutism by a declaration issued on 24 June 1661.[22]

Taxation of the lands of the main farm of a manor lasted only nine years. On 23 July 1670 all main manorial farms owned by the nobility were exempted from tax on condition that the landowners assumed responsibility for the payment of taxes by their subordinate tenant farmers instead – and also handled the levying of taxes themselves.[23] By an ordinance of 16 December 1682, this regulation was extended to apply to all manors whose tenant farms within a radius of 2 Danish miles from the main farm were of 200 *tønder hartkorn* or more, regardless of whether the owner was a noble or not. In broad terms, these regulations meant that in the matter of taxation the situation had reverted to what had been in force prior to the introduction of absolutism. At the same time, the central administration had become dependent upon the landowners by requiring them to act as tax collectors on behalf of the state.[24]

In the same way that the central administration had to rely on landowners for the collection of taxes it was also obliged to rely on them for the conscription of soldiers, though this too resulted in a corresponding loss of power for the government. In 1663 a form of compulsory military service was introduced, shortly after which it became the duty of landowners to provide a specific number of soldiers according to the extent of their lands. Apart from a brief interruption at the end of the seventeenth century, this arrangement lasted until the abolition of adscription in 1788. The routine purpose of adscription legislation was to confirm the natural (and essential) right of landowners to control the movements

[22]   Edvard Holm 1885–6, I, pp. 119–20; Thomas Munck 1979, p. 66.
[23]   Edvard Holm 1885–6, I, pp. 155–6; Thomas Munck 1979, p. 66.
[24]   Edvard Holm 1885–6, I, p. 158.

Power   205

of the male farming population, seeing that it was their duty to provide soldiers.[25]

In other areas where absolutism, during the hectic years after 1660, had failed to settle accounts with the past, everything continued as before, regardless of possible inconsistencies with the principles of the system. An example was the landowners' right to nominate judges to lower courts and the right of patronage, that is, the right to appoint a priest to a church of which the landowner was both patron and owner. A large number of landowners continued to hold the right to appoint judges to district courts after the introduction of absolutism. More judges were even added, for during the first decades of absolutism a number of royal lower courts were abolished, partly in connection with the sale of Crown lands and, as will be discussed, the establishment of countships and baronies. In the same way, extensive sales of royal churches under Christian V and Frederik IV led to a considerable increase in the number of churches over which landowners held the right of patronage.[26]

The right of private patronage, in conjunction with other delegations of royal authority, such as the collection of taxes and conscription of soldiers, obviously lowered the esteem in which the ostensibly omnipotent absolutist government was held. Conversely, the system served to strengthen the landowners' power and prestige.[27] A landowner who took charge of tax collection and the conscription of soldiers, and perhaps even appointed priests, parish clerks, and judges, had, as the Danish historian Hans Jensen expressed it, "to some extent reason to regard himself as a royal vassal or vice-regent in the region."[28]

An extensive concession of power by the central administration to decentralized authorities took place in 1671 with the formation of a new class of counts and barons. It was decreed that these new nobles on their large estates – countships of at least 2,500 *tønder hartkorn* of tenant farmland and baronies of at least 1,000 *tønder hartkorn* – were to enjoy exemption from taxes not only for their main farms, as in the case of any manorial lord, but also for part of their tenant farmlands, more specifically, for 300 *tønder hartkorn* in countships and 100 *tønder hartkorn* in baronies. In addition, they

[25] Thomas Munck 1979, pp. 88–92, 166–8; Edvard Holm 1885–6, I, pp. 158–9 and 1883–4, p. 540.

[26] Thomas Munck 1979, p. 51; John T. Lauridsen and Thomas Munck 1981–2, p. 640; Anne Riising 1976, p. 199; P. Severinsen 1920, pp. 61–4.

[27] Edvard Holm 1885–6, I, p. 92.   [28] Hans Jensen 1936–45, I, p. 16.

206 *The New Denmark*

were to enjoy extensive liberties; counts and barons were given authority to act as chief administrative officers in their respective districts, which placed their holdings out of bounds to the king's officials. An important feature of the new countships and baronies was that they could not be divided on inheritance in the same way that ordinary private estates were, but were entailed, like the kingdom itself, and therefore subject to special regulations covering succession. This endowed the countships and baronies with great stability, which further strengthened their independence in relation to the central administration.[29]

It is probable that the newly created counts and barons, "to the greater Lustre of our Court," were introduced first and foremost to provide a counterweight, under the king's control, to the old Danish aristocracy, whose loyalty towards the new government was doubted by all absolutist rulers up to and including Frederik IV (who reportedly felt "a veritable hate" for the old aristocracy).[30] But seen from the point of view of the absolute monarchy's demand for absolute power, the establishment of a new group of nobles as a counterweight to the old aristocracy was tantamount to wanting to drive out Satan with the help of Beelzebub.

An almost comic example of how the king, even over the most minor details, attempted to exploit the newly created nobility as a means of frustrating and irritating the old Danish aristocracy, was Christian V's prohibition in 1690 of a proposed marriage between Jørgen Skeel of Estrup, perhaps the richest aristocrat of the day, and a Countess Ahlefeldt. The argument was that this would be a mésalliance – for her.[31] The members of the self-respecting old Danish aristocracy were duly provoked and deeply offended. This emerges, for example, in a political satire called *The Comedy of the Count and the Baron*, written by Mogens Skeel, a distant relation of Jørgen Skeel, probably towards the end of the 1670s. Skeel's comedy, which for political reasons remained unpublished until 1793, heaped ridicule on the new nobles.[32]

In addition to establishing countships and baronies, the Danish Law of 1683 (Book 5, Ch. 2, §65) opened up the possibility, under certain circumstances, for other properties, even those of as little as 400 *tønder hartkorn*, to be converted, by means of a private declaration of intent by the owner, into entailed estates in the same

---

[29] Birgit Bjerre Jensen 1968–9; Lotte Dombernowsky 1983, pp. 31–48. Cf. Nils G. Bartholdy 1971, pp. 583–4.

[30] Edvard Holm 1885–6, I, p. 134, and 1891–1912, I, p. 255; Nils G. Bartholdy 1971, p. 610.

[31] Edvard Holm 1885–6, I, p. 136.　　　　[32] John T. Lauridsen 1987.

Power   207

way that countships and baronies were.[33] If an ordinary landowner
had grounds for feeling like a royal vassal or a vice-regent in his
area, then counts and barons – and to a certain extent even owners of small entailed estates – could feel almost like states within
the state.[34]

Eighty years after the introduction of absolutism, during the
years 1739–40, a trial of strength took place between the central
administration and the decentralized authorities. The occasion
was a new elementary village school system, decreed on 23 January 1739, in which the state not only expanded the demands made
on tuition but also, through bishops and prefects, assumed far-
reaching control of curricula, the number of schools, and school
financing. However, opposition to this new school act by landowners was so massive that the law had to be withdrawn the very next
year and tuition again left to local initiative. It is unlikely to have
been any the worse on this account, for, in general, tuition was
well taken care of by landowners and perceptive tenant farmers.
On the other hand, the resolution of this conflict was highly detrimental to the government's prestige. The purpose of the new
school act had undoubtedly been to secure a much-needed political triumph. Instead, it turned out to be a serious political defeat.[35]

As regards the quality of basic education in Denmark it may be noted that
the number of schools grew steadily after 1735. At the end of the eighteenth century there were about seventeen hundred village schools,[36]
which was undoubtedly a sufficient number to give practically all children a satisfactory basic education.

The tension between centralization and decentralization in
Denmark under the absolute monarchy was not exclusively bound
up with the conflict between the government and the landowner
class. However, as a simple consequence of the social and economic dominance of the agricultural sector and the landowner
class's central position in agriculture, this was in fact the core of
the matter.[37] An additional aspect of the overall picture of decentralization is that other institutions in society enjoyed great independence as well. In rural districts, village life continued to
function more or less autonomously in relation to the central government, for there was wide scope for independent local legisla-

---

[33] Lotte Dombernowsky 1975, pp. 122–3.   [34] Cf. Anne Riising 1976, p. 205.
[35] Ole Feldbæk 1990a, pp. 185–6.
[36] Joakim Larsen 1916, p. 294; Hans Christian Johansen 1979, pp. 248–50; Johannes C.
Jessen 1938 and 1942; L. Koch 1882, p. 24. Cf. Laurits Engelstoft 1961, p. 93.
[37] Erik Arup 1916, p. 432.

208   *The New Denmark*

tion in the form of bylaws.[38] In the market towns, the guilds, which had existed since the Middle Ages, constituted independent bodies over which the state exercised only limited influence; they have been aptly characterized as "entailed estates for a small number of families."[39]

The centralistic absolutism laid down by the Royal Law of 1665, which in theory hardly permitted a bird to fall to the ground without royal permission, in practice quickly became bogged down. One of the main reasons was an infrastructure that was far too weak to sustain the level of ambition. The lines of communication that extended out to the populace, though far better than during the Middle Ages, were inadequate to handle the dissemination of the constant, dense stream of information essential to a centrally governed society. Even after the introduction of the new postal organization in 1694, which was a marked improvement on the old system, there were only two weekly postal services between Copenhagen, Altona, and Hamburg, and only one weekly service along the northern part of the kingdom's main axis, that is, from Copenhagen to Kristiania (Oslo). Only between Copenhagen and Elsinore was there a daily postal service.[40]

In addition, the bureaucratic machine, despite frequent expansion, was still far too small to handle the wealth of the correspondence that had to be conducted if citizens and local authorities were both to be kept informed of the government's wishes and to feel constantly aware of the government's prying eye. The sound of the government's voice throughout the kingdom was pitifully thin, so much so that, for example, an important figure such as the bishop of the diocese of Ålborg received only seven letters from Copenhagen in the whole of 1702.[41]

Besides the fundamental problems stemming from inadequate communication there were a number of other difficulties facing Denmark's absolute monarchy after 1660. Above all, the young absolutist rule lacked powerful political allies. As Margrethe I, Christian I, and Christian II had realized long before, both the farming class and urban citizens were potential allies for the central power in its struggle against decentralized aristocratic tendencies. The farmers were especially important. However, prospects of an alliance with the farmers were not exactly good during the first decades of the absolute monarchy. First, apart from sporadic

[38] Poul Meyer 1949, especially pp. 343–69.
[39] Edvard Holm 1891–1912, III, 2, p. 201. Cf. Anne Riising 1976, p. 188.
[40] Edvard Holm 1885–6, I, pp. 199 –200.   [41] Ibid., II, pp. 96–7.

Power   209

episodes, some of which were under Christian II, there had never been close cooperation between the farmers and the government. Second, the government, as the source of demands for dramatic increases in taxes, could hardly expect much sympathy from the farmers. In addition, the increasing burden of taxation and the resultant chronic economic difficulties for agriculture meant that farmers were so hard-pressed during these years that they became less attractive as political partners. The government seems to have understood this – no evidence can be traced of any attempts on its part to gain the sympathy of the farmers during the first decades of absolutism.[42]

The only action dating from the first years of the absolute monarchy that could indicate a wish on the part of the government to establish goodwill with the farmers is the abolition of serfdom in 1702. However, it is debatable how much importance should be attached to the abolition of this system on the islands of Zealand, Møn, Lolland, and Falster. For one thing, the practical consequences of the act were limited because serfdom was immediately replaced by de facto adscription applicable to the whole country.[43] Furthermore, motives unrelated to agriculture and the condition of farmers may well have played a part in the government's decision to abolish serfdom.

It was important for the absolute monarchy to have well-organized, uniform legislation throughout the country. Serfdom was a striking irregularity, for it applied only in the area covered by the old Zealand Law (the islands of Zealand, Møn, Lolland, and Falster) and not to the rest of the country and, therefore, obviously had to be abolished sooner or later in the same way that other provincial legislation had long since been annulled. Either it would be necessary to extend serfdom to cover the whole country – in the way that legal practice was apparently well on the way to doing [44] – or else it would have to be terminated. Frederik IV, perhaps with due consideration for the free goodwill the government could hope to obtain, decided to abolish serfdom, which his popular great-grandfather, Christian IV, had wanted to do but failed to carry through in the face of resistance from his aristocratic councillors.[45]

Among the factors hampering the central administration during the first decades of the absolute monarchy was the spirit of the times, which was dominated to an overwhelming degree by aristocratic ideas and concepts. The extroverted, self-confident, patriar-

---

[42] Finn Stendal Pedersen 1982–3, pp. 285–6.
[43] Chapter 6 n. 123; Thomas Munck 1979, pp. 198, 204–6.
[44] Jens Holmgaard 1983.   [45] Thomas Munck 1979, pp. 177–8.

210   *The New Denmark*

chal ideology of the aristocracy, with its roots in antiquity and the Middle Ages,[46] had been praised at the end of the sixteenth century and the beginning of the seventeenth century by any number of personalities, including Admiral Herluf Trolle, the author of what was probably the most famous formulation on Danish soil of the fundamental principles of classical aristocratic thinking:

> Know ye wherefore we be called lords of manors, wear golden chains, own lands and wish to be superior and more highly respected than others? Because when our king and master, our country and kingdom, are in need, we have the honour, before others, of being required to repel our kingdom's enemies, protect and shelter the kingdom of our fathers by force of arms and with all our fortune, so that our subjects may dwell and remain in peace and tranquillity. Indeed, we must be prepared to take the rough with the smooth.[47]

This aristocratic world of ideas, which also underlies the interpretation of the history of Denmark published in 1595–1603 by a Danish noble, Arild Huitfeldt, under the title *Danmarckis Rigis Krønnicke* (Chronicle of the Kingdom of Denmark), had been brought into some discredit during the anti-aristocratic period towards 1660. But the dust had barely settled after the introduction of absolutism before aristocratic ideology began to regain ground. A treatise appeared in 1663 entitled *Nobilitatis responsum ad famosum factiosi calumniatoris libellum* (Reply from the nobility to a notorious, defamatory, and seditious pamphlet), which defended the old Danish aristocracy against various accusations, notably, those contained in another treatise by one of the chief ideologists of the new absolutist government, Paul Tscherning. *Nobilitatis responsum*, which was published anonymously, was possibly written by Oluf Rosenkrantz, a member of the old Danish aristocracy. At all events, Rosenkrantz was the author of *Apologia nobilitatis Danicae* (Apologia for the Danish nobility), which came out a few years later, in 1681, and provoked such intense fury on the part of the government that all his titles as well as his fortune were confiscated.[48] The English diplomat Sir Robert Molesworth, whose anti-absolutist treatise published in 1694 under the title *An Account of Denmark as it was in the Year 1692* became an international success, made himself a spokesman for

[46] Otto Brunner 1949.
[47] Quoted by Tycho de Hofman 1777–9, I, pp. 174–5.
[48] On aristocratic culture in seventeenth-century Scandinavia: Dieter Lohmeier 1978. Cf. Andrea Boockmann 1985.

Power   211

the same circles as those represented by Rosenkrantz. He too
aroused the government's wrath, though in his case it was of
course ineffectual.[49]

The traditionally aristocratic world was able to unfold itself more
freely and therefore more clearly in the spheres of architecture and art than it could in the literary field, which was long
kept at bay by the merciless punishment enforced by censorship
during the early period of absolutism. New manor houses, including Nysø, Lerchenborg, Ledreborg, and Bregentved (all on the island of Zealand) were built during the first hundred years of the
absolute monarchy. Their extroverted, self-confident, almost
princely style made them comparable to a medieval stronghold like
Gjorslev (Zealand) or to Renaissance houses like Rosenholm (Jutland), Egeskov (Funen), and Gisselfeld (Zealand).[50]

Many landowners raised memorials to themselves by rebuilding
the village churches to which they held the right of patronage.
A fine example was the way an East Jutland magnate, Gerdt de
Lichtenberg, set about this task. With a display of energy and self-
confidence reminiscent of the delight in building shown by the
nobility of the sixteenth century, even of the church-building aristocrats of the Middle Ages, de Lichtenberg rebuilt numerous
churches in East Jutland during the middle third of the eighteenth
century. With his passion for the onion-shaped cupola, so rare in
Danish architecture, he left his mark – still visible – on the villages
surrounding Horsens and Vejle. In other areas, village churches
were transformed during the first hundred years after the introduction of absolute monarchy into veritable mausoleums for
noble families, including, for example, Auning in East Jutland (for
the Skeel family) and Karise on the island of Zealand (for the
Moltke family).

Portraits of aristocrats, conscious of their power and social
standing, also enjoyed a splendid period during the first hundred
years of the absolute monarchy. Frederik II's problem in the
1580s, namely, the nobility's insistent desire to commission works
of art rivalling those of rulers, in no way diminished under the absolute monarchy during the first half of the eighteenth century. In
1742, for example, Christian VI had to intervene in the case of
J. L. Holstein, who had commissioned a portrait of his mother
standing in a long cloak beneath a drapery and with an armchair
behind her. In the king's opinion, a pose of this kind was only be-

---

[49] Poul Ries 1978.   [50] Hakon Lund 1980.

212   *The New Denmark*

fitting for a royal person, and subsequently, when Holstein had an engraving made, he was obliged to destroy both the copperplate and all the prints.[51]

An important manifestation of the classical aristocratic lifestyle was the setting up of foundations and scholarships for all kinds of cultural and social purposes. In this way the aristocracy could emphasize its worth and at the same time help to build up valuable loyalty among those who benefited from these funds. In this area, too, the years after the introduction of absolute monarchy proved to be an extremely fruitful period, as demonstrated by Hans de Hofman's *Samlinger af Publique og Private Stiftelser, Fundationer og Gavebreve* (Collections of public and private foundations, scholarships and deeds of gift) (1755–65). This ten-volume work lists hundreds of foundations in existence around the middle of the eighteenth century, the majority having been set up by big landowners after 1660.

Few people failed to be fascinated and charmed by the aristocracy. Not even the chief architect of the anti-aristocratic absolutist rule, Peder Schumacher, a commoner who wanted to "place ourselves and our people on the same bench and on an equal standing with the nobility,"[52] could resist the aristocracy's discreet charm. Schumacher, who was a great womanizer, married into an upper-class Copenhagen family, which was the correct thing for him to do. But it was mostly among the ladies of the nobility that he found his mistresses, and when the chance presented itself he saw no reason why he should not let himself be raised to the nobility as the Count of Griffenfeld.[53] Many followed in Schumacher's footsteps. Snobbishness towards the aristocracy and high rank, which as Holberg observed in 1731, "afflicts people in this country like bouts of fever," was as rife as ever during the first century of absolutism.[54] The rapier, which indicated a person of distinction, was an indispensable part of a man's attire in Holberg's day, and therefore in Copenhagen it was worn by nearly all men of a certain standing.[55]

The rural population also had many links to the aristocratic world. In contrast to the absolutist state's unfounded claim to possess, after God, all power on earth, the role played by the landowners was the embodiment of reality. The manors were there, and aristocrats existed in the flesh. Furthermore, the immediate, visi-

---

[51] Edvard Holm 1891–1912, II, pp. 265–6.
[52] Quoted by Edvard Holm 1885–6, I, p. 125.
[53] Knud Fabricius 1910, pp. 178, 218–20.
[54] Ludvig Holberg 1919–63, IV, p. 636 (*Den honnette Ambition*, II, 7). Cf. Nils G. Bartholdy 1971, pp. 586, 606.
[55] Edvard Holm 1891–1912, I, p. 467; H. Nyrop-Christensen 1971, pp. 153–6.

Power   213

ble reality that each and every person could see corresponded to the fictive world encountered by the rural classes in the stories that they read for pleasure: Since ancient times these had been romances of chivalry and heroic deeds. As early as about 1600, the historian Arild Huitfeldt had complained about the profusion of such books in Denmark,[56] and matters were not to improve for the next two hundred years. Rasmus Nyerup, the first Danish scholar to take an interest in the sociology of literature, wrote in 1794:

> The story of Ogier the Dane is to be found in nearly every peasant cottage and is frequently read aloud in the evenings during church festivals, wool-carding sessions, hop-picking and similar social activities.[57]

It was not difficult to associate the tale of the deeds performed in Europe by Ogier the Dane (a mighty, legendary warrior at the time of Charles the Great, and the most famous Dane for centuries),[58] with the reality that daily confronted most rural Danes: imposing manor houses and distinguished, powerful, and yet gracious families whose members moved with equal ease in royal courts and in the farming parishes that formed their base. Everything was as it always had been, and the aristocratic world possessed the natural and obvious authority of both myth and immediate reality.

The concealed rule of the aristocracy culminated around 1750–60 with the so-called rule of excellencies, which had been developing since the days of Christian VI and which gradually led to a group of aristocratic counsellors close to the king becoming the holders of absolutist power.[59] This development served to annul the central wielding of power at the very top of the system, something that previous absolutist rulers had protected jealously as it was the last substantial element of the absolutism introduced so ostentatiously in 1660.[60] Instead of his being an active centre of power as before, the king, during the 'rule of excellencies,' became the symbolic focal point for a group of aristocratic ministers; officially they were referred to as the Council.

---

[56] Svend Ellehøj 1964, pp. 347–8.
[57] Quoted in J. P. Jacobsen et al. 1915–36, XIII, p. 241. On popular reading, the main work is still Rasmus Nyerup 1816. On the Ogier the Dane legend, which appeared in numerous editions, pp. 99–105.
[58] The Danish Egyptologist Erik Iversen relates that during a stay in Sicily in about 1950 he was treated with particular respect because he was a compatriot of Ogier the Dane (1951, pp. 493–4).
[59] Edvard Holm 1891–1912, III, 2, pp. 10–11; Axel Linvald 1921, p. 261.
[60] Birgit Bjerre Jensen 1987.

214   *The New Denmark*

Although not repealed, the Royal Law of 1665 had largely been abandoned, both in theory and in practice. This is evidenced by the memorial raised by 'their excellencies' to themselves in Frederikstaden, the new quarter in the northern outskirts of Copenhagen as it was at the time.[61] Its centre, whose foundation stone was laid in 1749 to mark the 300th anniversary of the Oldenborg family's accession to the throne, was Amalienborg, a group of four splendid, identical mansions surrounding an equestrian statue of the king; each was owned by an aristocratic family. The Amalienborg complex (fig. 19) accurately represented Denmark under the 'rule of excellencies.' The symbol of power was the king, but the real power was held by 'their excellencies,' the group of counts and barons close to the throne. The new group of nobles created by the absolutist king to protect himself against the old Danish aristocracy turned out to be a viper in his bosom. It now emerged as the main guarantor of the decentralized, 'feudal' exercise of power that had become established behind the façade of absolutism since 1660. In the phrase coined a few years later by the then prime minister C. D. Reventlow, Denmark had "an aristocratic constitution under the rule of sovereign monarch."[62]

This was as far as the undermining of absolutism went – and no further. The 'rule of excellencies' was on the brink of collapse. The "aristocratic constitution under the rule of a sovereign monarch" was not to last for even as long as it took to complete Amalienborg. When the unveiling of the equestrian statue of Frederik V by the French sculptor Jacques Saly finally took place in 1771, their excellencies had fallen from grace. The royal family's disapproval of the whole Amalienborg project indeed was so strong that its members refused to take part in the festivities. The celebration was therefore reduced to a banquet given in one of the four mansions by one of the fallen excellencies, Count Adam Gottlieb Moltke, who came up to Copenhagen from his country residence, Bregentved in South Zealand, for the occasion.[63] Times had changed, and the central administration, which had overexerted itself by the introduction of absolutism to such an extent that it had been on the defensive ever since, once more moved into the forefront. The ecological revolution, which by a series of blind, nonlinear processes had changed the face of the landscape and turned both the social structure and the pattern of disease upside

[61] John Erichsen 1972.
[62] C. D. Reventlow 1786, p. 269. Cf. Edvard Holm 1891–1912, IV, 1, pp. 15–16.
[63] Carl Bruun 1887–90, III, pp. 266 –7; John Erichsen and Emma Salling 1976, pp. 70–1.

Figure 19. Amalienborg.

216   *The New Denmark*

down, also affected the struggle for power in Denmark in favour of centralized bureaucracy.

8.2 THE BREAKTHROUGH OF CENTRALISTIC GOVERNMENT, 1766–1814

The breakthrough of centralistic absolutism took place at both the top and the bottom of the system. The revolution at the top, which once more concentrated power in the person of the king, took place shortly after Christian VII's accession to the throne in 1766, the first step being the dismissal, in quick succession, of the members of the Council – 'their excellencies.' After this followed a series of drastic changes in the central administration with the aim of achieving an almost military streamlining of the exercise of power below the top leadership. It had to be borne in mind, as one member of the new group of powerful bureaucrats expressed it, that

> in a monarchistic state such as ours, such stern restrictions on intermediate authorities must be prescribed as to preclude harm being done, in any wise or manner whatsoever, to the sovereign power, which rests solely in the person of the King, being based on him alone.[64]

These changes were realized even before the end of the brief period of 'enlightened' dictatorship, from 1770 to 1772, under the extraordinary figure of Johann Friedrich Struensee, who was the king's favourite as well as his physician in ordinary. Struensee succeeded not only in taking the king's place politically but also in becoming the lover of the English-born queen, Caroline Mathilde; finally, Struensee was denounced and beheaded.[65] However, Struensee's achievement represented the conquest of only the first and most prominent bastion of aristocratic government, behind which was a decentralized society protected by defences that were difficult to penetrate – as centuries of experience had proven. But this time the attempt proved successful. After having displayed formidable powers of resistance and regenerative prowess, the old decentralized social pattern crumbled away in the course of half a century.

A start was made with two ordinances issued in May 1769, covering villeinage regulations and encouraging freehold.[66] A provi-

---

[64] Axel Linvald 1921, pp. 268–372, quotation pp. 286–7; Ole Feldbæk 1982, pp. 75–6; Edvard Holm 1891–1912, IV, 1–2, passim.

[65] Axel Linvald 1921, pp. 371–3.

[66] Ordinance of 6 May 1769 on the conditions of villeinage in Denmark and ordinance of 13 May 1769 on freeholders in Denmark.

Power   217

sional conclusion was reached with the Village School Act of 1814, which consolidated government control of the elementary village school system and in this way eradicated the memory of the ignominious defeat suffered in 1739–40 in connection with the reorganization of the educational system. Between these two extremes lay an extensive complex of legislation that was, broadly speaking, identical to the so-called agrarian reform legislation, whose gradual introduction marks the various phases in the real assumption of power by the absolutist state.

Ever since Hans Jensen published in 1936 the first volume of *Dansk Jordpolitik* (Danish land policy)[67] covering the years 1757–1810 there has been some appreciation of the fact that, behind the slogans extolling liberty and the right of private ownership, the agrarian reforms at the end of the eighteenth century were the immediately visible aspects of absolutism's confrontation with decentralized authority.[68] Practically the entire complex of agrarian reform legislation – even the parts that appeared to be purely technical – may indeed be regarded as a series of varied and mutually complementary manifestations of the growth of absolutist power.

The reform legislation can be divided into two parts. One of them consisted of a series of measures that were mainly 'negative,' that is, their principal function was the dispersal of units representing local autonomy. The other part embraced 'positive' legislation whose function was to transfer power from the crumbling decentralized authorities to the central administration and so establish specific ways of exercising power in the future.

a. Legislation that Dissolved Decentralized Forms of Power

The measures introduced to encourage freehold property and enclosure are among those that must be regarded as part of the complex of agrarian reforms whose primary function was to dissolve decentralized units of power. Freeholders, who came under the surveillance of royal officials and therefore constituted a kind of Trojan Horse beyond the control of the local landowners, had not been encouraged since the end of the seventeenth century, when the nobility had regained full control.[69] After 1761, when it was for-

---

[67] Hans Jensen 1936–45, I, for example, pp. 231–3, 244–5.
[68] Sigurd Jensen 1950, pp. 15–16; Birgit Løgstrup 1983, p. 369; Finn Stendal Pedersen 1988, p. 50; Ole Feldbæk 1982, pp. 164–78.
[69] Hans Knudsen 1927, p. 392; Sigurd Jensen 1950, pp. 15–16; Claus Bjørn 1981b, pp. 82–6.

218   *The New Denmark*

bidden during the palmy days of 'their excellencies' to separate a manor from its farmers, it had been impossible in practice to set up new freehold farms.[70] A few years later, after the fall of 'their excellencies,' the situation looked very different. Instead of restraining farmers' attempts to buy freehold property, the government now encouraged farmers to do so. By an ordinance of 13 May 1769 entitled "Om Selvejerbønder i Danmark og de dem allernaadigst forundte Fordele" (On freeholders in Denmark and the advantages graciously accorded to them), which has been rightly characterized as an important change of direction in Denmark's political system,[71] the encouragement of freehold purchases became official policy.

This new policy was wrapped up in standard formulations derived from natural law and assertions on the subject of private ownership as an expression of universal economic rationality. The petition submitted to the king on 3 May 1769 concerning freehold legislation included the following passage:

> It would seem to be a natural consequence of an ordinary human outlook that private ownership must be one of the most powerful and convenient means of emboldening a farmer and giving him the courage and desire to work hard. One can hardly blame a tenant farmer for thinking primarily of the present, nor can one really assume that he will divert any expense towards the improvement of his farm with the aim of reaping the fruits thereof in the future. The uncertainty in which he constantly lives, or believes he lives, wholly precludes anything of this nature. On the other hand, a freeholder realizes quite well, without even being very enlightened, that whatever money, and, equally, time, diligence and labour spent on the improvement of his farm and his land, is safely invested capital from which he and his children will be able in time to expect twofold interest.[72]

The ordinance of 1769 was the first of a number of measures taken during the ensuing years to encourage the purchase of farm freeholds. These measures followed the principle of allowing opponents, as far as possible, to dig their own graves by conceding them short-term advantages that tempted them to ignore the long-term disadvantages. In 1784 it became possible for landowners who sold tenant farms as freehold property to retain their tax ex-

---

[70] Hans Jensen 1936–45, I, p. 76. This law seems to have been prompted by a few individual cases of freehold sales of estates in West Jutland in 1757–61. Sigurd Jensen 1950, pp. 16–19. Cf. Lotte Dombernowsky 1988, pp. 351–3.

[71] Hans Jensen 1936–45, I, p. 76.   [72] Henrik Stampe 1793–1807, VI, p. 116.

Power 219

emption for lands belonging to the main farm even though the total acreage of underlying tenant farms was reduced to less than 200 *tønder hartkorn*, (the lowest limit to qualify for tax exemption, in force since the seventeenth century).[73] Further action towards a liberalization of access to establish freeholds was taken during ensuing years. The most important step was the ordinance of 15 June 1792, which made it possible, providing certain conditions were fulfilled, to sell off not only tenant farmlands but also plots of land belonging to the main farm of an estate.[74]

In addition, the government encouraged freehold purchases by placing credit facilities at the disposal of farmers who wished to buy their own land, initially in 1771,[75] and later through the state financial institute, the Kreditkasse, among whose main objectives, from the very outset in 1786, was precisely the financing of freehold acquisitions.[76] Because the last half of the eighteenth century was marked by violent rises in food prices – which, as is always the case, causes land prices to rise even more[77] – there was everything necessary for an extremely speculative real estate market. It is therefore hardly surprising that the number of freehold farms increased rapidly after 1770.

Whereas right up to 1769 freehold had been a marginal phenomenon openly opposed by the government (except on the island of Bornholm, where it had been common practice for centuries), by 1810 it embraced more than forty thousand farms, in other words, about two-thirds of all the farms in Denmark.[78] The tenant system, which for centuries had served to unite the big estates that formed such a prominent feature of Denmark's decentrally governed society, was disintegrating. In 1810 a number of large estates still remained unaffected by the development towards freehold properties, especially countships and baronies, whose entailed assets were fairly well protected against being split up by strict rules covering their disposal. But in between these units the ice had melted, and, because of its thousands of small, independent, owner-occupied farms, what had previously been a very closed rural society now lay much more exposed than before to political intervention and manipulation by the government.

[73] Hans Jensen 1936–45, I, p. 224. As soon as the political possibilities of this advantage had been exhausted it was withdrawn by the ordinance of 1 Oct. 1802 covering *hartkorn* taxation. Ibid.

[74] Jens Holmgaard 1970, p. 130. [75] Lotte Dombernowsky 1988, pp. 355–6.

[76] Sigurd Jensen 1950, pp. 35–9. As from 1797 the Kreditkasse was replaced as a major lender for freehold purchases by a superannuation fund called Den almindelige Enkekasse. Ibid., pp. 39–47.

[77] V. Falbe Hansen 1889, I, pp. 83, 99–100. [78] Lotte Dombernowsky 1988, p. 359.

220   *The New Denmark*

At the same time as the increasing number of freehold properties was gradually disrupting the relationship between landowners
and tenant farmers by transforming the latter into 'citizens,' the
enclosure movement shattered communal village life, which had
been another mainstay of Denmark's decentrally governed society. As already mentioned, the ecological revolution created social
tensions that led almost spontaneously to enclosures whenever the
opportunity presented itself, an example being the Copenhagen
military district after privatization in 1766.[79] In order to accelerate
the dissolution of village life and end the far-reaching village autonomy that went with it, the government had merely to take advantage of tendencies already existing in rural society.

After initial steps introduced by an ordinance of 13 May 1776,
which in various ways encouraged enclosure and the moving
of farms out of the villages, a law was passed on 23 April 1781 to
abolish the communal cultivation system. The aim was that every
farmer in a village should have his own plot of land, clearly separated from those of other farmers. Whenever possible, farmers
were encouraged to move their farms out of their villages – in fact,
money was made available for this purpose.[80] Farmers needed no
further incitement to go ahead with enclosures. The situation was
different for landowners in cases where they still had a say in the
matter, in other words, in cases where farmers had not yet obtained freeholds and the landowners, as owners of the plots, therefore had to pay the expenses. For one thing, enclosure was a costly
affair for which it was difficult to obtain compensation within the
framework of the inflexible Danish tenancy system dominated by
tenures and fixed manorial dues. Furthermore, a number of examples are recorded of landowners with a paternal outlook op-
posing enclosure on grounds of its negative social consequences
for cottagers.[81]

An attempt was made to counteract the hesitancy of the landowners by linking enclosure with freehold, in this way utilizing the
incitements encouraging freehold to pave the way for enclosure as

---

[79] Chapter 6.2, section b; Jørgen Dieckmann Rasmussen 1977, pp. 100–7 and passim.
[80] Hans Jensen 1936–45, I, pp. 107–8; Lotte Dombernowsky 1988, p. 321.
[81] See, for example, Anna Rasmussen 1985, pp. 20–1. Cf. Fridlev Skrubbeltrang 1940,
     p. 281. In Kalundborg there was strong opposition to enclosure of municipal lands be-
     cause the result would be antisocial. Tore Nyberg and Thomas Riis 1985, pp. 274–7. See
     also G. L. Baden 1796, p. 90. Examples of estate management enforcing favourable mea-
     sures for cottagers against the wishes of farmers: Christian H. Brasch 1859–63, III, p.
     194. Cf. Fridlev Skrubbeltrang 1940, p. 298 (n. 49). In other places estate management
     gave up in the face of massive resistance by farmers to concessions being made to cot-
     tagers. Claus Bjørn 1981b, p. 145.

Power

well. This was effected by a royal resolution of 8 December 1784 covering freehold, which stated that permission to sell tenant farmland as freehold property could be obtained most easily if enclosure had already been arranged.[82] A few years later, economic advantages were made available to landowners who did not wish to sell freehold land, or could not do so because the land in question was entailed, provided they arranged enclosure. An ordinance dated 15 June 1792 permitted estate owners not only to distribute the expenses involved in enclosure and the moving of tenant farms out of the villages on to the farmers but also to raise manorial dues for enclosed farms in the event of new tenancies. Enclosure thus offered the possibility of breaking the rigid system of manorial dues that hitherto had obliged all rent increases to be imposed in the form of villeinage work.[83]

Endeavours to promote enclosure were not in vain. Before 1800, enclosure had been arranged in the majority of Danish villages, and the close social contact of village life had been undermined by the scattering of farms. After having existed for several hundred years, communal cultivation of fields and sharing of village amenities faded away within three or four decades, and so did the widespread village autonomy that had existed until then.

Among the measures that dissolved existing structures in rural society was the strange, protracted conflict over villeinage that arose in 1769, leaving its mark on Danish politics, social life, and public debate during the 1770s, 1780s, and 1790s. The conflict was strange because the policy pursued by the authorities in regard to villeinage seemed irrational. No official with insight into agricultural conditions can seriously have believed that it would be possible to regulate the extent of villeinage work as long as manorial dues were unchangeable. There had to be some way of regulating the tenant farmer's overall burden so that landowners could also obtain a share of the profits reaped during periods of prosperity. In the absence of any other possibility, this had to be arranged through villeinage work.[84]

Nevertheless, one ordinance was issued after another, purportedly in attempts to regulate villeinage work. The first, dated 6 May 1769, was subsequently replaced by a very detailed version dated 20 February 1771. This was replaced in turn by the somewhat less ambitious ordinance of 12 August 1773. Villeinage work soon be-

---

[82] Jens Holmgaard 1970, p. 130.
[83] Hans Jensen 1936–45, I, p. 109; Thorkild Kjærgaard 1980, p. 69.
[84] Thorkild Kjærgaard 1980, pp. 43–7.

222   *The New Denmark*

came a major issue in the Greater Agrarian Commission, which was appointed in 1786. In 1787–8 C. D. Reventlow drew up a comprehensive report on the subject. After long discussions, yet another list of new regulations was presented in 1791, but they proved to be almost as ineffectual as those previously issued.[85] It was not until 1792, when manorial dues were made adjustable, that legislation became constructive in the sense that a basis was provided for regulating villeinage work, gradually permitting its conversion into fixed payments in money;[86] villeinage work finally disappeared in the course of the nineteenth century.

Precisely what lay behind twenty-five years of energetic but almost grotesquely ineffectual villeinage legislation remains something of a riddle. During the many years when the question was being discussed almost incessantly, villeinage work increased steadily, and in many places doubled or perhaps increased even more.[87] A possible explanation of the apparently irrational villeinage policy could be that for a long time the central administration simply did not attempt to solve the problem at all, but instead deliberately procrastinated, because the continued existence of villeinage work acted as an effective catalyst in the general process of undermining the decentralized authorities.

The macroeconomic tendency towards a greater demand for labour automatically made villeinage work a sensitive area in which conflicts easily arose between tenant farmers and landowners. The landowners were always anxious to increase villeinage work, especially because the rigid system of fixed manorial dues made it difficult if not impossible for them, as landowners, to obtain their share of the rising income from farmlands in any way other than by demanding additional villeinage work on the main farm. On the other hand, the farmers, despite making stable economic progress, were always on their guard against this trend.

If the purpose of the villeinage conflict from 1769 to 1791 was to create dissension within the rural community rather than to find permanent solutions to recurring problems, and also to mobilize opinion among farmers in favour of the government and against the landowners (damaging what would appear to have been the generally trusting relationships hitherto prevailing between farmers and landowners),[88] it was certainly an overwhelming success. Whereas records reveal only sporadic villeinage conflicts

[85] Ibid., pp. 53, 68, and passim.   [86] Ibid., p. 69.
[87] Ibid., pp. 32–5. Cf. Claus Bjørn 1981b, p. 87.
[88] Christian H. Brasch 1859–63, III, p. 162.

Power 223

during the foregoing decades,[89] the period from the end of the 1760s is full of villeinage strikes and other altercations between farmers and landowners.[90]

At the same time, a certain degree of loyalty was built up among the farmers towards the government, which now, thanks to its admittedly rather theatrical efforts to regulate villeinage work, could claim to be protecting the farmers against the landowners.[91] The villeinage issue served the government as an implement with which to overcome a bothersome political problem, namely, the authorities' inadequate degree of contact with tenant farmers, who were traditionally hostile towards the state.[92]

At the end of the eighteenth century the central administration's policy of dissolving the decentralized power structure was directed primarily at the rural districts. But attention was also focused on the situation in the market towns. The guild system, which in many ways corresponded to village autonomy, was under constant attack from the government.[93] The government also strongly opposed all efforts to create new corporations in the form of workers' or journeymen's associations of the kind attempted during the carpenters' strike in Copenhagen in 1794, which was energetically put down.[94]

To sum up, the government's policy during these years was aimed at dissolving local power structures and privilege systems and creating a more fragmented and individualized society. This policy can also be discerned in the abolition in 1788 of the right solely held by landowners and market towns to fatten oxen in stalls and in the new, liberalized Customs Act of 1797.[95] Liberalism, the new economic doctrine of the eighteenth century, by encouraging the free, economically independent entrepreneur and showing enthusiasm for the free, deregulated market as the only legitimate mechanism for controlling the economic life of the nation, represented a perfect rationalization of the wish of the new civil service elite to split up all local power and privilege structures.[96] No wonder Danish was one of the first languages into which Adam Smith was translated.[97]

[89] Claus Bjørn 1981b, pp. 87–93.
[90] Claus Bjørn 1977, 1978, 1979–81, 1981b, and 1983.
[91] Claus Bjørn 1981b, pp. 93–6; Christian H. Brasch 1859–63, III, p. 162.
[92] Cf. Chapter 8.1.   [93] Anne Riising 1958, pp. 109–11, 126–7, and passim.
[94] Jens Christian Manniche 1972–4.
[95] Hans Jensen 1936–45, I, p. 156; Aage Rasch 1955.
[96] Gail Bossenga 1988, pp. 422–4.   [97] Hans Degen 1936.

224　*The New Denmark*

b. Legislation that Transferred Power into the Hands of the Central Administration

It can be observed how, during the 1780s, the power of the state gradually imposed itself on rural society, which was steadily being weakened by freehold purchases, enclosures, and conflicts about villeinage work and the rights of cottagers. The first major steps were the Colbiørnsen ordinances of 8 June 1787, so named after their originator Christian Colbiørnsen, a Norwegian-born, aggressively anti-aristocratic civil servant. In an introductory declaration, Colbiørnsen stated that

> the King regards the promotion of agriculture as the most natural and lasting source of prosperity for the State, and the upholding of the rights due to each one of his subjects according to his position in society as the most reliable foundation for the liberty and security of its citizens.[98]

He went on to enumerate regulations whose principal aim has since been described as the wish to "abolish all sovereignty for landowners in relation to their tenant farmers and place this whole situation under ordinary legislation and rules of law."[99]

Obviously this could not be achieved by means of two ordinances, for the powers of landowners were very complex and ramified. But important steps were taken in this direction when the state-appointed judges of lower courts as well as the chief administrative officers of counties gradually gained more insight into tenancy contracts and the administration of wills, which hitherto had been handled largely without the intervention of the central administration. From now on, lower court judges were to be involved at both the commencement and termination of tenancy agreements, and chief administrative officers were to act as defendants for farmers accused of neglecting their land. Finally, landowners lost their sovereignty as executors of wills left by tenants on their estates, and this loss in turn helped extend the power held by the judges of the lower courts, who were government officials.

The last regulation in the Colbiørnsen ordinances was the paragraph, now familiar to all Danes, that abolished the right of landowners to inflict corporal chastisement on farmers and their wives.[100] Henceforth, only children, farmhands, and servants could be thrashed in the interests of domestic discipline. In this way the state assumed what was almost a monopoly on harsh physical vio-

---

[98] Hans Jensen 1936–45, I, p. 139.　　[99] Ibid., pp. 139–43, quotation p. 142.
[100] Ibid., I, pp. 141–2.

Power 225

lence, a right that it was to exploit widely. Hitherto, society had managed without any form of domestic army lined up against the civilian population. But the situation now changed. Ever since the late eighteenth century, the building up of an increasingly stronger police force and the expansion of what was previously only a rudimentary prison system have been constant and characteristic features of Denmark's domestic history.[101]

The next offensive to be launched by the government took place the very next year with the abolition of adscription on 21 June 1788 and the subsequent setting up of a state-run military conscription board. This new board was empowered to keep the movements of all young men under surveillance, a regulation that was virtually a new form of adscription: §20 of the ordinance, covering the abolition of adscription, decreed that any young man, having been confirmed on reaching the age of discretion, was to be brought before a medical board and declare on oath "that he would not without permission move away from the district [that is, the recruitment district] without first having obtained a certificate of dismissal or freedom."[102] The only difference was that the new form of adscription was applied within the government's administrative boundaries instead of those of individual manors as previously.

For the male farming population, the abolition of adscription was an event of no or only slight importance, except that (as in the case of enclosure) the farmer class was favoured. Because of the regulation that permitted a man to pay someone else to do his military service for him, far-reaching opportunities arose for heaping the burden of military service on to the poor sector of the rural population.[103]

On the other hand, in terms of the relative strengths of the central administration and decentralized authorities, the abolition of adscription was an event of great significance. It was not only a manifestation of the central administration's victory over the de-

---

[101] Cf. Frederik Stuckenberg 1893–6.
[102] At the same time, the regulations in the ordinance of 14 Sept. 1774, §40, enjoined punishment of deserters and those who helped them. Cf. Finn Stendal Pedersen 1988, p. 41.
[103] The rural population's indifference to the abolition of adscription: None of the three extant farmers' diaries of 1788 makes any mention whatsoever of the abolition of adscription. See Jens Holmgaard 1969, p. 18; Karl Peder Pedersen 1985; and Holger Rasmussen 1982; cf. Finn Stendal Pedersen 1988, p. 42. The mechanisms provided in the new conscription law for burdening the poor sector of the rural population with military service are mentioned in Finn Stendal Pedersen 1988, p. 41; cf. also Rudi Thomsen 1949, pp. 51–2, and Johan Hvidtfeldt 1938, pp. 13–14.

226   *The New Denmark*

centralized authorities but also a step towards obliterating the profound influence exercised for centuries by the big manors on the minds of the rural population, who now slowly came to realize that the boundaries of the big estates meant nothing, and that the state, 'the nation,' was all that counted. The abolition of adscription was an important phase in the process of transforming the rural population of Denmark into Danes. A few years later, a number of citizens of Copenhagen, mostly members of the civil service, had good reason to commemorate the abolition of adscription by raising an obelisk outside Copenhagen's Vesterport (West Gate), at that time out in the countryside, the final conquest of which by the central government was now in sight.[104]

During the ensuing years the central administration consolidated its position on the basis that had been established in 1787–8 by means of a series of initiatives. The landowners retained their authority as tax collectors as long as the tenancy system continued to exist, but in 1793 the rules for imposing distraint for arrears of taxes were tightened in a manner that effectively reduced the landowners' discretion in such matters.[105] By 1802, tax exemption for main farms had come to an end.[106]

Next, a campaign was launched against private judicial districts and *jus vocandi*, that is, the right to appoint a priest. With the ordinance of 3 June 1809, a landowner's right to appoint a judge to the local court and a vicar to the church of which he held the patronage was reduced to the right solely to nominate three suitable persons. Such strict demands were also made on the financial capacity of private judicial districts that they gradually had to be abolished; by the end of the 1850s they had nearly all disappeared.[107] As regards education, the Village School Act of 29 July 1814 deprived landowners of control of an area in which only seventy-five years previously they had triumphantly asserted their power in opposition to the central administration.[108]

A particular problem was posed by the countships and baronies. Sales of freehold plots from these estates could normally not take place because they would automatically come into conflict with the strict regulations that existed to prevent deterioration of assets. On the other hand, there was nothing to prevent enclosure, which indeed took place to a large extent.[109] At the same time, the au-

---

[104] Karin Kryger 1986, pp. 165–71 and passim.
[105] Birgit Løgstrup 1983, pp. 233–5 (also n. 7, p. 425).   [106] See n. 73.
[107] Harald Jørgensen 1970–1; Paul G. Ørberg 1978–9.   [108] Erik Nørr 1981, pp. 225–7.
[109] See, for example, Harald Jørgensen and Fridlev Skrubbeltrang 1942, pp. 330–41.

Power   227

thority of counts and barons as chief administrative officers was undermined in the course of a dogged struggle against the central authorities. The countships and baronies were gradually degraded to inferior administrative and judicial districts. In 1789 the count of Langeland wrote:

> The rights of counts are being docked. We produce proofs dating back hundreds of years, but in vain, for no arguments are brooked. . . . Should this continue, the devil may take all countships, baronies and noblemen, for now we shall all become peasants.[110]

His prediction proved correct. A long time was to pass before the Constitution of 1849 would prohibit the setting up of new fiefs, and even longer until the law passed in 1919, by which the remaining countships and baronies were converted to fee simple. But a change of course had been effected, and there was time to wait. The age-old struggle for power was over: The civil servants had overcome the old Danish aristocratic elite.

Traditional village autonomy collapsed along with the old elite. Earlier, each parish had had a local parish bailiff, but the office was only rudimentary. The ordinance of 11 November 1791 established it as a permanent feature of public administration, the government's outpost in small communities; its holder, as 'local chief of police', gradually replaced the locally appointed alderman.[111] Furthermore, in 1795, a nationwide system of local justices of the peace was established under the surveillance of the chiefs of the various administrative districts to handle the increasing number of small litigations that village councils and/or the patriarchal dictates of landowners no longer had the authority to deal with. These state-appointed magistrates had, as one Copenhagen functionary observed in 1803, "unmistakably, a beneficial influence on the common people's way of thinking."[112] The final phase of governmental regulation and disciplining of conditions in rural areas was introduced by the Rural District Council Act of 1841,[113] which removed the remains of age-old village autonomy based on bylaws.

From having been small autonomous republics, with direct access to the European world via the network of hundreds of local centres of culture spread over the country by the old cosmopolitan elite, these local communities were now reduced to lonely is-

---

[110] Anne Riising 1976, p. 198; Lotte Dombernowsky 1983, p. 11 (quotation) and passim.
[111] Jørgen Dieckmann Rasmussen 1978, pp. 16–22; Poul Meyer 1954–6, p. 129.
[112] Lotte Dombernowsky 1985, pp. 20–7, 191.   [113] Poul Meyer 1954–6, pp. 133–9.

228   *The New Denmark*

lands, administrative units under the careful control of a jealous and small-minded central administration.

8.3 CONDITIONS THAT PAVED THE WAY
FOR THE BREAKTHROUGH OF CENTRALISTIC
BUREAUCRATIC GOVERNMENT

At the beginning of the 1760s very few observers probably realized that centralistic government was about to make its definitive breakthrough in Denmark and that it would conquer the old aristocratic elite within the course of a generation.[114] However, with the benefit of historical hindsight it is easier to understand.

Two different groups of conditions determined the breakthrough of centralistic bureaucratic government. One group embraced conditions that were independent of the ecological revolution and the other those resulting from the ecological revolution and the processes initiated by it. The first of these two groups includes the increased capacity of the governmental apparatus and the transformation of the printing press into a mass medium capable of providing the basis of a public opinion. The second group includes not only a growing desire on the part of the nobility to lead their own private lives but also social polarization in rural society.

a. Independent Conditions

The lack of a well-developed bureaucratic apparatus and the inadequacy of available systems of communications together had been the central administration's Achilles' heel for centuries. These deficiencies reemerged during the first years after the introduction of absolute monarchy in 1660, when the bureaucracy found it impossible to maintain power.

This situation was slowly rectified during the first century of the absolute monarchy. The civil servant class grew, while at the same time its members became more professional and homogenized as a result of the various forms of training introduced from time to time, such as the training of naval officers in 1701. The University of Copenhagen, which had previously concentrated on educating young men who wished to enter the church, introduced law studies in 1736.[115] The postal services were continually being ex-

---

[114] Cf. Birgit Løgstrup 1983, p. 359.
[115] Ole Feldbæk 1982, pp. 83–7. On the growth, professionalization, and homogenization of the civil servant class: Axel Linvald 1921, pp. 257–8; Gunner Lind 1987, pp. 223–4

Power   229

panded.[116] Finally, during the course of the eighteenth century, the central administration obtained a wider knowledge of the kingdom it was administrating through an increasing volume of topographical and statistical literature and the detailed mapping of the country in accordance with advanced trigonometrical principles.[117] Whereas previously the central administration had to a certain extent been fumbling blindly, in the eighteenth century it found itself increasingly able to work on the basis of solid, detailed knowledge. Proof of the growing capacity of the governmental apparatus during the eighteenth century as well as of its sounder grasp of the details of the country's social structure was the increase in the number of pages of law texts per year. Following a steadily rising tendency, output during the eighteenth century became four or five times as large as before (fig. 20).

Another important condition for the breakthrough of centralized government was the emergence of public opinion during the second half of the eighteenth century. At the beginning of the century it was still impossible to speak of Danish public opinion in the sense of a broad awareness of matters of public interest. This was because there was no medium capable of conveying the detailed insight necessary for the formation of such opinion. At that time, newspapers and magazines were read by 1 percent of the adult population at most. This changed in the course of the eighteenth century: The regular press became a mass medium and by the end of the century was being read by an estimated 10 percent of the adult population.[118]

Public opinion arose in the wake of this development. It was difficult to interpret precisely, but there was no doubt about its existence. Tangible evidence of the population's interest in politics and communal affairs was provided by the formation of a great many associations and clubs during the second half of the eighteenth century.[119] A rarely noticed, but not insignificant aspect of this growing interest in public affairs is an increasingly eager exchange of opinions as demonstrated by an explosion in correspondence during the eighteenth century: Between 1718–19 and

and 1986b, especially p. 178. On the training of naval officers: H. C. A. Lund 1901. On law studies: Erik Reitzel-Nielsen and Carl Popp-Madsen 1936, especially pp. 84–114, 271–95.

[116] Fritz Olsen 1903, pp. 48–68, 162–77, 255–303.

[117] The basic topographical work was Erik Pontoppidan's *Danske Atlas* (1763–81), followed by a number of lesser works, e.g., J. N. Wilse 1767. On statistical literature: Axel Holck 1901. On cartography: Ole Feldbæk 1982, p. 10.

[118] Thorkild Kjærgaard 1989b, p. 223.

[119] Jørgen H. Monrad 1978; Niels Clemmensen 1987.

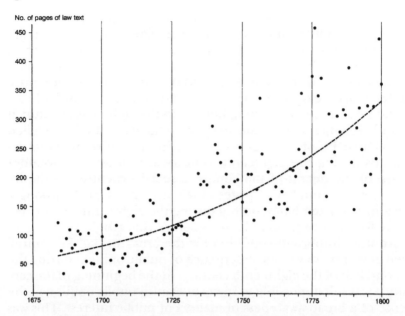

Figure 20. Number of pages of law texts per year, 1683–1800.

1807, the number of private letters handled by the postal services increased by about 500 percent.[120]

b. Conditions Resulting from the Ecological Revolution

One of the most remarkable features of the eighteenth-century history of mentalities is the way the nobility gradually gave up being public figures and became private individuals instead. The term 'bourgeoisification' has been coined to describe the clear tendency among aristocrats of the century to abandon their traditional role as a distinguished social elite upon whom all eyes focused and instead behave merely as slightly superior citizens.[121]

One of the areas in which this tendency left its mark was architecture. Manor houses with dignified, formal exteriors and interiors of the kind that had been built since the Middle Ages were still being erected in the 1740s but went out of fashion during the last half of the eighteenth century. They were replaced by villas of the *maison de plaisance* type, devoid of large reception rooms and

[120] Fritz Olsen 1903, pp. 73, 327.
[121] G. Chaussinand-Nogaret 1984; Dieter Lohmeier 1980. On traditional aristocratic culture: Norbert Elias 1975; Otto Brunner 1949; Dieter Lohmeier 1978.

Power 231

equipped solely for private dwelling purposes. Examples are Frederiksgave (Funen, 1775), Langesø (Funen, 1774–8), Dronninggård near Furesøen (Lake Fure) (north of Copenhagen, completed in 1783), Hindemae (Funen, ca. 1790), and Stenalt (East Jutland, 1799).[122] Instead of being set in formal, baroque gardens, they were surrounded by landscape gardens in the new English style, which helped to emphasize their informal, private character.[123]

Portraiture was another area in which the trend towards bourgeoisification was clearly noticeable. The imposing portrait of a grand seigneur with his time-honoured iconography – armour, coat of arms, and other clear marks to denote membership in the kingdom's highest estate – was still being commissioned unhesitatingly in the 1750s and 1760s, but during the 1770s these accoutrements disappeared in paintings as if by the wave of a magic wand. A new type of unostentatious portrait reflecting bourgeois intimacy and emotions came into fashion, a genre mastered brilliantly by the Danish painter Jens Juel, whose fame spread throughout Europe – his 'portrait factory' became a tremendous success.[124]

As already mentioned, the growing interest displayed during the eighteenth century in the nuclear family and in emotions, and in marriage as a bond based on romantic love instead of merely on duty and mutual respect between spouses in a *mariage de convenance*, may be seen in conjunction with changes in the disease pattern.[125] But the steadily increasing acceptance of individual emotions manifested by the members of aristocratic circles was also linked to a wish to abandon a flamboyant lifestyle in favour of greater privacy. Among the traditional aristocracy, whose members spent their lives as if on a stage, forever exposed to the public gaze, private feelings were largely of no importance; if they did exist, they were almost a hindrance. Spouses had separate wings in buildings, matrimonial bedrooms did not exist,[126] and people not only were permitted to watch their lords and ladies at table[127] but were even permitted to watch newly married members of the nobility retiring to bed.[128] Things were very different when spouses

---

[122] Hakon Lund 1980, pp. 91–177; Arthur G. Hassø 1943–5, II, pp. 668–76; III, pp. 281–5; IV, pp. 261–4; Dieter Lohmeier 1980, pp. 132–3; Christian Elling 1939, p. 16 and figs. 55–8. On Dronninggård: Eiler Nystrøm 1938, pp. 474–94. Cf. Christian Elling 1942, p. 58.

[123] Chapter 5.1. [124] Vagn Poulsen et al., 1972–5, III, pp. 174–80.

[125] Chapter 7.5.

[126] Spouses having separate bedrooms until the end of the eighteenth century: Dieter Lohmeier 1980, p. 132.

[127] Harald Langberg 1951, p. 58.

[128] See, for example, the bed of state executed for Count Christian Danneskiold-Samsøe's

232 The New Denmark

and children lived together *en famille*. Without love and mutual compatibility, life could become disastrous.

Not all aristocrats were as fortunate as Count C. D. Reventlow and his wife, Sophie. Letters written by the countess in the 1790s describe a life of bourgeois cosiness hardly surpassed by the Biedermeier culture of the following century:

> Domestic bliss reigns in our home. . . . We spend our evenings amongst our children: my husband studies at his writing-desk; we dance, draw, gossip and read in the same room, and when my husband wishes to re-fresh himself for a moment he capers through the room with the chil-dren, taking part in their hilarity. Often, at the end of a day's work, indeed almost daily, when the children have been put to bed and we sit together for an hour or so, my husband thanks God for all the kindness He has shown him . . . and then tears of gratitude run down our cheeks. . . . I pray to God that many a pleasure as yet unknown to us may await us in our old age, which our children will sweeten in due course when we *breathe a second spring* [in English in the original letter] in their happy company.[129]

Even linguistic style changed. The language of the nobility, which during the sixteenth and seventeenth centuries had been la-conic, authoritative, and extroverted,[130] became effusive, emo-tional, and sentimental during the last decades of the eighteenth century. A characteristic example is Count Reventlow's often-quoted letter of 1786 to his sister on the occasion of the setting up of the Greater Agrarian Commission:

> Joyfully, and grateful to God, do I pen these lines. No, my wife has not been delivered, she has given birth to no son. . . . No doubt she will trail around for another fortnight. But a thousand sons have been borne to me, a thousand daughters. . . . Joyfully do they drive well-fed horses to work with light ploughs, singing a little song about the yellow giant,[131] who in his cave seemed like a monster to the dwarfs who had held them bound, but to them was a joyful messenger of freedom, bringing the tid-ings that God's blessings have come, that He loves the country He has blessed and that He will crown the soil of this land, small though it may be, with renewed blessings. There lies the rubbish: the chains, the yokes, the dungeons, the long whips, the timber-mares, the Spanish capes: all are gone. Hurrah, hurrah, hurrah! Shout, cry out with me in order that

wedding in 1724 to Catharine Christiane von Holstein, Frederiksborg Museum, Hillerød, inv. no. B 592.

[129] Christian B. Reventlow 1902–3, I, pp. 157–8 (letter of 20 Nov. 1790).
[130] See, for example, G. L. Wad 1893.
[131] "The yellow giant" (Der gelbe Riese) was the writer's nickname in his family.

Power 233

> our voices may intercept where the great gentlemen wearing blue ribbons are sitting.[132]

The almost self-denying distance which Reventlow here places between himself and the "great gentlemen wearing blue ribbons," in other words, his own class, along with the lifestyle, rights, and obligations that had been theirs for centuries, was also demonstrated by the recipient of this letter, Countess Louise Stolberg, who put her family tree into the fire. Another noble who shared the same views was Count Adam Ditlev Moltke, who, during a dinner party at Bregentved Manor in 1790 shortly after the outbreak of the French Revolution, spoke warmly in the presence of his grandfather, A. G. Moltke (the last survivor of the old 'excellencies') in favour of abolishing all entailed property, and also changed the design of his seal so that the three birds in the Moltke coat of arms became three Phrygian caps.[133] In the same aristocratic circles the francophile poet Jens Baggesen won applause by declaring that he "hated the aristocrats from the bottom of his heart" and "would gladly have taken part in killing them."[134]

As a consequence of the new trend among the nobility to start living their lives in privacy instead of in the public view, members of the old elite began to lose interest in their role as local 'vice-regents,' which was not only burdensome and expensive but now also was regarded by many nobles as illegitimate. This attitude emerged clearly in the person of C. D. Reventlow, who, in one of his reports to the Greater Agrarian Commission of 1786, after having remarked that "the aristocratic republics have always been the hardest and most unfortunate societies," continued:

> No matter how fortunate the state of being a landowner may seem to me, and how much pride I take, by promoting the welfare of my subordinates, in establishing a basis for the constant happiness of many families, I nevertheless hate all the many rights by which such subordinates may be subjected to discretionary treatment by myself, my children or my officers, and even more must they be hated by the Master of the Land [i.e., the king] and other members of the State who either suffer under them themselves or see their fellow-citizens abused and humiliated by them.[135]

Opinions such as these obviously made matters easier for an aggressively advancing central government.

[132] Louis Bobé 1895–1932, I, p. 87. "The great gentlemen wearing blue ribbons": Knights of the Order of the Elephant.
[133] Dieter Lohmeier 1980, p. 142; Axel Pontoppidan 1939, p. 68.
[134] Christian Hermann Jensen 1989, pp. 4–5. [135] C. D. Reventlow 1786, pp. 269–70.

234   *The New Denmark*

It is difficult to account convincingly for this tendency towards bourgeoisification in aristocratic circles. It would appear to have taken place for no apparent reason, like a deus ex machina, and therefore it has been regarded in a rather vague, general way as being the result of the ideological influence of eighteenth-century Enlightenment philosophy.[136] This is probably part of the explanation. However, it is also reasonable to see the trend as being connected with the new, objective conditions imposed by the green revolution.

The increased amount of labour that was being invested in agriculture also manifested itself as a strongly increased demand on the landowners themselves to keep abreast of farming methods and even to participate in the business of farming. Professionalization in agriculture resulted in fewer opportunities for indulging in a time-consuming, opulent, aristocratic lifestyle.

An additional part of the explanation comes from the effects of the transformation of the landscape as a result of the ecological revolution. The classic lifestyle of the aristocracy was in many ways symbiotically bound up with the old countryside. This applied, for example, to hunting. Alongside war, hunting on horseback with dogs had been the preferred sport of the aristocracy since antiquity. It symbolized the life led by the lords of manors and was a regular subject in the extensive range of handbooks on agriculture and the aristocratic way of life published during the sixteenth and seventeenth centuries.[137] A description written in 1757 reveals that hunting was still a principal feature in the life of a noble in the middle of the eighteenth century:

> When the 12th of September arrives, being the date on which the hunting season commences, as announced by the public notice of 6th of August 1744, it is as if the enemy had attacked the country. At least the hares must think so. Each and every man must needs mount his horse and ride out, be he one-eyed, bent double, hunch-backed, or lame. He who brings with him the largest number of people and the largest number of dogs is most to be admired.[138]

But all this was soon to fade into the past. Hunting had been declining for a long time as a result of forest clearance and a shortage of game, little being left but hares. This was bad enough, for

[136]   Cf. Ib Olsen 1983, especially pp. 166–75.
[137]   Vitus Gay 1944; Thorkild Kjærgaard 1984. Among the most magnificent works of the period on hunting is Johann Täntzer's *Der Dianen hohe u. niedere Jagtgeheimnüsz*, published in Copenhagen between 1682 and 1689 in three large volumes.
[138]   Anon. 1757, pp. 11–12. Cf. F. Ahlefeldt-Laurvig 1927–31, III, pp. 173–200.

Power 235

hares could hardly be expected to provide the best sport. Even worse was that it was hardly possible any longer for a hunt to move across the countryside, for the green revolution in progress was creating a network of deep ditches, high, thick fences, and dense forest reserves.[139] The new landscape forced the nobility to assume a more static lifestyle, one that demanded less space; the classic, expansive manner formerly displayed by Denmark's aristocrats was gradually abandoned.

Hunting had long been a colourful element in the landscape and social life of the country, but its disappearance failed to cause many regrets, for public opinion, both at the time and later, regarded the sport as a parasitic upper-class phenomenon detrimental to the interests of the ordinary working farmer. This view was expressed by the Danish poet B. S. Ingemann in an 1816 poem called "King Valdemar's Hunt":

> Hunters and their hounds alike
> Would gallop gaily past.
> All bare they laid the forest
> To reach the frightened deer.
> The farmer's golden crop withal
> Lay trampled in the dust.
>
> Then sighed the mourning farmer
> And wrung his hands in grief.
> On swept the hunters and their hounds
> Not noticing a thing . . .[140]

Not many people gave a thought to the fact that the sport was also a last, wistful reminder of the Danish people's early beginnings as a freeborn race of hunters. Nor were there many who realized that with the disappearance of hunting an immediate point of contact between landowners and the population withered away. The landowner, from having been a man on horseback who rode everywhere and was seen by all,[141] became, to an increasing extent, a distant, unreal person who spent his time either in his office or on the road in a closed carriage. And thus, also via this winding path, the ecological revolution contributed to a dissolution of the old patriarchal society by creating a more distant and reserved relationship between the old elite and the population.

The landowners on the eastern islands of Denmark were among the first to feel the impact of the green revolution on their old-

---

[139] C. Weismann 1931, pp. 435, 453, 457.
[140] Quoted by F. J. Billeskov Jansen 1985–7, II, p. 136. See also Povl Hansen 1889, p. 12; C. Christensen (Hørsholm) 1879, pp. 88–9. Cf. Knud J. V. Jespersen 1988, p. 150.
[141] F. Ahlefeldt-Laurvig 1927–31, V, p. 112.

236   *The New Denmark*

fashioned, aristocratic lifestyle. Owing to the proximity of the capital, whose rhythm and ideals were dominated more and more by bourgeois civil servants, this way of life not only became quite impossible to sustain but also perhaps began to appear slightly ridiculous and antiquatedly rustic. The last bastion was Jutland, where the greater distance from the capital, in conjunction with the slower progress of the ecological revolution, permitted old aristocratic ideals and habits to survive a little longer. One of the last places in Denmark where large-scale hunting of a wide range of game (including wild boar, wolves, deer, and any number of smaller animals) was still practised during the 1750s and 1760s was Dronninglund Manor in North Jutland.[142] In this connection, it is of interest to note that a coalition of landowners formed in 1790 in protest against the agrarian reforms, and which became the last, ineffectual attempt by the old elite to unite against the new elite, arose in Jutland and failed to gain any appreciable support on the islands of eastern Denmark.[143]

Several participants in the Jutland landowner protest upheld old aristocratic ideals to a pronounced degree. One of the leaders was F. L. C. Beenfelt, who later gained distinction in various ways, including through his generosity in setting up charitable foundations. The old aristocratic set of norms behind the protest in Jutland was also revealed by the procedure chosen by the landowners. They did not address themselves to the Crown as represented by the crown prince in Copenhagen, the seat of government, but waited until the heir to the throne should happen to come to their own part of the country. This took place in September 1790, when a deputation sought out the crown prince while he was staying at Louisenlund Manor in Schleswig on the occasion of his wedding.

This medieval procedure was not appreciated everywhere, as was to emerge in an almost tragicomic fashion during the subsequent political confrontation when the Jutland landowners were accused, among other things, of having disturbed the crown prince during his honeymoon.[144] These provincial nobles had most likely never envisaged the possibility that this aspect of their protest could represent a problem. They adhered to norms that stemmed from the time before spouses shared the same bedroom, and could not imagine that their feudal lord and master could possibly be prevented from receiving them just because he was newly married.

The terribly old-fashioned outlook maintained by the Jutland landowners was a reality which the progressive elements of the day, to their

[142] L. T. Fogtmann 1927–8.   [143] Claus Bjørn 1979–81.
[144] Christian Colbiørnsen 1790, p. [3].

Power 237

annoyance and surprise, were forced to acknowledge time and again.
When Laurits Engelstoft (a Jutland vicar's son and supporter of the
French Revolution) travelled through North Zealand he was delighted to
see so many landscape gardens in the English style and recalled in hor-
ror the gardens of the past

> when the fashion was to impose upon nature the self-same stiff, formal
> pattern as that displayed by members of the court, by which I mean
> heavily trimmed, arrow-straight avenues, ingeniously arranged mono-
> grams, etc., of the kind still to be seen, on a smaller scale, at most manor
> houses in Jutland.[145]

Another factor, also resulting from the ecological revolution
and of decisive importance to the breakthrough of centralistic
government, was the line of development in rural society. The
increasing power wielded by the farmer class opened up the
possibility of an alternative basis of power. Instead of constantly
having to run their heads against a brick wall of resistance as
represented by the old landowner class, the government attempted to win the support of the farmers. As already mentioned,
this came about partly by destabilizing the existing relationship between landowners and farmers (especially as regards
the question of villeinage work) and partly by supporting farmers
in their altercations with cottagers and farm labourers – conflicts that had been developing since the beginning of the eighteenth century.

In 1762, even before the 'rule of excellencies' had fallen, the
law covering the so-called extra tax, or poll tax, had the effect of
heaping the burdens on to the cottager and farm labourer group
to the advantage of the farmer class.[146] Gradually, as the eighteenth
century drew to its close, government support for the farmers became more systematic. In the question of *lønnesæd* (see Chapter
3.5) and the conflict about *skulteuger* (see Chapter 6.1) the government desired a solution that, as it was formulated in a report
submitted on 21 March 1770, would mean that the farmer could
"once more assume his natural place as master."[147] In June 1771
the government made its relations with cottagers even cooler by
declaring that the villeinage ordinance of 20 January 1771 (which
was favourable to the farmers) did not apply to persons whose
properties amounted to less than 1 *tønde hartkorn* – in other words,

[145] Laurits Engelstoft 1961, p. 34   [146] Chapter 6.3.
[147] Fridlev Skrubbeltrang 1940, p. 235.

238   The New Denmark

did not apply to cottagers.[148] The year 1781 saw the introduction of the important enclosure legislation, which gave farmers carte blanche to expropriate cottagers' rights provided that they could talk the landowner into it.[149] This was followed by a series of regulations that also discriminated strongly against cottagers and farm labourers, including, as has been mentioned, a new adjustment of military service regulations after the abolition of adscription of 1788.

The conflict between the farmers and the lower classes was not due solely to the actual struggle for access to resources, but was nurtured also by the anxiety being diffused throughout society as a result of increased social polarization and negative social mobility. Even among the farmers, who had drawn the longest straw, social anxiety was widespread because they were confronted in their daily lives with the losers in the social struggle, often within their own family circle.[150] As a cleric on the island of Funen expressed it,

> generally there is a fear that the large number of cottagers which already exists, and which will increase when crops fail and we experience difficult times for a few years in succession, will be like a tidal wave of beggars, spreading throughout the country, and in some cases dangerous beggars (for they are fit and strong) who could easily think of getting together and – if I may venture to say so – forming gangs of thieves and robbers.[151]

An important – and for many farmers, attractive – consequence of enclosure was the resultant physical separation of the farmer and cottager classes. Either the farmers moved out to the newly enclosed fields and left the cottagers behind in the villages, or vice versa. A common practice was for cottagers to be removed to colonies on the outskirts of the areas belonging to the village, near a bog or on a stony piece of land. Alternatively, their new homes could be spread over the lands belonging to the farmers of the village, for example, by placing one or two cottages on the borders of plots belonging to individual farmers.[152] This purely physical

[148] A. Sørensen 1941–2, pp. 120–1; J. L. Lybecker 1772–84, II, pp. 312–13. On the government's attitude when it was caught between promises made to cottagers and political expediency: Fridlev Skrubbeltrang 1940, p. 289.

[149] Chapter 6.2, section b.

[150] Chapter 6.2, section b. Cf. Hans Vammen 1990, p. 292 and passim.

[151] Quoted by Gregers Begtrup 1803–12, III, pp. 69–70.

[152] Examples of this are provided on nearly every enclosure map. For the main types, i.e., removal of cottagers and removal of farmers, respectively, see Karl-Erik Frandsen 1988a, p. 50, and Lotte Dombernowsky 1988, p. 322. Cf. Erland Porsmose 1988, p. 241 (map of the parish of Skamby, Funen, ca. 1800) and Fridlev Skrubbeltrang 1940, p. 291.

Power   239

separation of the classes, which placed the threatening lower class literally out of sight, soothed the farmers' social anxiety.

Domestic servants and farmhands could not be kept out of sight in the same way, but farmers could at least keep them at a certain distance, partly by arranging separate living quarters for them – often in or adjacent to the cowhouse or stables – and partly by establishing a clear social distinction. Whereas previously servants and farmhands had enjoyed positions as more or less 'one of the family' on farms, this practice was now discontinued. As one Funen farmer put it: "It was no longer any of their business whether the master of the house had visitors."[153]

Parallel with a violent wave of anti-aristocratism, a widespread fear of 'the mob' could be observed throughout Europe at the end of the eighteenth century. An opportunity to vent both these feelings uninhibitedly was in the form of commentaries on the French Revolution. In Denmark, for example, in a monthly called *Minerva*, the editor, on behalf of "the honourable class of citizens, the friends of peace and good order and enemies of tyranny just as much as of rebellious movements,"[154] rejoiced at the abolition of the privileges of the aristocracy,[155] while at the same time making violent attacks on the lower classes, who were referred to as "the quick-tempered dregs of society," "a wild rabble," "the scum of humanity, the most despicable robbers."[156]

Jens Baggesen, too, as mentioned earlier, hated the aristocrats with all his heart and would gladly have taken a hand in killing them if only Paris were a little closer. But this did not imply that he sympathized with the lower classes and their cause – on the contrary. Marat, the leader of the Parisian proletariat, was in Baggesen's eyes "the despicable author of a newspaper: *L'Ami du Peuple*, ... which is generally referred to by the more appropriate name: *l'ennemi de la nation*."[157] Events in France also provided another Danish author, K. L. Rahbek, with an opportunity to express anxiety:

> This revolution undeniably contains a terrible warning to princes, who can see here the lengths to which a mistreated people can go; but it also contains a no less horrible and emphatic warning to all those concerned for the welfare of their country: not to touch the dams that hold back the onward rush of the common people, for once the stream of rebellion rages, no human hand can say: you are only to come this far and no further.[158]

---

[153] Thorkild Kjærgaard 1979–80, pp. 190–1; N. Rasmussen Søkilde 1875–8, p. 123.
[154] Christen Pram 1789, p. 129.   [155] Ibid., pp. 290–2.
[156] Ibid., p. 129, and 1792, pp. 395–6.
[157] Christian Hermann Jensen 1989, pp. 4–5.
[158] K. L. Rahbek 1792, p. 545. Cf. Thorkild Kjærgaard 1989a, pp. 89–100.

240   *The New Denmark*

c. The Melting Down of the Old Political System

The tendencies that lay deep in the social structure – the expansion of the capacity of the governmental apparatus, the gradual crystallization of public opinion, and the accumulating effects of the ecological revolution – took a long time to emerge. They were not to gather real momentum until they became so powerful that they made contact with and reinforced each other. The situation came to a head after 1750; all that was needed at this point was some additional form of heat to spark the process that would melt down the old political system. The kindling was provided in 1766 with the accession of the new king.

Christian VII was young and impressionable. He had been brought up to have the loftiest ideas of royal power and was, therefore, sympathetic to approaches from groups who clung to the suppressed but always latent anti-aristocratic tradition in the Danish central administration. During the 1760s, anti-aristocratic attitudes were strongly represented in the military sector, which had found a hero in a senior French officer, Claude Louis Saint-Germain, who had been summoned to Denmark during the last years of the reign of Frederik V. Saint-Germain made valiant but fruitless attempts to break the influence exercised by the Danish aristocracy on the army.[159]

Shortly after his accession, Christian VII dismissed 'their excellencies' one by one, whereupon the way was paved for the opposition to move in. A group of ambitious, anti-aristocratic persons under the leadership of Johann Friedrich Struensee stepped to the forefront. Realizing swiftly where the political battle must be fought in a society dominated by the agrarian sector, this new group of leaders outlined the fundamentals of an aggressive reform policy whose ostensible aim was to strengthen agriculture, but whose real purpose was to strengthen the central administration.[160]

This basic strategy remained unaltered. Despite exhausting struggles for power within the higher ranks of the central administration, the old elite was completely outmanoeuvred within the next three or four decades. In contrast to the situation after 1660, the administration's success was possible now partly because the governmental apparatus had been expanded and was therefore capable of shouldering its new burdens and partly because the central administration was aided by some extremely advantageous political circumstances.

---

[159] John Danstrup 1947–9a.   [160] Thorkild Kjærgaard 1989b, pp. 225–6.

Power 241

The first of these circumstances was the weakening of the aristocracy through their desire to start leading private lives. The landowners lost both the aptitude and the wish to be landowners in the old-fashioned 'feudal' sense, and many allowed themselves to be tempted by the opportunities to dispose of their tenant farms in an advantageous manner in order to concentrate on their new role as landowning, capitalistic, private individuals. The other circumstance was public opinion. The mass media, which to a large extent were controlled by civil service circles,[161] exploited the waverings and doubts of the old elite in order to whip up an increasingly unrestrained anti-aristocratic public opinion. At the same time the media started to glorify the bourgeoisie and, especially, the farmer class, the new major factor in Danish home politics. The free, independent, owner-occupier farmer on enclosed lands was represented as an economic and moral ideal.

The prorevolutionary author P. A. Heiberg's formulation of the anti-aristocratic manifesto is still well remembered in Denmark:

> Orders and decorations are hung on idiots
> Stars and ribbons are reserved for the nobility.[162]

Less known today is M. G. Birckner's withering criticism of the nobility, though it made a strong impression at the time. In his "Answer to the question: Should the nobility be suppressed?" Birckner accused, amongst others, "the mighty aristocracy, the highly influential allies who surrounded the Throne and were landowners" for having thwarted for decades the king's and the people's wish to "abolish the oppressive slavery endured by farmers." In Birckner's view, the aristocracy "as has been said in France, is often a veritable barrier between the king and his people."[163] Evidence of the self-glorification of the bourgeoisie includes the emergence of a number of new terms at the end of the eighteenth century, for example, *borgerdyd* (literally, 'civic virtue'), which has survived to the present day in the names of two Copenhagen schools.[164]

An early climax in the exaltation of the free, independent farmer was reached by Charlotta Dorothea Biehl's emotional poem of 1771 entitled "Liberty and Property."[165] A later example was Thomas Thaarup's lyrical

[161] During the decade 1789–99, about two-thirds of the persons engaged in political publishing as writers, translators, or magazine editors were government employees. Thorkild Kjærgaard 1973, I, pp. 52–3.
[162] Quoted by F. J. Billeskov Jansen 1985–7, I, p. 277.
[163] M. G. Birckner 1790, pp. 25–6.
[164] Østre Borgerdyd and Vestre Borgerdyd. Cf. Thorkild Kjærgaard 1989b, p. 229.
[165] Charlotta Dorothea Biehl 1771. See also a poem written in the same year by the Norwegian Hans Bull, "Om Landmandens Lyksalighed ved Friheds og Eiendoms Nydelse" (On the Farmer's Happiness at enjoying Freedom and Property).

242 The New Denmark

drama opera of 1790, *Høst-Gildet* (The harvest festival), whose idealized representation of the farmers of Zealand was a tremendous success.[166] The ideal farmer of the new era was found in the Norwegian hereditary freeholder, who, unlike the Danish tenant farmer, was not tied to a landowner. During the last half of the eighteenth century this gave rise to a veritable mania for Norway in Denmark, one of its many manifestations being the fifty-five statues of Norwegian peasants erected during the 1760s in Nordmandsdalen (Norwegian Valley) in the grounds of Fredensborg Palace in North Zealand; copies were also made in porcelain.[167] Adulation of the independent freeholder was a natural part of the systematic worship of the free, economically independent entrepreneur that formed part of the new economic doctrine of liberalism at the end of the eighteenth century.[168]

The political constellation working for the central administration released a series of uncontrollable, accelerating feedback mechanisms. The movement did not let itself be stopped by opposition but virtually fed on it instead. This lesson was learned by the Jutland landowners who, at the beginning of the 1790s, tried to stem the tide of developments by seeking audience with the crown prince but merely achieved the opposite, for anti-aristocratic propaganda was whipped up to new heights. A few days after the visit paid by the deputation of Jutland landowners, Heiberg commented on the event as follows:

> Here[169] we do not teach despotic dogmas.
> Liberty for human beings is our aim.
> No slaves do we desire, nor ruined farmers
> As is the goal of Jutland's lofty lords
>   We feed ourselves;
>   And do not waste
>   Like fools the produce of our fields.[170]

8.4 WINNERS AND LOSERS

A striking feature of the political revolution during the last decades of the eighteenth century is the way the central administration managed to impose its will everywhere. The old power structures

---

[166] Arthur Aumont and Edgar Collin 1897–1900, V, 1, p. 396.
[167] Johann Gottfried Grund 1773; S. B. Fredstrup 1939, pp. 124–41. Wooden copies of Grund's statues were set up in the grounds of Brahesborg Manor, Funen. Christian Elling 1939, p. 31.
[168] Cf. Chapter 8.2, section a.　　　　　　　　[169] I.e., in Copenhagen.
[170] Quoted by F. J. Billeskov Jansen 1985–7, I, p. 277.

Power 243

were crushed without the emergence of new ones that could impede the central administration's demand for hegemony. The farmers, upon whose support the government to a large extent depended, also emerged victorious, even though they were obliged to see their interests thwarted in important respects. The dissolution of village autonomy can hardly have been to their liking, and they were also disappointed in the matter of villeinage work, for they found it hard to accept that the whole purpose of all the fuss and talk about villeinage was social destabilization and not, as they had hoped and expected, a reduction of their burdens, which never took place.[171]

In dealing with the landowner class, it is striking to note how mercilessly the government behaved when it came to expropriating decentralized political power. The landowners lost, but not everything – the government carefully avoided clashing with their economic interests at any time.[172] The real losers were the cottagers, servants, and farm labourers. Macroeconomic development was against them, so nobody was interested in their situation, least of all the Machiavellian state.[173]

During the period from 1750 to 1800 the parallelogram of political strengths underwent significant changes. The landowners and the cottagers lost power. The farmers and the bureaucrats gained power. The landowners, who in reality had previously controlled Danish home politics, had been ousted by the central administration. The changing of the guard within the Danish elite was complete. The Danish Revolution of 1500–1800 was over: A world had collapsed, and a new one had arisen in its place.

[171] Fridlev Skrubbeltrang 1973, p. 24; Thorkild Kjærgaard 1980, p. 70.
[172] Thorkild Kjærgaard 1989b, p. 229; Jens Holmgaard 1977–8, pp. 43–4.
[173] Jens Holmgaard 1977–8, p. 43; Hans Jensen 1936–45, I, pp. 210–16; Finn Stendal Pedersen 1989.

Part IV

THE DRIVING FORCES BEHIND THE DANISH REVOLUTION, 1500–1800

9

THE AGRARIAN REFORMS

The prevailing view in Danish historiography is that the agrarian reforms represented the great turning point in Denmark's history. The freehold legislation of 1769, the enclosure ordinance of 1781, the abolition of adscription in 1788, the Forest Reserve Act of 1805, and the Village School Act of 1814 formed, together with a number of less conspicuous laws, the point of departure for the rapid economic, cultural, social, and political development of the whole of Danish society during the nineteenth and twentieth centuries.

In the course of the present examination of Denmark's transformation from a society gradually sinking into an abysmal ecological crisis to one in permanent growth, nothing has emerged to confirm the accuracy of this view. The agrarian reforms emerge only at a late stage in the course of events, both chronologically and analytically, because they are the result of the ecological revolution and not its cause. There is no demonstrably positive connection, for example, between, on the one hand, progressive measures such as water level regulation and the introduction of clover and, on the other, the order imposed on the organization of agriculture by the agrarian reforms.

Had there been such a connection one might have presumed that key innovations such as water level regulation and clover cultivation would have initially appeared on estates where enclosure had taken place, in freehold areas, and in areas where little or no villeinage existed. This would imply that the primary centres of innovation should have been peripheral areas such as West Jutland and various islands such as Læsø, Fanø, and Bornholm, where freehold tenure, enclosed, consolidated farms, and farms unhampered by villeinage were common, and only a few small manors existed, or none at all. But this was not the case.

On the contrary, these were the last areas to wrest themselves from the clutches of the ecological crisis, a circumstance un-

247

248   *Driving Forces of Revolution*

doubtedly bound up with the fact that it was particularly difficult to carry out coordinated improvements in these strongly individualistic regions.[1] There are indications to the effect that in these areas it was much more difficult, for example, to carry out water level regulation, which nearly always called for a common, coordinated effort, that was the case in villages with communal arrangements. Whereas the Agricultural Society's records are full of prizes awarded for group work carried out by villagers, such as the nineteen inhabitants of the village and parish of Kundby in Zealand, who in 1789 were awarded 60 rix-dollars for having dug 4,970 *favne* of ditches, examples of water level regulation are seldom to be found in freeholder areas. The prevailing attitude among the independent farmers of Bornholm, for example, seems to have been one of complete disdain for any form of cooperative enterprise.[2] And it was certainly not in West Jutland or on the islands of Læsø or Bornholm that clover was first introduced (see figs. 8–11).

It must of course be conceded that ecological degradation as a result of sand drift and heath formation was particularly serious in West Jutland and on Læsø, and to some extent also on Bornholm, and that the task of regeneration was therefore particularly difficult in these regions – but then it was also particularly urgent. However, one has to ask, yet again, whether there was not a connection between the individualism that had characterized farming in these districts since olden times and the early and very violent forms of ecological degradation. The lack of regulating mechanisms such as communal village life, the tenancy system, and landowner control that could restrain the uninhibited egoism of the individual farmer may well have been one of the reasons why ecological degradation in these districts started at such an early stage and was allowed to continue to almost suicidal lengths before any action was taken.

In many parts of the world it has been observed that cooperative farming methods promote a sense of ecological responsibility. An example is agriculture on the highland plains of the Andes in Peru. Here, in one of the ecologically fragile regions of the world, there existed until the Second World War an agricultural system, which, owing to its highly cooperative working methods developed over thousands of years, had had an incredible record of stability and dependability. After 1945, however, in-

[1] Cf. Johannes Mølgaard 1988, pp. 90, 94.
[2] Anders Holm Rasmussen 1988, pp. 18–19.

Agrarian Reforms 249

dividualized agrarian reforms were introduced and led the unique agriculture on this highland plain into tragic difficulties.[3]

In many cases, freehold tenure and enclosure led to agricultural stagnation and chaos – not, as has been popularly believed, to growth, progress, and the liberation of hitherto restrained forces. Examples of the negative effects of freehold have already been mentioned in connection with forests, which farmers, as soon they became freeholders, were allowed to buy, fell, and turn into money.[4] Destructive disturbances in crop rotation after enclosure would appear to have been a serious problem.[5] In 1795 H. J. C. Høegh no doubt had good reason to warn farmers to be careful when starting to cultivate newly enclosed plots of land, for

> as a rule we observe that when a farmer has had his land enclosed he attacks everything within reach that he thinks may be suitable for grain crops, choosing the best for barley and rye and the remainder for oats. He cultivates this land as long as it provides even the smallest yield, and each year tills more land, not only what he can fertilize, but much more, because he feels that it must at all events at least be able to produce oats. If he has a number of good plots in his holding, he probably manages in this way at first, yet each year he prepares his own decline, for the yield grows smaller with the exhaustion of the soil; and the grass has gone.[6]

In general, freehold tenure caused the farmer class to start taking an interest in capital and speculative acquisition of land rather than in farming. Together with the parcelling out of small lots,[7] dividing up of property on inheritance, chronic debt, and/or failure to make investments, this proved to be the scourge of freehold and the explanation why it was by no means always bound up with agricultural expansion but, on the contrary, often led to stagnation and ecological difficulties.[8]

Rather than look for a positive connection between the agrarian reforms and growth in agriculture one may ask whether it is possi-

---

[3] Peter Bunyard 1988, pp. 197–8. For a Danish example, see Wilhelm von Antoniewitz 1944, pp. 85–7, 103–4, 126 (Frejlev Forest on the island of Lolland).

[4] Chapter 4.3, section a.

[5] See, for example, C. Christensen (Hørsholm) 1878, pp. 205–6; and Christian H. Brasch 1859–63, III, p. 190.

[6] H. J. C. Høegh 1795, p.60.

[7] Parcelling out of small plots from freehold farms as a means of financing, for example, the purchase of farms, already common practice during the first decades of the nineteenth century: Thorkild Kjærgaard 1979–80, p. 191.

[8] T. C. Smout 1987, p. 96; Aage Rasch 1964, pp. 326–7; Maurice Agulhon et al. 1976, pp. 10–11. Cf. Erik Helmer Pedersen 1983, pp. 48–9.

250 Driving Forces of Revolution

ble to observe a negative connection between these reforms and growth, that is, whether growth in the agricultural sector would have been greater without them. The answer is probably in the affirmative. As early as in 1760 a writer on economics argued that the effect of enclosure would be negative, because it would impose an expensive infrastructure upon agriculture that would demand a great deal of space and involve high and continuous maintenance expenses.[9]

This indeed proved to be the case. After the introduction of enclosure, and the moving of farms out of villages, unnecessarily long distances took their toll on the rural community. The first to suffer were children and cottagers, the former because they had an unreasonably long way to go to school and the latter because they often had a long way to go to work, which made an already inhumanly long working day even longer. But provided only children and cottagers suffered, nobody cared. Later, when agriculture's need to be in contact with its market and the processing industry became a daily affair, the structure created by enclosure and moving farms out of villages proved to be a burden on the production system: Milk routes, postal routes, transport of fertilizer and feedstuffs, electricity wires and telephone cables – even water pipes – became longer and more expensive than they would otherwise have been and in this way imposed upon agriculture an additional and unnecessary level of expense that was to affect the country's economy as a whole.

One indication of the high level of expense that followed in the wake of enclosure and farmers moving out of their villages is that rural districts in Denmark became electrified at a relatively late date. Whereas in 1935 rural districts in Holland were 100 percent electrified and in France 95 percent, in Denmark only 85 percent were electrified.[10]

There is probably a connection between the structural weaknesses created during the reform period and the fact that Danish agriculture, compared with agriculture in the rest of Europe, did not do particularly well during the nineteenth century. Among the countries that experienced greater agricultural growth was Hungary, which had retained the classic system of big estates; Scotland,

---

[9] O. D. Lütken 1760, II, pp. 29–68. In 1785 the farmers who were cultivating clover in the village of Nørre Broby on the island of Funen explained that the reason for their retaining the open-field system was that enclosure demanded too much space. Rtk. 2485.12: Sallinge herred, indberetning om Vejlegård, 29 March 1785. Danish National Archives.
[10] Robert T. Beall 1940, p. 790.

Agrarian Reforms

where the copyhold system had survived, also did extremely well. Countries whose agriculture fared worse than Denmark's included Belgium, which had a very large number of freeholders.[11]

That it proved possible to keep Danish agriculture on a more or less competitive level internationally was partly because Denmark still had a great number of efficient and dynamic large-scale producers and partly because of the cooperative movement, which was a conservative revolution involving a partial return to a more communal pattern of village life.[12] However, this movement embraced only the processing and marketing phases of agricultural production, not the actual cultivation of the soil, and by no means solved all the problems. Danish agriculture has indeed continued to find itself in difficulties, particularly after 1945. The extremely high and speculative prices of land in conjunction with the constantly high production costs have made it difficult for Danish agriculture to hold its own internationally. This has become more than clear since Denmark joined the European Community in 1973 and was faced with particularly strong competition from other countries, especially Holland, which has a widespread state-controlled copyhold system.

Seen from an agroeconomic viewpoint, the agrarian reforms have been a millstone round Danish society's neck for two hundred years. The fact that they have been regarded as economically advantageous is partly because the dynamism inherent in agriculture and the social position of the farmers prior to the reforms have both been underestimated, and partly, because attention has been devoted to the conditions of the farmers. No attention has therefore been paid to freehold tenure and enclosure as mechanisms for economical expropriation. The damage this inflicted upon the lower rural class has not been taken into consideration. Finally, a factor of decisive importance has been ignored, namely, the economically liberating effect of being able to solve the demand for energy and raw materials by means of coal and increasing imports of iron.

The dynamics of the green revolution and the energy and raw materials revolution were so violent that for long periods they were able to conceal completely the negative effects that the agrarian reforms exercised on the national economy. This has led to any number of absurd claims being made about the excellence of Den-

[11] T. C. Smout 1987, p. 96.
[12] Axel Garde 1938, pp. 133–4, 142–3. On the cooperative movement in Denmark: Claus Bjørn 1974.

252 *Driving Forces of Revolution*

mark's agrarian reforms. As recently as 1981 a Danish historian claimed, in a Festschrift in commemoration of the 200th anniversary of the enclosure ordinance of 1781, that enclosure and other reforms on the Danish model, in conjunction with the type of adult training colleges known in Denmark as Folk High Schools, were all that was necessary to solve the agricultural problems of the Third World.[13]

This is not to say that the reforms were unsuccessful on their own terms. They were concerned with political power, not economy. They were to be a device for the redistribution of power within the Danish elite; as such, they were indisputably successful.

[13] Claus Bjørn 1981a, p. 29.

10

TECHNOLOGY AND
COMMUNICATION SYSTEMS

Politics was only the uppermost sphere in the Danish revolution. If we pass downwards through this sphere and through changes in the disease pattern, in social structure, in working hours, in the landscape, and in production methods in agriculture and in the energy and raw materials sector, we finally come to rest on the firm ground of technology.

It was the growing technological potential that made it possible during the eighteenth century to mine coal not only for domestic heating but also for smelting iron,[1] so that the destructive nexus between wood and iron, whereby the latter could be obtained only by using the former, could be broken. Without this colossal technological development the energy and raw materials revolution would never have been possible. This in turn would have halted the green revolution, which could only be carried through if an answer were found to the energy and raw materials problem.

The green revolution was also dependent upon technological progress in another, more direct manner. Without agronomics, which is a combination of applied botany, zoology, chemistry, physics, geology, and veterinary medicine, agriculture would not, as the Danish landowner C. W. von Munthe af Morgenstierne put it in 1773, have been able to develop "from a thoughtless craft . . . to a cultivated science established on a firm basis."[2]

At that time, as today, technology was primarily the practical application of the results of basic research in the natural sciences.[3] Consequently, behind the technological development (which thus emerges as a decisive prerequisite for the major changes) lay the advances made in the natural sciences during

[1] John U. Nef 1977, pp. 142–50; R. P. Sieferle 1982, pp. 151–60.
[2] C. W. von Munthe af Morgenstierne 1783, pp. 41–2; Christian H. Brasch 1859–63, III p. 182. Cf. Mauro Ambrosoli 1992.
[3] A. E. Musson and Eric Robinson 1969, especially pp. 87–189; D. S. L. Cardwell 1972, pp. 210–20 and passim; Peter Mathias 1976; Margaret Gowing 1984, p. xii. Cf. Chapter 7.4.

253

254   Driving Forces of Revolution

the sixteenth, seventeenth, and eighteenth centuries and, in the final instance, the art of printing, the new system of communication that spread both the growing wealth of scientific knowledge and the resultant technological development. Without printing there could have been no unlimited dialogue on an international level (the basis for the rapid progress of the basic sciences since the Renaissance), nowhere near as many technological innovations, and no efficient means of spreading knowledge of them.

In connection with technology and the transfer of knowledge, the importance of the printed word was immense in all sectors – and agriculture was no exception. A simple quantitative analysis of the books and treatises on farming published in Denmark between 1500 and 1800 reveals that literature on this subject enjoyed an increasingly wider distribution, and that there was a considerable and steadily increasing interest in works of this type.[4]

One of the earliest known examples of interest in agricultural literature in Denmark is the translation of the first two volumes of the well-known German agronomist Konrad Heresbach's *Rei rusticae libri quatuor* (Four books of husbandry) of 1570, commissioned by the Jutland landowner Maurits Stygge of Holbækgård in 1601 from the otherwise unknown Morten Andersen Horsens. The translation was entitled *Conradi Heresbachij Bondeverck* (Konrad Heresbach's Guide to Husbandry).[5]

An example of what a well-supplied Danish manorial library contained around the year 1700 is provided by that assembled by Count Carl Ahlefeldt of Langeland, a catalogue of which was compiled in 1710. The collection included *Agricultura nuova e casa di villa* by Carlo Stefano (Charles Estienne), *Agricultura tratta di diversi antichi* by Gabrelo Alfonso (Gabriel Alfonso de Herrera), *Economia del cittadino in villa* by Vincenzo Tanara, *Economie générale de la campagne* by Louis Liger, *Instruction pour les jardins fruitiers et potagers* by Jean de la Quintinie, and a gardening handbook, *The English Gardener*[6] – all well-known classics in European agronomic literature.[7] By the end of the eighteenth century, large collections of

---

[4] Thorkild Kjærgaard 1986; Corinne Beutler 1973.

[5] For unknown reasons the manuscript, which still exists, was never published. Today in the Royal Library, Copenhagen, Manuscript Collection, NKS 351^d 4°. Cf. Konrad Heresbach 1944–5 and Corinne Beutler and Franz Irsigler 1980.

[6] Langeland Manor archives: Lensgreve Carl Ahlefeldt (1670–22) og hustru . . . deres arkiv 1693–1754, div. år. C.VI: Katalog over Bibliotheket paa Gravensten 1710, Provincial Archives of Funen.

[7] Thorkild Kjærgaard 1984.

Technology and Communications 255

farming literature were to be found in manor house libraries all over the country.[8]

From the beginning of the 1780s, local classes in agriculture for farmers were common, often based on Esaias Fleischer's excellent *Agerdyrknings-Katekismus* (Catechism of agriculture). The Agricultural Society awarded several prizes for tuition of this kind.[9] Members of the upper classes of society were taught the latest agronomical advances as part of their general education. At Sorø Academy, lectures on the use of clover to improve grass cultivation were given to pupils not later than 1773.[10]

It is not possible to present here a detailed examination of the complicated and – in its widest ramifications – analytically insoluble interplay between studies of agricultural literature and agricultural innovation. But many examples serve to prove that such literature was not merely bought but also read, and that attempts were made to put its lessons into practice. A few examples from the eighteenth century will suffice. A. C. Teilmann, one of the greatest Danish agricultural innovators of the eighteenth century, refers expressly to the writings of Carl von Linné as the source of his idea to use marl. His experiments were immediately imitated, initially by tenant farmers doing villeinage work, who were the first to observe the good results, then by tenant farmers doing no villeinage work, and finally by freeholders in the district, who in this case were the last to accept innovative methods.[11] At Vissenbjerg on the island of Funen, the Reverend J. K. Trojel experimented in 1773 with forage crops, partly inspired by the writings of the well-known English agronomist John Mortimer.[12]

The vicarage at Vær (northeast of Horsens in Jutland), where clover was cultivated in the 1770s, contained a large collection of farming literature.[13] A few years later the owner of Valdemar's Castle on the island of Tåsinge (for decades a centre of agricultural innovation), after reading a number of books on English agriculture, initiated large-scale experiments with broad beans, vetch, mangold, and turnips.[14] Similar experiments were conducted on the main farm at Silkeborg Manor (Central Jutland), whose owner at the end of the eighteenth century, Henrik Muhle Hoff, was a keen reader of the writings of Arthur Young, Jethro Tull, and Albrecht Thaer.[15]

---

[8] Engelholm Manor archives: Dokumenter vedrørende Grevensvænge 1758/1810–1865/69: Fuldstændig Fortegnelse over mine Bøger, forfattet på Grevens Vænge 20. April 1798, Provincial Archives of Zealand; H. K. Kristensen 1968, p. 81; Hans Berner-Schilden-Holsten and Albert Fabritius 1940–70, I, 2, p. 239.

[9] Agricultural Society prizewinners 1783–9, Danish National Business History Archives.

[10] Axel Nielsen 1948, p. 118. [11] A. C. Teilmann 1789, p. 568.

[12] *Odense Adresse-Contoirs Efterretninger* 1773, no. 38.

[13] Knud Prange 1972, p. 9. [14] Thorvald Hansen 1934, p. 117.

[15] Otto Bisgaard 1937, p. 12.

256   Driving Forces of Revolution

In the 1760s, farmers on the island of Lolland used constructional drawings from *Danmarks og Norges Oeconomiske Magazin* as models for making new skeps.[16] Fleischer's beekeeping manual of 1777 and Høegh's *Anviisning* are known to have been copied directly.[17] All this is of course part of a broader pattern: In other European countries there are numerous examples of attempts during the sixteenth and seventeenth centuries, in practical farming, to use recommendations found in agronomical treatises, including those by writers on agronomical subjects in antiquity.[18]

All in all, the revolution of 1500–1800 was therefore to a large degree a result of the art of printing, which thanks to the practical European alphabet became a communication system with hitherto unrealized possibilities. The situation was quite different in China, where the art of printing had originated and been known for a long time, but where its potential remained unexploited due to the complicated structure of the Chinese written language, involving a code of about fifty thousand characters as compared with the approximately thirty letters in the European alphabet.[19] The process of development in Denmark from 1500 to 1800 would appear to fully confirm the American historian Elizabeth L. Eisenstein's theory to the effect that the stage reached by systems of communication is one of the most important parameters for the development of human society.[20]

The new system of communication gave the European world enormous strength without which the general process of development could scarcely have been transformed from stagnation and decline into sustainable growth during the eighteenth century. Instead of sustainable, rising production, Europe would have experienced a falling rate that probably would have reached its lowest point at the beginning of the nineteenth century and then triggered a crisis which, broadly speaking, would have been a repetition of that which arose during the late Middle Ages.

10.1 THE DANISH REVOLUTION, 1500–1800: A CHAOTIC PROCESS

Historical hindsight makes it possible to demonstrate the connection between a great many of the factors that contributed to the

[16] Erik Pontoppidan 1763–81, III, p. 252.
[17] *Kiøbenhavns Kongelige allene priviligerede Adresse-Contoirs Efterretninger* 1782, no. 69; Bolle Willum Luxdorph 1915–30, II, p. 116; Gregers Begtrup 1803–12, III, p. 282.
[18] Joan Thirsk 1983. Cf. Thorkild Kjærgaard 1984.
[19] Thorkild Kjærgaard 1986, pp. 592–3.
[20] Elizabeth L. Eisenstein 1979.

Technology and Communications   257

Danish Revolution, but this is not the same as saying that the developments could have been foreseen. On the contrary, in its actual course it was a network of unpredictable, nonlinear, complex processes within dynamic systems in which the individual processes were no doubt logical and understandable in relation to their causes, but the results of the many accumulated, interacting processes eluded prediction and calculation.

Nobody could have foreseen that one of the accumulated effects of larger herds of cattle would be the disappearance of malaria. Nor was it possible to foresee that economizing on energy, in conjunction with the ecological recovery, would lead, among other things, to tuberculosis and longer working hours with repercussions, still observable, on the working morale of the Danish population. And it was equally impossible to foresee the formation of a new landscape as a final result of the ecological revolution. It was pure luck that the necessary technology was available and that pit coal was ready to take over the task of supplying energy when wood ran out. The Middle Ages had not been as fortunate. An analysis of the actual development between 1500 and 1800 lends no support to the widespread notion that social and economic development proceeded in accordance with a fixed, progressive plan. The most appropriate word to describe this period is not 'plan' but 'chaos.'

Part V

THE INHERITANCE

L'aristocratie fait de tous les citoyens une longue chaîne qui remonte
du paysan au roi; la démocratie brise la chaîne et met chaque anneau
à part.

Alexis de Tocqueville, 1835

11

THE SOCIAL AND POLITICAL INHERITANCE

The Danish Revolution not only created a new Denmark, ideologically legitimized by an emerging sense of national identity,[1] but at the same time furthered the idea of political democracy.[2] The political transformations resulted in a marked intensification of the central administration's influence on society, and hence led to a much greater interest in the exercise of centralized power. By the end of the eighteenth century demands were being made to the effect that the people should have their own continuous influence on the process of government. These wishes were met by allowing public opinion to exercise greater influence; the end of the eighteenth century has indeed been called "the era of absolutism under the control of public opinion."[3]

This construction, however, was too imprecise and too informal to be satisfactory in the long run, quite apart from the fact that whenever public opinion might cause difficulties it could always be suppressed by press laws, as happened in 1799. The demand for public influence on the way in which the government conducted its business was therefore reformulated as a wish for political democracy. This was obtained within an astonishingly short number of years. With the consultative assemblies of the so-called Estates of the Realm, Denmark had already by the beginning of the 1830s acquired political bodies that to some extent were democratically elected; by the end of the 1840s the country had secured a democratic constitution that granted the right to vote to a considerable part of the population.

One of the most interesting and quite definitely unexpected consequences of extending the franchise to steadily wider groups of society was the welfare state, which from the 1880s gradually replaced the deregulated, liberalistic state that had developed out

[1] Cf. Ole Feldbæk 1984.
[2] Johan Hvidtfeldt 1949–52, p. 359; Ole Feldbæk 1990b, p. 45.
[3] Jens Arup Seip 1957–8.

261

262   *The Inheritance*

of the dissolution of all local centres of power.[4] The welfare state can be regarded as the result of a strange alliance between the losing parties from the last half of the eighteenth century, that is, an alliance between on the one hand the cottagers and labourers and on the other hand the aristocracy. What united these discrepant sectors of the population was their common yearning for a revival of a patriarchal society, characterized by a continual search for solutions that were, if possible, socially acceptable – something the liberal, laissez-faire central administration had deliberately neglected.

The disdain felt by liberal ideologists for the softness of the patriarchal society can be traced far back into the eighteenth century. In an often-quoted piece in the magazine *Den danske Tilskuer* (The Danish spectator) of 1763, Jens Schielderup Sneedorff, a leading figure of the Danish Enlightenment, advocated that farmers be given "freedom and property," and to the question of who was to help the farmer when in need his answer was simply: "Nobody."[5]

Christen Pram, who was the editor of the monthly magazine *Minerva*, dwelt on the same question. He believed that society should give citizens freedom by abolishing privileges and other barriers to personal development and moreover should protect their personal safety – but that was all. To demand that society should also take care of its citizens' welfare was a misconception, if not to say a manifestation of envy:

> For one thing there are people everywhere suffering from poverty, or some other form of misfortune, who, being sensible of their condition, may easily begin to accuse the government, in fact believe that it must be responsible for their sufferings. For another, there are, everywhere, unruly characters who are either envious of the persons commissioned by the government to rule, on account of their ostensible or real glory or happiness, and therefore wish to overthrow these enviable people, or else they hope, by means of revolutions, to attain positions of grandeur and affluence themselves.[6]

This total lack of social understanding prevailed in government circles throughout most of the nineteenth century. In 1848 it aroused the fury of the old poet, Adam Oehlenschläger:

> Here [in Copenhagen] high government officials smile at the promise "to procure work for the workers," which they regard as an impossibility; but I think that when people *can* work and *are willing* to work, and would not be able to *live* without work, and yet are unable to *find* it, then the government has turned them into legitimate robbers and rebels.[7]

---

[4] Vagn Skovgaard-Petersen 1985, pp. 74–81, 269–76.   [5] J. S. Sneedorff 1776, p. 480.
[6] Christen Pram 1789, Oct.–Dec., p. 110.   [7] Adam Oehlenschläger 1990, p. 336.

Social and Political 263

After the aristocracy and the lower strata of society had become paralysed by the agrarian reforms, a revival of the old ways of thinking can be observed during the 1830s and 1840s. There is a strange parallelism between, on the one hand, the attempts of the landowner class to revert to the past (exemplified by the castellated Neo-Gothic and palatial Neo-Renaissance architecture displayed in mid-nineteenth-century manor houses)[8] and, on the other hand, the revived interest shown by the lower classes in the guild system, which reemerged only lightly disguised as the trade union movement and socialism.[9] The welfare state was founded during the last decades of the nineteenth century on the basis of a tacit alliance between the Højre (Right) party, which represented the old patriarchal instincts, and the emerging Social Democratic party, which was supported by those who were alienated from society so that they too yearned for a regulated and reasonably secure patriarchal society.

The era of the welfare state was heralded by old age pensions and a publicly supported health insurance system. At the same time, the first important steps were taken towards the protection of workers with the forbidding of child labour and regulation of working conditions.[10] The central administration, long the enemy of both the aristocracy and the proletariat, was tamed and used for a completely different purpose from that originally intended by the liberalistic civil servants and ideologists of the eighteenth century. The founder of the Carlsberg Breweries, J. C. Jacobsen, himself a splendid representative of patriarchal thinking, was able to write in 1885 – not without justification – that

> Højre [is] not a party in the normal sense, for it strives for nothing on its own account and only enters the lists as citizens whose aim it is to protect the entire population against overwhelming dominance on the part of the egoistic leaders of the Venstre [Left = Liberal] Party.[11]

The alliance between the Højre party and the Social Democrats established a political line that was continued until the middle of the twentieth century. Not until the early 1970s did the pressure from a growing middle class become so strong that it shattered the solidarity of the welfare state. The middle class, whose narcissistic

---

[8] Mette Smed 1988; Hakon Lund 1980, pp. 178–90. Pederstrup, on the island of Lolland, an ideal example of 'bourgeoisification' of a noble's home at the time of the agrarian reforms, had large corner towers added in 1858, which converted it into a Renaissance palace.

[9] Henry Bruun 1938; Niels Finn Christiansen 1986, pp. 51–7, 89–98.

[10] Daniel Levine 1978; Hans Christian Johansen 1962, pp. 151–67.

[11] Kristof Glamann 1991, p. 134.

264   *The Inheritance*

tendencies may be regarded as a consequence of the individualization at the end of the eighteenth century, paved the way for an individualistic, liberalistic, deregulated, competitive society with widening social differences, reminiscent in many ways of the society that arose before the foundation of the welfare state at the end of the nineteenth century. At that time too, in the same way as today, people smiled whenever it was suggested that there should be work for everybody.

After the long interlude with a regulated welfare state it now seems as if the system established at the end of the eighteenth century will prevail. Lined up against a strong central administration is an atomized, narcissistic population so absorbed in its individualistic struggle that it has completely lost interest in the life of the community. This is reflected in reduced involvement in matters affecting society as a whole, a trend manifested in various ways, including a decrease in the amount of support given to trade unions and political parties. The increasing acceptance of a narrow, formal concept of democracy must also be seen in this context.[12]

[12]   Cf. Henning Fonsmark 1990.

12

THE ECOLOGICAL INHERITANCE

The ecological revolution solved problems of incalculable serious-ness by converting social and economic decline into sustainable growth, leading in the long run to improved living standards for most people; in historical terms, these have reached incredible heights in the course of the twentieth century. However, this has not been achieved without creating new problems. For one thing, it must be assumed that the subterranean forests upon which en-ergy supplies now mainly depend will be used up in the same way as ordinary forests were. At the moment, subterranean energy is being used very rapidly: As much energy is now being consumed annually, worldwide, as was deposited in the course of a million years during the carboniferous period.[1] Furthermore, the increas-ing discharge of carbon dioxide (CO_2) that is a consequence of using fossil fuel endangers the climate. In the middle of the eigh-teenth century the concentration of CO_2 in the atmosphere was about 260 ppm. Since then, as a result of burning coal and oil, close on 500 billion tonnes of CO_2 have been released, which means that the carbon dioxide concentration today is 345 ppm, and by the year 2000 will have risen to 370 ppm; in the event of an unaltered rate of increase the concentration will have reached 600 ppm by the year 2050.[2]

One of the first to warn of the potential danger to the stability of the world climate represented by anthropogenic carbon diox-ide was the Danish physiologist August Krogh (1874–1949.)[3] Nev-ertheless, much time was to pass before the problem became visible. This happened during the 1980s, when the risk of a green-house effect produced by anthropogenic carbon dioxide in con-junction with the increasing amount of methane – another greenhouse gas that is similarly a result of the ecological revo-

[1] R. P. Sieferle 1982, p. 61.
[2] Peter Bunyard 1988, pp. 199–200; Thomas E. Graedel and Paul J. Crutzen 1989, p. 33.
[3] August Krogh 1904, pp. 419, 426–7.

266 *The Inheritance*

lution – emerged as a serious threat to the Earth's ecological system in general and to the continued existence of the human race in particular.

The amount of methane is related to the number of ruminants, primarily cattle. After thousands of years of stability the methane content in the atmosphere began to rise during the eighteenth century because of the considerable increase in cattle stocks made possible by the green revolution.[4]

In addition there is the pollution of soil, water, and the atmosphere by industrial and consumer waste as well as by electrochemically produced nitrogen fertilizer, which to a large extent has replaced the nitrogen generated by clover. These problems are among the long-term negative results of the methods developed during the seventeenth and eighteenth centuries. Present-day serious ecological problems are directly connected with the green revolution and the energy and raw materials revolution that took place two hundred years ago.

The fact that we now have new problems does not mean that we have disposed of the old ones. Soil drift, which was restricted in the eighteenth century, has returned as a result of the very powerful working of the soil possible with modern agricultural machinery. When work on the fields of Jutland starts in the spring and the wind is blowing from the west, the soil is blown over the Kattegat in such thick clouds that sometimes the lightships have to set their foghorns going.[5] Now that the stone walls and thick hedges of the eighteenth century have nearly all gone there is no longer anything to hold the soil back, and it will only be a matter of a few decades before large parts of the topsoil accumulated over thousands of years will have been blown away.[6]

If we take our eyes off Denmark and Europe and the European world's offshoots in North America, Australia, and New Zealand and turn our attention to the rest of the world, we see that there are about two billion people, or 40 percent of the world population, who have access to only one source of energy, namely, wood.[7] Whereas the postrevolutionary society has imposed new, over-

---

[4] Thomas E. Graedel and Paul J. Crutzen 1989, pp. 33–4.
[5] Helle Askgaard and Kurt Pedersen 1987, p. 18.
[6] A comparison of the contour lines in the village of Sønder Vestud on the island of Møn in 1880 and at the end of the 1980s showed that during the intervening period 1 metre of topsoil had disappeared. Reported by Karl-Erik Frandsen, University of Copenhagen, Department of History. Disappearance of hedges: Chapter 4.2, Section b.
[7] UN Chronicle 1988, p. 49.

Ecological 267

whelming problems on our globe, we still have large regions of the world – the Indian subcontinent, parts of southeast Asia, South and Central America, and Africa – where the old agrarian society's problems still exist: population growth and a shortage of energy, resulting in forest clearance, which in turn produces hydrological problems and causes deserts to be formed, while at the same time impoverishing the flora and fauna. The pattern is the same as it was in Europe during the sixteenth, seventeenth, and early eighteenth centuries. To complete the parallel it may be added that the development of the social and disease patterns in the Third World today is reminiscent of what took place in eighteenth-century Europe. Together with a rapidly increasing occurrence of tubercular diseases, the features that characterize living conditions outside the European world today are the proletarization of large parts of the population, prolonged working hours, and increasing undernourishment.

Whether or not it will prove possible for the international community of nations to overcome this malignant, mutually reinforcing combination of a repetition of the ecological and social problems of the past and the new ecological and social problems of the present is the all-important question facing us as we approach the end of the second millenium of the Christian Era.

Appendix 1

CURRENCY, WEIGHTS, AND MEASURES

CURRENCY

A rix-dollar was a small silver coin of varying value and current in several European countries during the period. In Denmark: 1 rix-dollar = 6 marks = 96 *skilling*.

MEASURES

1. Linear measure
   1 *alen* (pl. *alen*) (ell) = 2 feet = 62 cm
   1 (Danish) mile = 12,000 *alen* = 7,532 m
   1 *favn* (pl. −*e*) (fathom) = 1.88 m
2. Square measure
   1 hectare = 10,000 m²
   1 *tønde* pl. −*r*) = 8 *skæpper* = 14,000 *alen²* = 5,516 m² = 1.36 acres = 0.55 ha
   1 *tønde hartkorn*. This term (literally, 'barrel of hard corn', traditionally rye or barley) was frequently used to describe the extent of farmlands, especially as a basic unit of soil evaluation for taxation purposes. The land register of 1688 valued Denmark's 3,750,000 hectares at 357,571 *tønder hartkorn*. On average, depending on the fertility of the soil, 1 *tønde hartkorn* corresponded to 10.5 hectares, or about 26 acres.
3. Cubic measure
   1 *favn* of firewood = 2.2m³
   1 *favn* of peat = 2.5 m³

WEIGHTS

1 *lispund* (pl. *lispund*) = 16 *pund* (pounds) = 8 kg
1 *skippund* (pl. *skippund*) = 20 *lispund*
1 centerweight (cwt.) = 50.8 kg

Appendix 1 269

1 *tønde* (pl. −*r*) of pitcoal = 158½ kg
17 Danish *tønder* pitcoal = 1 Newcastle chaldron = 2,692 kg
1 *læst* (pl. −*er*) (cargo) of pitcoal = 12 Danish *tønder* = 1,900 kg

NUTRITION VALUES

1 Scandinavian feed unit = nutritional value of 1 kg barley.

Appendix 2

REIGNS OF DANISH KINGS AND QUEENS MENTIONED IN THIS BOOK

Canute the Holy	1080–1086
Valdemar I (the Great)	1157–1182
Valdemar II (the Victorious)	1202–1241
Erik V (Klipping)	1259–1286
Valdemar IV (Atterdag)	1340–1375
Margrethe I	1387–1412
Christian I	1448–1481
Christian II	1513–1523
Frederik I	1523–1533
Christian III	1534–1559
Frederik II	1559–1588
Christian IV	1588–1648
Frederik III	1648–1670
Christian V	1670–1699
Frederik IV	1699–1730
Christian VI	1730–1746
Frederik V	1746–1766
Christian VII	1766–1808
Frederik VI	1808–1839 (de facto regent from 1784)

SOURCES AND BIBLIOGRAPHY

This list of sources and bibliography is shorter than the one given in the Danish edition because the appendix, "Domesticeret kløver i Danmark 1749–1805" (Domesticated clover in Denmark, 1749–1805), has been omitted from the English edition.

1. UNPUBLISHED

A. Danish National Archives

Rentekammeret (Rtk.). 2484. Landvæsenskontorenes sandflugtssager 1793–1840.

2485.6–19. Indberetninger om forbedringer i landvæsenet og fællesskabets ophævelse 1773–1809.

2485.21–23. Indberetninger fra lensbesiddere om forbedringer i lensvæsenet og nedlagte bøndergårde m.m. 1774–1807.

434.10. Diverse dokumenter ang. hoveri og tiendesagen.

B. Provincial Archives of Zealand

The archives of Engelholm Manor. Dokumenter vedr. Grevensvænge 1758–1810/1865–9.

The archives of Gammelgård Manor. Diverse dokumenter 1751–1849.

The archives of Gerdrup-Lyngbygård Manor. Diverse dokumenter 1725–1830.

The archives of Giesegård Manor and others. Forpagtningskontrakter vedr. Spanager 1720–1879.

The archives of Gjorslev Manor. Kasseekstrakter over indtægter og udgifter 1793–1802. Do. 1803–8/1819–24.

The archives of Juellinge Manor. Godsforvalter Chr. Sørensens arkiv 1728–43.

The archives of Ringsted Convent. Godsbeskr. og synsforretn. 1769–1817.

C. Provincial Archives of Funen

The archives of Langeland Manor. Lensgreve Carl Ahlefeldt (1670–1722) og hustru Ulrica Antoinette, f. Danneskjold-Laurvig (1686–1755), deres arkiv 1696–1754, various years.

D. Provincial Archives of Northern Jutland

The archives of Boddum Bisgård Manor. Hoveribestemmelse iht. forening af 16.4.1792.

271

272 Sources and Bibliography

The archives of Glomstrup Manor. Forskellige dokumenter 1653–1849.
The archives of Hesselmed Manor. Sandflugt og klitbeplantning 1749–1874.
The archives of Marselisborg Manor. Forskellige sager 1662–1851.
The archives of Store Restrup Manor. Forskellige dokumenter 1674–1844.
The archives of Vedelslund Manor. Diverse dokumenter 1767–1826.
The archives of Vedø Manor. Forskellige sager 1691–1822.
The archives of Volstrup Manor. Forskelligt 1530, 1753–1872.

    E. Danish National Business History Archives
The Archives of the Agricultural Society. Landhusholdningsselskabets præmie-
    protokol, various years.
    Agricultural Society prizewinners. 1770–1968. Typewritten card index
    compiled by Ole Degn.

    F. The Royal Library, Copenhagen, Manuscript Collection
NKS 351ᵈ4°. Conradi Heresbachij Bondeverck.
NKS 3446 4°. C. Raunkiær, Samlinger vedrørende Planterne i dansk Poesi.

    G. The Royal Veterinary and Agricultural College, Copenhagen, Manuscript
    Collection
4° V 41.g. N. Jensen, Agerdyrkningslære opskrevet paa Tune Landboskole 1873.

    H. *The University of Copenhagen, Department of History,* Collection of
unpublished documents for a history of prices.

    I. Other
Letter of 27 July 1990 from Michael Bræstrup.
Letter of 10 August 1990 from Finn Eiland.
Notes taken during lecture given by Karl-Erik Frandsen at the University of
    Copenhagen on 18 February 1988.
Letter of 4 September 1990 from Jagt- og Skovbrugsmuseet, Hørsholm.
Letter of 26 September 1990 from Hans Christian Johansen.
Letter of 9 February 1989 from the Laboratory for Energy Technology, Techni-
    cal University of Denmark.
Letter of 15 May 1990 from Hans Rose, Danish Brick & Mortar Board.
Letter of 2 January 1989 from Axel Steensberg.

    2. PUBLISHED

Note: Unless stated to the contrary, the place of publication is Copenhagen. Laws,
ordinances, decrees, and posters are listed under *Forordninger og Aabne Breve* (various years); from 1848 in *Departementstidende;* from 1871 in *Lovtidende.* Other legal sources in Laurids Fogtman, *Kongelige Rescripter, Resolutioner og Collegialbreve for
Danmark (og Norge) 1660–(1870);* from 1871 in *Ministerialtidende.*

A.***. 1760. Antegning over Askes Brug i Almindelighed og særdeles efter den
    Maade Forpagterne betiene sig af omkring Woolhampton i Berch Shire
    udi Engelland, til at faa Clever, Lucerne og Burgundisk Høe i stor Mængde
    [with editorial comments by Erik Pontoppidan p. 116]. *Danmarks og Norges
    Oeconomiske Magazin,* 4. 105–16.

Sources and Bibliography

273

Abel, Wilhelm. 1967. *Geschichte der deutschen Landwirtschaft vom frühen Mittelalter bis zum 19. Jahrhundert.* Günther Franz, ed., *Deutsche Agrargeschichte.* 2. ed., II. Stuttgart.

1972. *Massenarmut und Hungerkrisen im vorindustrielle Deutschland.* Göttingen.

Abildgaard, Søren. 1761. Beskrivelse over Kiøbstæden Skagen, dens nærværende oeconomiske Tilstand, og Fiskeriets Beskaffenhed sammesteds. *Danmarks og Norges Oeconomiske Magazin,* 5. 343–60.

1776. Afhandling om Mergel. In *Det Kgl. Danske Landhuusholdnings-Selskabs Skrifter,* 1. 147–286.

Agulhon, Maurice, Gabriel Désert, and Robert Specklin. 1976. *Apogèe et crise de la civilisation paysanne 1789–1914.* Histoire de la France rurale, 3. Paris.

Ahlefeldt Laurvig, F. 1927–31. *Generalen,* I–IV.

Ahlefeldt-Laurvig, Jørgen, and Anne-Mari Steimle. 1977. *Fajancer og stengods fra fabriken i Kastrup.*

Albertus Magnus. 1867. *De vegetabilibus libri VIII,* eds. Ernst Meyer and Carl Jessen. Berlin.

Alexander, John T. 1980. *Bubonic Plague in Early Modern Russia. Public Health and Urban Disaster.* The John Hopkins University Studies in Historical and Political Sciences, 98. series, 1. Baltimore and London.

1986. Reconsiderations on Plague in Early Modern Russia, 1500–1800. *Jahrbücher für Geschichte Osteuropas,* New Series, 34. 244–54.

Ambrosoli, Mauro. 1992. *Scienziati, contadini e proprietari. Botanica e agricoltura nell'Europa occidentale 1350–1850.* Biblioteca di cultura storica, 190.

Amstrup, Niels. 1955. Den ældste tørlægning af Søborg sø. *Fra Frederiksborg Amt.* 100–19.

Andersen, Valdemar. 1953. *Alheden med Frederiks sogns historie.* Kolding.

1975. *Fra Alheden. Lyng. Landbrug. Plantager.*

Andresen, C. C. 1861. *Om Klitformationen og Klittens Behandling og Bestyrelse.*

Anonymous. 1747. Nogle Anmerkninger om det saa kaldede Esparcette Frøe, tillige med en Skrivelse derom [includes a discussion of clover]. *Kiøbenhavnske Samlinger om adskillige, til Land- og Stad-Væsenet, Agerdyrkningen, Qvægningen, Naturlæren og andre nyttige Konster og Videnskaber henhørende Sager,* I. 52–62.

1757. En Reisendes Betragtninger over Uleylighederne af de Fyenske Proprietariers og Bønders Fælleskab i Byer og Marker, samt Fordeelen af en muelig Forandring. *Danmarks og Norges Oeconomiske Magazin,* 1. 3–36.

1758a. Betragtninger over Skovenes Tilstand i Fædernelandet. *Oeconomisk Journal,* 3: 1. 312–44.

1758b. Velmeente Forslag til Landgodsets Forbedring i Siælland. *Danmarks og Norges Oeconomiske Magazin,* 2. 85–102.

1771. *Upartiske Tanker om Land-Oeconomien i Dannemark, og billige Forslag til sammes ufeylbare Forbedring.*

1798. Brev til Udgiveren om Agerdyrkning og Landvæsen i Schodborg Herred paa ***Gaard. *Tilskueren for Landvæsenet,* 1. 31–42.

Antoniewitz, Wilhelm von. 1944. *Frejlev Skoves Historie.*

Arup, Erik. 1916. Danmarks ældste Landbrug. *Tidsskrift for Landøkonomi.* 400–33.

1925–55. *Danmarks historie.* I–III.

1947. Kong Christiern 2. Et Portræt. *Scandia,* 28. 73–80.

274   Sources and Bibliography

Askgaard, Helle, and Kurt Pedersen. 1987. Eds., *Regionalgeografi*. Herning.

Augé-Laribé, Michel. 1955. *La révolution agricole*. L'Evolution de l'humanité, 83. Paris.

Aumont, Arthur, and Edgar Collin. 1897–1900. *Det danske Nationalteater 1748–1889*. 1–5.

Axelgaard, Tue. 1922–5. Om Kvægsygen paa Hindsholm i det 18de Aarhundrede. *Aarbog for Odense og Assens Amter*, 3. 269–74.

Baden, Gustav Ludvig. 1796. *Nakskovs nu værende Forfatning, dens Mangler, med Forslag til sammes Forbedring*.

Balvig, Flemming. 1987. *Den tyvagtige dansker. Brudstykker af kriminalitetens udvikling gennem tre århundreder, fra 1725 til 2025*.

Bartholdy, Nils G. 1971. Adelsbegrebet under den ældre enevælde. Sammenhængen med privilegier og rang i tiden 1660–1730. *Historisk Tidsskrift* 12th series, 5. 577–650.

Barton, H. Arnold. 1988. The Danish Agrarian Reforms, 1784–1814, and the Historians. *Scandinavian Economic History Review*, 36, 1. 46–61.

Beall, Robert T. 1940. Rural Electrification. In *Farmers in a Changing World. Yearbook of Agriculture*. 76th Congress, 3d Session – House Document No. 695. Washington DC. 790–808.

Bech, C. 1817. Bemærkninger om den røde Kløver og dens Afarter. *Landoeconomiske Tidender*, 6. 63–74.

Becker, Hermann Friedrich. 1804. Om Skibsbygningstømmers Kultur, konstige Dannelse og Fældning. In *Det Kgl. Danske Landhuusholdnings-Selskabs Skrifter*, 7. 155–256.

Begtrup, Gregers. 1801. *Beskrivelse over Hovedgaardene i Sjelland saavel komplette som ukomplette*.

1803–12. *Beskrivelse over Agerdyrkningens Tilstand i Danmark*. 1–7.

1804. Strynøe. In *Det Kgl. Danske Landhuusholdnings-Selskabs Skrifter*, 7. 307–21.

Bellmann, Carl Michael. 1790. *Fredmans Epistler*. Stockholm.

Bendix-Almgreen, Svend Erik. 1964. Palæopathologien. *Naturens Verden*. 129–41.

Bendixen, H. C. 1944. *Forelæsninger over speciel Patalogi og Terapi: Infektionssygdomme hos Husdyrene*.

1973. *Den Kongelige Veterinærskole den 13. Juli 1773*.

Bergsøe, A. F. 1837. *Geheime-Statsminister Greve Christian Ditlev Frederik Reventlovs Virksomhed som Kongens Embedsmand og Statens Borger*. I–II.

1844–53. *Den danske Stats Statistik*. 1–4.

Berner-Schilden-Holsten, Hans, and Albert Fabritius. 1940–70. *Lehnsbaron Hans Berner Schilden Holsten's Slægtebog*. 1–3 and volume of tables and index.

Berntsen, Arent. 1650–6. *Danmarckis oc Norgis Fructbar Herlighed*. 1–4. Reprint 1971.

Berry, Wendell. 1981. *The Gift of Good Land: Further Essays Cultural and Agricultural*. San Francisco.

Berstrand, Hans Erik. 1925. *Fra Fraugde Sogn. Historisk-topografisk Skildring*. Odense.

Bethell, Lesli. 1984–86. Ed., *The Cambridge History of Latin America*. 1–5. Cambridge.

Beutler, Corinne. 1973. Un chapitre de la sensibilité collective: la littérature agricole en Europe Continentale au XVIe siècle. *Annales E. S. C.*, 28. 1280–1301.

Sources and Bibliography 275

Beutler, Corinne, and Franz Irsigler. 1980. Konrad Heresbach (1496–1576). *Rheinische Lebensbilder*, 8. Cologne. 81–104.

Beyer, Seyer Mahling. 1791. *En geographisk-historisk og oeconomisk, physisk-antiqvarisk Beskrivelse over Bringstrup og Sigersted Sogne ved Ringsted.* Sorø.

Biehl, Charlotta Dorothea. 1771. Om Frihed og Eiendom. In *Forsøg i de skiønne og nyttige Videnskaber,* 5. 161–76.

Billeskov Jansen, F. J. 1985–7. Ed., *Den danske lyrik.* 1–5.

Birch, H. J. 1786. *Statistiske og Oekonomiske Tanker til høyere Eftertanke.*

Birckner, M. C. 1790. Svar paa det Spørgsmaal: Skal man undertrykke Adelen? *Minerva,* July–September. 11–52.

Bisgaard, H. L. 1902. *Den danske nationaløkonomi i det 18. århundrede.*

Bisgaard, Otto. 1937. *Af Silkeborg Hovedgaards Historie 1794–1846.* Silkeborg.

Bjerre Jensen, Birgit. 1968–9. Christian V's greve- og friherreprivilegier. *Arkiv,* 2. 89–130.

  1987. *Udnævnelsesretten i enevældens magtpolitiske system 1660–1730.* Administrationshistoriske studier, 12.

Bjeregaard, Hans Jensen. 1771. *Brev fra Hans Jensen, Selv-Eier Bonde paa det Bernstorffske Gods, til sine Landsmænd, de øvrige Danske Bønder, om de Nye Indretninger til Landvæsenets Forbedring i Danmark.*

Bjørn, Claus. 1974. The Cooperative Movement. In *Denmark: An Official Handbook.* 207–13.

  1977. The Peasantry and Agrarian Reform in Denmark. *The Scandinavian Economic History Review,* 25. 117–37.

  1978. Bondeuro på Fyn 1768–70. *Fynske Årbøger.* 73–87.

  1979–81. Den jyske proprietærfejde. En studie over godsejerpolitik og bondeholdninger omkring 1790. *Histoire,* XIII. 1–70.

  1981a. Udskiftningsforordningen af 23. april 1781 og dens plads i dansk landbrugs historie. In *Forordning om Jord-Fælledskabets Ophævelse . . . 1781 – 23. April – 1981.* 5–30.

  1981b. *Bonde, Herremand, Konge. Bonden i 1700-tallets Danmark.*

  1983. "De danske cahiers." Studier i bondereaktionerne på forordningen af 15. april 1768. *Bol og by,* 2nd series, 5. 145–70.

  1988a. 200 års historieskrivning om landboreformerne. *Historie & Samtid,* 1 7–15.

  1988b. Ed. *Landboreformerne – forskning og forløb.*

  1990. *Fra reaktion til grundlov 1800–1850.* Olaf Olsen, ed., *Gyldendals og Politikens Danmarkshistorie,* 10.

Bligaard, Mette. 1987. *Frederiksborg Slot. Kongeborg og Museum.* Herning.

Bobé, Louis. 1895–1932. Ed., *Efterladte Papirer fra den Reventlowske Familiekreds i Tidsrummet, 1770–1827.* 1–10.

  1898. Ed., *Johan Caspar Lavaters Rejse til Danmark i Sommeren 1793.*

  1935–7. *Rom og Danmark gennem Tiderne.* I–II.

Boesen, Ludvig. 1769. *Beskrivelse over det smukke og fornøyelige Stamhus og Herresæde Lundsgaard.*

Bolens, Lucie. 1981. *Agronomes andalous du Moyen-Age.* Geneva.

Boockmann, Andrea. 1985. Das Wirtschaftsbuch der Abel Dorthea von Thynen. In Aage Andersen et al., eds., *Festskrift til Troels Dahlerup.* Arusia – Historiske skrifter, 5. Århus. 375–402.

276 Sources and Bibliography

Boserup, Ester. 1965. *The Conditions of Agricultural Growth*. Chicago.

1981. *Population and Technology*. Oxford.

Bossenga, Gail. 1988. La révolution française et les corporations: trois exemples lillois. *Annales E. S. C.*, 43, 2. 405–26.

Brasch, Christian H. 1859–63. *Vemmetoftes Historie som Herregaard, Slot og Kloster.* I–III.

Braudel, Fernand. 1949. *La Méditerranée et le Monde méditerranéen l'époque de Philippe II*, Paris.

Bremer, A. F. 1848. Om Koldfeber-Epidemierne i Danmark i Aarene 1825–34. *Det kongelige medicinske Selskabs Skrifter*, new series, 1. 124–38.

Bricka, C. F. 1870–72. [Review of] E. Erslev: Om de glubende Dyrs Undergang i Nørrejylland. *Historisk Tidsskrift*, 4th series, 2. 841–60.

Bro Jørgensen, J. O. 1943. *Industriens Historie i Danmark 1730–1820*. Axel Nielsen, ed., *Industriens Historie i Danmark*, I, 2.

1972. Ed., *Ove Høegh Guldbergs og arveprins Frederiks brevveksling med Peter Christian Schumacher 1778–1807*.

Bruce-Chwatt, Leonard Jan. 1985. *Essential Malariology*. 2d ed., London.

Bruce-Chwatt, Leonard Jan, and Julian de Zulueta. 1980. *The Rise and Fall of Malaria in Europe: A Historico-epidemiological Study*. Oxford.

Brüel, Jens. 1918. *Klitterne i Vestjylland og paa Bornholm*.

Brunner, Otto. 1949. *Adeliges Landleben und europäischer Geist*. Salzburg.

Bruun, Carl. 1887–90. *Kjøbenhavn*. I–III.

Bruun, Henry. 1938. *Den faglige Arbejderbevægelse i Danmark indtil Aar 1900*. I: til ca. 1880. Skrifter udgivet af Institutet for Historie og Samfundsøkonomi, 5.

Bryld, Carl-Johan, and Harry Haue. 1982. *Det agrare Danmark 1680–1980'erne*.

Brøndegaard, V. J. 1978–80. *Folk og flora: dansk etnobotanik*. 1–4.

1985–6. *Folk og fauna. Dansk etnozoologi*. 1–3.

Buderath, Bernhard, and Henry Makowski. 1986. *Die Natur dem Menschen untertan. Ökologie im Spiegel der Landschaftsmalerei*. Munich.

Bugge, Alexander. 1925–33. *Den norske Trælasthandels Historie*. I–II. Skien.

Bull, Hans. 1771. Om Landmandens Lyksalighed ved Friheds og Eiendoms Nydelse. In *Forsøg i de skiønne og nyttige Videnskaber*, 5. 139–60.

Bundgaard Lassen, T. 1932. Om Kaffedrikning blandt Almuen i Aarhus Stift i 1783. *Aarbøger udgivne af historisk Samfund for Aarhus Stift*, 25. 154–63.

Bunyard Peter. 1988. Gaia: The Implications for Industrialised Societies. *The Ecologist*, 18. 196–206.

Butterfield, H. 1957. *The Origins of Modern Science 1300–1800*. London.

Böcher, Steen B. 1942. *Vandkraftens Udnyttelse i det sydlige Nørrejylland før og nu*. Det Kgl. da. Geogr. Selskab's kulturgeogr. Skr., III.

Callisen, Henrich. 1807–9. *Physisk Medizinske Betragtninger over Kiøbenhavn*. 1–2.

Caprioli, Francesco Grasso. 1982. Camillo Tarello – Agostino Gallo – Giacomo Chizzola e l'Accademia di Rezzato. Contributo a nuovo studio dell'agricoltura bresciana, nel quadro della "rivoluzione agronomica" europea. *Rivista di Storia dell'Agricoltura*, 22, 2. 37–122.

Cardwell, D. S. L. 1972. *Technology, Science and History: A Short Study of the Major*

Sources and Bibliography

Developments in the History of Western Mechanical Technology and Their Relationships with Science and Other Forms of Knowledge. London.

Carlsen-Skiødt, J. C. A. 1931–6a. Nogle historiske Optegnelser om Sønderby Sogn. *Aarbog for Historisk Samfund for Odense og Assens Amter,* V. 3–48.

1931–6b. Nogle historiske Optegnelser om Helnæs Sogn. Sst. 187–214.

Carlsson, Sten, and Jerker Rosén. 1961–2. *Svensk Historia.* I–II. Stockholm.

Cavling, Henrik. 1897. *Fra Amerika.* I–II.

Cedergreen Bech, Svend. 1975. *Brev fra Dorothea. Af Charlotta Dorothea Biehls historiske breve.*

Chalke, H. D. 1962. The Impact of Tuberculosis on History, Literature and Art. *Medical History,* VI. 301–18.

Chalklin, C. W., and M. A. Havinden. 1974. *Rural Change and Urban Growth 1500–1800. Essays in English Regional History in Honour of W. G. Hoskins.* London.

Chambers J. D., and G. E. Mingay. 1966. *The Agricultural Revolution.* London.

Chaussinand, R. 1948. Tuberculose et lèpre. Maladies antagoniques. Éviction de la lèpre par la tuberculose. *International Journal of Leprosy,* 16. 431–8.

Chaussinand-Nogaret, G. 1984. *La Noblesse au XVIIIᵉᵐᵉ siècle. De la Féodalité aux Lumières.* Bruxelles.

Chorley, C. P. H. 1981. The agricultural revolution in Northern Europe, 1750–1880: nitrogen, legumes, and crop productivity. *Economic History Review,* 34. 71–93.

Christensen, Aksel E. 1943. *Industriens Historie i Danmark indtil c. 1730.* Axel Nielsen, ed., *Industriens Historie i Danmark,* I, 1.

1945. *Kongemagt og aristokrati. Epoker i middelalderlig dansk statsopfattelse indtil unionstiden.*

1977. Tiden 1042–1241. In Åksel E. Christensen et al., eds. *Danmarks historie,* 1. 211–399.

Christensen, Harry. 1983. *Len og magt i Danmark 1439–1481. De danske slotslens besiddelsesforhold analyseret til belysning af magtrelationerne mellem kongemagt og adel. Med særlig fokus på opgøret i slutningen af 1460'erne.* Skrifter udg. af Jysk Selskab for Historie, 42. Århus.

Christensen, Jens. 1985. *Landbostatistik. Håndbog i dansk landbohistorisk statistik 1830–1900.*

Christensen, P. 1962–3. Urmagere og Tusindkunstnere i Vendsyssel ca. 1750–1850. *Vendsysselske Aarbøger,* 1962. 1–116; supplement 1963, with separate pagination.

Christensen (Hørsholm), C. 1879. *Hørsholms Historie, fra 1305 til 1875.*

1886–91. *Agrarhistoriske Studier.* I–II.

Christiansen, Niels Finn. 1986. *Arbejderbevægelsens forhistorie.* SFAH's skriftserie, 18.

Clemmensen, Mogens. 1937. *Bulhuse. Studier over gammel dansk træbygningskunst.* I–II.

Clemmensen, Niels. 1987. *Associationer og foreningsdannelse i Danmark 1780–1880. Periodisering og forskningsoversigt.*

Clemmensen, Tove. 1942. *Borreby.*

Clemmensen, Tove, and Mogens B. Mackeprang. 1980. *Kina og Danmark 1600–1950. Kinafart og Kinamode.*

278   Sources and Bibliography

Cockburn, Aidan. 1963. *The Evolution and Eradication of Infectious Diseases.* Westport, CT.

Cohen, Mark. 1977. *The Food Crisis in Prehistory: Overpopulation and the Origins of Agriculture.* New Haven and London.

Colbiørnsen, Christian. 1790. *Betragtninger i Anledning af endeel jydske Jorddrotters Klage til Hans Kongelige Høihed Kronprindsen.*

Collins, Harvey Shields, and Donald Armstrong. 1986. Tuberculosis. *Encyclopedia Americana,* 27. 193–202.

Crescenzi, Pietro de'. 1305. *Liber ruralium commodorum.* (Quoted from the Italian translation *De agricoltura.* Venice, 1495.)

Crosby, Alfred W. 1972. *The Columbian Exchange: Biological and Cultural Consequences of 1492.* Contributions in American Studies, 2. Westport, CT.

1986. *Ecological Imperialism: The Biological Expansion of Europe, 900–1900.* Studies in Environment and History. Cambridge.

D. H. 1758. Patriotiske Tanker om Landvæsenets Forbedring i Siælland. *Oeconomisk Journal,* 3: 1. 396–421.

Dahlerup, Troels. 1971. [Den nordiske Adel i Senmiddelalderen:] Danmark. In *Den nordiske Adel i Senmiddelalderen.* Rapporter til det nordiske historikermøde i København 1971 9–12 august. 45–80.

1986. Den folkelige Danmarkshistories fødsel. *Skalk,* nr. 6. 18–26.

1989. *De fire stænder 1400–1500.* Olaf Olsen, ed., *Gyldendal og Politikens Danmarkshistorie,* 6.

Dalsgaard, Kristian. 1984. Matrikelkortet fra 1844 anvendt til rekonstruktion af det udrænede landskab. *Aarbøger for nordisk Oldkyndighed og Historie.* 282–301.

Damsholt, Torben. 1972. De gode kejsere og den oplyste enevælde. In *Festskrift til Povl Bagge.* 1–32.

Danstrup, John. 1947–9a. Kampen om den danske Hær 1740–66. *Historisk Tidsskrift,* 11th series, 2. 1–60.

1947–9b. [Review of] Aksel E. Christensen: Kongemagt og aristokrati. Ibid. 139–57.

de Vries, Jan. 1974. *The Dutch Rural Economy in the Golden Age.* New Haven and London.

Degen. Hans. 1936. Om den danske Oversættelse af Adam Smith og Samtidens Bedømmelse af den. *Nationaløkonomisk Tidsskrift,* 74. 223–32.

Degn, Ole. 1969. Flids og vindskibeligheds belønning. Præmiesystemet, præmievinderne og deres arbejde 1769–1967. In Vagn Dybdahl, ed., *For Fædrelandets bedre flor.* 192–254.

Deutsch, Karl W. 1966. *The Nerves of Government. Models of Political Communication and Control.* New York and London.

Devèze, M. 1961. *La vie de la forêt française au XVIe siècle,* II. Paris.

Dicckmann Rasmussen, Jørgen. 1977. *Bønderne og udskiftningen. En undersøgelse af udskiftningen i det københavnske rytterdistrikt med særlig henblik på bøndernes holdning.*

1978. Ed., *Sognefoged i Stavnsholt Lars Nielsens dagbog (1771) 1789–1794.*

Dodoens (Dodonæus), Rembert. 1563. *Crüjdeboeck.* (1st ed. 1554). Antwerpen.

Doll, Hans, H. Giese, S. K. Rasmussen, and L. Skøt. 1987. Genteknologi i forskning og planteforædling. *Naturens Verden.* 185–91.

Sources and Bibliography 279

Dombernowsky, Lotte. 1975. *De fynske godsarkiver* (under the name Lotte Jansen). Odense.

1983. *Lensbesidderen som amtmand. Studier i administration af fynske grevskaber og baronier 1671–1849.* Administrationshistoriske studier, 8.

1985. *"Slagsmaale ere nu om Stunder langt sjældnere. . . ." Retsopfattelse og adfærd hos fynsk landalmue omkring år 1800.*

1988. [Tiden] ca. 1720–1810. In Claus Bjørn et al., eds., *Det danske landbrugs historie*, 2: 1536–1810. 211–394.

Dons Christensen, Johannes. 1952. *Gødningslære.* 7th ed.

Drejer, S. 1837. *Anviisning til at kjende de danske Foderurter.*

Drewsen, Helge, et al. 1943. *Agerdyrkningslære* III: Kulturplanterne. Odense.

Drewsen, Johan Christian. 1815. Hvorfor lykkes Kløveren ikke mere saa fuldkommen vel, som før da den blev indført hos os? *Landoeconomiske Tidender*, 2. 173–93.

Dubos, Réné, and Jean Dubos. 1953. *The White Plague: Tuberculosis, Man and Society.* London.

Dumont, René. 1977. A world gone mad. In S. Gopinathan, ed., *Population.* Tangents/UNESCO, 8. Singapore. 78–89.

Eisenstein, Elizabeth L. 1979. *The Printing Press as an Agent of Change, Communications and Cultural Transformation in Early-Modern Europe.* Cambridge.

Ejlersen, Torben. 1979. Københavns møller. *Historiske Meddelelser om København.* 18–77.

Elias, Norbert. 1975. *Die höfische Gesellschaft.* Soziologische Texte, 54. Darmstadt.

Eliassen, P. 1906. Fra Hans de Hoffmans Dage. Nogle Papirer fra det 18. Aarhundrede om Vejle Amt. *Vejle Amts Aarbøger.* 77–110.

1923. *Historiske Strejftog i Kolding og Omegn.* Kolding.

Ellehøj, Svend. 1964. *Christian 4.s Tidsalder 1596–1660.* John Danstrup and Hal Koch, ed. *Danmarks Historie*, 7.

Elling, Christian. 1939. *Klassicisme i Fyen. En arkitekturhistorisk Studie.*

1942. *Den romantiske Have, Danske Studier.*

1961. *Et yndigt Land. Billeder og Minder fra det romantiske Sjælland.*

Elton, G. R. 1953. *The Tudor Revolution in Government: Administrative Changes in the Reign of Henry VIII.* Cambridge.

Engberg, Jens. 1973. *Dansk guldalder eller oprøret i tugt-, rasp- og forbedringshuset i 1817.*

Engelstoft, Laurits. 1961. *Mine Vandringer i Sjælland i Juni 1797*, ed. Povl Eller. Fra Frederiksborg Amt. Årbog.

Engqvist, Hans Henrik. 1974. *Tjele. En midtjysk herregårds bygningshistorie.*

Erichsen, John. 1972. *Frederiksstaden. Grundlæggelsen af en københavnsk bydel 1749–1760.* Skrifter udg. af Lokalhistorisk Afdeling, 1.

Erichsen, John, and Emma Salling. 1976. *Fyrste & hest. Rytterstatuen på Amalienborg.*

Erici, Nicolaus. 1688. *Disputatio medica inauguralis de phthisi.*

Eriksen, Palle. 1987. Kampen for gravhøjene. *Skalk*, no. 6. 18–27.

Erslev, Kr. 1879. *Konge og Lensmand i det sextende Aarhundrede.*

1882. *Dronning Margrethe og Kalmarunionens Grundlæggelse.*

Essen, K. von. 1807. *Mærkværdige Jordbrug i Danmark og Tydskland*, 1.Odense.

Estienne, Charles. 1570. *L'agriculture et Maison Rustique . . . plus un bref recueil des chasses du Cerf, du Sanglier, du Lieure, du Regnard, du Blereau, du Counin, & du Loup: Et de la Fauconnerie.* Paris.

280 Sources and Bibliography

Estrup, Jørgen. 1976. Præsten i Fyhn – Otto Diderich Lütken. In *Danske økonomer. Festskrift i anledning af Socialøkonomisk Samfunds 75 års jubilæum.* 61–93.

Evald, Anders. 1989. Skovbrug bremser drivhuseffekten. *Politiken*, 8. February.

Ewald, Johannes. 1969. *Samlede Skrifter.* 1–6.

Faber, Knud. 1926. *Tuberkulosen i Danmark.*

Fabricius, Johan Christian. 1774. Forsøg til en Afhandling om Planternes Sygdomme. In *Det Kgl. Norske Videnskabernes Selskabs Skrifter,* 5. 431–92.

Fabricius, Knud. 1910. *Griffenfeld.*

1920. *Kongeloven. Dens Tilblivelse og Plads i Samtidens natur- og arveretlige Udvikling.*

1932–4. Corn. Hamsfort og den danske Bonde. *Historisk Tidsskrift,* 10th series, 2. 540–54.

Fabricius, Nina. 1975. Kineseri. *Skalk,* no. 5. 18–27.

Falbe-Hansen, V. 1889. *Stavnsbaands-Løsningen og Landboreformerne. Set fra Nationaløkonomiens Standpunkt.* 1–2. Reprint 1975.

Falbe-Hansen, V. and William Scharling. 1885–91. *Danmarks Statistik.* 1–5 and supplement.

Fallesen, L. S. 1836. *Chronologisk Samling af de kongelige Forordninger og aabne Breve, Forst- og Jagtvæsenet i det egentilge Danmark angaaende, som fra Aaret 1660 til vore Tider ere udkomne.*

Feldbæk, Ole. 1982. *Tiden 1730–1814.* Aksel E. Christensen et al., eds., *Danmarks historie,* 4.

1984. Kærlighed til fædrelandet. 1700-tallets nationale selvforståelse. *Fortid og nutid,* 31. 270–88.

1990a. *Den lange fred 1700–1800.* Olaf Olsen, ed., *Gyldendals og Politikens Danmarkshistorie,* 9.

1990b. Christian VIIs Danmark. In *Flora Danica og det danske hof.* 45–69.

Fenger, Ole, C. Rise Hansen et al. 1979. Eds. *Sagregister til Herlufsholm Birks Tingbog 1616–19 og 1630–33.*

1980. Eds. *Sagregister til Skast Herreds Tingbøger 1636–1640.*

1985. Eds. *Sagregister til Sokkelund Herreds Tingbog 1621–22 og 1624–37.*

Fitter, Richard, and Alastair Fitter. 1974. *Nordeuropas vilde Planter.* Danish edition translated and edited by Bodil and Morten Lange.

Fjelstrup, August. 1909. *Borreby og dets Ejere. Af et sjællandsk Herresædes Arkiv.*

Fleischer, Esaias. 1777. *Udførlig Afhandling om Bier, og en for Dannemark og Norge nyttig Bie-Avls Anlæg.*

1779. *Forsøg til en Underviisning i Det Danske og Norske Skov-Væsen.*

1780. *Agerdyrknings-Katekismus til Underretning for Landmanden i Dannemark efter det Kongelige Danske Landhuusholdnings-Selskabs Indbydelse. . . . Trykt og uddeelt paa Selskabets Bekostning.*

Flensburg, Kjeld. 1969. *Egaliseringer og markomlægninger på bøndergodset i Merløse herred (Holbæk amt) i det 18. århundrede.* Thesis, University of Århus, available on demand.

Fogtmann, L. T. 1927–8. Spredte Træk af Jagtens Historie paa Dronninglund Gods i det 18de Aarhundrede. *Dansk Jagttidende,* XLIV 285–7, 305–6, 359–60.

Fonsmark, Henning. 1990. *Historien om den danske Utopi.*

Sources and Bibliography

Frandsen, Karl-Erik. 1977–8. Udsæd og foldudbytte i det 17. århundrede. *Fortid og nutid*, 27. 21–36.

1983. *Vang og tægt. Studier over dyrkningssystemer og agrarstrukturer i Danmarks landsbyer 1682–83.*

1984. Ved Ellehøj. Bebyggelse og agrarstruktur i Barup. In Grethe Christensen et al., eds., *Tradition og kritik. Festskrift til Svend Ellehøj den 8. September 1984.* 13–23.

1988a. Kulturlandskabet under forandring – Landboreformerne på Falster. In Claus Bjørn, ed., *Landboreformerne – forskning og forløb.* 44–53.

1988b. [Tiden] 1536–ca. 1720. In Claus Bjørn et al., eds., *Det danske landbrugs historie*, II: 1536–1810. 9–209.

Frandsen, Steen Bo. 1984. *Teglproduktion og tidlig industrialisering. Studier omkring teglværkerne i Jylland og Hertugdømmerne ca. 1750–1864.* Thesis, University of Århus, available on demand.

Fridericia, J. A. 1888. *Den danske Bondestands Undertrykkelse og Frigjørelse i det 18de Aarhundrede.*

Friis, Astrid, and Kristof Glamann. 1958. *A History of Prices and Wages in Denmark 1660–1800.* Copenhagen, London and New York.

Friis, Lars. 1968. Den sjællandske landbebyggelses ildsteder 1677–1800 – En arkivalsk undersøgelse. In Ivan Boserup et al., eds., *Extracta*, 1. 87–96.

Friis, Palle. 1967. Til sandet lagde mig øde. *Skalk*, nr. 3. 11–17.

1970. Sandflugt. *Kulturhistorisk leksikon for nordisk middelalder*, 15. 37–8.

Friis, Aage. 1903–19. *Bernstorfferne og Danmark.* I–II.

Fritzbøger, Bo. 1989a. *Skove og skovbrug på Falster 1652–1685.*

1989b. Om skovdyrkning i 1670'ernes Danmark. *Jagt- og Skovbrugsmuseet. Årsskrift.* 3–25.

Fuglsang, Anthon. 1943. Sandflugtens Dæmpning i Gern Herred. Haarup Sande i Linaa Sogn. *Aarbøger for Aarhus Stift*, 36. 30–76.

1947–9. Bidrag til Sandflugtens Historie. *Jyske Samlinger*, 5th series, 8.162–94.

Furetière, Antoine. 1960. *Dictionaire universel.* 1–3. The Hague and Rotterdam.

Fussell, G. E. 1958. *Crop Nutrition in the Late Stuart Age* (1660–1714). *Annals of Science*, 14. 173–84.

1972. *The Classical Tradition in West European Farming.* Newton Abbot.

Fussing, Hans H. 1957. *Bybefolkningen 1600–1660.* Skrifter udg. af Jysk selskab for historie, sprog og litteratur, 1.

Gadd, Carl-Johan. 1983. *Järn och potatis. Jordbruk, teknik och social omvandling i Skaraborgs län 1750–1860.* Meddelanden från ekonomisk-historiska institutionen vid Göteborgs Universitet, 53.

Gallo, Agostino. 1572. *Le vinti giornate dell'agricoltura et de'piaceri della villa* (many editions under varying titles, 1st ed. 1550.) Venezia.

Gamrath, Helge, and E. Ladewig Petersen. 1980. Perioden 1559–1648. In Aksel E. Christensen et al., eds., *Danmarks historie*, 2. 359–617.

Garde, Axel. 1938. *Fra Fællesskab til Fællesskab.*

Garde, H. G. 1832–5. *Efterretninger om den danske Søemagt.* 1–4.

Garnier, Bernard. 1975. La mise en herbe dans le Pays d'Auge aux XVIIᵉ et XVIIIᵉ siècles. *Annales de Normandie*, 25. 157–80.

Gay, Vitus. 1944. Jagtlitteratur. In *Dansk Jagtleksikon*, II. 698–708.

282   Sources and Bibliography

Geill, Torben. 1972. Peder Thun. En foregangsmand indenfor human og veterinær medicin. *Dansk medicinhistorisk årbog.* 82–112.

Gerner, Henrick. 1670. *Hesiodi Dage eller Rijmstock* (quoted from Hans Ellekilde's ed. 1942).

Gissel, Svend. 1956. Ed., *Sjællands Stifts Landebog 1567.*

1968. *Landgilde og udsæd på Sjælland i de store mageskifters tidsalder.* Landbohistoriske skrifter, 3.

1972. Forskningsrapport for Danmark. In *Nasjonale forskningsoversigter.* Det nordiske ødegårdsprojekt, 1.

Glamann, Kristof. 1960. The Danish Asiatic Company, 1732–1772. *Scandinavian Economic History Review,* VIII. 109–49.

1962. *Bryggeriets historie i Danmark indtil slutningen af det 19. århundrede.*

1966. *Otto Thott's Uforgribelige Tanker om Kommerciens Tilstand. Et nationaløkonomisk programskrift fra 1735.*

1991. *Jacobsen of Carlsberg: Brewer and Philanthropist.*

Glob, P. V. 1949. Barkær. Danmarks ældste landsby. *Fra Nationalmuseets Arbejdsmark.* 5–16.

Goethe, Johann Wolfgang von. 1962. *Italienische Reise.* Gedenkausgabe der Werke, Briefe und Gespräche 28. August 1949, ed. Ernst Beutler, 2nd printing, 11. 7–613. Zürick.

Gowing, Margaret. 1984. En gammel og intim forbindelse. *Naturens Verden,* 11. ix–xvi.

Graedel, Thomas E., and Paul J. Crutzen. 1989. The Changing Atmosphere. *Scientific American,* Sept. 28–36.

Gram, K., Hjalmer Jensen, and A. Mentz. 1937. *Nytteplanter.*

Gram, K., and Knud Jessen. 1957–9. *Vilde Planter i Norden.* 3rd ed. 1–4.

Graves, Karoline. 1921. *Ved Halleby Aa. Optegnelser af Karoline Graves,* ed. Henrik Ussing. Fra Holbæk Amt, XV.

Grund, Johann Gottfried. 1773. *Afbildning af Nordmands-Dalen, i den Kongelige Lyst-Hauge ved Fredensborg.*

Grunth, P. 1928. Om Peter Christian Abildgaards Forhold til Beslagkunsten. In *Festskrift til Bernhard Bang 1848 – 7. Juni – 1928.* 41–94.

Grøn, A. Howard. 1955–61. *Skovenes og skovbrugets historie. Kompendium.* I–II and supplement ved P. Chr. Nielsen.

1959. Egeskib og Egeskov. *Jyllands-Posten,* 23. april.

Hald, J. C. 1833. *Ringkjøbing Amt.* Bidrag til Kundskab om de danske Provindsers nærværende Tilstand i oeconomisk Henseende, 8.

Halskov-Hansen, V. 1968–9. Omkring St. Nørlund plantage. *Hedeselskabets Tidsskrift,* 89. 311–21, 351–60; 90. 13–27, 38–43.

Hansen, H. P. 1959. *Hedebønder i tre slægtled.* 2nd ed.

Hansen, K. 1920. Gødning. *Salmonsens Leksikon,* 10. 524–8.

1924–5. Ed. *Det danske Landbrugs Historie.* 1–5.

Hansen, Poul. 1942. *Fra Ødemarker til Storskove. Kronvildtomraadet i Ringkøbing Amt.*

Hansen, Povl. 1889. *Bidrag til det danske landbrugs historie: jordfællesskabet og Landvæsenskommissionen af 1757.*

1900. Bidrag til hegnenes historie. *Aarbog for dansk kulturhistorie.* 155–63.

Hansen, Thorvald. 1934. *Mellem sydfynske Sunde,* ed. Henrik Ussing.

Sources and Bibliography

Hansen, Viggo. 1957. Sandflugten i Thy og dens indvirkning på kulturlandskabet. *Geografisk Tidsskrift*, 56. 69–92.

1964. *Landskab og bebyggelse i Vendsyssel. Studier over landsbybebyggelsens udvikling indtil slutningen af 1600-tallet.* Kulturgeografiske Skrifter, 7.

1976. Thy – Et sandflugtsområde. In Ruth Helkiær Jensen and K. Marius Jensen, eds., *Topografisk Atlas Danmark.* 56–7.

1979–82 Hedens opståen og omfang. In Arne Nørrevang and Jørgen Lundø, eds., *Danmarks natur*, 3rd ed., 7. 9–28.

Hansen, W. A. 1790. *Beskrivelse over de efter en Kongelig Commissions Forslag paa Friderichsborg og Cronborg Amter foretagne Indretninger.*

Hassø, Arthur G. 1943–5. Ed., *Danske Slotte og Herregaarde.* I–IV.

Hastrup, Frits. 1970–3. Danske vangelag – i nordisk perspektiv. *Kulturgeografi*, 8. 65–100.

Hatt, Gudmund. 1937. *Landbrug i Danmarks Oldtid.*

Havinden, Michael. 1974. Lime as a Means of Agricultural Improvement: The Devon Example. C. W. Chalklin and M. A. Havinden, eds., *Rural Change and Urban Growth, 1500–1800.* London. 104–34.

Hazard, Paul. 1939–40. *La crise de la conscience européenne (1680–1715).* I–II and volume of notes.

Heiberg, Steffen. 1984. Samtidige portrætter af Frederik II. In Grethe Christensen et al., eds., *Tradition og kritik. Festskrift til Svend Ellehøj den 8. september 1984.* 183–204.

1988. *Christian 4, Monarken, Mennesket og Myten.*

Heide, Frits. 1913–16. Eds. Et Bidrag til Fyns Flora i det 18. Aarhundrede [by H. J. Trojel]. *Aarbog for Historisk Samfund for Odense og Assens Amter*, I. 592–606.

Heinild, Svend. 1979. *Sygdomsmønstrets ændring gennem 100 år.*

1989a. Afskaf Den Store Bastian. *Politiken*, 24. July.

1989b. Sundhed og sygdom. *Ugeskrift for læger*, 151. 1253–4.

Hellesen, Jette, and Ole Tuxen. 1984. "Fattige Børns Antagelse i de publique Latinske Skoler og Forsendelse til Academiet" i det 18. århundrede. In Grethe Christensen et al., eds., *Tradition og kritik. Festskrift til Svend Ellehøj den 8. september 1984.* 321–50.

1988. Eds., *Historisk Atlas Danmark.*

Helmer Pedersen, Erik. 1983. Dansk landbrugsudvikling i det 18. århundrede. En oversigt. *Bol og By*, 2nd series, 5. 43–75.

1988. Bønder og penge – reformer og landbrug 1750–1800. In Claus Bjørn, ed., *Landboreformerne – forskning og forløb.* 54–69.

Henningsen, Henning. 1960. "Papegøje" og vippefyr. Det danske fyrvæsen indtil 1770. *Handels- og Søfartsmuseet på Kronborg. Årbog.* 1–40.

Henningsen, Sven. 1944. *Studier over den økonomiske liberalismes gennembrud i Danmark: landhaandværket.* Göteborg.

Henschen, Folke. 1965. *Sygdommenes historie.*

Hentze, Arne. 1974. Planmæssig drift på fæstegods i Holbæk, Sorø og Præstø amter ca. 1790–1840. *Bol og by*, 8. 58–133.

Heresbach, Konrad. 1944–5. Om Bondeværk, ed. Peter Skautrup, *Sprog og Kultur*, 13. 129–31; 14. 56, 152.

Hermann Jensen, Christian. 1989. Jens Baggesen som øjenvidne i revolutionens Frankrig. *Folkets jul.* 3–7.

284 Sources and Bibliography

Hermansen, Niels K. 1955. Om Fredskovsforordningen af 1805. *Dansk Skovforenings Tidsskrift*, 40. 379–93.

Herrera, Gabriel Alfonso de. 1513. *Obra de Agricultura*. Biblioteca de Autores Españoles, 225. Madrid, 1970 (1st ed. 1513).

Hertel, H. 1919–20 *Det kgl. danske Landhusholdningsselskabs Historie*. I–II.

Hoffmeyer, Jesper. 1985. *Samfundets naturhistorie*. 2nd ed.

Hofman, Hans de. 1755–65. *Samlinger af Publique og Private Stiftelser, Fundationer og Gavebreve . . . udi Danmark og Norge*. I–X.

1757. *Oeconomiske Betragtninger om Aarhus-Stift*. [1]–4.

1758. Om Heederne i Jylland. *Oeconomisk Journal*, 3: 1. 20–38.

Hofman, Tycho de. 1777–79. *Historiske Efterretninger om velfortiente Danske Adelsmænd*. I–III.

Holberg, Ludvig. 1913–63. *Samlede Skrifter*. 1–18.

Holberg-Ordbog. 1981–8. Aage Hansen et al., eds., *Holberg-Ordbog. Ordbog over Ludvig Holbergs Sprog*. 1–5.

Holck, Axel. 1901. *Dansk Statistiks Historie 1800–1850*.

Holm, Edvard. 1883. *Om det Syn paa Kongemagt, Folk og borgerlig Frihed, der udviklede sig i den dansk-norske Stat i Midten af 18de Aarhundrede (1746–1770)*. Københavns Universitets Indbydelsesskrift.

1885–6. *Danmark-Norges indre Historie under Enevælden fra 1660 til 1720*. I–II.

1888 *Kampen om Landboreformerne i Danmark i Slutningen af 18. Aarhundrede (1773–1791)*. Festskrift i Anledning af Den Nordiske Industri, Landbrugs- og Kunstudstilling 1888.

1891–1912. *Danmark-Norges Historie fra Den Store Nordiske Krigs Afslutning til Rigernes Adskillelse (1720–1814)*. I–VII.

1907. *Sandflugtens Dæmpning i Tisvildegnen 1724–1738*.

Holm, Rita. 1983. Breve til amtmanden. Kilder til 1700-tallets lokalhistorie. *Fortid og nutid*, 30. 191–206.

Holm Rasmussen, Anders. 1988. Det bornholmske landbosamfund i 1700-tallet. *Bornholmske Samlinger*, 3rd series, 2. 9–20.

Holmgaard, Jens. 1962. Ed. *Indberetninger om kornavlen i Danmark 1778 og forslag til dens forbedring*. Bol og by, 3.

1969. Ed. *Fæstebonde i Nørre Tulstrup Christian Andersens Dagbog 1786–1797*.

1970. En jysk godsslagtning. Bagge Lihmes salg af Stårupgårds bøndergods til selveje 1794–1804. In Svend Gissel, ed., *Landbohistoriske studier tilegnede Fridlev Skrubbeltrang*. Landbohistoriske Skrifter, 4. 129–41.

1977–8. Landboreformerne – drivkræfter og motiver. *Fortid og nutid*, 27. 37–47.

1983. Går den, så går den . . . Løskøbelse fra et ikke eksisterende jysk vornedskab i 1729. *Fra Viborg Amt*. 114–19.

1986. Eksercitsen bag kirken efter gudstjenesten. Var landmilitstjenesten i stavnsbåndstiden en ringe byrde? *Bol og By. Landbohistorisk Tidsskrift*, fascicle 1. 44–64.

1988. Er stavnsbåndet først indført 1733? En undersøgelse af forordningen af 5. marts 1731 og dens tilblivelse. *Bol og By. Landbohistorisk Tidsskrift*, fascicle 1. 7–31.

1992. Et par kontrarevolutionære kommentarer til en revolutionær bog. *Fortid og Nutid*. 41–6.

Sources and Bibliography

Hornby, Ove and Erik Oxenbøll. 1982. Proto-Industrialisation before Industrialisation? The Danish Case. *The Scandinavian Economic History Review*, 30. 3–33.

Horstmann, Paul. 1986. Malariaens forsvinden fra Danmark. *Bibliotek for læger*, CLXXVIII. 69–101.

Hove, T. T. 1983. *Tørvegravning i Danmark. Fra håndgravning til moseindustri*. Herning.

Humlum, Johannes. 1943. *Danmarks Minedrift*. Erhvervsgeografiske Skrifter, 2.

Hurtigkarl, N. 1757. Nogle faa Observationer og Anmerkninger over Land-Væsenet. *Danmarks og Norges Oeconomiske Magazin*, 1. 37–66.

1762. En kort Undersøgning anstillet over Tørve-Moser. *Danmarks og Norges Oeconomiske Magazin*, 6. 419–32.

Huusfeld, Daniel. 1771. *Patriotiske Breve til Adskillige om (1) Een States Gield, (2) Samme Materie, (3) Skovenes Aftagelse og Opælskning, (4) Hoverie, (5) Bønder-Gaarders Udfløttelse paa deres Mark Deele, (6) Consumption og Brændevins- Brænderiet i Kiøbstæderne*.

Hvidtfeldt, Johan. 1938. Stavnsbaandet, dets Forudsætninger og Virkninger. *Vejle Amts Aarbog*, 34. 4–49.

1949–52. Dansk lokalhistorie gennem 50 år. *Fortid og Nutid*, 18. 357–63.

Hübner, Martin. 1774. *Ære-Minde for Patriotisk Nidkierhed. I Anledning af Det Kgl. Landhuusholdings-Selskabs Høitidelige Handlinger den 3die Februarii 1774. Med Tillæg af S. T. Hr. Etats-Raad Hübners Tale, da Han den 14de April nestefter nedlagde sit Embede som Selskabets Vice-Præsident*.

Høegh, Hans Jørgen Christian. 1795. *Anviisning til et velindrettet Jordbrug for Gaardmænd og Huusmænd paa Landet, som have faaet deres Jorder udskiftede af Fælledskab*.

Højrup, Ole. 1961. Hegn. *Kulturhistorisk leksikon for nordisk middelalder*, VI. 279–82.

1979–82. Hedens udnyttelse. In Arne Nørrevang and Jørgen Lundø, eds., *Danmarks natur*. 3rd ed., 7. 73–106.

Haarløv, Niels. 1979–82. Skovklimaet. In Arne Nørrevang and Jørgen Lundø, eds., *Danmarks natur*, 3rd ed., 6. 105–10.

Ilmoni, Immanuel. 1846–53. *Bidrag till Nordens Sjukdoms-Historia*. 1–3. Helsingfors.

Ilsøe, Harald. 1989. Bestsellere og Bogbelønninger – Biskop Balle på Bogmarkedet. *Magasin fra Det kongelige Bibliotek og Universitetsbiblioteket I*, 4, 1. 17–29.

Ilsøe, K. 1975. Bælgsæd. In *Plantedyrkning*. Landbrugets Informationskontor. 561–76.

Ingers, Enoch, and Sten Carlsson. 1943–56. *Bonden i svensk historia*. 1–3.

Iversen, Erik. 1951. Sicilianske Marionetter. *Gads danske magasin*. 487–96.

Iversen, Johannes. 1979–82. Naturens Udvikling siden sidste Istid. In Arne Nørrevang and Jørgen Lundø, eds., *Danmarks natur*, 3rd ed., 1. 345–445.

Jacobsen, Erik. 1987. Kopper og vaccination. *Medicinsk Forum*, 40. 137–44.

Jacobsen, Fritz. 1940. Nogle Oplysninger om Skovene paa Antvorskov Gods. *Aarbog for Historisk Samfund for Sorø Amt*, 28. 34–59.

Jacobsen, J. P., Jørgen Olrik, and R. Paulli. 1915–36. Eds. *Danske Folkebøger fra 16. og 17. Aarhundrede*. 1–14.

Jensen, Frede. 1941. *Af den danske Frøavls Historie*.

286 Sources and Bibliography

Jensen, Frede P. 1978. *Bidrag til Frederik II's og Erik XIV's historie.* Skrifter udg. af det historiske institut ved Københavns Universitet, VII.

1982. *Danmarks konflikt med Sverige 1563–1570.* Ibid., 12.

Jensen, Hans. 1917. A. G. Moltkes Forbedring af Agerdyrkningen paa Bregentved. *Aarbog for Historisk Samfund for Sorø Amt*, 6. 95–109.

1936–45. *Dansk Jordpolitik 1757–1919.* I–II. Reprint 1975.

Jensen, Jens Villiam. 1983–5. [Review of] E. Ladewig Petersen: Fra standssamfund til rangssamfund 1500–1700. *Historie. Jyske Samlinger*, new series 15. 514–21.

Jensen, Jørgen. 1979. *Oldtidens samfund. Tiden indtil år 800.* Dansk social historie, 1.

Jensen, P. E. 1902. *Gavnø Kloster og Herregaard fra Aar 1402–1902.*

Jensen, S. P. 1984. Lindencrones landboreformer på Gjorslev gods 1767–71. Baggrund og virkninger. *Historisk samfund for Præstø Amt. Årbog.* 7–30.

1985. Træk af udviklingen i landbrugsproduktionen gennem 200 år. *Tidsskrift for landøkonomi*, CLXXII. 273–90.

1986. Landbruget på Stevns fra udskiftningen til 1914. In *Landsbyer på Stevns – før og nu*, 4. 38–80.

1987. Agrarøkologi og landbrugsudvikling i det 18. og 19. århundrede. *Bol og By. Landbohistorisk Tidsskrift*, fascicle 2. 82–136.

Jensen, Sigurd. 1950. *Fra Patriarkalisme til Pengeøkonomi. Studier over dansk Bondeøkonomi i Tiden mellem Midten af det 18. og Midten af det 19. Aarhundrede.*

Jespersen, Knud J. V. 1975. *Skaføgårds adkomstbreve og jordebøger 1647–1797.* Hornslet.

1988. "Dristig skal sig Funken te, til den vorde Lue." Omkring oprettelsen af Dansk Adelsforbund 1908. In *Festskrift til Tage Kaarsted. Om Danmarks historie 1900–1920.* Odense University Studies in History and Social Sciences, 110. 147–64.

Jespersen, Svend. 1961. *Studier i Danmarks bønderbygninger.*

Jessen, Johannes C. 1938. *V. og Ø. Flakkebjerg Herreders Skolehistorie. Blade af den danske Skoles Historie fra ca. 1690 til vore Dage.* Slagelse.

1942. *Slagelse Herreds Skolehistorie 1721–1830.* Sorø.

Jessen, Knud, and Jens Lind. 1922–3. *Det danske Markukrudts Historie.* Kgl. Danske Videnskabernes Selskabs Skrifter, Naturvidensk. og Mathem. Afd., 8th series, 8.

Johansen, Bo. 1987. Inerti og vækst. Det danske landbrugs strukturelle udvikling ca. 1760–ca. 1810 – belyst gennem et udvalgt område på Falster. I–II. Thesis, University of Copenhagen, available on demand.

Johansen, Hans Christian. 1962. *Den økonomiske og sociale udvikling i Danmark 1864–1901.*

1968–80. *Dansk økonomisk politik i årene efter 1784.* I–II. Aarhus.

1975. *Befolkningsudvikling og familiestruktur i det 18. århundrede.* Odense University Studies in History and Social Sciences, 22.

1979. *En samfundsorganisation i opbrud 1700–1870.* Dansk social historie, 4.

1983. *Odense bys historie: Næring og bystyre. Odense 1700–1789.* Odense.

Juel, Povel. 1721. *En god Bonde, hans Avl og Biæring.*

Sources and Bibliography 287

Juncker, Flemming. 1985. *Humus. Dynamisk økologi. Fra fattig hede til frodig løvskov.*

Jutikkala, Eino. 1983. Spridningsmönstren hos smittkopporna under andra hälften av 1700-talet i Finland. In Ole Feldbæk and Niels Thomsen, eds., *Festskrift til Kristof Glamann.* Odense. 213–33.

Jørgensen, Grethe. 1986. De fynske haver på Frilandsmuseet. *Nationalmuseets Arbejdsmark.* 49–61.

Jørgensen, Harald. 1970–1. De private birkers endeligt. En oversigt. *Arkiv,* 3. 92–110.

Jørgensen, Harald, and Fridlev Skrubbeltrang. 1942. *Det Classenske Fideicommis gennem 150 Aar.*

Jørgensen, Karl A. 1921. Da Rødkløveren kom til Danmark. Et Bidrag til en uskreven Kulturhistorie. *Elevforeningen for Landboskolen ved Lyngby. Aarbog.* 5–31.

1930. Rødkløveren i Danmark. 1730–1930. *Ugeskrift for Landmænd,* LXXV. 369–71.

Jørgensen, Svend. 1984. *Danske industridamplokomotiver.* 1: Faxe jernbane, danske smalsporslokomotiver, mergelbaner.

Karup Pedersen, Ole. 1958. *Dansk Landbrugsbibliografi.* I: indtil 1814.

Karup Pedersen, Ole, and Karen Marie Olsen. 1958–74. Eds., *Sokkelund Herreds Tingbøger 1628–36.* [1–4].

Kerridge, Eric. 1967. *The Agricultural Revolution.* London.

Kjærgaard, Thorkild. 1973. *En undersøgelse af den offentlige kritik af den danske enevælde 1789–1799, dens indhold, skrifternes antal, forfatternes sociale placering og hvilken læserkreds, de henvendte sig til.* 1–3. Thesis, University of Copenhagen.

1977–8. Gårdmandshoveriet i økonomisk og social sammenhæng. I anledning af en bog om hoveriet på Egeskov. *Fortid og nutid,* 27. 419–27.

1979–80. Gårdmandslinien i dansk historieskrivning. Ibid., 28. 178–91.

1980. *Konjunkturer og afgifter. C. D. Reventlows betænkning af 11. februar 1788 om hoveriet.*

1981–2 Fridlev Skrubbeltrang og det danske landbosamfund. *Fortid og nutid,* 29. 276–84.

1984. *Farming Encyclopedias for the Western European Landowner: The "hausväter-literature", 1550–1750.* [At the end, with separate pagination: Chronological Bibliography of Farming Encyclopedias in Western Europe 1550–1750]. Duplicated. Florence.

1985a. The Farmer Interpretation of Danish History. *Scandinavian Journal of History,* 10. 97–118 [rev. ed. 1979–80].

1985b. Vejen til velstand og katastrofe. *Jyllands-Posten,* 27. November.

1986. Origins of Economic Growth in European Societies Since the XVIth Century: The Case of Agriculture. *Journal of European Economic History,* 15. 591–8.

1989a. *Le Danemark et la Révolution française.*

1989b. The Rise of Press and Public Opinion in Eighteenth-Century Denmark-Norway. *Scandinavian Journal of History,* 14. 215–30.

1991a. Ukrudt. In *Dansk Kulturhistorisk Opslagsværk.*

1991b. Gødning. Ibid.

288   Sources and Bibliography

Kjærgaard, Aage J. 1987. Et folk der lever bygger for sin fremtid. *Holstebro Dagblad*, 30. June.

Klitgaard, C. 1933–4. Ed., En skarp Formaning. Stiftamtmand Chr. Reitzers Interesse for Klitfredning. *Vendsysselske Aarbøger.* 333–6.

Knudsen Hans. 1927. Danske Lovs Bestemmelse om Selvejerbønders Hoveri. In *Festskrift til Kristian Erslev.* 371–92.

Koch, Elers. 1892. Brahetrolleborg Skovdistrikt 1786–1886. *Tidsskrift for Skovvæsen*, 4, series B. 89–222.

Koch, L. 1882. *Den danske Landsbyskoles Historie til 1848.*

Kragelund, Patrick. 1988. Abildgaard around 1800: His Tragedy and Comedy. *Analecta Romana Instituti Danici*, 16. 137–85.

    1989. Abildgaard, Homer and the Dawn of the Millennium. Ibid., 17–18. 181–224.

Kragelund, Aage. 1976. *Den humanistiske renæssance og antikken.* Berlingske leksikon Bibliotek, 113.

Krarup, J. B., and S. C. A. Tuxen. 1895–1912. *Beskrivelse af Landbrugets Udvikling i Danmark fra 1835 indtil Nutiden.* I–VI.

Kriedte, Peter, et al. 1978. *Industrialisierung vor der Industrialisierung.* Göttingen.

Kristensen, H. K. 1944. *Øster Horne Herred.*

    1968. *Hovedgården Estrup i Malt herred. Med bidrag til bøndergodsets historie.* Varde.

    1975. *Nørre Horne Herred.* Tarm.

Kristensen, Poul Halkjær. 1946. Et Bidrag til Belysning af Bondeinventariet paa Lolland i Begyndelsen af det 18. Aarhundrede. *Lolland-Falsters Historiske Samfunds Aarbog*, 5th series, 1. 123–42

Kristiansen, Kristian. 1979–80. [Review of] Ruth Tanderup and Klaus Ebbesen: Forhistoriens historie. *Fortid og nutid*, 28. 491–3.

Krogh, August. 1904. The Abnormal CO_2-Percentage in the Air in Greenland and the General Relations between Atmospheric and Oceanic Carbonic Acid. *Meddelelser om Grønland*, 26. 407–34.

Krogh, Tyge. 1987. *Staten og de besiddelsesløse på landet 1500–1800.* Odense University Studies in History and Social Sciences, 105. Odense.

Kroon, Sigurd. 1964. Medeltid och nutid. Helg och vardag. *Kyrkohistorisk årsskrift.* 194–210.

Kruse, Christian. 1988. Agroforestry i Afrika. In Helle Askgaard et al., eds., *Skovbogen.* Herning. 66–70.

Kryger, Karin. 1986. *Frihedsstøtten.*

Kuhlman, Hans. 1979–82. Kystklitterne. In Arne Nørrevang and Jørgen Lundø, eds., *Danmarks natur*, 3rd ed., 4. 160–86.

Kupzow, A. J. 1980. Theoretical Basis of the Plant Domestication. *Theoretical and Applied Genetics*, 57. 65–74.

Kaae, Alfred. 1948. *Laasby Sogn.* Ulfborg.

Ladewig Petersen, Erling. 1980. *Fra standssamfund til rangssamfund 1500–1700.* Dansk social historie, 3.

Lampe, Jens. 1980. *Urmagere og ure i Randers amt.*

    1982. Træk af urmageriets historie i Vendsyssel og Øster Hanherred. *Vendsyssel årbog.* 7–26.

Landbrugets Ordbog. 1937–8. Thomas Madsen-Mygdahl, ed., *Landbrugets Ordbog.* 3rd ed. I–II.

Sources and Bibliography

289

Landbrugets Ordbog. 1951–2. Thomas Madsen-Mygdahl, ed., *Landbrugets Ordbog.* 4th ed. I–II.

Langberg, Harald. 1951. Arkitektonisk Baggrund. In *Dronning Anna Sophie.* 1955. *Danmarks bygningskunst.* I–II.

Lange, Axel. 1937. Fredshaven i La Plata som Samlingssted for Jordens Nationalplanter. *Gartner-Tidende,* LIII. 182–4.

Lange, Johan. 1959–61. *Ordbog over Danmarks Plantenavne.* I–III.

1961. Hestebønner. *Kulturhistorisk leksikon for nordisk middelalder,* 6. 523–24.

1966. Vilde madplanter. Ibid., 11. 205–12.

1976. Ærter. Ibid., 20. 578–9.

Larsen, Henrik. 1937–8. Nordfyens Bebyggelse og Skove. *Aarbog for historisk Samfund for Odense og Assens Amter,* 6. 25–39.

Larsen, Jens (I). 1977. Myggestik. *Skalk,* no. 3. 18–26.

Larsen, Jens (II). 1983. *Nyopdyrkning i 1700-tallet.* Thesis, University of Copenhagen, available on request.

Larsen, Joakim. 1916. *Den danske Folkeundervisnings og Folkeskoles Historie fra 1536 til 1916.* Reprint 1984.

Lassen, Aksel. 1965. *Fald og fremgang. Træk af befolkningsudviklingen i Danmark 1645–1960.* Skrifter udg. af Jysk Selskab for Historie, 13.

Lassen, Erik. 1989. Thorvaldsen og H. C. Andersen. In *På Klassisk Grund. Tilegnet Dyveke Helsted.* Meddelelser fra Thorvaldsens Museum, 1989. 119–46.

Laumann Jørgensen, E., and P. Christian Nielsen. 1964. *Nordsjællands skove gennem 200 år.*

Lauridsen, John T. 1987. Adelsreaktion og politisk satire under den tidlige enevælde. *Danske studier.* 9–25.

Lauritsen, J. 1890. Frederik Buchwald som Godsejer. *Samlinger til Fyens Historie,* 10. 111–30.

Lerche, Grith. 1969. Bøndernes boliger. In Axel Steensberg, ed., *Dagligliv i Danmark i det syttende og attende århundrede.* I: 1620–1720. 551–84.

1985. Bramminge-skæret og andre nyere fund af pileformede ardskær. *Mark og Montre.* 78–98.

1987. Ed. *Bøndergårde i Danmark 1789–90.*

Levi, Carlo. 1947. *Cristo si è fermato a Eboli.* Saggi, 55. Turin.

Levine, Daniel. 1978. Conservatism and Tradition in Danish Social Welfare Legislation. 1890–1933: A Comparative View. *Comparative Studies in Society and History,* 20. 54–69.

Lind, Gunner. 1986a. Den dansk-norske hær i det 18. århundrede. Optimering, modernisering og professionalisering. *Historisk tidsskrift,* 86. 26–73.

1986b. Navn, stand, rang og slægt: Navneskik i en gruppe embedsmænd under enevælden. *Fortid og nutid,* 33. 165–79.

1987. Military and Absolutism: The Army Officers of Denmark-Norway as a Social Group and Political Factor, 1660–1848. *Scandinavian Journal of History,* 12. 221–43.

Lindbæk, Johannes. 1909–13. ed. Italienske Bidrag til Kristian den Fjerdes Historie. *Danske Magazin,* 6th series, 1. 344–68.

Lindhardt, P. G. 1939. *Peder Hersleb, I (689–1737). Studier over Dansk-norsk kirkeog kulturhistorie i første halvdel af det 18. århundrede.*

1978. *Vækkelse og kirkelige retninger,* 3rd ed. Århus.

290 Sources and Bibliography

Linné, Carl von. 1874. *Skånske Resa förrättad År 1749.* Lund.

Linvald, Axel. 1905–11. Antvorskov og Vordingborg Krongodser 1768–1774. *Fra Arkiv og Museum*, 3. 234–89 [I]; 4. 175–226 (II).

1921. Struensee og den danske Centraladministration. Statsstyrelse og Statsforvaltning i det 18. Aarhundrede. In Aage Sachs, ed., *Den danske Centraladministration*. 253–393

1942. Oplysningens Tidsalder. In Aage Friis et al., eds., *Schultz Danmarkshistorie*, 4. 1–300.

Lindvald, Steffen. 1962. *Brønshøj, Husum og Utterslev. De rige bondebyer.*

Liversage, David, and David E. Robinson. 1988. Mens havet æder ind i det nordjyske hedelandskab. *Naturens verden.* 262–71.

Lohmeier, Dieter. 1978. Ed. *Arte et Marte. Studien zur Adelskultur des Barockzeitalters in Schweden, Dänemark und Schlewig-Holstein.* Kieler Studien zur Deutschen Literaturgeschichte, 13. Neumünster.

1980. Der Edelmann als Bürger. Über die Verbürgerlichung der Adelskultur im dänischen Gesamtstaat. In Christian Degn and Dieter Lohmeier, eds., *Staatsdienst und Menschlichkeit. Studien zur Adelskultur des späten 18. Jahrhunderts in Schleswig-Holstein und Dänemark.* Kieler Studien zur Deutschen Literaturgeschichte, 14. Neumünster. 127–49.

Loomis, R. S. 1978. Ecological Dimensions of Medieval Agrarian Systems: An Ecologist Responds. *Agricultural History.* 478–85.

Lund, H. C. A. 1901. *Søkadet-Korpsets Historie 1701–1901.*

Lund, Hakon. 1963. *Danske Haver i det syttende og attende Aarhundrede.*

1980. Ed. *Danmarks arkitektur. Landbrugets huse.*

Lund, N. 1809. *Underretning om Tørvemosers Opmaaling, Undersøgelse, Beregning og Afbenyttelse.*

Lunn, F. 1876. *Knabstrup i ældre og nyere Tid. Et Bidrag til gamle Herregaardes Historie.*

Luxdorph, Bolle Willum. 1915–30. *Luxdorphs Dagbøger*, ed. Eiler Nystrøm. I–II.

Lybecker, Johann Ludvig. 1772. *Korte Betragtninger over Aarsagerne til Kornmangelen og de høie Kornpriser i Danmark, samt om de beste Hielpemidler til at forekomme samme.*

1772–84. *Applications-Udtog af alle de Kongelige Forordninger, Placater, Rescripter.* 1–3.

Lüders, P. E. 1758a. Om Bie-Avlen. *Danmarks og Norges Oeconomiske Magazin*, 2. 293–304.

1758b. Om det Røde Klever-Græs, og om Tørve-Jordens Brug til Giødning. Ibid., 2. 305–12.

1760. *Kort Samtale imellem en Landmand og en Præst hvorudi den Materie om Hør-Potatos- Humle- og Klever-Avlen bliver afhandlet.*

1761. *Kurze Nachricht von dem Klever-Bau.* Flensburg.

Lütken, O. D. 1760. *Undersøgninger angaaende Statens almindelige Oeconomie.* I–II. Sorø.

1762. Undersøgning i Almindelighed om de til Brændsels behørige Vedligeholdelse i Dannemark nærmeste og tienligste Midler, og i Særdeleshed om Tørve-Mosernes egentlige Væsen og Natur, deres Fremvæxt paa nye, samt den til deres Vedligeholdelse behøvende Forsigtighed. *Danmarks og Norges Oeconomiske Magazin*, 6. 249–96.

Lütken, P. W. 1808. Om Danmarks Skove. *Ny Minerva.* 38–50.

Sources and Bibliography

291

Lütken, Vilhelm 1909–10. *Bidrag til Langelands Historie.* Rudkøbing.

Løgstrup, Birgit. 1983. *Jorddrot og offentlig administrator. Godsejerstyret inden for skatte- og udskrivningsvæsenet i det 18. århundrede.* Administrationshistoriske studier, 7.

1986. Landsbyfællesskabet i det 18. århundrede. En studie i vider og vedtægter. *Bol og By. Landbohistorisk tidsskrift,* fascicle. 2. 34–74.

McEvedy, Colin, and Richard Jones. 1978. *Atlas of World Population History.* Harmondsworth.

McNeill, William H. 1977. *Plagues and Peoples.* Oxford.

Maczak, Antoni, and William N. Parker. 1978. Eds. *Natural Resources in European History.* Washington, DC.

Malling, Gerd. 1982. Teori og praksis i dansk landbrug i 1700-tallet. Thesis, University of Copenhagen, available on request.

Malthus, Thomas Robert. 1966. *The Travel Diaries of Thomas Robert Malthus,* ed. Patricia James. Cambridge.

Mandix, Jacob. 1830. *Danmarks Tilstand for omtrent tredsindstyve Aar siden sammenlignet med den nuværende.*

Mann, R. D. 1990. Time Running Out: The Urgent Need for Tree Planting in Africa. *The Ecologist,* 20. 48–53.

Manniche, Jens Christian. 1972–4. Den københavnske tømrerstrejke 1794. *Historie. Jyske Samlinger,* new series 10. 523–61.

Mansa, F. V. 1842. *Pesten i Helsingør og Kiøbenhavn 1710 og 1711.*

1873. *Bidrag til Folkesygdommenes og Sundhedspleiens Historie i Danmark.*

Markussen, Ingrid. 1988. *Visdommens lænker. Studier i enevældens skolereformer fra Reventlow til skolelov.*

Mathias, Peter. 1976. Wer entfesselte Prometheus? Naturwissenschaft und technischer Wandel von 1600 bis 1800. In Rudolf Braun et al., eds., *Industrielle Revolution. Wirtschaftliche Aspekte.* Neue Wissenschaftliche Bibliothek, 50. Cologne. 121–38.

Matsen, Bjørn. 1978. *Gode viljer, gode konjunkturer eller ressourcepres? Et bidrag til forklaring af de danske landbrugsreformer i 1700-tallet.* Thesis, University of Copenhagen, available on request.

Matthiessen, Hugo. 1942. Det gamle Land. Billede fra Tiden før Udskiftningen.

Medicus, Ludwig W. 1829. *Zur Geschichte des künstlichen Futterbaues, oder des Anbaues der vorzüglichsten Futterkräuter, Wiesenklee, Luzerne, Esper, Wicke und Spergel.* Nürnberg.

Mentz, A. 1912. *Studier over danske Mosers recente Vegetation.*

Meuvret, Jean. 1955. L'agriculture en Europe aux XVIIème et XVIIIème siècles: Aperçu d'ensemble. In *Relazioni del X Congresso Internazionale di Scienze Storiche,* 4. Florence. 137–68.

Meyer, Poul. 1949. *Danske bylag.*

1954–6. Bylag og sogn. Bondeting og bylag. Landsbystyret indtil udskiftningen. Sognekommunerne opstår. Den første landkommunalordning. In Wm. S. Rasmussen and Tage Mortensen, eds., *Danmarks kommunale styre,* I. 106–39.

Michell, A. R. 1974. Sir Richard Weston and the Spread of Clover Cultivation. *The Agricultural History Review,* 22. 160–1.

Michelsen, Peter. 1968. *Ildsteder og opvarmning på Frilandsmuseet.*

Mikkelsen, Keld. 1989. *Københavns Fattigvæsen 1770–1840. Fattigdommen, det københavnske fattigvæsens og fattigpolitikkens udvikling i perioden fra omkring*

292   Sources and Bibliography

1770 til omkring 1840. Thesis, University of Copenhagen, available on request.

Mineccia, Francesco. 1982. *Da fattoria granducale a communità Collesalvetti 1737–1861*. Napoli.

Mogensen, Margit, and Poul Erik Olsen. 1984. *Godsejerrøster. Landøkonomiske indberetninger fra Roskilde amt 1735–1770*.

Molbech, Christian. 1846. Ed., *Uddrag af Biskop Jens Bircherods historiskbiographiske Dagbøger for Aarene 1658–1708*.

Molesworth, Robert. 1694. *An Account of Denmark as it was in the Year 1692*. London.

Monrad, Jørgen H. 1978. *Den københavnske klub 1770–1820*. Århus.

Monrad Møller, Anders. 1981. *Fra galeoth til galease. Studier i de kongerigske provinsers søfart i det 18. århundrede*. Esbjerg.

1988. *Jagt og skonnert. Studier i den danske provinssøfart i tiden fra 1814 til 1864*.

Montesquieu. 1748. *De l'Esprit des Lois* (quoted from Gonzague Truc's ed., Paris, 1961, 1–2) (1st ed. 1748).

Mortensen, R. 1917. Skovplantningen paa Hederne før Dalgas. *Aarbøger for Aarhus Stift*, 10. 1–39.

Mossin, Hans. 1773. *Beretning om Agerdyrknings-Maaden i Jylland, Holsteen og Lolland*. Bergen.

Mulvad, Søren. 1988. Fourlund – en husmandskoloni fra 1788. *Fra Ribe Amt*, 24, 2. 223–7.

Munck, Thomas. 1979. *The Peasantry and the Early Absolute Monarchy in Denmark, 1660–1708*.

Munk, Holger. 1951. *Hesten i Sydsjælland gennem 200 Aar. 1700–1900*.

1962. *Færgegaarden gennem fire hundrede aar*.

Munksgaard, Elisabeth, and J. Troels-Smith. 1968. *Den hellige Mose*.

Munthe af Morgenstierne, C. W. von. 1783. *Det Danske Landvæsens Forfatning*. Sorø.

Musson A. E., and Eric Robinson. 1969. *Science and Technology in the Industrial Revolution*. Manchester.

Myers, J. Arthur, and James H. Steele. 1969. *Bovine Tuberculosis Control in Man and Animal*. St. Louis, Missouri.

Mølgaard, Else, and Ole Schou Vesterbæk. 1987. Kulsvierne og administrationen. In Poul Vestergaard, ed., *Kulsvierlandet*. 68–79.

Møller, Carl Marius. 1950. *Mycorrhizia and nitrogen assimilation. With special reference to Mountain Pine* (Pinus Mugo Turra) *and Norway Spruce* (Picea Abies (L.) Karst). Det forstlige forsøgsvæsen i Danmark, 19. 105–203.

Møller-Christensen, Vilhelm. 1959. Feber. *Kulturhistorisk leksikon for nordisk middelalder*, 4. 208–10.

1961–2. Lepra og dens historie. *Medicinsk Årbog*, 5. 17–81.

1963. *De store sygdomme*. Søndagsuniversitetet, 35.

Møller-Holst, E. 1877–83. Ed. *Landbrugs-Ordbog for den praktiske Landmand*. 1–6.

Møllgaard, Johannes. 1988. Det "mørke" Jylland og "verdensmarkedet." *Folk og Kultur*. 61–99.

Mønster, Erik. 1951–2. Sygdommen, der gav hospitalerne navn. Hos de spedalske i Paris. *Vor Viden*, 2nd series, 1. 689–94.

Mørch, Søren. 1982. *Den ny Danmarkshistorie 1880–1960*.

Sources and Bibliography

Nannested, Kirsten. 1990. Bolle Willum Luxdorph, 1716–1788. *Carlsbergfondet. Årsskrift.* 136–40.

Nassini, Carla. 1985. Moti popolari e criminalità in Arezzo tra fine '700 e inizi '800. In Ivan Tognarini, ed., *La Toscana nell'età rivoluzionaria e napoleonica.* Napoli. 175–96.

Needham, Joseph. 1984. *Science and Civilisation in China,* 6, II. Cambridge.

Nef, John U. 1932. *The Rise of the British Coal Industry.* I–II. London.

1977. An Early Energy Crisis and Its Consequences. *Scientific American.* 237:5. 140–51.

Nielsen, Axel. 1944. *Industriens Historie i Danmark. 1820–70.* 1st half-volume, Axel Nielsen, ed., *Industriens Historie i Danmark,* 3, 1.

1948. *Det statsvidenskabelige Studium i Danmark før 1848.*

Nielsen, Lauritz. 1935. *Registre til dansk Bibliografi 1482–1550 & 1551–1600.*

Nielsen, Niels. 1928. Danske Jærnværker fra Aar 1500 til vore Dage. *Naturens Verden,* 12. 257–76.

Nielsen, P. 1878. Græsmark. In E. Møller-Holst, ed., *Landbrugs-Ordbog for den praktiske Landmand,* 2. 433–55.

1879. Kløver. Ibid., 3. 467–90.

Nielsen, P. Christian. 1960. Skibets krav til skoven. *Handels- og Søfartsmuseet på Kronborg. Årbog.* 169–202.

1979–82. Skovens Historie. In Arne Nørrevang and Jørgen Lundø, eds., *Danmarks natur,* 3rd ed., 6. 9–64.

1982. Johan Ulrich Røhl. *Dansk Biografisk Leksikon,* 3rd ed., 12. 510.

Nielsen-Kold, R. 1932. Strynø. Strynø Hvidkløver! – Strynø Barres! *Kærhave Elevforenings Aarsskrift.* 3–6.

Nordberg, Michael. 1987. *Den dynamiske Middelalder.*

Nüchel Thomsen, Birgit, Thomas Brinley, and John W. Oldam. 1965. Dansk-engelsk samhandel 1661–1963. *Erhvervshistorisk Årbog,* 16. 7–438.

Nyberg, Tore, and Thomas Riis. 1985. Eds., *Kalundborgs historie.* 1: Tiden indtil 1830. Kalundborg.

Nyerup, Rasmus. 1816. *Almindelig Morskabslæsning i Danmark og Norge igjennem Aarhundreder.*

Nyrop-Christensen, H. 1971. Den honnette ambition. In Axel Steensberg, ed., *Dagligliv i Danmark i det syttende og attende århundrede: 1720–1790.* 153–81.

Nystrøm, Eiler. 1938. *Fra Nordsjællands Øresundskyst.*

Nørr, Erik. 1981. *Præst og Administrator. Sognepræstens funktioner i lokalforvaltningen på landet fra 1800 til 1841.* Administrationshistoriske studier, 4.

Oakley, Stewart. 1972. *The Story of Denmark.* London.

Oehlenschläger, Adam. 1896–99. *Poetiske Skrifter i Udvalg,* ed. F. L. Liebenberg and A. Boysen, 1–15.

1990. *Breve fra og til Adam Oehlenschläger okt. 1829–jan. 1850.* III: 1844–1850, ed. Daniel Preisz.

Olsen, Albert. 1932. *Bybefolkningen i Danmark paa Merkantelismens Tid:* Merkantelistiske Studier, I. Acta Jutlandica, VI, 2. Århus.

1936. *Danmark-Norge i det 18. Aarhundrede.*

Olsen, Fritz. 1889. *Det danske Postvæsen, dets Historie og Personer indtil dets Overtagelse af Staten 1711.*

1903. *Postvæsenet i Danmark som Statsinstitution indtil Christian VIIIs Død. (1711–1808).*

294 Sources and Bibliography

Olsen, Gunnar. 1950–2. Stavnsbåndet og tjenestekarlene. *Jyske Samlinger*, new series, 1. 197–218.

1957. *Hovedgård og bondegård.* Landbohistoriske skrifter, 1. Reprint 1975.

1961. *Kronborg Vestre Birk. Holbo herred fra oldtiden til vore dage.*

Olsen, Gunnar, and Poul Alkærsig. 1965. *Pest over landet.*

Olsen, Ib. 1983. De nyeste hovedretninger indenfor den familiehistoriske forskning om Vesteuropa i perioden ca. 1400 til ca. 1800. *Historisk Tidsskrift*, 83. 166–94.

Olsen, Johannes. 1937. Vand- og Vindmøller i Svendborg Amt. *Svendborg Amt*, 29. 3–23.

Olufsen, Christian. 1797. Rødkløver og Raygræs. *Oeconomiske Annaler*, I. 42–6.

1809. Om de forskjellige Arter af Markbrug. *Oeconomiske Annaler*, 11. 139–244.

1811. *Danmarks Brændselsvæsen, physikalskt, cameralistiskt og oeconomiskt betragtet.*

Oppermann, A. 1887–9. *Bidrag til det danske Skovbrugs Historie 1786–1886.* Tidsskrift for Skovbrug, X.

1923. Af Skovgræsningens Historie. *Dansk Skovforenings Tidsskrift*, 8. 53–74.

1923–31. Skove og Søer. In *Sorø: Klostret, Skolen, Akademiet gennem Tiderne*, II. 1–86.

1929. *Den danske Skov-Lovgivning 1660–1924.*

Oppermann, A., and V. Grundtvig. 1931–5. *Den danske Skovbrugs-Litteratur indtil 1925.* Bibliograhia Universalis Silviculturae, I.

Orth, F. 1921. Klee. In *Paulys Real-Encyclopädie der Classischen Altertumswissenschaft*, 11, 1. Stuttgart. 585–91.

Osborn, Fairfield. 1948. *Our Plundered Planet.*

Palladius, Peder. 1872. *Biskop Peder Plades visitatsbog*, ed. Svend Grundtvig.

Paludan, Helge. 1977. Tiden 1241–1340. In Aksel E. Christensen et al., eds., *Danmarks historie*, 1. 401–511.

Paludan, Johan. 1822–4. *Beskrivelse over Møen.* 1–2.

Paludan-Müller, Astrid. 1923. *Generalmajor Classen 1725–1792.*

Paulli, Simon. 1648. *Flora Danica. Det er: Dansk Urtebog.*

Pedersen, Christiern. 1533. *Christiern Pedersen's Lægebog* (facsimile ed. with an introduction by Poul Hauberg, 1933).

Pedersen, Henrik. 1907–8. Udsæden og det dyrkede Areal paa Falster i sidste Halvdel af det 17de Aarh. *Historisk Tidsskrift*, 8th series, 1. 101–37.

1928. *De danske Landbrug, fremstillet paa Grundlag af Forarbejderne til Christian V.'s Matrikel 1688.* Reprint 1975.

Pedersen, Karl Peder. 1985. En vestfynsk fæstebonde. Peder Madsen, Munkegårds optegnelser 1744–98. *Bol og By. Landbohistorisk tidsskrift*, fascicle 2. 18–55.

Pedersen, Søren. 1983. *En fæstebondes liv. Erindringer og optegnelser af gårdfæster og sognefoged Søren Pedersen, Havrebjerg (1776–1839)*, ed. Karen Schousboe.

Petersen, Julius. 1896. *Kopper og Koppeindpodning.*

Petersen, Viggo. 1967. Stengærder og grøfter og gærdselshugstens formindskelse i det 18. århundredes første halvdel. *Dansk Skovforenings Tidsskrift*, 52. 311–20.

1969. Agernhaver og andre skovdyrkningsforanstaltninger i Danmark før v. Langens ankomst 1763. Ibid., 54. 261–70.

Poni, Carlo. 1982. *Fossi e cavedagne benedicon le campagne. Studi di storia rurale.* Bologna.

Sources and Bibliography 295

1989. Struttura strategie e ambiguità delle "Giornate": Agostino Gallo fra l'agricoltura e la villa. *Intersezioni*, 9, no. 1. 5–39.

Pontoppidan, Axel. 1939. *Adam Gottlob Detlev greve Moltke.*

Pontoppidan, Erik. 1759. *Eutropii Philadelphi Oeconomiske Balance eller Uforgribelige Overslag paa Dannemarks Naturlige og Borgerlige Formue til at gjøre sine Indbyggere lyksalige.*

1762. Fortale til Læseren. *Danmarks og Norges Oeconomiske Magazin*, 6. [1–16].

1763–81. *Den Danske Atlas.* 1–7 (vols. 4–7 ed. Hans de Hofman). Reprint 1969–72.

Porsmose, Erland. 1987. *De fynske landsbyers historie – i dyrkningsfællesskabets tid.* Odense University Studies in History and Social Sciences, 109.

1988. Middelalder 0. 1000–1536. In Claus Bjørn et al., eds., *Det danske landbrugs historie*, 1. 205–417.

Poulsen, Vagn, Erik Lassen, and Jan Danielsen. 1972–5. Eds. *Dansk Kunsthistorie.* I–IV.

Prahl, Jacob Peter. 1777. *Agerdyrknings Catechismus, efter Bornholms Agerdyrknings-Maade.*

Pram, Christen. 1789. Historien. *Minerva*, July–Sept. 120–36, 281–96; Oct.–Dec. 102–12.

1792. Om Hovedtildragelserne af Dagens Historie, siden de i sidste Hefte nævnte. *Minerva*, July–Sept. 394–423.

Prange, Knud. 1972. Ed. *Bog over avlingen til Vær præstegaard 1771–1780.* Bol og by, 6.

Prange, Wolfgang. 1971. *Die Anfänge der grossen Agrarreformen in Schleswig-Holstein bis um 1771.* Quellen und Forschungen zur Geschichte Schleswig-Holsteins, 60.

Radkau, Joachim. 1983. Holzverknappung und Krisenbewusstsein im 18. Jahrhundert. *Geschichte und Gesellschaft*, 9. 513–43.

1986. Zur angeblichen Energiekrise des 18. Jahrhunderts: Revisionistische Betrachtungen über die "Holznot." *Vierteljahrschrift für Sozialgeschichte und Wirtschaftsgeschichte*, 73. 1–37.

Rafner, Claus. 1986. Fæstegårdmændenes skattebyrder 1660–1802. *Fortid og nutid*, 33. 81–94.

Rahbek, Knud Lyne. 1792. [Om den franske Revolution]. *Den danske Tilskuer*, II. 537–46.

Ramskou, Thorkild. 1960. *Lindholm Høje.*

Rasch, Aage. 1955. *Dansk toldpolitik 1760–1797.*

1964. *Niels Ryberg 1725–1804.*

Rasch, Aage, and P. P. Sveistrup. 1948. *Asiatisk Kompagni i den florissante Periode 1772–1792.*

Rasmussen, Anna. 1985. *Hylke sogn i det nittende århundrede.* Skanderborg.

Rasmussen, Holger. 1970. Vindmøllerne på Harboøre. In: Svend Gissel, ed., *Landbohistoriske studier tilegnede Fridlev Skrubbeltrang.* Landbohistoriske Skrifter, 4. 142–56.

1974. The Use of Seaweed in the Danish Farming Culture. In *In Memoriam Antoñio Jorge Dias*, 1. Lissabon. 385–98.

1982. Ed. *Optegnelser fra Holevadgården 1767–1863.*

Rasmussen, Poul, and August F. Schmidt. 1955. *Frøslev og Mollerup Sognes Historie.* Nykøbing M.

296 Sources and Bibliography

Rasmussen Søkilde, N. 1875–8. *Holstenshus og Nakkebølle med tilliggende Sogne og Øer.* Odense.

1888. *Landboreformerne og den danske Bondestands Frigjørelse før og efter 1788.*

Raunkiær, C. 1930. *Hjemstavnsfloraen hos Hedens Sangere Blicher og Aakjær.*

Ravn, Thomas Bloch. 1983. Arbejdet mellem nødvendighed og dyd. Et mentalitetshistorisk projekt om arbejdsmoralens udvikling i Danmark. *Den jyske historiker,* 26. 4–21.

Ravnholt, A. 1934. *Historiske og topografiske Efterretninger om Thorning Sogn.* Nr. Nebel.

Reitzel-Nielsen, Erik, and Carl Popp-Madsen. 1936. Eds. *Festskrift i Anledning af Tohundrede Aars Dagen for Indførelsen af juridisk Eksamen ved Københavns Universitet.*

Reventlow, Christian B. 1902–3. *En dansk Statsmands Hjem omkr. Aar 1800.* I–II.

Reventlow, Christian Ditlev. 1786. [Bemærkninger af 4de December 1786 til Kammerherre Lehns Forestilling af 25. November 1786]. In *Den for Landboevæsenet nedsatte Commissions Forhandlinger,* I. 1788. 267–71.

Rhode, P. 1776–94. *Samlinger til de Danske Øers Laalands og Falsters Historie.* 1–2.

Riegels, N. D. 1796. *Indskuds-Plan for danske Patrioter til det falsterske Noors Omdannelse fra en flade Vand til Ager og Eng.*

Ries, Paul. 1798. Robert Molesworths Analyse des dänischen Absolutismus. In Dieter Lohmeier, ed., *Arte et Marte. Studien zur Adelskultur des Barockzeitalters in Schweden, Dänemark und Schleswig-Holstein.* Kieler Studien zur deutschen Literaturgeschichte, 13. Neumünster. 43–66.

Riis, Thomas. 1977. *Les institutions politiques centrales du Danemark 1100–1332.* Odense University Studies in History and Social Sciences, 46. Odense.

1990. Le temps du travail: une esquisse. *Diogène,* no. 149, Jan.–Mar. 64–81.

Riising, Anne. 1958. Den økonomiske debat om lavs- og købstadsprivilegier i sidste halvdel af det 18. århundrede. *Erhvervshistorisk Årbog,* 10. 98–134.

1976. Dansk lokaladministration i 1700-tallet (Fyns Stiftamt). In *Från medeltid till välfärdssamhälle. Nordiska historikermötet i Uppsala 1974.* Stockholm. 187–219.

Riismøller, Peter. 1952. Kan mennesker bygges om? *Danske Museer. Aarbog for Dansk kulturhistorisk Museumsforening,* III. 25–32.

1972. *Sultegrænsen.*

Rise Hansen, C. 1968. *Hoveriet på Ringsted Kloster 1570–1620.* Landbohistoriske skrifter, 2.

Rise Hansen, C., and Axel Steensberg. 1951. *Jordfordeling og Udskiftning. Undersøgelser i tre sjællandske Landsbyer.* Det kgl. danske Videnskabernes Selskab. Historisk-filologiske skrifter, 2, no. 1.

Roche, Daniel. 1981. *Le peuple de Paris. Essai sur la culture populaire au XVIIIᵉ siècle.* Paris.

Rockstroh, K. C. 1909–26. *Udviklingen af den nationale Hær i Danmark i det 17. og 18. Aarhundrede.* I–III.

1911. Om Frederiksværkegnen for 200 Aar siden. *Fra Frederiksborg Amt.* 39–107.

Roesdahl, Harald. 1977. *Gamle glas og karafler. Historie, Beskrivelse, Bestemmelse.*

Rothe, Tyge. 1795. *Karen Biørns Minde. Ved hendes Mand: Tyge Rothe.*

Rudé, George. 1975. *Revolutionary Europe, 1783–1815.* New York and London.

Sources and Bibliography

Rumar, Lars. 1966–7. Jordbrug og brændevinsbrænding. *Erhvervshistorisk Årbog,* 17. 7–95; 18. 46–131.

Rønne Kejlbo, Ib. 1974. Ed. *Kobberstikkene fra Peder Hansen Resen: Atlas Danicus 1677.*

Rørdam, H. F. 1883–9. Ed. *Danmarks Kirkelove.* I–III.

Raabyemagle, Hanne. 1988. "Den engelske have." A. G. Moktke and Glorup. In Kjeld de Fine Licht, eds., *Forblommet antik. Klassicismer i dansk arkitektur og havekunst. Studier tilegnet Hakon Lund 18. oktober 1988.*

Sand, Petrine. 1945. Da man søgte efter Stenkul – og fandt Brunkul i Stedet. *Andelsbladet.* 1121–2.

Schade, Caspar. 1811. *Beskrivelse over Øen Mors.*

Schadewaldt, H. 1972. Hermann Hellriegel. In Charles C. Gillispie, ed., *Dictionary of Scientific Biography,* 6 New York. 237–8.

Schiermer Andersen, Bent. 1986. Mejeri- eller staldgård. En studie i dansk herregårdsdrift i det 18. århundrede. *Bol og by,* fascicle 2. 75–114.

Schiöt, Jørgen Andersen. 1759. Om Eng-Bundens Forbedring samt Have-og Skov-Væxt, saa og et par Exempler paa priselige Land-Mænd i Fyen. *Danmarks og Norges Oeconomiske Magazin,* 3. 127–38.

Schiöth, David. 1760. Om Val af Sædekorn og i sær om den Norske Rug [with an editorial comment by Erik Pontoppidan, pp. 237–8]. *Danmarks og Norges Oeconomiske Magazin,* 4. 217–38.

Schmidt, August F. 1939. Møddinger og Gødskning. Et Stykke Bondehistorie. *Tidsskrift for Landøkonomi.* 64–72, 701–32, 785–804.

1948. *Moser og Tørv. Et Stykke Bondehistorie.* Brabrand.

1949. *Brørup Sogns Historie.* Brørup.

1953. *Hegn og Markfred.* Brabrand.

Schmidt, Thorvald. 1878. Om Tangens Anvendelse i Agerbruget. *Ugeskrift for Landmænd,* I (5th series, 5). 492–4.

Schröder-Lembke, Gertrud. 1953. Die Hausväterliteratur als Agrargeschichtliche Quelle. *Zeitschrift für Agrargeschichte und Agrarsoziologie,* I. 109–19.

1978. Die Einführung des Kleebaues in Deutschland vor dem Auftreten Schubarts von dem Kleefelde. In Gertrud Schröder-Lembke, *Studien zur Agrargeschichte.* Quellen und Forschungen zur Agrargeschichte, 31. Stuttgart. 133–81.

Schumpeter, Elizabeth Boody. 1960. *English Overseas Trade Statistics 1697–1808.* Oxford.

Schumpeter, Joseph A. 1963. *History of Economic Analysis.* London.

Schwarz Lausten, Martin. 1987. *Biskop Peder Palladius og kirken 1537–1560.* Studier i den danske reformationskirke, 2.

Seip, Jens Arup. 1957–8. Teorien om det opinionsstyrte enevelde. (Norwegian.) *Historisk tidsskrift,* 38. 397–463.

Sereni, Emilio. 1958. Spunti della rivoluzione agronomica Europea nella scuola bresciana cinquecentesca di Agostino Gallo e di Camillo Tarello. In *Miscellanea in onore di Roberto Cessi,* II. Rome 113–28.

Severinsen, P. 1920. *Folkekirkens Ejendoms-Historie.*

Shorter, Edward. 1975. *The Making of the Modern Family.* New York.

Sieferle, Rolf Peter. 1982. *Der unterirdische Wald. Energiekrise und Industrielle Revolution.* Munich.

298 Sources and Bibliography

Siggaard, Niels. 1945. *Fødemidlerne i ernæringshistorisk Belysning.*
Sioli, Harald. 1987. The Effects of Deforestation in Amazonia. *The Ecologist*, 17. 134–8.
Skougaard, Mette, and Karl-Erik Frandsen. 1988. Herregård og bønder i Fjellerup. *Arv og Eje.* 117–26.
Skovgaard-Petersen, Vagn. 1985. Tiden 1814–1864. In Aksel E. Christensen et al., eds., *Danmarks historie*, 5.
Skrubbeltrang, Fridlev. 1940. *Husmand og Inderste. Studier over sjællandske Landbo-forhold i Perioden 1660–1800.* Reprint 1974.
—— 1954. *Den danske Husmand.* I–II.
—— 1961. Strejftog blandt østjyske bønder i det 18. århundrede. *Østjysk Hjemstavn*, 26. 20–33.
—— 1966. *Det indvundne Danmark.*
—— 1969–70. [Review of] C. Rise Hansen: Hoveriet på Ringsted Kloster 1570–1620. *Historisk Tidsskrift*, 12th series, 4. 229–35.
—— 1972–3. [Review of] Jens Holmgaard: Fæstebonde i Nørre Tulstrup Christen Andersens dagbog 1786–1797. Ibid., 6. 261–4.
—— 1973. Ed. *M. H. Løvenskiolds hoveridagbog 1795–1797.* Bol og By, 7.
—— 1978. *Det danske Landbosamfund 1500–1800.*
Slicher van Bath, B. H. 1955. Agriculture in the Low Countries (ca. 1600–1800). In *Relazioni del X Congresso Internazionale di Scienze Storiche*, 4. Florence. 129–263.
—— 1960a. The Rise of Intensive Husbandry in the Low Countries. In J. S. Bromley and E. H. Kossmann, eds., *Britain and the Netherlands.* London. 130–53.
—— 1960b. *De agrarische geschiedenis van West-Europa (500–1850).* Utrecht and Antwerpen.
Slottved, Ejvind, and Mogens Thøgersen. 1980. Universitetets gods. In Svend Ellehøj and Leif Grane, eds., *Københavns Universitet 1479–1979*, 4. 1–126.
Smed, Mette. 1988. "Godsejernes Lykketime." Om renæssance- og barokmotiver i dansk herregårdsarkitektur og portrætmaleri 1850–1900. In Nina Damsgaard, ed., *Danmarks Christian. Chr. IV i eftertiden.* Aarhus. 98–111.
Smid, Henrick. 1577. *Lægebog.* I–VI. Reprint 1976.
Smout, T. C. 1987. Landowners in Scotland, Ireland and Denmark in the Age of Improvement. *Scandinavian Journal of History*, 12. 79–97.
Sneedorff, Jens Schielderup. 1776. *Samtlige Skrivter.* 6: Den patriotiske Tilskuer, no. 256–308 (1. July–30. Dec. 1763).
Sombart, Werner. 1916–27. *Der moderne Kapitalismus.* I–III. Leipzig.
Sontag, Susan. 1978. *Illness as Metaphor.* New York.
Sorterup, Jørgen. 1698. Tenck paa Mig. Eller Ærbødigt og Frie-postigt Tancke-Brev. Riimviis forfattet, og overleveret Etats-Raad Christian Scheel den 16. December 1698. In J. Wieland, ed., *Samling udaf smukke og udvalde Danske Vers.* 1725–6. 99–129.
Stampe, Henrik. 1793–1807. *Erklæringer, Breve og Forestillinger, General-Prokureur-Embedet vedkommende.* 1–6.
Stangerap, Hakon. 1936. *Romanen i Danmark i det attende Aarhundrede. En Komparativ Undersøgelse.*
Starcke, Viggo. 1946. *Danmark i Verdenshistorien. Danmarks Historie udadtil fra Stenalder til Middelalder.*
Steenberg, Jan. 1950. *Christian IVs Frederiksborg.* Hillerød.

Sources and Bibliography

Steensberg, Axel. 1940. Middelalderens og Renaissancetidens Bondeboliger. *Naturens Verden*, XXIV. 109–21.

1956. Ager. *Kulturhistorisk leksikon for nordisk middelalder*, I. 32–54.

1958. Dræn. Ibid., 3. 352–4.

1968. Plov. Ibid., 13. 330–42.

1969. Natur og landskab. In Axel Steensberg, ed., *Dagligliv i Danmark i det syttende og attende århundrede*, I: 1620–1720. 489–522.

1974. *Den danske bondegård*.

1980. *New Guinea Gardens. A Study of Husbandry with Parallels in Prehistoric Europe*. London and New York.

Steensgaard, Niels. 1969–70. Det syttende århundredes krise. *Historisk Tidsskrift*, 12th series, 4. 474–504.

Stendal, Pedersen, Finn. 1982–83. [Review of] Thomas Munck: The Peasantry and the Early Absolute Monarchy in Denmark 1660–1708. *Historisk Tidsskrift*, 82. 382–6.

1988. Stavnsbåndet og dets løsning på Fyn. Myte og realitet. *Fynske Årbøger*. 33–52.

1989. Husmænd på landboreformernes tid. In Helle Damgaard and Per Grau Møller, eds., *Huse og husmænd i fortid, nutid og fremtid. Småbrugets udbredelse og vilkår i Norden*. Odense.

Stoklund, Bjarne. 1965. Deres bedste brænde. *Skalk*, no. 6. 8–11.

1969a. Læsøboerne og det daglige brød. *Nationalmuseets Arbejdsmark*. 5–16.

1969b. *Bondegård og Byggeskik før 1850*.

1985. "Det er et sælsomt syn at se deres pløjning." Jorddyrkning på Læsø før ca. 1850. In Birte Friis et al., eds., *Bønder og fiskere*. Folkelivs Studier, 9. 101–15.

1986. Hakkemøg, foldtørv og træk. Om brugen af tørvegødning i de jyske hedeegne. *Norveg. Folkelivsgransking*, 29. 51–69.

Stone, Lawrence. 1977. *The Family, Sex and Marriage in England 1500–1800*. London.

Storgaard, Einar. 1952–3. Nylandsmosen. Et Inddæmningsforetagende fra Christian V's Tid. *Geografisk Tidsskrift*. 276–91.

Stuckenberg, Frederik. 1893–6. *Fængselsvæsenet i Danmark*. 1–2.

Sundbärg, Gustav. 1905. Dödligheten af Lungtuberkulos i Sverige åren 1751/1830. *Statistisk tidskrift*. 163–97.

Sveistrup, P. P., and Richard Willerslev. 1945. *Den danske Sukkerhandels og Sukkerproduktions Historie*.

Sørensen, A. 1941–2. Et par Hoverikonflikter fra Aggersborggaard og Asdal. *Vendsysselske Aarbøger*, 14. 119–31.

Tamm, Ditlev. 1988. *Christian den Fjerdes kanslere*.

Tanderup, Ruth, and Klaus Ebbesen. 1979. *Forhistoriens historie*. Højbjerg.

Tang Kristensen, Evald. 1928. *Danske Sagn som de har lydt i Folkemunde*, new series, Part 1.

Tarello, Camillo. 1567. *Ricordo d'agricoltura*. Venice.

Taylor, N. L. 1985. Ed., *Clover Science and Technology*. Agronomy, 25. Madison, WI.

Teilmann, A. C. 1771. *Et Brev fra Anders Christensen til - - - - om Kornpriser, Folkemængde, Proprietærer, Bønder, med videre Landhuusholdningen angaaendis, hvorved tillige adskillige Modens Fordomme bestrides*.

1772a. Forslag til suur og ubrugelig Jords Forbedring ved Mergel. *Bibliothek for nyttige Skrifter*, 1. 9–16.

300 Sources and Bibliography

1772b. *Betænkninger over Hr. Lütkens og Hr. Clausens Afhandlinger om Bøndergaardes tienligste Størrelse.*

1789. Svar til Recensenten N. i de Berlingske Lærde Efterretninger No. 14, 1789. Hoveriet med dets Følger egentlig angaaende. *Morgen-Posten. Et Ugeblad*, IV, 2. 562–8, 575–83, 591–9.

Thaulow, Thorkil. 1957. *Stamhuset Ravnholt-Nislevgaard-Hellerup's Godshistorie.*

Thestrup, Poul. 1971. *The Standard of Living in Copenhagen 1730–1800.*

Thestrup, Søren. 1760. Om Jord-Marv- eller Mærgel som findes paa adskillige Steder, særdeles i Nørre Jylland, samt dens nyttige Brug. *Danmarks og Norges Oeconomiske Magazin*, 4. 61–71.

Thirsk, Joan. 1983. Plough and Pen: Agricultural Writers in the Seventeenth Century. In T. H. Aston et al., eds., *Social Relations and Ideas: Essays in Honour of R. H. Hilton*. Cambridge. 295–318.

Thomsen, Robert. 1975. Om Myremalm og Bondejern. In V. Fabritius Buchwald, ed., *Glimt af Metallurgiens Udvikling i Danmark*. 151–63.

Thomsen, Rudi. 1949. *Den almindelige værnepligts gennembrud i Danmark.*

Thuborg, Karen. 1928. *Det gamle Harboøre*. Danmarks Folkeminder, 36.

Thune, L. G. W. 1848. Om den fuldvoxne værnepligtige Bondeungdoms Legemshøide i Danmark. *Det kongelige medicinske Selskabs Skrifter*, new series, 1. 242–64.

Toft Andersen, Lis. 1986. Bondens almanak. *Bol og by. Landbohistorisk Tidsskrift*, fascicle 1. 79–115.

Toftgaard Poulsen, Søren. 1988. "En rig fader, men en fattig søn" – mergling gennem 200 år i Ringkøbing amt. *Arv og Eje*. 199–218.

Trap, Jens Peter. 1953–72. *Trap Danmark*, 5th ed., 1–31.

Troels-Lund, Troels. 1879–1901. *Dagligt Liv i Norden* (quoted from the 6th ed. 1968–9, 1–7).

Trojel, Frans Wilhelm. 1784. *Fuldstændig Afhandling om alle Slags Indhegninger omkring Marker, Haver og Plantaser, som kan anvendes i disse Lande. Belønnet af Det Kongel. Danske Landhuusholdings-Selskab.*

Täntzer, Johann. 1682–9. *Der Dianen hohe und niedere Jagtgeheimnüsz, darinnen die gantze Jagt-Wissenschaft ausführlich zu befinden.* I–III.

Tørning, Kjeld. 1945. *Tuberkulosen og Samfundet.*

Uldall, Kai C. 1913–16. Indberetning om den økonomiske Tilstand i Vestfyen i 1735. *Aarbog for Historisk Samfund for Odense og Assens Amter*, I. 548–77.

Ulsig, Erik. 1985. Valdemar Atterdags mænd. In Aage Andersen et al., eds., *Festskrift til Troels Dahlerup*. Arusia – Historiske skrifter, V. Århus. 257–76.

UN Chronicle. 1988. Will Earth Survive Man? A Planetary Life or Death Struggle Is Unfolding. *UN Chronicle*, 25, 2. 40–51.

Utenhof, Wolfgang von. 1539. Samtidig Beretning om Forhandlingerne imellem Kong Christian den Anden og Hertug Frederik, samt dennes Kongevalg. Ed. N. M. Petersen, *Danske Magazin*, 3rd series, 3. 1851. 1–26.

Vammen, Hans. 1990. Bourgeois Mentality in Denmark 1730–1900. In Bo Stråth, ed., *Language and the Construction of Class Identities: The Struggle for Discursive Power in Social Organisation: Scandinavia and Germany*. Condis Project, report no. 3. Göteborg. 283–309.

Sources and Bibliography

Vaupell, Christian. 1862. Om de Forandringer, som det danske Skovlands Udstrækning har været underkastet i den historiske Tid. *Tidsskrift for populære Fremstillinger af Naturvidenskaben*, 2nd series, 4. 389–436.

1863. *De danske Skove*. Repro. 1986.

Venge, Mikael. 1980. Tiden fra 1523 til 1559. In Aksel E. Christensen et al., eds., *Danmarks historie*, 2, 1. 271–356.

Vensild, Henrik. 1985. Den bornholmske hjulplov. In Birte Friis m.fl., udg., *Bønder og fiskere*. Folkelivs Studier, 9. 116–29.

Viborg, Erik. 1795. *Botanisk Bestemmelse af de i den danske Lov omtalte Sandvexter samt Efterretning òm Sandflugtens Dæmpning*.

Vibæk, Jens. 1964. *Reform og Fallit 1784–1830*. John Danstrup and Hal Koch, eds., *Danmarks Historie*, 10.

Villadsen, J. G., and Villads Villadsen. 1941. *Træk af Egaa Sogns Historie gennem Tiderne*. Aarhus.

Vogt, J. H. E. 1908. *De gamle norske Jernverk*. Norges geologiske Undersøgelse, 46. Kristiania.

Volsøe, Helge. 1979–82. Dyrenes udbredelse. In Arne Nørrevang and Jørgen Lundø, eds., *Danmarks natur*, 3rd ed., 2. 415–46.

W. E. 1763. Betænkning om at forbædre Græsningen især med at saae Klever-Frøe. *Danmarks og Norges Oeconomiske Magazin*, 7. 357–66.

Wad, Gustav Ludvig. 1893. Ed., *Breve til og fra Herluf Trolle og Birgitte Giøe*. I–II. 1916–24. Ed., *Fra Fyens Fortid*. I–IV.

Walgensten, Thomas. 1664. *En kort og Almindelig Bonde Practie Om Afvels-handel, Som paa andre Steder er observeret, oc udi Gierningen god befunden*.

Weber, I. C. 1919. *Fra Hjulskibenes Dage*.

Weber, Max. 1920. Die protestantische Ethik und der Geist des Kapitalismus. In Max Weber, *Gesammelte Aufsätze zur Religionssoziologie*. Tübingen. 17–206.

Wedel, Lago Matthias. 1792–6. *Samlinger om Agerdyrkning og Landvæsen i Korthed uddraget af de beste oeconomiske danske og fremmede Skrifter*. 1–5.

Wegener, C. F. 1855–6. *Historiske Efterretninger om Abrahamstrup Gaard i ældre og nyere Tid*. 1–2.

Weisheipl, James A. 1980. *Albertus Magnus and the Sciences*. Toronto.

Weismann, C. 1931. *Vildtets og Jagtens Historie i Danmark*. Reprint 1986.

Wesenberg-Lund, C. 1921. Undersøgelser over danske Malariamyg og dansk Malaria. *Nordisk hygieinisk tidsskrift*, II. 229–47.

Westenholz, J. D. W. 1772. *Priisskrift om Folkemængden i Bondestanden* (quoted from A. Rasmussen's ed., 1919).

White, K. D. 1970. *Roman Farming*. London.

Willerslev, Richard. 1983. Beboelsestætheden i København omkring år 1800. In Ole Feldbæk and Niels Thomsen, eds., *Festskrift til Kristof Glamann*. Odense. 395–410.

Wilse, J. N. 1767. *Fuldstændig Beskrivelse af Stapel-Staden Fridericia*.

Windfeld Lund, Niels. 1975. Kartoffeltyskerne. Livsvilkår i de jyske hedekolonier i det 18. årh. *Folk og kultur*. 31–66.

1984. Udviklingsfaktorer i Vestjylland i det 18. århundrede. In *CDR Seminar Papers B. 84.2.: Oplæg præsenteret ved seminaret d. 23–24. maj 1984 om landdistrikternes udvikling i Danmark og i U-landene* (Center for Udviklingsforskning).

302   Sources and Bibliography

Winther, Christian. 1828. *Digte.*

With, N. Randulff. 1758. Tractatus physico-oeconomicus om de Midler, hvorved Jordens Frugtbarhed kand befordres, og dens Frugter formeeres. *Danmarks og Norges Oeconomiske Magazin,* 2. 117–50.

Woll, V. 1931–6. Et Inddæmnings-Projekt fra 1726 (Tårup Strand ved Kerteminde). *Aarbog for Historisk Samfund for Odense og Assens Amte,* 5. 147–51.

Wolter, Hans Christian. 1982. *Adel og embede. Embedsfordeling og karrieremobilitet hos den dansk-norske adel 1588–1660.* (Skrifter udg. af det historiske institut ved Københavns Universitet, 13.

Woolf, Stuart. 1986. *The Poor in Western Europe in the Eighteenth and Nineteenth Centuries.* London and New York.

Worm, Ole. 1965–8. *Breve fra og til Ole Worm.* Trans. H. D. Schepelern. 1–3.

Worster, Donald. 1979. *Dust Bowl: The Southern Plains in the 1930s.* Oxford.

Worsøe, Eiler. 1979. *Stævningsskovene.*

Worsøe, Hans H. 1982. *Vonsild Kirkebog 1659–1708.*

Yde-Andersen, D. 1953. *Bornholmere og andre gamle Ure.*

Zahrtmann, M. K. 1917. Sandflugten paa Bornholm og Peder Jespersen. *Bornholmske Samlinger,* 11. 26–106.

1934–5. *Borringholms Historie.* I–II. Rønne.

Zangenberg, H. 1935. Gamle Gaarde og Huse i Sydvestjylland. *Turistforeningens Aarbog.* 227–48.

Zohary, Daniel, and Maria Hopf. 1988. *Domestication of Plants in the Old World: The Origin and Spread of Cultivated Plants in West Asia, Europe, and the Nile Valley.* Oxford.

Ørberg, Paul G. 1978–9. De private birkers endeligt. En korrigeret oversigt. *Arkiv,* 7. 39–46.

Østergaard, Jens. 1956. Træk af svingplovens historie fra det vestlige Fjends herred. *Skivebogen,* 47. 34–64.

Aaby, Bent, and Bent Odgaard. 1988. Miljøet og mennesket siden istiden. MS, Denmark's Geological Investigations.

Aaris-Sørensen, Kim. 1988. *Danmarks forhistoriske dyreverden. Fra Istid til Vikingetid.*

INDEX

Abildgaard, P. C., 52
Abildgaard, Søren, 52
absolutism, 203–4, 205, 207–9,
    214, 217
*Account of Denmark as it was in the
    Year 1692, An* (Molesworth),
    115, 210
acidification, 21, 25, 26, 41, 49–50, 51
adscription, 158–9, 178, 204–5, 209
    abolition of, 225–6, 247
Agrarian Commission, of 1784, 53,
    169, of 1786 (Greater Agrarian
    Commission), 169, 222, 232, 233
agrarian reform, 4, 247–52
    and agricultural growth, 249–52
    and ecological revolution, 247–8
    and enclosures, 220–1
    and freehold property, 217–20
    and villeinage, 221–3
Agricultural Society, 38, 47, 48, 52,
    53, 57, 79, 101, 102, 105, 118,
    121, 124, 248, 255
agriculture
    agrarian reform impact
        on, 249–52
    at ascension of Christian IV, 9
    books on, 254–6
    buildings, 94–5, 138
    cooperative movement in,
        248–9, 251
    crop rotation, 74–5, 78, 79, 81, 83,
        86, 87
    drainage, 40–1, 42, 44–7, 48–9
    ecological stabilization of, 129–30

energy/raw materials crisis and,
    89, 90
fallowing, 81–2, 146
fencing, 99–105, 137
implements, 2, 116–18, 266
irrigation, 47–8
labourers, 147–51, 159, 160, 237
land reclamation, 25–6
lønnesæd system, 60, 150–1, 237
multiple-field system, 45–6, 47,
    49, 102
prices, 16, 17, 27, 60, 158, 159,
    160, 164, 174
production, 16, 22–3, 26, 84–7,
    146, 157–8
professionalization in, 234
revolution, 4
sand drift related to, 11
slash-and-burn method, 145–6
tenant farmers, 165–78, 219, 222–3
three-field system of, 44–5, 77
    see also cattle; land ownership; soil
agronomics, 253–6
Ahlefeldt, Carl, 254
Åkær Manor, 39
Ålborg, 34, 208
Alfonso, Gabrelo, *see* Herrera, Gabriel
    Alfonsode
Alheden, 36
Als, 82, 85
Amager, 62, 63, 64, 89, 90, 122
Amalienborg complex, 214, 215
Andalusia, clover domestication
    in, 69–70

303

304 Index

Andersen, Christian, 36, 171
Anholt, 13, 14, 19, 23
animals
  game, 9, 10, 234–5, 236
  in new landscape, 137
  see also specific names
Antvorskov Manor, 23
Antvorskov Palace, 10
Anviisning til et velindrettet Jordbrug for Gaardmænd og Huusmænd paa Landet (Høegh), 79, 256
Apologia nobilitatis Danicae (Rosenkrantz), 210
architecture, 92–5, 202, 211, 230–1, 263
aristocracy, see nobility
armaments, 14–15, 158
Arresø, 24, 34, 41, 49
art, 202, 211–12, 231
Asbjørn, 201
Asserbo, 34
atmosphere, and greenhouse effect, 265–6
Åtte, 48

Baggesen, Jens, 233, 239
Balle, Nikolaj Edinger, 172
Balvig, Flemming, 164
Barnewitz, Joachim von, 75
barns, 94–5
baronies, 205–6, 219, 226–7
beans, broad, 65, 67, 72, 74, 83–4
beech trees, 1, 2, 13, 115, 138–9
Beenfelt, F. L. C., 236
bees, 136–7
beggary, 156, 163, 164
Begtrup, Gregers, 23–4, 48, 82n, 86, 101, 103, 116–17, 156, 169
Behr, Niels, 44
Bellman, Carl Michael, 193
Benzonslund Manor, 43
Berntsen, Arent, 10
Bibelske Søn- og Helligdagslæsninger (Balle), 172
Biehl, Charlotta Dorothea, 96, 241
Bircherod, Jens, 159

Birch, H. J., 163
Birckner, M. G., 241
bird's-foot trefoil, 143
Birkelse Manor, 36
Black Death, 10, 12, 181, 191
Blekinge, 5
Blichfeldt, Henrik, 124
Boddum Bisgård Manor, 149
bogs, 25, 27, 43, 47, 49, 52
  peat, 112, 113–14, 115
books
  on farming, 254–6
  law texts, 229
  on medicine, 192
  in tenant farms, 172
  see also literature
Bornholm, 19, 20, 83n, 89, 101, 124, 125, 219, 248
Borreby Manor, 89
Boserup, Christian Jacob, 61–2
Boserup, Ester, 145, 146
Bøtø Bay, 40
bourgeoisification, 230–2, 233–5
Brahetrolleborg Manor, 110–11
Bregentved Manor, 47, 76, 211, 214
brick-built houses, 93, 94
brickworks, fuel in, 113, 122, 130
Brønshøj, 167
Buchwald, Peder Matthias von, 42
buckwheat, 143
building materials/methods, 2, 92–5
  half-timbered construction, 93, 94
  roof construction, 93
  turf-built houses, 93
Bülow, Johan, 96
bureaucracy, 208, 216, 228–9
butterflies, 137

calcium carbonate, 50
Callisen, Heinrich, 186, 187–8
Canute the Holy, 199
carbon dioxide, in atmosphere, 265
Caroline Mathilde, 216
Cato, 65
cattle, 23, 25, 136, 266
  fences, 98, 102

Index

305

fodder, 23, 27
forest grazing, 106, 109, 110, 111, 138
impact on disease patterns, 184, 186, 257
in movable pens, 61, 63
plague, 27–8, 157
population, 27, 84, 119, 184
stall feeding, 61–2, 63, 147, 184
centralistic government, 216–28
Chorley, C. P. H., 84
Christensen, Christian, 38
Christensen, Hans, 57
Christian I, 199, 208
Christian II, 201, 208, 209
Christian III, 11, 201
Christian IV, 9, 10, 12, 201, 202, 203, 209, 211
Christian V, 205
Christian VI, 211, 213
Christian VII, 216, 240
Christiansborg Palace, 13
church architecture, 211
civil servants, 199, 226, 227, 228, 236, 241, 263
Clausholm Manor, 95
climate, world, 265–6
clocks/clockmakers, 171
clover, 1, 2, 23, 58, 59, 142, 144, 266
bees and, 136–7
domesticated vs wild, 70–1
domesticated in America, 69
in England, 71–2
in France, 71
in Italy, 68, 71
domestication of, 67–72, 73–4
fatigue, 86, 87
harvesting, 151–2
impact on agricultural production, 84–7
introduction into Denmark, 73–7, 248
in landscape, 135
size of clover area, 76–83
coal, 13–14, 120–2, 124–5, 126, 128, 130–1, 253

Colbiørnsen, Christian, 224
Colbiørnsen ordinances, 224–5
coltsfoot, 136
Columella, 50, 65
Comedy of the Count and the Baron, The (Skeel), 206
commons, 80, 136
communications, 200, 202, 208, 254, 256
Complaint; or Night Thoughts on Life, Death and Immortality, The (Young), 195–6
Conditions of Agricultural Growth, The (Boserup), 145
Constitution of 1849, 227
Copenhagen
coal as fuel in, 120–1
disease patterns in, 182, 188, 189
night soil manure from, 62, 63–4
population, 62, 63
postal service in, 208
standard of living in, 162, 163–4
workers' organizations in, 223
corn marigold, 136
cottagers, 160–2, 173, 175, 176–7, 237–9, 243, 250
countships, 205–6, 219, 226–7
crime, 164

Danmarckis Rigis Krønnicke (Huitfeldt), 210
dams, 39
Danmarks Brændselvæsen, physikalskt, cameralistiskt og oeconomiskt betragtet (Olufsen), 97, 122
Danmarks og Norges Oeconomiske Magazin, 52, 60, 70, 256
Danske Atlas (Pontoppidan), 42, 43, 52, 124
Dansk Jordpolitik (Jensen), 217
Dante Alighieri, 192–3
deforestation, see forest clearance
Den danske Tilskuer, 262
De vegetabilibus (Magnus), 68–9
diet, 162–3, 164–5, 169–70

306 Index

Discours of Husbandrie used in Brabant and Flanders (Weston), 71
disease, patterns of, 3, 179–97
 fuel shortage and, 97
 impact on social life, 192–7
 malaria, 182–5, 193, 257
 plague, 179–82, 193–5
 smallpox, 191–2, 194–5
 tuberculosis, 3, 97, 185–91, 193, 195, 197, 257, 267
ditches and canals, drainage, 40–1, 42–5, 46, 47, 48–9, 57, 151, 248
Divina Commedia (Dante), 192
Djursland, 19, 52, 122
Dodoens, Rembert, 67–8
Drachmann, Holger, 136
drainage, 24–5, 41–9, 50, 57
Drewsen, J. C., 85
Dronninggård, 231
Dronninglund Manor, 236
Dubos, René, 186
dune plantations, 35, 39, 144
Dybvad, Christoffer, 203

earthfast fences, 99–105
ecological revolution
 agrarian reform and, 247–8
 aristocratic lifestyle and, 234–6
 disease patterns and, 181–2, 184, 186–7, 189, 257
 labour and, 145–52, 154, 257
 landscape and, 135–44
 long-term negative results of, 265–6
 technology and, 253–6
 see also energy/raw materials revolution; green revolution
education, 156, 228, 252
 in agriculture, 255
 in village schools, 207, 217, 226, 247
Egeskov Manor, 101, 211
Einsidelsborg, 39–40
Eisenstein, Elizabeth L., 256
electrification, 250
enclosure, 80, 98, 102, 104, 160–2, 220–1, 238, 250, 252
energy/raw materials crisis, 88–92

in Third World, 266–7
energy/raw materials revolution, 92–132
 economizing measures and, 92–106
 forestry production and, 106–12
 forest stabilization and, 129–31
 peat resources in, 112–15
 scientific revolution and, 192
 water-power/wind-power in, 115
 wood substitutes in, 116–29, 130
Engelstoft, Laurits, 237
Erasmus of Rotterdam, 156
Erik V, 199, 201
erosion, 19, 21
Essay on the Principle of Population (Malthus), 155
Estienne, Charles, 254
European Community, 251
Ewald, Johannes, 196

Faeroe Islands, 4
fallow land, 81–2, 146
Falster, 23, 40, 46, 53, 74–5, 78, 82, 89, 169–70, 184, 209
family tenancy, 165–6, 172–3
Fanø, 96
farmer class, 165–73, 208–9, 237–9, 241–2, 243, 249
farming, *see* agriculture
farm labourer, 147–51, 159, 160, 237, 243
Fehmarn, 72, 76
fences, 98–105, 109, 135, 137, 148
fertilizers
 nitrogen, 266
 seaweed as, 64–5
 see also manure; nitrogen; nitrogen assimilating plants
fiscal-military state, 13–16
Fleischer, Esaias, 106, 255, 256
flooding, 21, 24, 25, 26, 42, 112
Fønss, Hans, 43–4
forage crops, 255
forest
 at ascension of Christian IV, 9, 10
 expansion of production, 107–12
 grazing, 107, 109, 110, 111, 138

Index

307

oak, 14n
  stabilization of, 129–31
  see also trees
forest clearance, 10, 18, 23, 71
  disease patterns and, 181
  energy/raw materials problems
    and, 88–92
  export of timber and, 91n
  hunting and, 234–5
  in Spain, 91
  long term effects of, 25–7
  shipbuilding and, 14–15
  water level and, 26, 112
Forest Reserve Act of 1805, 111, 112,
    129, 130, 131, 247
Forestry and Game Department,
    108, 109
foundations, 212
Fredensborg Palace, 242
Frederik II, 201, 202, 211
Frederik III, 203
Frederik IV, 205, 209
Frederiksborg Palace, 13, 197, 202
Frederiksgave Manor, 40, 76,
    94–5, 231
Frederik V, 240
freehold property, 217–20, 242,
    247, 249
French Revolution, 239
Frijsenborg Manor, 121
fuel
  coal as, 13, 120
  economizing on wood, 95–8
  fossil, 265
  imported, 122–9
Funen
  agricultural innovation in, 255
  clover cultivation in, 74, 77, 78,
    79, 82
  coal in, 125
  fence construction in, 100, 102,
    104
  forest clearance in, 23, 89, 94
  land reclamation in, 39–40, 42, 48
  marling in, 53
  sand drift in, 19
  seaweed in, 65

social development in, 164, 167,
    169, 211, 231, 238

Gallo, Agostino, 68, 71
Gammelgård Manor, 43
gardens
  landscape, 139–42, 196,
    231, 237
  farmers', 172
Gavnø Manor, 39
Gerdrup-Lyngbygård Manor, 148–9
Gilbert, L. W., 59
Gjorslev Manor, 78–9, 121
Glomstrup Manor, 149
Glorup Manor, 100
Goethe, Johan Wolfgang von, 63
Grabow, Rudolf von, 44
Gram, Christian, 109
Gram-Langen forestry system,
    109–10, 129, 130
grass, 12, 33, 36
Gråsten-Tranekær estates, 16
grazing, 19, 25, 106, 109, 110,
    111, 138
Greater Agrarian Commission, *see*
    Agrarian Commission
greenhouse effect, 265–6
Greenland, 4
green revolution, 4, 33–87
  energy/raw materials revolution
    and, 128
  land reclamation in, 39–40
  marling in, 50–6
  nitrogen-assimilating crops in,
    65–87
  resource utilization in, 57–65
  sand drift control in, 33–9
  water regulation in, 40–9
grey leaf, 56
guano, 59, 128
Gudumlund, 113, 130
guilds, 208, 223, 263

half-timbered construction, *see* build-
    ing materials/methods
Halland, 4
Hansen, Hans, 105

308   Index

Hansen, Povl, 103
hares, 234–5
Harritslev, 48
Hårup, 37–8
heating, domestic
  chimneys, 96
  fireplaces, 95–6
  stoves, 96, 116
hedgerows, 1, 2, 45, 135
Heiberg, P. A., 241, 242
Hellriegel, H., 58
heredity tenure, 110–11
Heresbach, Konrad, 254
Herningholm Manor, 52, 58n
Herrera, Gabriel Alfonso de, 254
Hersleb, Peder, 156
Hersleb, P. L., 166–7, 170
Hesseballe, 48
Hindemae, 231
Høegh, H. J. C., 79, 82, 173, 256
Hoff, Henrik Muhle, 255
Hofman, Hans de, 90–1, 212
Højre party, 263
Holberg, Ludvig, 106, 138, 194, 212
Holm, Edvard, 178n
Holmgaard, Jens, 178n
Holstein, 4, 5, 72
Holstein, J. L., 211–12
Holsteinborg Manor, 121
hop medic, 143
Horsens, 48
Horsens, Morten Andersen, 254
horses, 119–20, 149
Høsten, 47
Høst-Gildet (Thaarup), 242
Hübner, Martin, 118
Huitfeldt, Arild, 210, 213
humus, 25–6
hunting, 18–19, 234–5, 236
Huusfeld, Daniel, 128n
Hvidkilde Manor, 101

Iceland, 4
implements, agricultural, 2,
  116–18, 119, 266
inflation, 174

Ingemann, B. S., 235
inoculation, 191, 192
Institutio principis Christiani
  (Erasmus), 156
intercommoning system, 98
iron, 116–20, 124, 125, 126, 128, 253

Jacobsen, J. C., 263
Jægerspris Manor, 103
Jenner, Edward, 192
Jensen, Hans, 205, 217
Johansen, Hans Christian, 188
Jørgensen, Karl A., 87
"Joys of Denmark, The" (Møller), 1
Juel, Jens, 231
Juel, Niels, 39, 152
Juellinge Manor, 74n
Juliane moors, 52
justices of the peace, 227
Jutland
  building construction in, 93, 95
  clover cultivation in, 82, 83, 85,
    142, 144
  farmer class in, 167, 168, 170
  fence construction in, 101
  forest clearance in, 89, 90
  iron production in, 124
  iron use in, 116–17
  landowner protest in, 236–7, 242
  land reclamation in, 39
  landscape of, 142–4
  marling in, 51–2, 53, 56, 142
  peat production in, 113, 114
  sand drift in, 24–5, 248
  sand drift arrest in, 33, 34, 36, 37–8
  water regulation in, 43–4, 46, 48, 49
Jutland Law of 1241, 202

Kalø (Djursland), 43
Kalundborg, 10
kiln waste, 52
"King Valdemar's Hunt"
  (Ingemann), 235
Knabstrup, 43
knotgrass, 143
Kolindsund, 40

Index

Køng, 78
Korselitse Manor, 46, 74n, 75, 78
Krenkerup Manor, 44
Kristensen, Evald Tang, 74
Krogh, August, 265
Krollerup, 53
Kronborg Castle, 202
Kullen, 13
Kynde, O., 154

labour
  demand for, 146–7, 154–5, 158, 174, 177
  morale of, 152, 154, 159
  proletarianized, 172, 173
  restriction on free movement of, 158–9, 178n, 204–5, 209
  rhythm of work, 151–2
  in rural industry, 152
  wages, 159, 160, 174, 177
  and work ethic, 156–7
  working hours/days, 147–51, 160
  work as source of wealth, theory of, 155
  yield ratio, 145–6
Læsø, 19, 23, 35, 89, 122, 248
Lammefjorden, 40
land ownership
  entailed estates, 206–7
  freehold tenure, 217–20, 242, 247, 249
  heredity tenure, 110–11
  and patronage rights, 205, 226
  by speculators, 110
  and tenancy system, 174–6, 204, 219, 222, 224–5, 226
land reclamation, 25–6, 39–40
landscape
  moors, 142–4
  transformation of, 1, 2, 135–42, 234–5
landscape gardens, see gardens
Lange, Philip, 121
Langeland, 16, 74, 77
Langen, J. G. von, 109
Langesø, 231

La Plata, Argentina, garden of peace in, 1
Lassen, Bendix, 39
Lavater, Johann Caspar, 154
law courts, 202, 205
Lawes, J.B., 59
Ledøje, 57
lentils, 65
leprosy, 190–1
Levi, Carlo, 157
liberalism, 223, 242, 262
Lichtenberg, Gerdt de, 211
Liebig, Justus von, 59
Liger, Louis, 254
lighthouses, 13, 120
Lillelund, Mads, 52
Lille Vildmose, 43, 49, 113
lime, 50, 52, 90, 113
Limfjorden, 42, 65, 121
Lindenborg Manor, 43, 121
Lindhardt, P. G., 197
Linné, Carl von, 255
literature
  chivalry/heroic deeds in, 213
  melancholy mood in, 195–6
Lolland, 23, 40, 43, 44, 53, 74–5, 78, 82, 89, 111, 152, 167, 170, 183, 184, 209
lønnesæd system, 60, 150–1, 237
Louisenlund Manor, 236
love, 195, 231–2
Løvenholm Manor, 43–4, 116
Løvenskiold, M. H., 145
lucerne, 65, 67, 72
Lüders, Philip Ernst, 70, 85, 135
Lund, 49
Lund, G. H., 53
lupins, 65, 67, 72
Lütken, Otto Diderik, 128, 155
Lykkesholm Manor, 33, 36

McNeill, William H., 145, 185
Madsen, Johan, 39, 40
Madsen, Peder, 171, 173
Magnus, Albertus, 68–9
malaria, see disease, patterns of

310   Index

malnutrition, 162–3, 164–5
Malthus, Thomas, 155, 163
manganese deficiency, 56
manorial dues, 174, 220, 221, 222
manorial farms
  houses of, 211, 230–1, 263
  libraries of, 254–5
  tax exemptions on, 204, 226
Mansa, F. V., 182, 187
manure, 22, 27
  distribution of reserves, 60–1
  as fuel, 23
  night soil, 62–4
  waste avoidance, 61–2
Margrethe I, 199, 208
Mariager, 90
marling, 50–6, 136, 142, 151
  and deficiency diseases, 56
marram grass, 33, 39n
marriage, 195, 231–2
marshland, 39–40, 41
Martfelt, Christian, 124
Marx, Karl, 155
media, 229, 241
medicine, 191–2
melilot, yellow, 143
methane, in atmosphere, 265–6
middle class, 264
military expenditures, and wood consumption, 14–15
military service, 204, 225
Minerva, 239, 262
Molbech, Christian, 197
Molesworth, Robert, 115, 210–11
Møller, Poul Martin, 1, 135
Moltke, Adam Ditlev, 233
Moltke, Adam Gottlieb, 43n, 45,
  214, 233
Møn, 176, 209, 266n
Mønsted, 37
Montesquieu, 194
moors, 10, 52, 142–4
Mors, 25n, 52
mortality
  child, 194

fear of loving, 195
  tuberculosis and, 188, 190, 195
Mortensen, Lars, 102
Mortimer, John, 255
mosquito, malaria, 183–4, 185
Mossin, Hans, 82
mould drift, 19–20
movable pens, 61, 63
Müller, Henrik, 16
multiple-field system, 45–6, 47,
  49, 102
Munthe af Morgenstierne, C. W. von,
  81, 166, 253

Natte-Tanker (Ewald), 196
Nature Conservation Act of 1937, 1
naval expenditures, and wood consumption, 14–15
newspapers and magazines, 229, 239,
  241, 262
N-fixation, 22, 58, 59, 67n
Nielsen, Jens, 143
Nielsen, Peter, 87
nitrogen
  existing resources of, 57–60
  fertilizer, 60–5, 71, 266
  role in plant nutrition, 58–9
nitrogen assimilating plants, 22, 66
  of pea family, 58, 59, 65–7, 72–87,
  see also clover
*Nobilitatis responsum ad famosum factiosi
  calumniatoris libellum*, 210
nobility
  anti-aristocratic attitudes, 203, 233,
  239, 240, 241
  in art and architecture, 202,
  211–12
  bourgeoisification of, 230–2,
  233–5
  and central administration,
  226–7, 243
  foundations and scholarships
  of, 212
  ideology of, 209–11
  Jutland landowners, 236–7, 242

Index

language of, 232–3
new class of, 205–6, 214
patriarchal, 263
and royal power, 198–9, 201, 202, 203, 213–14
and relations with other classes, 212–13
see also manorial farms
Nordens Guder (Oehlenschläger), 2
Norway, 4, 5, 91, 94, 242
Nyerup, Rasmus, 213
Nylandsmosen, 39

oak trees, 2, 3, 107, 108, 109, 138
Øbjerggård Manor, 43
Oeconomisk Journal, 101
Oehlenschläger, Adam, 1, 2, 262
Ogier the Dane, 213
Olsen, Jens, 53
Olufsen, Christian, 86n, 97, 122–3
Orupgård Manor, 74n, 75
overmarling, 56

Palladius, 65
Palladius, Peder, 150
patronage, right of, 205, 226
Paulli, Simon, 74
pea family, 58, 59, 65–7, 72, 74–5, 83–4, *see also* Clover
peas, 65, 72, 74–5, 83, 84
peat
    formation, 25, 26, 27
    as fuel, 112–15, 130
Pedersen, Christiern, 182
Pedersen, Hans, 102
Pedersen, Iver, 53
Pedersen, Johannes, 38
Pedersen, Knud, 53
Pedersen, Niels, 52
Pedersen, Søren, 48
Pederstrup, 263n
pH balance, 49–50, 56
phosphoric acid, 57, 58
pigs, 25
plague, *see* disease, patterns of

plant nutrients, 22
    accessible, 57–8
    in cleared forestland, 25–6
    see also nitrogen; nitrogen assimilating plants
Plasmodium, 183
Plett, Peter, 192
Pliny, 50
ploughs, iron, 117–18
police, 225
pollution, 266
Pontoppidan, Erik, 25, 42, 43n, 96, 98, 124, 156, 167
population growth, 10, 12–13, 145–6, 158, 176–7
populationism, 154–5
portraiture, 211–12, 231
postal service, 208, 228–30
potash, 57, 58
poverty
    attitude to, 155–7
    spread of, 162–5
    and tuberculosis risk, 186–7
power structure, 198–243
    aristocratic rule *vs* absolutism, 198–216
    centralistic bureaucratic absolutism, 216–43, 261
    and welfare state, 261–4
Pram, Christen, 262
printing, 192, 200, 254, 256
prisons, 225
protein deficiency, 164, 165
Protestant work ethic, 156–7
proto-industry, 152
public opinion, 229, 241, 261

quarantine system, 194
Quintinie, Jean de la, 254

Rahbek, K. L., 239
Randers, 52
Rasmussen, O. F. C., 178n
rats, and plague, 180, 181, 182, 194
Recchia, Torquato, 9–10, 116

312   *Index*

Reichardt, Christian, 76
Reitzer, Christian, 34
religion
  attitude toward poor, 156
  church architecture, 211
  and patronage rights, 205, 226
  Protestant work ethic, 156–7
  revivalist movement, 197
  working days and, 150
Rentekammer, 37, 38n, 47, 90, 115
Resen, Peder Hansen, 50
Reventlow, C. D., 111, 214, 222,
  232–3
Reventlow, J. L., 110, 111
Rhode, Peder, 184
Ricardo, David, 155
Richardson, Samuel, 195
Ricordo d'agricoltura (Tarello), 68
Riegels, Niels Ditlev, 40
Ringkøbing Fjord, 25, 34, 36, 42, 49
Ringsted, 10, 50
Ringsted Convent, 96n, 147
River Skjern, 40
road surfacing, 107
rococo style, 194
Rødby Fjord, 40
Røhl, Johan Ulrich, 35–6, 37, 73, 77
Romanticism, 197
Rømø, 23
roof construction, *see* building materi-
  als/methods
Rosenkrantz, Oluf, 210, 211
Roskilde Fjord, 103
Rothe, Tyge, 167
Royal Law of 1665, 203, 208, 214
rule of excellencies, 213–14, 237
Rural District Council Act of
  1841, 227
rural industry, 152
Russia, 91

Sæbyholm Manor, 78
sainfoin, 72, 86
Saint-Germain, Claude Louis de, 240
Salling, 52
Saly, Jacques, 214

Samlinger af Publique og Private Stiftelser,
  Fundationer og Gavebreve (Hof-
  man), 212
sand drift, 10–12, 23, 26, 48, 248
  arrest of, 33–9, 73
  causes of, 19–21
  hydrological disturbances and,
    24–5, 41, 42
Saxo Grammaticus, 10
Schleswig, 4, 5, 16, 72, 82, 152
Schleswig-Holstein, 25n, 104n
scholarships, 212
schools
  in villages, 207
  School Act of 1814, 217, 226, 247
Schumacher, Peder, 212
scientific revolution, 192
seaweed, 64–5, 84
Selchau, Christian H., 43
Selmer, J., 154
serfdom, 158, 178n, 209
sheep, 119, 120
shipbuilding, 14–15, 105, 130
Shorter, Edward, 194–5
Silkeborg Manor, 255
Skaføgård Manor, 16n, 44
Skanderborg, 114
Skåne, 4, 94
Skaw, The, 13, 14, 89
Skeel, Jørgen, 44, 206
Skeel, Mogens, 206
Skjoldemose Manor, 104
Skrubbeltrang, Fridlev, 165
skulteuger, 150–1, 159, 237
slash-and-burn method, 145–6
smallpox, *see* disease, pattern of
Smith, Adam, 155, 223
Smith, Henrik, 182, 187
Sneedorf, Jens Schielderup, 262
Social Democratic party, 263
social mobility, 173
social structure, 3, 157–78
  agricultural production and,
    157–60
  cottagers, 160–2, 172, 173, 175,
    176–7, 237–9

Index

farmer class, 165–78, 208–9, 237–9
lower class, 162–65, 239
see also labour; nobility
soil
acidification of, 21, 25, 26, 41,
49–50, 51
drift, 266
erosion of, 19, 21
fertilizers, 59–64
marling, 50–6, 57
nutrient content of, 22, 23, 26,
57–8, *see also* nitrogen; nitrogen
assimilating plants
old power of fertilizing, 57–8
pH balance of, 49–50, 56
Sombart, Werner, 91–2
Sophie Amalie, 23
Sorø Academy, 203, 255
Sorterup, Jørgen, 24, 116
spurrey, 143
stall feeding, 61–2, 63, 147, 151, 184
standard of living, 146, 158, 162, 189
steam engines, 2–3
Stefano, Carlo, *see* Estienne, Charles
Stenalt, 231
Stolberg, Louise, 233
stone walls, 99–105, 135
Store Restrup Manor, 46
Store Vildmose, 49
Stounberg, Niels, 48
Støvringgård Manor, 121
Struensee, Johann Friedrich,
216, 240
Strynø, 77, 85, 89, 90
Stygge, Maurits, 254

Tanara, Vincenzo, 254
Tarello, Camillo, 33, 68, 71
Tåsinge, 39, 152, 154, 255
taxation taxes, 13, 15, 16, 64, 109,
158, 209
collection, 204, 226
exemptions, 204, 205, 218–19, 226
of nobility, 201
relief for farmers, 110, 177–8
tea, 170–1

technological development, 253–6
Teilmann, Andreas Charles, 51, 54,
95, 163, 255
Teilmann, Christian Hansen, 34,
36, 42, 51
tenancy system, 174–6, 204, 219, 222,
224–5, 226
tenant farmers, 165–74
Thaarup, Thomas, 241–2
Thaer, Albrecht, 255
Thaning, T., 45
Theophrastus, 65
Thorvaldsen, Bertel, 197
Thott, Lars, 34
three-field system, 44–5, 77
Thy, 51
Tibirke, 34
Tisvilde, 34, 39n, 73, 139
Tisvilde Hegn, 35, 39
Tjele Manor, 95
Tocqueville, Alexis de, 259
Torbenfeld Manor, 103
Torsted, 48
towns, 152
guilds in, 208, 223
trade
with China, 171
energy product imports, 123–6, 158
timber exports, 91n
triangular pattern of, 158
Treaty of Versailles, 4
trees
beech, 1, 2, 13, 115, 138–9
oak, 2, 3, 106, 108, 109, 138
Troels-Lund, Troels, 95
Trojel, F. W., 101–2, 103
Trojel, J. K., 255
Trolle, Herluf, 210
Tscherning, Paul, 210
tuberculosis, *see* disease, patterns of
Tull, Jethro, 255
turf-built houses, *see* building materials/methods

University of Copenhagen, 203, 228
Utenhof, Wolfgang von, 9, 28

314 Index

vaccination, 191–2
Vær, 255
Valdemar Atterdag, 199
Valdemar's Castle Manor, 76, 255
Valdemar the Great, 201
Valkendorf, Christoffer, 100
Varro, 50, 65
Vedel, Johan Frederik, 43
Vemmetofte Manor, 45, 49, 78,
116, 117
Venø, 52
Vesterborg Manor, 74n, 75
vetch, 65, 67, 72, 74, 83, 84, 143
Viborg, Erik, 20–21, 37
Viby Manor, 102
Vildmosegård, 43
villages, 138, 250
and central administration, 227–8
churches in, 211
and enclosure, 160–2, 220–1
villeinage, 148–9, 154–5, 167, 216,
221–3, 237
Vinti giornate della vera agricoltura e piaceri della villa, Le (Gallo), 68
Virgil, 65
Virgin Islands, 4
Vissenbjerg, 255
Voltaire, 194

wages, 159, 160, 174, 177
water
forest clearance and, 26, 112
levels, 21, 23, 25, 48
regulation, 40–9, 248
sand drift and, 24–5, 41, 42
watermills, 44, 115
Weber, Max, 157
Wedel, Lago M., 104
weeds, 136, 143
welfare state, 261–4

Westenholz, J. D. W., 91
Weston, Richard, 71
wheat, 75
Willumsen, Peder, 43
windmills, 44, 115
Winstrup, Peder, 201
Winther, Christian, 1
wire fencing, 104
wood
economizing on, 92–106
as raw material/energy source, 2,
10, 13, 14, 14–15, 18, 23, 88,
92–3, 94, 114, 115
shortage of, 88–92, 181
see also forest; forest clearance
work, *see* labour
work ethic, 156–7
working day, 147–51
Worm, Ole, 9, 34

Young, Arthur, 255
Young, Edward, 195–6

Zealand
clover cultivation in, 78, 82, 86
fence construction in, 98, 100, 101,
102, 103
forest clearance in, 10, 23
forests in, 109
land reclamation in, 39
marling in, 53
peat production in, 113
sand drift in, 19, 20, 24
sand drift arrest in, 34, 35–6, 73
serfdom in, 209
social development in, 163,
170, 176
stall feeding in, 61–2
water regulation in, 41–2, 43, 44,
47, 49, 57, 248

For EU product safety concerns, contact us at Calle de José Abascal, 56–1°, 28003 Madrid, Spain or eugpsr@cambridge.org.

www.ingramcontent.com/pod-product-compliance
Ingram Content Group UK Ltd.
Pitfield, Milton Keynes, MK11 3LW, UK
UKHW011323060825
461487UK00005B/308